D0300648

University of
Chester
Warrington Campus
LIBI

WARRINGTON Collegiate INSTITUTE
Padgate Campus • Crab Lane • Library

PEOPLE IN ORGANISATIONS - TUTOR'S PACK

Revised edition, 1989

Pat Armstrong and Chris Dawson

10 classroom-tested practical exercises for students of business
and management with notes, model answers and other material
for tutors to support and extend the book **People in Organisations.**
Student materials carry copying rights for purchasers.

Contents include:- attitude measurement, communication, employment
legislation, labour turnover/personnel records, negotiation,
pay administration, payment systems, recruitment and selection,
technological change, and training.

isbn 0 946139 60 1   £19.00   Looseleaf file for ease of copying

People IN Organisations

Pat Armstrong

&

Chris Dawson

This (fourth) edition is published by ELM Publications, 12 Blackstone Road, Huntingdon, Cambs PE18 6EF (Tel: 0480-414553) on the lst January, 1989; the first edition was published in August, 1981.

© Pat Armstrong and Chris Dawson, August/September, 1988.

Under the UK copyright laws (and international copyright laws to which the UK is a signatory), apart from extracts taken for critical assessment or review, no part of this publication may be copied, reproduced, broadcast or otherwise transmitted, stored electronically or in an information retrieval system without prior, written permission from the publisher who holds the copyright on behalf of the authors.

isbn 0 946139 55 5

Printed by St Edmundsbury Press, Bury St Edmunds, Suffolk and bound by Woolnough Bookbinding, Irthlingborough, Northants.

Contents

Figures

Introduction to the Fourth Edition

This book has been written to cover fully the BTEC Higher National Business Studies syllabus in the common study area People in Organisations.

Its wide appraisal of theory and application makes it a suitable textbook also for students on courses leading to IPM Stage 1 and the DMS. It has been adopted by many colleges and by the Institute of Bankers as a recommended text for their diploma syllabuses.

Where *he* is used, please assume that *she* could equally well apply, and vice versa.

This fourth edition has been updated and corrected and has been sent to press in December, 1988.

About the Authors

Pat Armstrong has been employed in higher education since 1972 and is currently Principal Lecturer in Applied Behavioural Sciences at Ealing College of Higher Education. A graduate in sociology from the London School of Economics, her M. Phil. thesis concerned women managers in bureaucratic organisations.

Chris Dawson gained most of his industrial experience working in the engineering industry within the personnel function of Lucas C A V. He joined the academic staff of Ealing College of Higher Education in 1978 as a lecturer in Personnel Management. He is a member of the Institute of Personnel Management and holds an MBA from The City University.

EMPLOYEE RELATIONS

an introduction

Ken Whitehead

Employee Relations describes the system by which employers
and Trade Unions seek to resolve their differences,
and reveals that disputes are not entirely concerned
with a particular workplace or set of rules.
Rather problems at work are a focal point of wider
issues arising from the very nature of industrial society.

CONTENTS

Why Trade Unions ?
Why so many Trade Unions ?
How are Trade Unions governed ?
What is an Employers' Association ?
The TUC and the CBI
International organisation
The role of management
The role of shop stewards
The organisation of bargaining
The practice of collective bargaining
The role of State and Government
Industrial democracy and participation
Pressures on the present system
Getting it together again

Book -   isbn 0 946139 76 8   £8.95

Tutor's Pack of tested exercises, notes, overhead projection
transparencies and other materials to support and extend
the textbook - isbn 0 946139 81 4   £39.00

Section 1

The Organisation : Goals And Structure

CHAPTER 1 : ORGANISATION GOALS

CHAPTER 2 : DETERMINANTS OF ORGANISATION STRUCTURE

CHAPTER 3 : VARIATIONS IN ORGANISATION STRUCTURE

CHAPTER 4 : HUMAN RESOURCE

In this Section we set the scene for *People in Organisations* by considering the characteristics and purposes of organisations. This is followed by an examination of some of the major theories which have influenced the structure of organisations and an overview of the main variations in organisation structure. The final chapter of this Section looks at the way in which goals are translated into manpower plans, through the medium of corporate plans. The practical aspects of manpower planning are further developed by a description of job analysis, job descriptions, and job specifications.

Chapter 1

Organisational Goals

Imagine you are standing in the Reception area of any large company headquarters. You have come for an interview for a job, and you are early, so you have time to look around before going up to the elegantly dressed young lady behind the reception desk. What do you think you might see?

You might see the board beside the lifts, telling you on which floor the various departments are to be found.

You might see a large glass display cabinet in which the products of this organisation are tastefully arranged.

You might see a uniformed chauffeur carefully opening the door for a man dressed in a soberly-toned three-piece suit.

You might see notices 'No Smoking', or 'Will all visitors please report to the reception desk', or 'representatives seen by appointment only'.

Characteristics of Organisations

What does all this tell us about Organisations?

1. Organisations consist of a number of people. Usually the reason why an organisation is created is because one person has not got the resources of time or skill or energy to do what he wants to do. Instead, therefore, he decides to ask other people to help him.

2. Organisations tend to have specialised tasks, and these are often grouped into departments. Imagine you and a friend have decided to open a restaurant. One way you could arrange this task is that you each do half of each job — cooking, washing up, serving at table and so on — but this is a waste of time, as only one person can be at the sink or cooker at one time. You could decide to have two sinks and two cookers so that you could both do your half at the same time — but this might be considered a waste of resources, since sink units and cookers are expensive, and they would not be in use all the time. So what you and your friend will probably decide is that one person will do one job and the other person will do another. In other words, one person specialises in cooking and the other person specialises in serving. We call this specialisation the division of labour, and in organisations too we find that people specialise in a part of the total task, for example in selling or in making the product, so that a list of Departments by a lift will tell you something about the division of labour in that organisation.

3. Organisations are formed with a purpose or goal in mind. The

2

cabinet which displays the company's products will provide some information about this purpose or goal — so will walking through the casualty department of a hospital or seeing the security arrangements of a prison.

4.   Organisations tend to have a hierarchy of authority — it is probable that the chauffeur mentioned above has less authority than the man in the suit, which means that the chauffeur will receive instructions from the other man just as in an army a corporal will receive instructions from a sergeant. In fact, most organisations are made up of layers or strata, to use a geological term, and so we can talk of organisations being stratified or 'layered' as shown in Figure 1. People in layer A will give instructions to people in layer B, who will give instructions to people in layer C and so

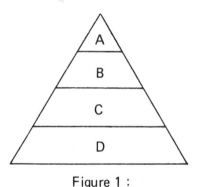

Figure 1 :
Stratified organisation

on. The trouble with instructions however, is that they are very time-consuming and it is somewhat annoying for a superior continually to tell a subordinate what to do and what not to do. Various devices have been developed to overcome this problem, some of which we will now examine.

5.   Organisations have rules and procedures. The notices which you saw in the Reception Area of the organisation stated certain organisational rules. Instead of a superior saying to me every hour of every day, 'You are not allowed to smoke here!', he might put up a notice — 'No Smoking'. But why does an organisation need rules anyway? If you remember, we said that organisations are created to meet a particular goal or purpose, and so in turn we need to arrange the work that people do to meet this goal or purpose. If every individual went about doing his work in any way that suited him at whatever time it suited him, the purpose of the organisation would never be achieved and, to remedy this, most organisations control the behaviour of employees in certain ways.

THE ORGANISATION : GOALS AND STRUCTURE

Having formal rules is one way to control behaviour, as long as you also have ways of enforcing them. Another, often more effective way, is to encourage people to see why they ought to behave in a certain way, and this can be achieved through training, which we examine in Chapter 15.

To summarise: What are the main characteristics of an organisation?

1. Organisations consist of a number of people;
2. Organisations operate a division of labour and coordinate the activities of their members;
3. Organisations are formed to achieve a goal;
4. Organisations have a hierarchical authority structure;
5. Organisations have a body of rules and procedures.

Definition of Organisation

Having described the major characteristics of an organisation we can link them together to form a definition.

Schein defines an organisation in this way:

> *'An organisation is the rational coordination of the activities of a number of people for the achievement of some common explicit purpose or goal, through the division of labour and function, and through a hierarchy of authority and responsibility.'* (E H Schein, 1972)

The Organisation Chart

At the beginning of this section we described an organisation as it looked to an individual standing in a Reception area. It is also possible to describe an organisation by drawing a map or chart — the organisation chart, as in Figure 2 on page 5

Such a chart tells us three things about an organisation:

1. It specifies what roles exist in the organisation;
2. It describes the hierarchy of authority;
3. It indicates the major communication channels.

1. *Organisational roles.* Figure 2 shows us that in this particular organisation there are many different 'jobs' — e.g. Salesman, Finance Director, Training Officer. Each of these jobs has a set of duties and responsibilities — for example the job of Training Officer may involve such duties as talking to managers about the need for training, planning training courses away from the office, and training new entrants to the organisation in particular skills. These duties and responsibilities are often listed in a job description, a document which can be very useful to

the job holder and his boss, since it gives a clear idea of what the job entails; to a training department, so that thay can ensure that the individual has had sufficient training to perform effectively; and also to a personnel specialist who might be trying to select an individual to fill that job.

Instead of using the word 'job' to describe these positions in an organisation and the duties and responsibilities that go with them, sociologists often use the term 'role', where a role may be defined as a set of rights and duties applicable to the holder of a particular position.

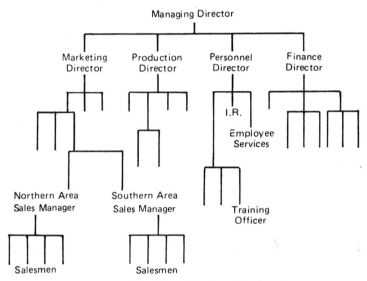

Figure 2 : Organisational roles

Thus an organisational chart may tell us what roles exist. It may also tell us about the degree of specialisation. We can see from Figure 2 that there are 4 Salesmen who work in the Southern area and who report to the Regional Sales Manager (South). Thus we know that these people specialise according to geographical area. It is likely that they sell *all* the products made by the company, otherwise we might have seen the left hand part of Figure 2 looking like Figure 3 on page 6

Similarly, we know that the Personnel Department has three sections — specialised divisions for training, industrial relations and employee services.

So, an organisation chart tells us what roles exist in the organisation, and it indicates the level of specialisation.

2. *Hierarchy of Authority.* Figure 1 showed a model of stratified organisation — the organisation chart in Figure 2 does the same thing, only in greater detail. Looking at the two together we can see that the organisational chart tells us who is at each level in the hierarchy:

A   Managing Director
B   Sales & Marketing Director
C   2 Regional Sales Managers — North and South
D   8 Salesmen

while Figure 1 only told us that there were 4 levels, with fewer people at the top than at the bottom.

But why do we need a hierarchy of authority? We have already learned that organisations exist to fulfil some purpose, and that they are made up

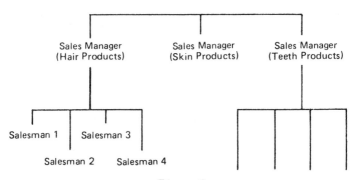

Figure 3 :
Specialised roles

of lots of different people doing a variety of specialised jobs. Consequently matching up the demands of the overall task and the contributions of the organisational members requires a significant amount of coordination. The Managing Director would be extremely busy if he had to supervise the work of all eight Salesmen as well as the staff in the Finance, Production, and Personnel Department, so he leaves it to his subordinates to do most of the day-to-day work, so that he can concentrate on matters of policy which affect the whole organisation. The Sales and Marketing Director is too busy to deal with the day-to-day problems of the eight Salesmen, as he has to consider matters of policy concerning the whole Marketing function, so he delegates these matters to his subordinates, the two Regional Sales Managers, and they each deal with four subordinates. Of course this system is useful for the Salesmen too. They know that the Managing Director has a hundred, perhaps even six hundred, people beneath him in the hierarchy and, though he might be efficient, kind and thoughtful, he is unlikely to be able to devote much time to each person and his problems. The Sales Staff probably feel much closer to the Regional Sales Manager and it is likely that he will be better able to appreciate their problems.

3. *Channels of Communication.* The organisation would be pretty chaotic if the Training Officer was at liberty to wander up to one of the Salesmen and say 'Hi! How would you like to attend one of our four day training sessions next week?' Apart from the possibility that the course might be of no relevance to the Salesman, particularly at that point in his career, it is probable that the Regional Sales Manager has alternative plans for the Salesman and he would be distinctly annoyed to have a member of another department arranging matters behind his back. To avoid this sort of problem, official communication channels exist in organisations, and these are outlined approximately on the organisational chart. The word *approximately* must be stressed here, because as we see in Chapter 8, unofficial communication channels also play an important part.

To summarise, an organisational chart is a diagram or map of an organisation, depicting three things:

1. What roles exist;
2. The hierarchies of authority;
3. The official communication channels.

Goals

In the last section we saw that organisations exist because one person, who is short of time or lacking in skills or whatever, is unable to achieve something he wants to do on his own — he needs other people to help him. We call the 'something he wants to do' his 'goal'. Often we talk about the 'goal of the organisation' but this is misleading, as we have already seen that setting up the organisation was the *means,* the method by which one *person* wanted to achieve a goal. Now this poses a possible problem. Does the goal of the founder fit in with the goals of the individuals who work in that organisation? Imagine a group of people who live in an area where there is not much to do at the weekends. One of them suggests setting up a football team so that they have something to do and so that they can meet other people by playing matches. They might go along very happily if they all want the same thing — but what happens if one individual, who fancies his chances as a potential Manchester United striker, decides that the others are holding him back because they are not sufficiently skilled or that the opposition are not strong enough to give him practice? Conflict will emerge over the purpose of the team and will possibly be resolved by the other players exerting pressure on the odd-one-out or 'deviant' to stick to the original purpose, or there might be a row leading to the break up of the team.

All organisations have to face this problem, because each individual has goals, and very often these goals conflict. The way in which an organisation copes with the problem of a variety of goals depends very much on its type. Etzioni (1961) suggests that there are three types of organisation, based on the sort of power they use:

1. Coercive
2. Normative
3. Remunerative

Coercive Power is used where the goal is to maintain order — a prison is a good example of this. Prisoners have to comply with the goals because there is the possibility that force and punishment will be used if they do not. Thus the prisoners may comply even if they do not really want to or indeed even if they think that their goals as individuals are in conflict with the goal of the prison governor — and so we call this type of compliance 'alienative'.

Normative Power may be used where there is likely to be a strong commitment on the part of the participating individuals to the purpose of the organisation. A hospital is a good example. If a nurse is unwilling to perform part of her duties because this does not fit in with one of her goals — for example resting her feet as much as possible because she wants to go dancing that evening — her superiors will start to talk about 'the good of the patient' and, because a nurse is trained to put the good of the patient above most other things, she will probably comply with this instruction. Where compliance rests on this type of value or ideal we call it 'moral compliance'.

Remunerative Power is the type which exists in most work organisations, because it is based on pay. In most work organisations there is an agreement between employer and employee about how much and what type of work is expected from the employee, and how much pay is expected from the employer. If my employer asks me to do something which conflicts with my personal goals, I must calculate whether sticking to my goals is worth losing out on my pay — hence we call this type of compliance 'calculative compliance'.

To summarise, the way in which the problems of conflicting goals are overcome depends on the type of organisation:

In a *Coercive* organisation physical pressure is used;
In a *Normative* organisation moral pressure is used;
In a *Remunerative* organisation financial pressure is used.

Up to now we have been talking about the founder of an organisation having a goal — but the majority of organisations continue long after the founder is dead. What happens to the goal over a long period of time?

Sometimes very little happens — the organisation is run by people who want the same goal as the founder, for example. A college may have been set up in the last century by someone who believed in the value of education, and on his death others may have carried on his work. It is possible that today that college may be run by a Local Education Authority, but their goal, and that of the other participants in the college, remains based on the value of education.

On the other hand, if the founder of a company dies and the company is sold there may be significant changes in the goal, and often the emergence of a number of conflicting goals. The company may now be owned by shareholders, and their goals might be to maximise the dividend paid to them — to obtain as much as they can for their investment. However, the people who manage the organisation might be oriented towards the goal of making their jobs as interesting as possible, or as secure as possible, or as well-paying as possible — and these goals may conflict with those of the shareholders. The manual workers in the company might similarly want interesting, secure and well paid jobs, plus a say in how the organisation is run, and these may also conflict with the goals of the other participants.

When we are looking at goals in the context of an organisation we must make sure that we know whose goals we are studying. To some extent the way in which we view an organisation and the goals it serves indicates our own personal values and the way in which we view the world of work in our society. Some people believe that organisations function, or *should* function, rather like a team — like 'one big happy family', a 'team approach', or 'we're all in this together'. These phrases are indicative of what is known as *the unitary approach* — a suggestion that there is no underlying or structural conflict between the different parts of the organisation and that a common goal unites all individuals into a cohesive unit.

However, other people perceive an organisation as comprising a number of groupings, all of whom have different goals and interests and who are constantly conflicting and negotiating with one another. Thus, instead of recognising one goal in an organisation, this approach recognises many goals — or a plurality of goals — and it is known as *the pluralist approach*.

To summarise, the unitary view of organisational behaviour assumes that organisations consist of many people all of whom are normally working with a common goal in mind. The pluralist view of organisational behaviour assumes that organisations consist of many people, who are members of a number of groups, and these groups might be working towards a variety of different goals — just as we saw in the example of the shareholders, managers and manual workers earlier in this section. (We examine the implications of these two approaches in Chapter 18.)

THE ORGANISATION : GOALS AND STRUCTURE

Hierarchy of Goals

In the last Section we saw that organisations tend to be stratified or layered into a hierarchy of authority. Goals too may be perceived as a hierarchy — with the overall goal or purpose of the organisation at the top and the goal or aim of the contribution of the individual worker at the bottom. In a college, for example, the hierarchy or goals might look rather like Figure 4 .

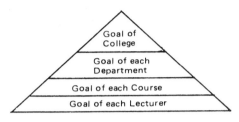

Figure 4 :
Hierarchy of organisational goals

Classifications of Organisations

So far we have seen that organisations may be classified according to the sort of power they use — Etzioni's Coercive, Normative or Remunerative organisations.

They can also be classified according to their goals — or who benefits from the organisation. This classification according to *prime beneficiary* was devised by P M Blau and W R Scott (1963). Their first type of organisation is a mutual benefit association, where the members themselves are the prime beneficiaries — for example, a Trade Union. The second type is a business concern, where the owners have the greatest benefit. Thirdly, there is the service organisation, which has its clients as the prime consideration — as in the case of a Building Society. Finally, Blau and Scott talked about the commonweal organisation — like a local library — where the public at large receives the major benefits.

To summarise, Blau and Scott's classification is based on the following four categories:

1. Mutual benefit associations;
2. Business concerns;
3. Service organisations;
4. Commonweal organisations.

A third way of classifying organisations is by looking at their overall purpose in society as a whole. Talcott Parsons (1960) suggested four such purposes or functions that organisations could fulfil:

ORGANISATIONAL GOALS

1.   Production organisations — to make things which are consumed by people in society — e.g. ICI, Unilever;

2.   Organisations oriented to political goals, e.g. Civil Service;

3.   The integrative organisation, whose goals are settling conflicts and making sure that parts of society work together. Our legal system with its various component organisations meets this criterion, and in some respects, so do religious organisations.

4.   The pattern maintenance organisation has as its goals the passing on of knowledge and values concerning the culture of society from one generation to the next or from one group to another. Schools, universities, libraries and theatres fall into this category.

The Parsons' classification depends on the overall use of the organisation to the whole society;

>   Production goals;
>   Political goals;
>   Integrative goals;
>   Pattern maintenance goals.

There are other classifications of organisations which depend on the type of structure or the type of technology used, and these will be outlined in later Chapters.

Chapter 2

Determinants of Organisational Structure

So far we have looked at the characteristics of organisations and the goals which organisations may have been established to achieve. In this section we will look at some of the theories which have been proposed to assist policy makers in deciding on the structure an organisation might take.

Bureaucracy — Max Weber

Some of the earliest work on organisation structure was carried out by Max Weber (1947), a German sociologist, early this century. Weber was particularly interested in the different types of authority which exist in industrial society, and he classified authority according to three main types:

Traditional authority — e.g. found in organisations in which the founder is still present.

Charismatic authority — stems from devotion to a particular person because of his personal characteristics.

Legal-rational authority — based on a view that those in high positions have a right to give instructions to those lower down in the hierarchy.

Weber considered that modern industrial society was moving towards a situation in which legal-rational authority would be the dominant form of authority. He went on to consider what type of organisation structure would be best fitted to this type of authority, and he constructed an 'ideal type' or model of bureacracy which possessed the following characteristics:

1.   A bureacracy aims essentially at rationality and efficiency in its administrative machinery.

1.   Authority derives from skill or expertise, not, for example, from whom your father knows or how much he earns.

3.   There is a high degree of specialisation of function. If we take a Personnel Department as an example, in most large organisations the Personnel specialists will be split up so that some people concentrate on training, some on Industrial Relations, some on payment systems and so on.

4.   Initial selection and subsequent promotion is dependent upon technical qualifications and experience, not, for example, simply because

you are a friendly person or because your brother has put in a good word for you (known as 'nepotism').

5. There is a pyramid shaped organisation hierarchy.

6. There is a formal set of rules governing procedures. This is particularly obvious in the treatment of clients, as it is considered important that each client should be 'fairly' or 'equally' treated and that there should be no favouritism.

7. Organisational members are encouraged to keep their relations with other members of the organisation on an impersonal footing. Again, the logic behind this becomes obvious if we consider that all parts of the organisation must work together if the goals are to be achieved, and that inefficiency would almost certainly follow from one departmental head providing better services to another simply because he happened to be particularly friendly with its head. It is obviously also a fear that personal friendships or animosity might take precedence over the good of the organisation and the achievement of goals.

8. All the various 'jobs' to be done in the organisation are allocated to various 'positions' or roles in the form of official duties, usually laid down in the job description for that role. It is important to note that these duties are not given directly to an individual to perform, but to the job that the individual is doing. The significance of this lies in the problems which might emerge if the individual leaves. In this way continuity of duties is assured.

We can see from these characteristics that Weber was insistent on the quality of *rationality* in bureaucracy, and he believed this quality to be penetrating all our social institutions. The modern army, the factory, the church and the college are all losing their 'traditional' character and are increasingly run through the operation of impersonal and rational rules which aim at maximum efficiency.

However the impact of these rules and the other characteristics of a bureaucracy may be far from stimulating as far as the individual employee or participant is concerned. In certain circumstances these bureaucratic procedures may cause the individual to see himself as significantly limited in terms of personal freedom and the opportunity to exercise creativity and responsibility. The specialisation referred to above may cause the bureaucratic administrator to experience a fragmentation of work very similar to that experienced by manual workers on an assembly line, who only do a very small part of the total manufacturing cycle. Marx predicted that the development of bureaucracy, particularly the state bureaucracy (e.g. the Civil Service in Britain), would lead to alienation, and that the majority of the population would see bureaucracy as a mysterious entity out of their control.

It would be inaccurate to consider that organisations work exactly in the way that Weber suggested, as Weber concentrated on the *formal* organisation or the official stance that the organisation might take, whereas we know that individuals can exert a considerable influence through the operation of the informal organisation.

Modifications to the Weberian Model of Bureaucracy

Alvin Gouldner undertook a very detailed piece of research in which he studied a gypsum mine in America. This mine was a subsidiary of a conglomerate and for many years was managed by an older manager who knew his staff very well, and who was somewhat lax in upholding the rules laid down by Head Office. When he left, the post was filled by a bright young man, who had been informed that, in effect, his future career depended on the success he made of this particular mine. This kind of situation has occurred in a great many organisations, frequently with the same sort of outcome. Being under pressure himself, the new young manager exerted pressure on the workforce, who were certainly unused to this style of managerial behaviour, and who did not particularly appreciate it. Suffice it to say that the title of one of Gouldner's books is *Wildcat Strike* (A W Gouldner, 1954).

One of the results of Gouldner's research was that he developed a three fold classification of bureaucracy, based on the type of coercion exerted by management and the type of consent offered by the workforce. He is basically saying, bureaucracy has rules, but in whose interests are these rules drawn up?

1. *Mock bureaucracy:* this often occurs in the subsidiary of a large conglomerate for example, or in any organisation where rules are made by an agency external to the organisation itself. It is probable that neither management nor workers have a vested interest in adhering to the rules and so they tend to be ignored, unless some inspection is to be made by the third party.

2. *Representative bureaucracy:* in this case the rules are drawn up in the interests of both management and workers, so that everybody gains by compliance to the rules.

3. *Punishment-centred bureaucracy:* this type is characterised by rules which serve the interests of only one group, although other groups may accept them through expediency. However, there is no moral commitment to accept them, except on the part of the originators, and evasion is common.

Obviously it would be inaccurate to assume that organisations have just one type of rule; according to Gouldner most have a mixture of all three, but Gouldner is suggesting that we look for the predominant type of rule when making our classification.

Another view of the changing nature of a bureaucracy is that put forward by Peter Blau (1963). He is particularly interested in the influence of the informal organisation on the formal structure, and he points out that, because the environment is constantly changing, and because an organisation takes a relatively long time to modify official rules and procedures to take into account these environmental changes, it has to rely on *unofficial* practices and communication channels if it is to remain effective. In other words, it relies on individual employees modifying the rules unofficially, in advance of the organisation doing so officially.

One of the most important developments from Weber's work was carried out by Tom Burns and G M Stalker (1961). During their study of British firms in the electronics and textile industries they became convinced that organisations could be seen in two typical forms — *mechanistic* and *organic*. The authors were interested in the difficulties

STABLE   UNSTABLE

MECHANISTIC   ORGANIC

Figure 5 : Burns and Stalker continuum

confronting firms which were operating in a rapidly changing market or technological environment, and they point out that a bureaucratic form of organisation, or a mechanistic form, as they term it, may be highly appropriate to stable conditions, but a far more flexible structure is required for fluctuating conditions. Burns and Stalker called this flexible structure an organic type of organisation. They suggest the extreme points on a continuum, as indicated in Figure 5, and that companies will adopt a position somewhere along that continuum, approximating to one or other type. It is probable that even within an organisation there will be differences, such that an advertising department is likely to be more organic than a finance department.

Thus the mechanistic type of organisation is similar to Weber's rational-legal type of bureaucracy, with a clear hierarchy of control, emphasis on vertical communication, narrow spans of control, and a large number of authority levels. The organic organisational structure is very much more decentralised; as the rate of change increases, so do the number of occasions which require quick and effective communication and decision making between people working in different departments.

Another development in the study of bureaucracy has come from Derek Pugh and his colleagues, originating at Aston University (1971).

THE ORGANISATION : GOALS AND STRUCTURE

The studies and theories mentioned so far have been based on a unitary concept in that bureaucracy has been regarded as a single dimension and organisations as being located somewhere along a continuum of more or less bureaucratisation. Pugh *et al* question the utility of this idea of bureaucracy and suggest that organisations may vary on six scales:

1. Specialisation — the extent of the division of labour;
2. Standardisation — of procedures and roles;
3. Centralisation — where decisions are taken;
4. Configuration — 'shape' of the organisation, e.g. flat or tall;
5. Formalisation — extent to which e.g. communications are in writing and filed.
6. Flexibility — amount and speed of change.

They then illustrate the work of other social scientists in terms of their scheme. For example, an interpretation (involving these dimensions) of Weber's theory would be that formalisation, specialisation (with professionalisation in particular), and centralisation would be highly correlated, but since bureaucracy rarely changes its structure, these variables would not be correlated with flexibility.

By using these six primary dimensions, it becomes possible to construct a profile characteristic of the structure of an organisation and to compare it directly with that of others.

One of the major disadvantages of this kind of study — one that Pugh *et al* themselves mention — is that it deals with what is officially expected SHOULD be done, and what is in practice ALLOWED to be done. It does not include what is ACTUALLY done, i.e. what really happens, in the sense of behaviour beyond that instituted in organisational forms.

Their studies were conducted by administering questionnaires to appropriate personnel in the organisation under study. These questionnaires were made up of a number of items concerning each of the dimensions, so that a 'score' could be attributed to each organisation in terms of each dimension.

It was found that organisations differed considerably according to these variables, and Pugh *et al* conclude that a unitary concept of bureaucracy, such as the Weberian one, is probably no longer useful.

Thus one of the central ideas guiding research into organisation structure has been that of Max Weber and bureaucracy. We will now consider another set of ideas — scientific management — the influence of which is also apparent today.

Scientific Management — F W Taylor

Frederick Taylor (1911) had a very clear philosophy about people's behaviour at work. He adopted a view of human motivation which is

16

called the principle of 'economic man'. According to this view, people act in isolation and without regard to others. They act in pursuit of their own interests so as to maximise their income and they act rationally, relating means and ends.

Tradition would have us believe that Taylor was the sort of person who could always think of a better way of doing things. When he was at college in America he tried to tell his fellow students about the most efficient way to throw a ball in baseball — he also designed a new style of tennis racquet. Sadly the reactions of his fellow students are not recorded! His career took him to the Midvale steel works where he was horrified to find that very little thought appeared to have been given to the design of jobs, and that the management did not appear to believe, as he did, that industrial organisations were governed by laws, as in science (hence the term 'scientific management'). He was amazed that while management had a clear idea of the output of a machine, they had very little idea of the output they could expect from a man.

Taylor believed he could increase the output of individuals by a series of improvements — or what he considered to be improvements — while at the same time increasing the wages of the workers, which would improve their motivation under his general philosophy of economic man. The steps involved:

1.   Selection — selecting the best person for the job;
2.   Design of equipment — for example, designing shovels that would be the right weight and size for the individuals using them;
3.   Design of method — Taylor believed there was 'one best way' of performing a given task, and that any redundant movements should be suppressed;
4.   Motivation by increased economic reward.

Taylor went to the management of the steel works and asked for a chance to try out his ideas. After some persuasion they agreed, and Taylor put his plan into operation initially with men who loaded pig iron. He simplified the work into its most basic form, he redesigned certain equipment and the layout of the shop floor to improve efficiency, and he trained the men in what he considered to be the best way of doing that particular job, using financial incentives to encourage them.

When Taylor reported to the management he could tell them that he had achieved a 362% increase in production, while the incentive payment system he had devised meant that the workers had received a 61% increase in wages. It is reasonable to suppose that the management might have been impressed.

There were, however, some fundamental problems arising out of Taylor's methods:

1.   The unions were singularly unimpressed by the amount of extra

money the workers received, compared to the amount of extra output they were producing. Indeed, even at the very earliest phases of Taylor's experiments a number of those taking part were subject to threats and intimidation from other workers who saw the danger to their interests in what Taylor was doing.

2. In devising 'one best way', Taylor ignored the field of individual differences, and the fact that the best working method for one individual might not be best for another.

3. In keeping with his 'economic man' philosophy, Taylor believed that workers only act as individuals, and so no account was taken of the impact of informal work groups, social needs of workers and so on.

4. Although Taylor did consider the use of scientifically designed rest pauses, he appears to have ignored both the effect of cumulative fatigue — i.e. fatigue which might build up progressively over the course of a day or a week, and the effect of trying to suppress certain actions which he considered unnecessary. To discover what this might mean, you can do an experiment. Try to read a chapter of this book whilst sitting absolutely still, with the exception of turning the page when necessary. You must not touch your face, fiddle with your fingers, or cross your legs — simply sit absolutely still. You will probably find that it is extremely difficult to do this — you have to concentrate on the subject matter in the book *and* on sitting still, and usually concentrating on the one will prevent concentration on the other. Thus Taylor was apparently unaware that significant energy was expended in remembering to suppress the redundant actions, which calls into question the efficiency of his methods.

In spite of these criticisms of his work, Taylor's influence has been significant in the organisation of work, particularly in the development of time and motion study, O & M, and indeed many managers today subscribe to the same philosophy of motivation as Taylor did — 'economic man'.

Although Taylor is perhaps the most widely publicised exponent of Scientific Management, there were many others whose philosophy was similar. The Gilbreths (1947), an engineer and psychologist couple, concentrated on efficient methods of work, breaking down tasks into their very simplest units, which they called 'therbligs'. Writers such as Fayol (1949), Mooney (1931), and Mary Parker Follet (1941) were particularly interested in the science of management, while Urwick(1947), Graicunas (1937), and others devised rules for efficient management, such as Unity of Command, i.e. that each individual should report to only one boss. Graicunas is specifically known for his work on Span of Control, and he devised rules concerning the optimum number of subordinates to each superior.

Thus scientific management may be considered the first attempt to tackle, in a systematic and rational manner, the problem of organisation of work. Although many writers of this persuasion concentrated on sets of methods and principles aimed solely at increasing production, their philosophy was founded on assumptions about people, their relationship with work, and their relationships with fellow workers — a philosophy which is frequently echoed today.

Human Relations School

In 1927 the Hawthorne factory of the Western Electric Company in America commissioned a study, according to 'Scientific Management' principles, on the effect of changes in illumination on production. The researchers were from Harvard, the senior researcher being Elton Mayo.

The research team observed the changes in output when illumination was improved, and found that it increased. At first they thought that a simple rule could be applied — that an increase in intensity of illumination led to a corresponding increase in output. Unfortunately for simplicity's sake, this was called into question when output increased even when the level of illumination remained constant and, even more dramatic still, output increased when the level of illumination *decreased*. The researchers had to admit that there were influences operating other than level of illumination and, for the next few years, they conducted a series of studies, observations and interviews to discover what these influences might be.

There were four major stages in the research after these initial findings from the illumination experiment:

1. *The Relay Assembly Test Room,* where specially selected girls worked in carefully monitored conditions. The supervision was friendly and participative and rest pauses were varied along with the length of the working day. Production increased, and this was attributed to a number of causes:

(a) friendly supervision;
(b) the existence of a small, cohesive work group; and
(c) the sense of importance felt by the girls — they were special because they were taking part in an experiment.

The researchers now realised that rather than objective factors, such as temperature or level of illumination, affecting output, subjective factors such as attitude and morale appeared to be important, and so the next phase was established.

2. *The Interviewing Programme* was conducted to examine further this relationship between worker attitudes and performance. In the course of this series of interviews it was discovered that an individual's attitudes to

19

wages or hours of work were significantly affected by his position in the group, and the group's attitude or 'norm' on this issue. Thus the main finding from this phase of the research was the importance of social relationships and group dynamics for production.

3. *The Bank Wiring Room* contained a number of men who were observed as unobtrusively as possible over a six month period. In this case very specific group attitudes or 'norms' were apparent concerning quantity of output. It was discovered that the group established its own acceptable level of production, and anyone who over-produced or under-produced experienced the displeasure of the group in the form of negative sanctions. Informal leaders were observed, and they could have a significant influence on the organisation and functioning of the work group. The researchers also claimed that group loyalty was more important to the members than financial incentives.

4. *The Employee Counselling Programme* was set up to improve communications in the company, especially from the shop floor upwards, and personal counsellors were appointed to talk to workers when requested. It was anticipated that this would lead to a more informed diagnosis of employee problems, and improved supervision.

As a result of the Hawthorne experiments (F J Roethlisberger & W J Dickson, 1939) the worker could no longer be regarded, as Taylor regarded him, as an isolated creature acting to maximise his income in a rational and independent way. Work was seen as a group activity, and thus the work place began to be regarded as a social system with an informal organisation which could work for or against the formal side. Informal work groups exercise considerable influence on workers' attitudes and output, and supervisory behaviour must be geared to the effective manipulation of group attitudes in ways that are favourable to the company interests.

It has frequently been claimed that the Human Relations School replaced one narrow view of the relationship between people and work — one which focused on the technical aspects of work — with a different, but equally narrow view by concentrating on the social aspects of work. This deficiency was considered and remedied by a number of researchers who are normally grouped together under the heading:

The Socio-Technical System Approach

This view of organisations, people, and work was developed mainly in Britain, and is particularly associated with the work of E L Trist, F E Emery and the Tavistock Institute of Human Relations. We devote Chapter 20 to the concept of systems as applied to organisations, so it is sufficient for the present to point out that systems are basically sets of interrelationships. Thus the socio-technical system approach is emphasising the interrelationship between the technical side of the organisation, which was previously studied by Taylor, and the social side, stressed in the Human Relations approach. Trist (E L Trist, G W Higgins, H Murray and A B Pollock, 1963) suggests that any productive organisation (or part of an organisation) is a combination of technology, including task requirements, physical layout and equipment design, and a social system, which is a set of relationships among those who perform the tasks. The technology and the social system influence one another, each shapes the other and is, in turn, shaped by the other. This approach gives equal weighting to the formal and informal structures, unlike other models of organisation we have considered, nor does it suggest that there is a single ideal structure.

One example of this kind of approach is the study of the Durham coal mines by Trist and Bamforth. They were interested in the effects on coal miners of a technological change involving the installation of mechanical coal cutting machinery. The original method of coal mining, called the shortwall method, involved small groups of between two and eight men working together as a team, independent of other teams. Each team was allocated a small section of the coalface and was responsible for the cutting, loading and removal of coal from this section. Teams were essentially self-responsible and members were picked by the team leader because they would be able to 'get on with' other members of the team. Because of this, very strong, friendly relationships existed between team members, to the extent that they would take care of a team member's family if he was hurt or killed. These personal bonds were strengthened by the anxieties generated by working underground and in the dark and dangerous conditions.

However, engineering advances made it preferable that mechanisation should be introduced for the cutting and removal of coal, and this became known as the long-wall method. The organisation of the miners themselves was greatly changed. The mine became more like a factory, with groups of forty or fifty men under a supervisor, and this new style of social grouping could not satisfy the social and emotional needs of the miners. However, the impact of mechanisation went further than social needs. The men were spread out along the coal face, and worked in three shifts. A high degree of coordination was necessary between the shifts, such that any inefficiency anywhere along the line on any shift could reduce drastically the output of the whole group. Morale was further damaged by the differential prestige allocated to the various tasks. Thus considerable emotional and physical strain resulted from the discruption of traditional group relationships with the advent of this highly differentiated, rigidly sequenced, mechanised mass production method. Because of the inherent dangers in the work environment, and the inherent difficulties of the work itself, the productivity of the miners fell.

We can see in this example the significant interrelationships of technology and the social system, and, in this case, social scientists were involved in re-designing the production system to overcome some of these difficulties.

Contingency Theory

In our discussion of the work of Trist and others it was stated that there was no single, ideal organisation structure. This is the basic view of adherents of the contingency theory of organisation, but they go a step further and outline some of the variables which will determine an effective structure.

An example of this approach is found in the work of P R Lawrence and J W Lorsch (1967). They consider organisations as operating in an environment made up of three segments: The Market, the Technological Environment, and Research and Development in their particular field. Each of these segments may experience a different rate of change, so that the Market may change more slowly than the Technology, for example.

Lawrence and Lorsch believe that the particular form and structure adopted for a particular organisation is dependent on the environmental conditions it faces, although they point out that size, tradition and other factors may also have an impact. They suggest that the effectiveness of an organisation is not achieved through adherence to any one model of structure and functioning, but is contingent upon, or depends on, environmental conditions.

Their research was carried out in three industries — plastics, processed foods, and containers.

The plastics industry is one which experiences a high level of competitive activity in the market place and also in the development of new and revised products and processes. The life cycle of any product is likely to be short, since all firms in the industry engage in intensive R and D activity, and can therefore make even a successful product rapidly obsolete. The six companies in the plastics industry, which Lawrence and Lorsch studied, operated in a turbulent environment and with a high level of uncertainty concerning market and development conditions. However, the process of production itself was more certain, as there was a well-established automated process.

From this we can see that internal differences in the level of certainty were attached to different departments — differences which Lawrence and Lorsch categorise in the following way:

1. *Formalisation* — i.e. the extent to which there were specific

procedures and standardised methods. Formalisation was highest in the production department and lowest in the research department.

2. *Interpersonal relations* — i.e. the extent to which the work of a department relied on the interpersonal skills of its members. The sales departments were most concerned with this area and the production departments least concerned.

3. *Time perspective* — i.e. the time horizons adopted by members of different departments. The shortest time perspectives were adopted by sales departments, followed by production departments, and the longest time perspective was adopted by research departments.

4. *Differentiation of departments according to goals* — sales departments were primarily oriented towards customers; production departments towards lowering costs and increasing efficiency; and research departments towards increasing the level of scientific knowledge.

Lawrence and Lorsch found significant interdepartmental differences on these four dimensions in the plastics industry companies, and they suggest that this high level of differentiation and complexity echoes the level of complexity and differentiation in the environment in which they operate.

The container industry, by comparison, operated in a relatively stable environment, and these organisations experience a low level of interdepartmental differences. The food processing industry occupied an intermediate position between these two extremes.

One notable area of variance was that of conflict resolution. Lawrence and Lorsch found that in the stable container industry, effective organisations dealt with conflict resolution at the top — i.e. at Board level or just below. However, the effective organisations in the highly differentiated plastics industry experienced a significant level of interdepartmental conflict, and these organisations tended to have established integrating positions or roles whose purpose was to resolve such conflict. These positions, in contrast to the container industry, tended to be located low down in the organisational hierarchy. So, in terms of conflict resolution, Lawrence and Lorsch are again stressing that no 'one best way' exists — effective structure depends on the environmental conditions.

The contingency approach of Lawrence and Lorsch fixes our attention on the interrelationship of organisation and environment, and on the fact that there are many means to the same end of effectiveness in terms of organisational structure.

Chapter 3

Variations In Organisational Structure

In the last section we traced the development of organisation theory, from the rigid rules of structure laid down by scientific management to the contingency approach, which claims that there is no 'one best way' to structure an organisation, and that effective structure is dependent on a number of variables such as R & D activity and market stability.

In this section we will look at some of the variations in structure and how these affect the experience of work for participants in the organisation.

Variations in the Hierarchy

T Burns and G M Stalker (1961) suggested that mechanistic organisations tended to have a great many different levels in the hierarchy, but that the span of control — the number of subordinates reporting to one boss — would be small. An organic organisation, on the other hand, might have few levels in the hierarchy but large spans of control. We call these varieties of hierarchy *tall* and *flat* respectively, and they may be illustrated diagramatically as in Figure 6.

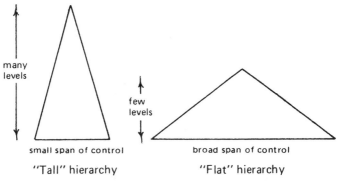

Figure 6 : Tall and flat hierarchies

What might be the advantages or disadvantages of working in a tall or a flat organisation?

In a *tall* organisation:

VARIATIONS IN ORGANISATION STRUCTURE

1.   You may have ready access to your boss, as he has only a few subordinates to supervise, but he may also exercise tighter control on your behaviour.

2.   Communication may be helped because your boss can talk to you personally, but there are a large number of other levels in between you and the top of the organisation through which communications must pass, and so the possibility of a message being distorted increases.

3.   As decisions are probably made at the top of the organisation, people at the bottom are unlikely to have any effective 'voice' or influence on these decisions.

4.   Because there are a large number of levels in the hierarchy, the probability of your being promoted from one level to the next is relatively high. However, this type of organisation is likely to be very specialised, thus your experience in each job and the range of abilities you develop at each level may be small.

In a *flat* organisation:

1.   Your dealings with your immediate boss may be relatively few and far between, as he will supervise a great many people. However, this means that more responsibility for problem solving will fall on your shoulders at an early stage in your career, and you may depend far more on your colleagues or peers for advice and consultation.

2.   Communication may be helped because there are few levels between you and the top of the organisation through which messages must pass, therefore there is little likelihood of distortion as they pass from level to level. However, because of the large spans of control it is unlikely that a superior would be able to pass all information to all his subordinates simultaneously — he may be selective as to who is told what or he may have to use impersonal means such as a 'memo' or letter, in which case your opportunity for asking questions etc. is limited.

3.   The few levels in the hierarchy increase the chances of each level contributing to the decision making process, particularly since decision making is often delegated downwards in this type of organisation.

4.   Because there are few levels in the hierarchy the probability of your being promoted from one level to the next is relatively low. However, as stated above, your experience of each job is likely to entail much greater responsibility and skill than in other forms of organisation.

Thus flat and tall organisations have advantages and disadvantages for participants, and their effectiveness depends greatly on the market and environmental conditions operating on the organisation.

THE ORGANISATION : GOALS AND STRUCTURE

Centralisation and Decentralisation

In your college it is unlikely that you have a separate library for every course or every subject - library services are often *centralised*, which means that they are all together in a common location and with one set of staff. Some organisations have found it more efficient and effective to have their personnel services centralised in the same way, or their typists, or their buying department. If we take a centralised buying department compared to a decentralised one as an example, some of the advantages and disadvantages may become apparent. If a central buying department obtains all the stationery — letter paper and envelopes, for example — for the whole organisation, they might be able to negotiate a lower price because of the greater bulk purchased, whereas each individual department would require only a fraction of that total.

It is possible to argue that a better quality of buyer is possible in a centralised department due to the likelihood of his being able to specialise in a particular range of goods and to receive some specialist training. From management's point of view it is more conducive to control to have centralisation of departments rather than decentralisation.

There may come a stage in the organisation's development when the task of buying becomes too great for anything other than a very unwieldy buying department. It may be that the organisation diversifies, as in the case of a cigarette manufacturer going in for the manufacture of potato crisps, and that very different types of knowledge and skill are required. This tends to lead to decentralisation. In a culture which, from time to time, wishes to remind itself that small is beautiful, the appeal of the smaller, more decentralised unit is obvious. Employee loyalty can be more readily tapped in the smaller, more personal, decentralised unit. In most organisations, therefore, the tendencies towards centralisation and decentralisation are very much the concern of policy makers, who have to trade off these particular advantages and disadvantages.

Variations in Departmental Structure

There are a number of ways in which groupings of people may be arranged to facilitate the achievement of the goals of the organisation.

In Figure 7 we can see that the organisation's departmental structure is arranged on functional lines with a department for finance people, a department for personnel people, and so on. As an employee of that organisation you would be allocated to a department solely on the basis of your particular specialism so, if you were an accountant, you would invariably work in the finance department.

This type of structure has the advantage that a large resource of

VARIATIONS IN ORGANISATION STRUCTURE

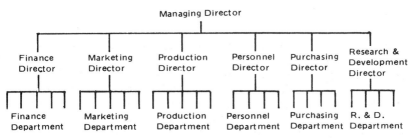

Figure 7 : Functional organisation structure

specialist talent is available to the organisation, and from the employee's point of view he has a considerable body of expertise to fall back on when he needs assistance in his work. However, again from the individual's point of view, his work is likely to be highly specialised, and it may take a number of years before he samples all the types of work which may fall to his particular function. A far more significant problem with this kind of structure is that loyalty often lies with the department rather than with the organisation as a whole. In a time of financial stringency, preserving the departmental budget may take precedence over viewing the situation in the light of efficiency of the company and the optimum use of resources.

Bearing these points in mind, some companies are structured along product, or product group, lines, as indicated in Figure 8.

This type of structure is frequently found in organisations with a heavy marketing bias, and the structure revolves around what is considered to

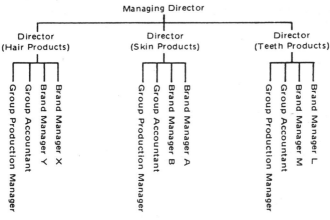

Figure 8 : Product group organisation structure

27

be the *raison d'etre* of the organisation, its products. From the management point of view, this structure has the advantage of developing a team of individuals with strong loyalties to a product or group of products. It minimises functional specialist conflict, for example between finance and production specialists, as the focus of interest is more immediate and more obviously of common concern. From the individual's point of view, he is likely to be a member of a relatively small group of specialists and so he is likely to obtain a wide range of experience relatively quickly in the early years of his career. However, because of this small number of specialists, his promotion opportunities could suffer and so, even if his immediate experience of job content is satisfactory, the individual might question the long term career implications of such a structure. From

	Finance Dept.	Marketing Dept.	R&D Dept.	Production Dept.
Project Manager A	Finance Specialist A	Marketing Specialist A	R&D Specialist A	Production Specialist A
Project Manager B		∗		
Project Manager C				

Figure 9 : Matrix organisation structure

management's point of view, this scheme has the disadvantage that it lacks the body of functional specialism and has diffused all its specialists throughout the organisation.

So both of these structures have advantages and disadvantages. Is there any structure which incorporates all the advantages and minimises the disadvantages? To an extent the answer is yes, in that a number of organisations in America and a few in Britain, particularly in the area of electronics, have developed a structure known as *matrix management* which is an attempt to combine these two.

Matrix management is a useful structural technique where a significant amount of new product development is undertaken in the organisation. Departments are organised on normal functional lines; so let us say for the sake of simplicity that we have a finance, marketing, research and development, and production department, as shown in Figure 9.

Let us assume that a new product (Product A) is being considered. A manager will be appointed from any department in the organisation that the board of directors, or their delegated representatives, think appropriate, and he is portrayed as Project Manager A in Figure 9. Now Project Manager A must gather together a team of experts from the relevant departments in order to develop, produce and market Product A effectively. The procedure is normally that he would go to the manager of the finance department and ask him to provide a finance specialist to work on the development team for Product A - we have called this person Finance Specialist A. The project manager then goes to the manager of the marketing department and asks for the provision of a marketing specialist, who becomes Marketing Specialist A, and this procedure is repeated with the research and development department and production department. At the end of this exercise a multifunctional team will have been formed to develop this new product. Obviously, it is unlikely that only one new product is being developed at a time, and so in Figure 9 you will see the structure provides for similar teams to work under the leadership of Project Manager B and Project Manager C.

The great strength of this structure is that the central focus for the individual is the product (instead of departmental loyalty) while support of the functional department is retained. Interested departments are involved from the very earliest days of the product's life.

However, there are a number of problems which may arise due to this particular structure. Much depends, for example, on the relationships between the individuals concerned.

Let us listen in to Project Manager A asking the finance manager for assistance.

Project Manager A	As you have probably heard, I have been appointed to head a team working on the development and launch of Product A. I really need a finance specialist to help, and I wonder if you could suggest someone?
Finance Manager	Well, we're pretty busy at the moment, but I think we could probably let you have Fred. O.K.?
PMA	No, not really, you see Joe is working on this product from the marketing side, and he and Fred hate each other — the meetings seem to be continually dealing with their problems.
FM	That is really up to you — as a manager you should be able to deal with a minor difference of opinion. As it so happens, I have a new bloke, joining next week, you could have him.
PMA	I don't want to be the trainer for your raw recruits — give him to someone else. Why can't I have Charlie — he's a great guy — really knows his stuff and gets on well with everyone.

FM   You can't have Charlie, because I have different plans for him. I am responsible for his career development, and if he always works on the same sort of project he'll find himself in a rut.

And so the negotiations continue until Finance Specialist A is agreed upon. It should now be possible to see that the goals of Project Manager A (to get the best person for his particular team) and of the finance manager (to arrange the development of his staff and to coordinate the work of the department) might be in conflict, and significant interpersonal skills may be required to overcome this problem, or a body of rules will have to be developed to legislate for such an eventuality.

Another problem may arise with an assessment of the performance of, for example, Financial Specialist A. His departmental manager may well be responsible for the performance appraisal of his staff (for a fuller coverage of performance appraisal see Chapter 13), and yet Project Manager A may have a much better idea of Financial Specialist A's performance as they have been working closely together for a year. An obvious solution is for the two managers to get together so that a full picture will emerge, but again this informal system relies on the goodwill and interpersonal skills of the individuals involved, and in many organisations specific rules and procedures will exist to cover this eventuality.

A third problem lies in the fact that matrix organisation breaks a fundamental rule which the classical organisation theorists laid down namely, unity of command - that a person should report to one boss. Yet matrix organisation has provided Financial Specialist A, and his colleagues with two bosses — the departmental manager and the project manager. It may be rare that the two managers conflict, but if this does occur poor Financial Specialist A may find himself in a very uncomfortable position. Again, this problem is tackled in some organisations by laying down carefully thought-out guidelines, suggesting whose views take precedence in specific situations, but other organisations take a much less structured approach and leave the individuals concerned to sort out their difficulties.

Matrix organisation is a form of structure which has significant advantages for an organisation operating in a rapidly changing market environment, combining as it does the strengths of both functional and product based departmental structures, but these advantages co-exist with the potential for various problems. Decisions concerning the extent of rules accompanying this structure will be made by the policy makers who must weigh up the advantages of clear-cut, if rigid, procedures against the greater ambiguity which will acompany flexibility.

VARIATIONS IN ORGANISATION STRUCTURE

Staff/Line Conflict

One final form of conflict which we will consider in this chapter is that between two types of manager — the *staff* manager and the *line* manager. Organisational life has become so complex that, as well as people who directly produce a good or service, it is frequently necessary to employ people to work in indirect or advisory functions, such as in a personnel or a finance department. Thus a staff manager is not directly involved in the production of output, but performs an advisory or service function; whereas the line manager, such as a production manager, is directly involved. M Dalton (1959) pointed out that these two types of manager might conflict, both because of their different roles in the organisation, and because they tend to have different characteristics as people. Staff managers are often members of professional associations who have spent some years in further education and training and who are specialists. Line managers have frequently 'worked their way up' an organisation, and are less likely to have had professional training.

These two types of managers may conflict, to use extreme examples, because the staff manager considers his specialist knowledge to be superior to the line manager's, while the latter considers his practical experience to be far more valuable than the 'book learning' of the staff manager. It is also the case that the staff manager has a much greater opportunity to find another position in a different organisation because of his qualifications and his dependence on, and possibly his loyalty to, his present organisation may be significantly lower. Line managers may see these qualified people as a threat and may resent the fact that they frequently attain high status in the organisation at a relatively early age.

Chapter 4

Human Resource Planning

In this chapter we are going to look in general terms at human resource planning, job analysis, job descriptions and job specifications. We will look at the techniques used in human resource planning in Chapter 14. First, let us define human resource planning as *the strategy for acquiring, using, improving and preserving the organisation's human resources.* That sounds fine, but, when you look at the definition more closely it almost amounts to 'everything to do with employees' — a definition which may be applied to personnel management itself. So where does human resource planning fit into personnel management? As the term suggests, it is the activity associated with planning rather than doing. In this sense human resource planning is concerned with determining what should or will happen in the future to the organisation with respect to the employees. It is only through the process of planning that future potential problems can be identified and remedial action taken. This aspect of the exercise becomes important when the action necessary may take a long time. So for instance it is useful for a company to anticipate how many craftsmen it will need in the future since the lead time on training craftsmen may be four or five years. If the organisation waited until it needed craftsmen and then recruited apprentices, it would have to wait four or five years before the apprentices were of use, by which time it could have gone out of business as a result of not having craftsmen when needed.

What we have said so far seems obvious and quite straightforward, however human resource planning depends upon *corporate planning*. In Chapter 1 we looked at the question of goals, which are of great significance in corporate planning.

Corporate Planning and Human Resource Planning

Let us consider corporate planning under two headings, strategic planning and tactical planning, the latter being derived from the former. Let us assume that the organisation exists to fulfil certain objectives and that these are known to senior management. It is the responsibility of senior management to deploy resources so that objectives are achieved. When senior managers or directors are drawing up strategic plans for the achievement of objectives they will have to take note of a number of factors, some of which will be completely beyond their control. Strategic planning may be shown in the form of a diagram (see Figure 10).

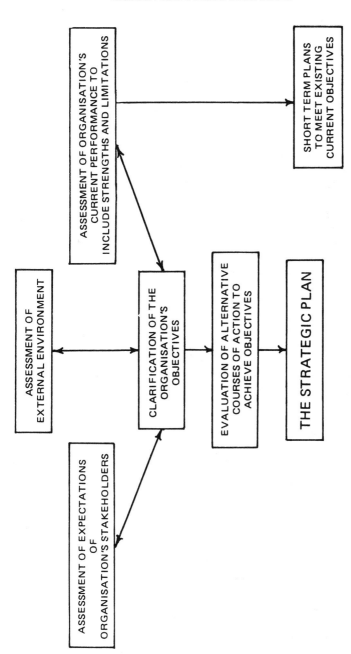

FIGURE 10 : STRATEGIC PLANNING CHART

If we consider the assessment of the external environment, we are looking mainly at the *markets* which the organisation serves and the *competitive environment* in which it operates. With respect to markets, the directors will want information on factors which affect the market in which the organisation sells its products or services. Are the markets growing or contracting; are they subject to economic change in the short or long term; what impact, if any, would political change have upon them? Clearly different organisations will need different information with respect to their markets, but whatever the organisation, be it the provider of goods like a manufacturer or the provider of services like a college, an assessment of the markets in which it operates is essential in drawing up a strategic plan. Just as the organisation needs to know what markets are potentially available, it also needs to know something about the competitive environment in which it will be operating. This competitive environment may be split into two component parts; competition for *customers* and competition for *resources*. Perhaps the best way to explain this is through the use of an example. Suppose there was a college which was considering running courses in business studies, then the director of the college could assess the market to see if there were potentially enough customers, in this case students. He may come to the conclusion that a big enough market exists for him to consider setting up courses in business studies. Before he does so however he must look at the state of competition for both customers and resources. The competition for *customers* may be another college six miles away, which is also considering running business studies courses. The competition for *resources* may be that there are not enough lecturers in business studies available. Thus, even if the market existed and perhaps was large enough (i.e. there were enough students) to make it possible for both colleges to run business studies courses, it would not be sensible for the directors to set objectives if there were not enough lecturers available.

It will be noted that in Figure 10 the line joining the 'assessment of the external environment' and the 'clarification of the organisation's objectives' has arrows pointing each way. The reason for this is that the objectives and the performance of the organisation may themselves affect the external environment as well as vice versa. So, if we go back to our example, and assume that plenty of business studies lecturers are available, we can see how the operation of the organisation may affect the environment. Suppose the director of the college is considering running BTEC higher national courses, then the fact that the college already operates *national* award courses will mean that the potential customers (i.e. students) for higher national award schemes will be greater, since entry qualifications for such higher level courses include a pass at the national award level.

Secondly, when clarifying the objectives of the organisation, the directors or senior managers will need to make an assessment of the expectations of the *stakeholders*. By the stakeholders we mean the owners, the employees, and the customers. Now, it is unrealistic to suppose that the expectations of each of these stakeholders will be identical. So, for instance, the owners or shareholders may have certain expectations about the profitability of their organisation, whilst the employees' expectations may be expressed in terms of their desire for higher wages and secure employment. The employees' goals of high wages may to some extent be in conflict with the shareholders' requirement for profits. Thirdly, the customers may be looking for services which are not very profitable. It is the duty of the directors or senior managers when assessing these expectations to clarify objectives; to balance out such conflicts of interest so that the organisation will prosper, whilst meeting at least the minimum requirements of all the different stakeholders.

Finally, before objectives can be set and alternative courses of action for their achievement can be evaluated, the current state of the organisation must be considered. This means an assessment of current performance. Is the organisation generating enough funds to provide finance for future investments, which may be needed to meet its objectives? There is clearly no point in setting grandiose objectives and drawing up plans for their achievement if there is no base to launch them from. Once again, this is a two way process, as noted by the two arrows in the diagram linking the boxes of 'clarification of the organisation's objectives' and 'assessment of the organisation's current performance'. The result of this two way process should be the drawing up of short term plans to increase immediate profitability.

Having carried out their assessment of the external environment, the expectations of the stakeholders, and the current performance of the organisation, the directors or senior managers clarify the objectives and evaluate the alternative courses of action available to them. Having done this the directors must draw up a *strategic plan* for their achievement. At this stage we should note that there are a number of human resource considerations to be taken into account in drawing up a strategic plan. We will recall that the expectation of employees and the availability of human resources are factors which must also be taken into account. It would be absurd for any organisation to ignore the human resource implications when drawing up a strategic plan, since these could provide constraints significant enough to make the plan unworkable. To put it another way we should see human resource planning as an integral part of corporate planning and not merely as a derivative.

After a strategic plan has been drawn up the next stage is *tactical planning,* or how the strategic plan is to be put into action and the organisational objectives achieved. There are four component parts of the detailed plans each being derived from the strategic plan:

THE ORGANISATION : GOALS AND STRUCTURE

1. Product Market development plans;
2. Resource development plans;
3. Organisation plans; and
4. Operations plans

The *product market plan* involves detailed analysis of the products of the organisation and the markets in which those products are to be sold. Clear plans for each product must be drawn up. This will be impossible unless a plan is drawn up for all *resources* needed (including labour). The human resources needed to execute the market and production plan must be organised to achieve the objectives. These four areas of planning must be conducted simultaneously so that overall detailed plans can be drawn up for the organisation.

When detailed plans have been drawn up these will normally be converted into objectives for individual senior managers. So, for instance, a manufacturing company may have decided upon a strategy of *diversification* into the plastic toy market, where previously they have manufactured only wooden toys. This strategic plan will have been drawn up after the directors have assessed the market and found that it is potentially profitable enough to warrant venturing into it. They will have satisfied themselves that they can obtain the resources they need to achieve this objective. The directors will ensure that this strategy is acceptable to the stakeholders and that their current trading position enables them to embark on such a strategy. Now they will have to draw up detailed plans for each of the operating areas. So, for instance, the chief design engineer may be asked to design appropriate toys with details of material and manufacturing specifications, by a given date. The production manager may be used to draw up production schedules for the new toys, noting his plant and manpower requirements. The personnel manager may be required to draw up specific plans to ensure that the right numbers of the right types of employees are ready and available at the right time (the human resource plan).

The Stages of Human Resource Planning

There are four stages to the operation of human resource planning each of which has qualitative and quantitative aspects. The four stages are:

(i)   Determination of the demand for workers;
(ii)   Human resource audit;
(iii)   Determination of external supplies of labour;
(iv)   The reconciliation of the demands for labour with the existing internal supplies of labour and potential external supplies of labour.

HUMAN RESOURCE PLANNING

This last stage involves planning the action to meet the demands for labour.

Demand for Labour

The demand for labour will be determined from marketing forecasts and subsequently derived production plans. The marketing or sales forecast will be based upon market research which will provide information on the types of products, the volumes in which they are required and the times at which they are needed by customers. Probably estimates of the size and nature of the workforce needed to ensure that production meets the demands of the sales forecast will be done jointly by the production manager and the personnel manager. To convert the sales forecast into a production forecast or plan these two people will need to know:

(i)   Will any new product, and perhaps, therefore, new production methods be started, and if so, when will these be introduced?

(ii)   If new production methods are to be employed, what types and numbers of personnel will be required for them? Answering these questions will involve them in discussions with the production engineer, who would be responsible for new methods of manufacture, and the acquisition of new plant and equipment.

(iii)   Will the production be carried out on existing sites or will new sites be needed, with the possibility of closure of existing facilities?

(iv)   Will the existing working arrangements be maintained, or will, for instance, new shift working arrangements have to be introduced?

(v)   What changes in job content are envisaged as a result of either new products or new methods of manufacture?

(vi)   Will the new production volumes and methods call for new ancillary services? For example, will there be a need for more or different types of maintenance engineers?

(vii) Will there be demand for improved labour productivity and, if so, is the current payment system flexible enough?

(viii) In general terms, is the current payment system appropriate for the new production requirements?

(ix)   Is the current organisation structure suited to the future needs? Does the organisation need to change its departmental structure?

It is only when these general questions have been answered that any serious attempt can be made to quantify the numbers of personnel required and, just as important, to make some assessment of the qualitative needs. Methods that can be employed in forecasting the demands for labour are considered in more detail in Chapter 14.

THE ORGANISATION : GOALS AND STRUCTURE

Human Resource Audit

Human resource audit is the critical analysis of the existing work-force. The success of this stage of human resource planning is dependent upon the personnel records that are maintained. The reason for conducting a human resource audit is that it is from the base of the current situation that the future must be planned, and an enormous amount of information needs to be available. This information must be of both a quantitative and a qualitative type. The quantitative information required will include:

(i)   The numbers of workers employed in each category of labour;

(ii)   Details of the age and length of service structure in each category of labour employed;

(iii)   Details of the labour turnover of all types of employees;

(iv)   Details of the absence records of all types of employees;

(v)   Details of the accidents and safety records of all employees;

(vi)   Details of industrial action within various parts of the organisation;

(vii)   Details of the amount of training given to employees;

(viii) Payroll details related to output and capital employed, including the amount of overtime worked.

Personnel records, their purpose and uses, will be considered in more detail in Chapter 14.

Qualitative information will also be required for a human resource audit to be carried out, this will include:

(i)   The level of performance being achieved by individual employees;

(ii)   The promotability of existing employees;

(iii)   The employees considered to have potential requiring development through training programmes;

(iv)   The effectiveness of the existing organisation structure in meeting current goals;

(v)   The effectiveness of the current payment system in meeting existing goals.

(vi)   The room for improvement in labour productivity;

(vii)   The state of industrial relations within the various parts of the organisation;

(viii) The effectiveness of the personnel policies and practices currently employed.

External Supplies of Labour

The personnel manager will normally be the person held responsible for obtaining information on the external supplies of labour available. The numbers and types of potential employees available in the labour market will be affected both by local and national factors. To take the *national* factors first, these are often longer-term and may have only a limited impact on the organisation and its potential supplies of labour, though sometimes the impact will be quite dramatic for instance, of legislation (e.g. Equal Pay Act). Other national factors include the activities of government agencies like the Training Commission through its operating division. The longest term national factors are related to the birth rate and death rate trends, with consequent effects upon the size of the total potential working population.

The *local* factors about which the personnel manager will want to obtain information include:

(i)   The number of people living in the catchment area of the organisation;

(ii)   The local levels of unemployment;

(iii) The amount of competition for labour in the area. This will be related not only to the numbers of other employers in the area, but to the type of work they have to offer, the pay they offer, and the general terms and conditions they provide;

(iv)   The accessibility of the organisation — how well is it served by transport services, is this likely to change or remain the same?

(v)   The pattern of immigration and emigration within the area — is the area growing or declining in terms of the size of its working population?

(vi)   The housing and schooling facilities within the area and whether they are likely to change.

(viii) The type of student emerging from the local educational system and his or her suitability for employment by the organisation.

The Reconciliation of Demand and Supply of Labour

The process of reconciling the demands for labour and supplies available (both internal and external) will result in a series of action plans. The detail into which these plans go will to some extent be determined by the time horizon over which the action is planned. The normal periods for detailed planning are three to five years: after this time so many features within the plan inevitably become so uncertain as to render the notion of going into detail a waste of time and effort. Plans at this stage should be expressed in both quantitative and qualitative terms and should be specific about what action is to take place and at what times. Whilst some plans will involve specific objectives in qualitative terms — for example, the reduction of the rate of labour turnover and absenteeism, by certain percentages, by specific times, and the actions that will be taken to achieve these objectives — others will be more specific in quantitative terms, where the qualitative considerations are implied. Examples of these sorts of plans are; recruitment plans, training plans, retirement plans, career development plans, transfer, promotion, and succession planning. (Examples of succession planning can be found in Chapter 16.)

When reconciling the supplies of labour to the demands for labour, the criterion used will be that of long term total cost minimisation. We will consider this in more detail when we look at human resource planning techniques in Chapter 14.

JOB ANALYSIS

Job analysis is *the systematic study and statement of all the facts about a job which reveal its content and all the modifying factors which surround it.* Managers require accurate information about all jobs within the organisation because only with this information can they efficiently manage the human resources. There are three main uses of job analysis, for the drawing up of job descriptions, for method study purposes, and for health purposes.

Job Analysis for Health Purposes

Under this general heading there are three main areas of interest, which require detailed analysis of what is actually involved in an employee doing a particular job:

(i)   a job may be analysed to understand its effect on the job-holder in terms of health and the fatigue he experiences whilst working;

(ii)   for determining which jobs may be suitable, for occupational therapy purposes, as part of a welfare programme;

(iii)   for identifying particular health or safety hazards within the job, so that remedial action to remove the hazards or minimise their effect may be taken.

Job Analysis for Method Study Purposes

Job analysis is used for time and motion study for the purposes of establishing a standard time for the job. The standard time for the operation of the tasks involved in the job will be based upon the most effective way of performing the tasks, as studied by the work study engineer. Such standard times may be a significant piece of information in the design of the payment system, especially where a *payment by results* system is in operation.

Job Analysis for the Purpose of Drawing up Job Descriptions

As we will find in the next few chapters, job descriptions are very important documents, since they are used for very many purposes. Here we shall just list the main uses to which they are put, looking briefly at some of their uses. Job descriptions obtained through job analysis are used in human resource planning and organisational planning. In the case of job description for organisational planning purposes, the very process of collecting the facts on jobs can uncover problems of motivation amongst job-holders, can show where problems exist with unclear divisions of responsibility; or can highlight problems of unclear accountability. During the process of job analysis it may become clear how organisational structures can be rationalised to promote closer contact between supervisors and their subordinates. Such closer contacts between individuals will help to achieve departmental, and ultimately organisational, objectives. Job descriptions are essential for job evaluation, performance appraisal and management by objectives. Job descriptions with the subsequently derived job specifications are essential for recruitment and selection purposes and for systematic training.

Methods of Job Analysis

We can look at three main methods of analysing jobs, industrial engineering methods, psychological methods, and physiological methods.

Industrial Engineering Methods of Job Analysis

In its most detailed form, this type of analysis involves breaking the tasks in a job into their smallest possible elements. The elements are looked at in discrete terms. So, for instance, if this method of analysis is being used for a clerical job, elements would include: the job holder firstly sight-glances paper, secondly sight-glances pen, thirdly picks up pen, fourthly writes his name. As can be seen, this method involves a tremendous amount of detail and is only normally used in limited circumstances like work measurement.

Another industrial engineering technique is that known as *charting*. In this method jobs are broken down into tasks by the job analyst who represents each task diagramatically on a chart. This method shows the flow of activities of the job holder, since there are different symbols

41

representing such activities as searching, selecting, inspecting, transporting loads. This method is such that the data about the job is presented in a compact way, making it possible to get an overall view of the whole job.

A third industrial engineering technique for job analysis is the *diary* method. In this method all daily activities of the job holder are recorded chronologically against elapsed time. Times are recorded either at the beginning and end of the particular activity or at fixed intervals throughout the day: typically, every fifteen minutes the diarist records what he or she is doing.

Psychological Methods of Job Analysis

The *interview* and *questionnaire* are included amongst these methods. The analyst questions the job holder, either face-to-face in the case of an interview, or by using a questionnaire, eliciting the details of what the job holder actually does. This is a skilled process, since it is easy for large portions of a job to be overlooked or given too little or too much weight by the job holder. It is up to the analyst to obtain a full and accurate picture of the job and, to achieve this, people other than the job holder may be interviewed about the job. For instance, the job holder's superior or subordinates may be interviewed to ascertain how they see the content and context of the job. Often after interview and/or questionnaire have been reviewed by the job analyst he will issue a checklist of what he considers the job involves. This will be given to the job holder to consider, comment upon, and perhaps update. The final method under this general heading is the one in which the job analyst does the job himself for a period of time. This has its limitations as a method if the job has a long cycle time of, say, a month or a year. Clearly the analyst cannot be exposed to all the aspects of the job if some of them only occur once a year. Though this method may at first seem attractive, it cannot be employed if the job involves special skills or knowledge, which the job analyst does not possess.

Physiological Methods of Job Analysis

These methods clearly constitute the most scientific approach to certain aspects of job analysis. Measures such as the expenditure of energy by the job holder or the electrical activity in the muscles of the job holder are made. This type of analysis has very limited application and may be used, for example, in analysing the job of an astronaut.

Whilst there are a number of methods available to the job analyst, no one method seems either to provide all the answers, or to be appropriate for all types of job. The normal practice tends to be to use more than one method of analysis, where possible, in the hope that a more valid analysis will be obtained.

JOB DESCRIPTIONS

A job description is a statement of the general purpose of the job, which also provides an outline of its scope, duties, and responsibilities. As the name implies, this is primarily a descriptive document. No job description can be expected to be comprehensive in terms of every minute detail of the job, but it should give enough information to be of use in the following ways:

(i)   it gives the job holder a pretty clear picture of what is expected of him;

(ii)   it gives some feel for the importance of the job, which will be important for job evaluation purposes;

(iii) by reading the job description we should be able to identify the important or critical areas within the job;

(iv) it will be of use in the development of training programmes since it will describe the required behaviour of the job holder.

Drawing Up Job Descriptions

We have noted that the process of job analysis is likely to be carried out by a specialist trained job analyst. This person will probably work either as a member of the Personnel Department, or the Management Services Department. Sometimes outside consultants are engaged to do job analysis within an organisation. The end product of the job analysis will almost certainly be a job description. It is usual for the job analyst to write up the job description in a standard format, in conjunction with the job holder and the job holder's superior. In this way, all the important features of the job can be given their proper relative weightings. Where there is more than one job holder, i.e. a number of people doing the same job, rather than discussing and agreeing the description with each of them in turn, it is more usual for the analyst to agree the description with a representative of the group, who will very often be the trade union shop steward or staff representative for the type of employees concerned. The job description should not be contentious, since it reflects what is actually done in the job. There may be extra difficulties if the job being described is not actually being performed at the time the job description is written. The most common reason for this is that the job is a newly created one. However it is uncommon for every task in the new job to be completely new, i.e. never having been done before as part of some other job. Where tasks were previously performed as part of other jobs, then clearly they can be analysed within those other jobs, and the job description can be drawn up as a composite of the various analysed tasks performed. Under these circumstances, it is essential that the job description is kept under review until all the parties concerned are happy that what is written in the job description accurately describes what is done by the job holder and, moreover, that the job holder is actually performing the job in the way that management intended.

As we have already noted, job descriptions will normally follow a standard format. The description gives the job title and the name of the department in which the job is located. There will normally be a brief description of the purpose of the job and its relationship to other jobs in the department and the organisation as a whole, stating the responsibilities of the job holder, both what he is responsible for, and to whom he should report. The use of an organisation chart can be of great help here in locating the job and identifying its reporting relationships. The main body of the job description will contain a statement of the duties and responsibilities of the job holder, i.e. detailing what the job holder actually does. Wherever possible standards of performance will be specified. The conditions under which the job is performed will be noted, so, for instance, the fact that the job involves driving or that the job holder will work inside or outside will be stated. The hours of work and location will also be noted in the job description. An example of a job description and organisation chart are given in figures 11 and 12 on p 45 and p46.

JOB SPECIFICATIONS

A job specification, which is derived from the job analysis and job description, is *a detailed statement of the skills knowledge and attitudes required by ANY holder of the job to perform the tasks that make up the job.* At this point we must stress that the job specification does not refer to the particular person who is doing the job but specifies what the management feel is required of any person who would perform it adequately.

Job specifications are normally drawn up by the job analyst and agreed with the manager of the department in which the job is located. Job specifications are used extensively in selection, training, job evaluation, and to some extent in performance appraisal. Clearly, what is written in the job specification, in terms of the qualifications and experience, must be capable of being related to and justified by reference to the duties and responsibilities noted in the job description. Because of the uses to which they are put, job specifications are nearly always written in a standard format within an organisation. An example of a job specification, for the job of personnel officer for which we have drawn up a job description, is given in Figure 13. The form of the example is biased towards its use for job evaluation purposes (in as far as it specifies the evidence of skills and knowledge required by anyone to do the job rather than the knowledge and skills *per se*). Job descriptions and specifications are developed into the person specification for the purposes of recruitment and selection (see Chapter 11).

HUMAN RESOURCE PLANNING

JOB TITLE: Personnel Officer

JOB HOLDER'S IMMEDIATE SUPERIOR: Personnel Manager

PRODUCT UNIT LOCATION: Baywood Factory

GENERAL PURPOSE OF JOB: The recruitment of all hourly paid personnel and weekly paid staff. Advising Line Managers of standard aspects of the Company's policies and practices. Dealing with the interpretation of Company policy as applied to absenteeism and simple disciplinary matters. The provision of the telephone, internal post, and employee sales services to the factory.

DUTIES AND RESPONSIBILITIES:

1. Monitor performance against the human resource plan, with respect to hourly paid and weekly paid personnel. Advise the Personnel Manager of any action required to keep within the Human Resource Plan.

2. Interview all potential staff employees with the member of Line Management concerned.

3. Draw up, and place advertisements in appropriate media, for hourly and weekly paid personnel vacancies, when appropriate.

4. Liaise with the Department of Employment and other agencies about vacancies.

5. Advise Line Management on all disciplinary matters to ensure that Company policy is followed.

6. Maintain records on all disciplinary matters for the factory.

7. Advise Personnel Manager of any potential industrial relations problems within the factory.

8. Advise Line Managers on aspects of Company personnel policy and practices as required.

9. Advise Managers of any changes in Company personnel policy.

10. Responsible for making arrangements for and monitoring the progress of the Company's performance appraisal system (once per year).

11. Responsible for the activities of the Personnel Assistant in the areas of:
    (a) All hourly paid recruitment to meet requirements of the Human Resource Plan.
    (b) Monitoring absenteeism and controlling sick visiting.
    (c) Running the Company sick pay scheme.

12. Responsible for the activities of the Clerical Assistant in the areas of:
    (a) Maintenance of the computerised personnel records system.
    (b) All returns made to outside bodies, including Department of Employment.

13. Responsible for the provision of telephonist services to the factory.

14. Responsible for the provision of internal postal service to the factory.

15. Responsible for the provision of an employee sales service to the factory.

16. In conjunction with the Training Officer, organise and run induction courses for all new employees to the Company.

WORKING CONDITIONS: Normal office conditions together with regular visits to the factory. Limited travel to other Company Product Units.

HOURS OF WORK: 37½ hours per week.

Figure 11

JOB DESCRIPTION

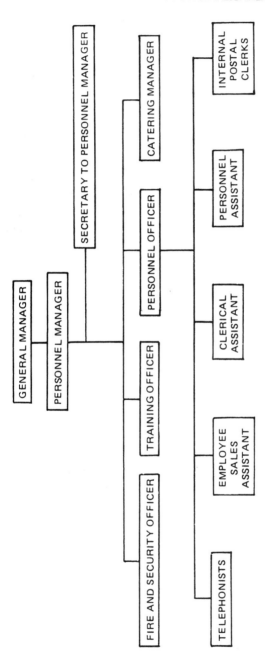

N.B This is an abstract of the Personnel Department Organisation structure
to show the relative position and reporting relationships of the
job of Personnel Officer

FIGURE 12 : PART OF ORGANISATION CHART SHOWING THE POSITION OF PERSONNEL OFFICER

EDUCATIONAL REQUIREMENTS: Degree in Social Sciences or Business Studies or some equivalent qualification.

SKILLS REQUIREMENTS:

Mechanical Skills: No exceptional mechanical skills required.

Intellectual Skills: The ability to deal with concepts is required. The ability to deal with ambiguous and complex situations is essential.

SOCIAL SKILLS: Extensive and well-developed social skills required for:
(a) Interviewing
(b) Supervising staff
(c) Dealing with personnel in difficult circumstances.
(d) Dealing with members of the public.

EXPERIENCE REQUIREMENTS: Experience required in the operation of the Company's personnel policies; experience in a manufacturing environment is highly desirable; previous experience in interviewing and in recruitment and selection essential; knowledge of Employment legislation essential.

INITIATIVE: Initiative required: in drawing up and placing advertisements; in identifying possible shortfalls in the Human Resource Plan; in identifying potential industrial relations problems, in dealing with disciplinary matters.

JUDGEMENTS: Required in decisions regarding employee selection; required in deciding on advertising; required in interpreting personnel policies.

PLANNING AND COORDINATING: Planning and coordinating of staff reporting to job holder; coordinating requirements in respect to annual performance appraisal exercise.

COOPERATION AND CONTACT: Essential that the job holder can elicit cooperation from employees at all levels of the organisation. Cooperation very important since the job is primarily advisory rather than executive in nature.

DECISION MAKING AFFECTING COSTS: Responsible for an advertising budget up to £20,000 per annum. Bad decision making in disciplinary matters can result in unnecessary company costs up to max £20,000 per annum. Bad decision making in recruitment can be costly.

MENTAL AND PHYSICAL FATIGUE: No significant physical fatigue. Short periods of sustained mental pressure.

Figure 13

JOB SPECIFICATION FOR THE JOB OF PERSONNEL OFFICER
(For Job Evaluation Purposes)

Section 2

Individual And Group Behaviour

Having considered the organisational setting in which people work, we turn in this Section to an examination of some important aspects of individual and group behaviour and the way in which they affect the process of work. In Chapter 5 we describe the concept of personality and the major theories which have been developed. This is followed by an examination of attitude formation and change — processes which determine the individual's expectations of, and responses to, employment. We then identify the principal types of needs relevant to people at work and link these to motivation. Moving away from the individual and towards interpersonal behaviour, the processes of communication and perception are described. Chapter 9 considers the characteristics of groups, with special reference to work groups, and Chapter 10 assesses leadership theory.

Chapter 5

Personality

Although we all have a general understanding of what we mean by 'personality' and use the expression quite freely, psychologists have tried to give specific definitions cf the term. A psychologist called G W Allport (1937) tried to synthesize these definitions in order to provide one which covered all the major aspects, but found the task almost impossible, and eventually concluded that there were about fifty major variants.

For our purposes, we can describe personality as those relatively stable and enduring aspects of the individual, which distinguish him from other people, and which form the basis of our predictions concerning his future behaviour. However, although we are concerned with stable and enduring aspects of the individual, we would be naive not to appreciate that an individual may exhibit different aspects of his personality in different environmental contexts. It does not deny the stability of personality to comment that an individual is bone idle in college, but demonstrates enormous energy on the football field. This variability associated with the environmental context has important implications for the use of personality assessment in the interview, for example, we may be shown the individual's 'interview personality' when we want to see his 'work place personality'. It is unwise, therefore, to rate aspects of behaviour such as industriousness or sociability on the assumption that, once assessed, they are likely to remain constant in any situation. On the contrary, we must be aware of the effects of changes in environment.

A number of different theories of personality have been proposed by psychologists, and the remainder of this chapter will be devoted to a consideration of some of the major ones.

Trait Theories

If you were asked to describe a colleague of yours you might use some of the following expressions:

> He is very conscientious;
> He has a mean streak;
> She is very inquisitive;
> She is a friendly soul.

By describing people in this way you would be using a set of personality characteristics or *traits,* as, according to trait theory, one can describe a personality by its position on a number of scales or dimensions, each of which represents a trait. Allport was one of the major exponents of this theory, and he defined a trait as 'some determining tendency to respond to a situation in a given way'. One of the fundamental features of Allport's theory was his insistence on the uniqueness and individuality of man, for he claimed that no two individuals could have the same personality, since no two people have the same set of traits.

Allport suggested that there are three kinds of traits:

1. *Cardinal traits,* which are so dominant that few activities cannot be traced to their influence;

2. *Central traits,* representing tendencies which are highly characteristic of the individual;

3. *Secondary traits,* which are more limited tendencies, and which may escape notice from all but the very closest of friends.

Allport defined personality as:

'the dynamic organisation within the individual of those psychophysical systems that determine his unique adjustment to his environment.'

One important question which is raised by this definition is how traits determine adjustment to the environment. Do traits themselves motivate behaviour? For example, does the fact that John has a sociable nature motivate him to go to a party? Or do traits initiate or cause behaviour? To clarify this point Allport distinguished between *motivational* traits and *stylistic* traits.

The final aspect of Allport's work which we will consider here is his theory of the *consistency of traits,* that is, people tend to react in the same way to the same situations. If someone bumps into me in the supermarket I am likely to react in the same way as I would if someone bumped into me in the street. However Allport pointed out that perfect consistency is impossible to achieve for three major reasons:

1. Different traits in the individual's personality may conflict, as in the case of a man who is very overbearing and aggressive among his equals or subordinates, and yet extremely timid and meek in the presence of his superiors at work.

2. No trait of personality operates in isolation for, if you remember, Allport defined personality as an *organisation* of traits, and thus a trait of truthfulness may be tempered by a trait of cowardice, as in the case of a normally truthful man who lies to escape from a dangerous situation.

3. Because the environment changes rapidly, we tend to experiment with behaviour in order to discover that which is most appropriate in an unfamiliar context. An array of traits may assume dominance in this new environment, and experience will indicate which one is most acceptable or effective.

PERSONALITY

In the course of his work, Allport compiled a list of personality traits, or words used in the English language to describe personality characteristics. This list eventually amounted to one thousand, eight hundred trait words.

It is possible to argue that a simple listing of traits descriptive of individual characteristics is not sufficient to provide a coherent science of personality; these traits need to be classified and measured. At this stage we can turn to the work of R B Cattell (1950). Cattell agreed with Allport on the existence of traits, but went beyond description to measurement, and in so doing he became associated with that branch of psychology known as *psychometry*. Cattell defined personality as:

'that which permits a prediction of what a person will do in a given situation'.

He devised tests of personality traits and, using the data derived from these tests, he studied the relationships between traits. He used a technique known as factor analysis to determine the underlying aspects of personality, and this led him to the proposition that two kinds of traits exist, surface traits and source traits.

Surface traits represent clusters of variables which are positively correlated, variables which are not only related to one another in a statistical sense, but also appear to be so. The following pairs of traits are indicative of Cattell's surface traits:

Disciplined	:	Foolish
Thoughtful	:	Unreflective
Austere	:	Profligate

Source traits, on the other hand, are discovered by factor analysis, and represent the basis or foundation of all other traits — they are the source of observable behaviour. Cattell gave each of the source traits a letter rather than a name, in much the same way as vitamins are known by letters such as Vitamin C, Vitamin B_{12} and so on. A list of Cattell's source traits is presented below:

FACTOR

A	Cyclothymia vs Schizothymia	— warm, sociable vs aloof, distant
B_1	Intelligence	
C	Ego Strength	— mature, stable vs unstable
D	Excitability	— excitable vs impassive
E	Dominance vs Submissiveness	
F	Surgency	— lively, cheerful vs depressed, gloomy
G	Superego Strength, Conscientiousness	
H	Adventurous vs shy, withdrawn	

I	Tough, Realistic, unsensitive vs sensitive, tender-minded
J	Neurasthenic, generalised obstructive dependence
K	Reasonableness
L	Suspicious, distrustful vs trusting
M	Conventional vs Unconventional
N	Shrewd, sophisticated
O	Guilt-prone, timid vs relaxed, secure
Q_1	Radical vs Conservative
Q_2	Self sufficient vs group dependent
Q_3	Strong-willed, self controlled
Q_4	Tense, anxious vs relaxed, assured

Cattell constructed a test, known as the '16 PF', to assess sixteen source traits.

In Cattell's approach to traits of personality we can see a very systematic analysis of the subject, but the approach has been criticised as being essentially one of *dissection* in that it studies individual components of personality, separating them from the whole. This piecemeal treatment of traits means that an additional factor is necessary to describe the organisation or ordering of traits within the individual.

The trait approach to personality is certainly a popularly recognised approach, and has appeal for that reason. It also has the advantage, by breaking down 'the personality' into manageable items, of allowing the consistencies of human behaviour to be readily studied. It does have a major disadvantage, however, one that is increasingly recognised as a problem by social workers, probation officers, and similar groups, and that is the problem of 'labelling'. There is a tendency to find a trait which you consider to be characteristic of an individual, and to use that trait as an identifying tag or label. This process may cause you to forget the environmental specificity of a trait, and so to generalise unfairly and inaccurately about his behaviour. Thus studies conducted on 'problem children' or 'aggressive boys' have found the problems of aggressiveness to be limited to a few contexts and certainly not to be the usual mode of behaviour.

Thus trait theories of personality have as their major advantage their facility for measurement and assessment of personality, but as their major weakness a tendency to dissect rather than present an integrated view, a tendency which may lead to labelling in certain situations.

Type Theories

One example of type theories is the constitutional approach to personality. The assumption underlying this approach is that physical and mental characteristics are related. Although this assumption has been inherent in studies since the Ancient Greeks and Hippocrates, E. Kretschmer (1925) first formalised it in 1925. He developed the theory from his observations of physical characteristics and mental disorders.

Kretschmer identified four physical types which he called:

Asthenic	—	a frail, thin physique;
Athletic	—	a muscular, strong physique;
Pyknic	—	a plump physique;
Dysplastic	—	an unusual or deviant combination of physiques.

From his observations of mental disorders and psychiatric patients, he concluded that the person with an asthenic physique had a tendency to schizophrenia and introversion, while the person with a pyknic physique had a tendency to manic-depression.

W.H. Sheldon and Stevens (1954) developed this theory further in the 1940s, making a more precise and detailed comparison of mental and physical characteristics. They took approximately four thousand photographs, at different angles, of male college students and, using this as their basic data, they identified four physical types which they termed the following:

Endomorphic	—	soft, round, plump;
Ectomorphic	—	tall, thin, fragile;
Mesomorphic	—	athletic, muscular, angular;
Dysplastic	—	an unusual combination of these.

They recognised that these are extreme types, and that the majority of individuals would possess some of all of these characteristics. They devised rating scales for each of these types, so that each individual can be attributed with a score on each of the three major categories. These three ratings give the individual's *somatotype*.

Parallel to this set of three physical categories, Sheldon identified three primary components of temperament, or mental characteristics. These were:

Viscerontonia	—	which is a general love of comfort, warmth of character and sociability;
Somatotonia	—	which is an active and aggressive temperament;
Cerebrotonia	—	which is a restrained and inhibited temperament.

Sheldon then looked at the relationships between these temperaments and physical characteristics and found strong positive relationships between them as follows:

53

Viscerontonia correlated .79 with Endomorphy;
Somatotonia correlated .82 with Mesomorphy;
Cerebrotonia correlated .83 with Ectomorphy.

This set of assumptions, linking physical characteristics and mental characteristics, has a wide popular usage. It is quite common to hear red hair linked with a fiery temper or a fat person described as 'jolly', and where such descriptions are used we have examples of the constitutional theories in practice. There is a more sinister aspect to this theory, however, in that it has also been used to predict a 'criminal type'. In everyday usage we hear people saying 'I don't trust him because his eyes are too close together', or 'he looks suspicious because he has thin lips', or 'never trust a man whose eyebrows meet in the middle'. In such cases we are again linking mental and physical characteristics, but the association is open to dangerous abuse for, unless it is completely proven that physical characteristics give an infallible indication of mental characteristics, it is possible that innocent people with 'criminal' physical characteristics may find themselves subject to unjustified harassment and suspicion.

Thus the constitutional theory of personality, which purports to link physical and mental characteristics, has had notable popular support, in spite of its worrying implications and low level of academic support.

Another psychologist who comes into the category of type theorists is C.G. Jung (1968). His division of people into extroverts and introverts is again widely known and extensively used in everyday conversation. These two categories represent two differing attitudes to life and ways of reacting to situations.

The *extrovert* is a sociable person who likes parties and being in a group of people. He is usually active and interested in anything and everything. He tends to be optimistic and enthusiastic, although his enthusiasm is often transitory in nature. Because of this transitory enthusiasm, the extrovert may be accused of superficiality. It is certainly true that the extrovert needs an audience to be at his best, and dislikes being on his own for any length of time.

The *introvert*, on the other hand, dislikes being in a large gathering of people, and can feel intensely lonely in a crowd. He is sensitive and afraid of making a fool of himself in front of other people. He tends to be very conscientious and dedicated to a few deep interests, as well as having a pessimistic outlook on life. The introvert has a noticeable independence of judgement, in that he makes up his own mind about something in the light of available evidence, and is not swayed by the advice or pressure of others. The introvert is in his element when he is alone or with a few people who are well known to him.

Jung did not claim that this distinction between introvert and extrovert explained all the possible differences in personality. He did, however, suggest that there are four functions which we use to orientate ourselves in the world and these are:

Sensation	—	perception through our senses;
Thinking	—	meaning and understanding;
Feeling	—	emotions and values;
Intuition	—	future possibilities.

Jung believed that introverts and extroverts differ in their approach to each of these four functions, and thus that this distinction is a highly significant one for our understanding and prediction of individual behaviour.

A later development of Jung's typology was undertaken by H.J. Eysenck (1947) in his two dimensional theory of personality. He proposed that many important aspects of personality could be understood through the combination of Jung's Extrovert/Introvert typology with a stable/unstable dimension. Thus four basic personality types are proposed:

> Stable extrovert;
> Unstable extrovert;
> Stable introvert;
> Unstable introvert.

All theories of personality which are classified as type theories suffer from a lack of scientific evidence to support or refute them and, because of this, they have not achieved widespread acceptance among academics. They also share the weakness of asserting too much about the individual, such that, by labelling an individual with a particular type name, there is an implicit assumption that he displays all the characteristics associated with that type in a consistent manner. This could lead to the problem of stereotyping. A third criticism which has been levelled at the type approach to personality is that it assumes that personality is inherited, that we are born with a particular personality and, in this assumption, the type theorists ignore or discount the effects of culture and environment on the development of the individual.

Psychoanalytic Theories

Sigmund Freud's (J.A.C. Brown, 1966) approach to personality was very different to that of Catell, for example, since instead of a 'dissecting' approach he was concerned with the development of the total personality. He also attacked the traditionally accepted view of psychology as the science of individual behaviour, and concentrated on the working of the mind.

INDIVIDUAL AND GROUP BEHAVIOUR

Freud believed that the mind is made up of three parts, which are:

The ID	—	consisting of basic instincts. It is amoral, non-rational and confined almost exclusively to our subconscious.
The EGO	—	that part of the mind of which we are usually aware. It operates on the reality principle, and its purpose is to mediate between the demands of the id and superego.
The SUPEREGO	—	our 'conscience', that part of our mind which has internalised the norms and values we are encouraged to cherish. The superego is a restraining influence on our behaviour.

Freud suggested that the individual's personality and his resultant behaviour was caused by the interaction of these three components of the mind. His work is particularly well known for his explanation of the development of the personality in the young child. Freud emphasised the importance of the early years of childhood in personality development, and he believed that 'the child is father to the man' — in other words that the basic structure of the adult personality is determined by childhood development. He proposed that the child goes through three stages in infancy, each one characterised by a particular zone of the body.

1. Oral stage — lasting from birth to around 18 months of age, the child's satisfaction is derived almost exclusively from his mouth — he sucks toys, his mother's breast, his fingers.

2. Anal stage — from 18 months to approximately 2½ years of age the child's interest centres on his excretory powers. During toilet training he learns that he can please or anger his mother by the appropriate or inappropriate use of these powers. Freud suggested that children who experience frustration in this stage may become excessively tidy or mean in later life.

3. Phallic stage — from 2½ to approximately seven years of age, the sex organs are of supreme interest to the child. This suggestion of childhood sexuality shocked Victorian society and Freud was severely criticised for this part of his theory in particular. Freud made matters worse by suggesting that the resolution of the Oedipus complex was a vital part of this stage of infancy. He suggested that little boys at this stage have a deep sexual feeling towards their mothers — a feeling which is not acted upon for fear of castration by the father. Instead the boy identifies with his father, and tries to become like his father in all attributes to overcome this obstacle to his affections.

In fact our personality in adulthood consists of an accumulation of a number of such identifications we make in early life.

Freud suggested that most men are unable to remember this particular phase in their childhood because they learn that such incestuous feelings are frowned on by society, so they lock these thoughts away, or suppress them. He believed in what is called *psychic determinism* — which means that everything we do or say is caused by the working of our mind. Thus every 'mistaken' slip of the tongue, every dream, has as its cause some desire of the id, ego or superego. You may have heard of a 'Freudian slip' by which we mean saying something wrong, or the opposite to what we mean, by mistake. Freud would argue that this does not happen 'by mistake', but that we are saying something we really mean, even if we do not recognise it as such. Thus when a female patient of Freud's claimed to have been brought up as a prostitute, a statement she very quickly altered to protestant, Freud was more inclined to believe her first comment, concluding that she had suppressed promiscuous sexual urges.

A similar line of argument is applied to the interpretation of dreams. We often dream about things that we suppress in the daytime, and often even the 'real' meaning of our dreams is hidden in the use of symbolism. A man may dream about wrestling with another man, which may in fact be an indication of latent homosexual tendencies, as portrayed in D.H. Lawrence's book *Women in Love.*

Freud's work has come in for wide-ranging criticism, not only because of its emphasis on sexuality, which offended his Victorian counterparts, but also because of its unscientific nature. Freud generalised from a small number of cases, simply accepting the word of his patients about their past life. However, it is possible to agree that Freud's theory of personality is unscientific and yet to consider it to be of significant importance and relevance today. His ideas are certainly challenging, and have led to a great deal of useful research by his followers (sometimes known as the post-Freudians) such as Adler and Horney (J.A.C. Brown, 1966).

Argyris — Personality and Organisation

The final set of ideas concerning personality to be examined here is that of Chris Argyris who looked at the relationship between the adult personality and the industrial organisation.

C. Argyris (1957) describes personality as being an organisation of components, not simply a sum of different parts or traits. This organisation of components may either be balanced internally, which Argyris considers leads to adjusted behaviour, or may be in harmony with the social environment, which leads to adapted behaviour. Where behaviour is both adapted and adjusted, it is called integrated behaviour. Thus:

INDIVIDUAL AND GROUP BEHAVIOUR

Internal balance	—	adjusted behaviour;
External balance	—	adapted behaviour;
Adjusted and adapted behaviours	—	integrated behaviour.

Argyris suggested that many problems could be explained by the lack of integrated behaviour. Let us take as an example the company director who has ulcers. To the outside world, to his immediate social environment, he displays adapted behaviour, and gains social approval and other rewards for doing so. Internally, however, this balance is missing — he is stressed, may be concerned about priorities, and may seek to compensate by overeating or drinking. In this case we have a good example of adapted behaviour without adjusted behaviour, leading to problems. Similarly, a problem might be caused by internal balance and harmony without external or environmental support. Many people who 'drop out' of society are perfectly clear what they are doing and why — they are well adjusted internally — but their actions earn them social disapproval.

This idea of personality being an organisation of components has significant implications for promotion and training. It is meaningless in Argyris' system to tell a potential foreman that if he displayed more initiative he would be promoted, for the apparently low level of initiative is presumably integrated into his whole personality, and to change this part would imply a change in the whole structure. So, too, in the case of training, the trainer must ensure not only the understanding of the material presented, but also the incorporation of the subject matter into the personality system of the trainees.

Argyris reviewed a number of works on personality and concluded that there was some measure of agreement on the existence of psychic energy as well as physical energy. This psychic energy conforms to the basic laws of physics in that it can neither be created nor destroyed. Thus if it is not used to fulfil one need, it will find expression in another way. If a person is only required to use half his psychic energy in his job, he will find an outlet through other means, such as arguments, aggression and so on.

The final part of Argyris' theory which we will consider is his concern for the development of the adult personality. Argyris lists seven of the most commonly accepted distinctions between childhood and adult behaviour:

1) Passivity in childhood vs activity in adults;
2) Dependence in childhood vs independent adults;
3) A repertoire of few behaviours in childhood vs many behaviours in adulthood;
4) Transitory interests in childhood vs deep and long-lasting interests in adulthood;

5) A short time perspective in childhood vs a long time perspective in adults;

6) The child is subordinate in a family, but the adult is an equal with other adults;

7) The child lacks an awareness of self, while the adult has an awareness of, and also control over, self.

It is possible to argue that the characteristics implicit in the structure and functioning of most large scale organisations are far more appropriate to the childhood personality than the adult one. Let us look at a few examples of this argument:

— It is claimed that mental passivity, not creativity and initiative, is required from most blue collar workers and many white collar workers. Physical passivity is a requirement of most assembly line forms of production.

— The industrial worker is frequently dependent on his union for power, on his employer for wages, and frequently on other workers in a similar sector of the economy for his work, as in the car industry, for example.

— The deskilling of many jobs and the decline of craft industries has meant increasing fragmentation of work, with subsequent demands on the worker to act in new ways and to maintain his interest in spite of increasingly shortened job cycles.

— The hierarchical structure of most organisations and the insistence on the part of some to have separate canteens, toilet facilities, and entrances for different types of employee, calls into question the characteristic equality of the adult.

In the same vein as D. McGregor (1960), Argyris is arguing that if management provides conditions of work suitable for a childhood personality, it cannot expect adult behaviour in return. Argyris has proposed that a basic conflict exists between the needs of the mature personality and the working conditions provided by the majority of industrial and commercial enterprises, and his study of personality suggests that changes in the work environment are needed before adult integrated behaviour can be expected from the workforce.

Chapter 6

Attitude Formation And Change

We all have a fairly good idea what an attitude is and we use the word 'attitude' freely. For example we might ask a friend about his attitude towards apartheid, or abortion. Among psychologists the word has many definitions, but it almost always indicates a readiness to respond towards a certain object in a favourable or unfavourable manner. Because of this 'readiness to respond' in a particular manner, numerous groups of people, for example market researchers, politicians and managers, have a special interest in discovering people's attitudes, as it is believed that this will enable behaviour to be predicted.

Attitudes are often described as having three components:

1. A *cognitive* component, i.e. an attitude is based on real or assumed *knowledge* about the object;
2. An *affective* component, i.e. an attitude includes a *feeling* or emotional response to the object;
3. A *behavioural* component, i.e. an attitude implies a predisposition to *act* in a particular way towards the object.

In addition to these three aspects or components of an attitude, we must also bear in mind that one rarely stands alone, but that attitudes tend to occur in clusters. For example, an individual who holds a negative attitude towards apartheid is also likely to hold a negative attitude towards a variety of forms of discrimination.

Having looked at these general aspects of the nature of attitudes, let us now turn to the subject of attitude formation. Our attitudes are formed through three main sources:

1. *Early socialisation* — many of our attitudes can be traced back to our childhood, and specifically to instruction by parents and at school. Attitudes concerning authority, the law and the purpose of work are often acquired through information received and behaviour observed in childhood. As an example, let us consider attitudes towards the police. Some children are brought up to consider the policeman as their friend, someone to turn to if they are lost, or someone to help them cross a busy road. Parents encourage their children, in this case, to develop a positive attitude towards the police. Many schools do likewise, and a policeman is often invited to give a talk on road safety, or children are encouraged to learn to ride a bicycle under a police training scheme. In the light of this set of circumstances, early socialisation leads to a favourable attitude

towards the police being formed in the young person's mind. However, there are some parents, particularly those whose own attitude towards the police is a negative one, who present information to their children which leads to a similar negative attitude being formed in this next generation. Some parents see the policeman as a threatening authority figure, whose role is punishment. It is possible to hear parents threatening a child that if he does not behave himself the parent will tell a policeman and he will lock up the child in prison. This direct form of influence, together with more subtle information which the child acquires by hearing his parents talk about incidents involving policemen, can readily lead to the development of a strong negative attitude at an early age.

2. *Group affiliation* — as we grow older we often becomes less concerned with what our parents think of us, and far more concerned with the esteem of our peers and friends. Thus a second source of attitude formation is the group affiliation we experience, the groups of friends or colleagues with whom we associate. It is not surprising that it is in adolescence, when we are given more freedom to mix with a wide range of different people of our own age, that we first experience serious clashes with our parents. We find that our friends, whose esteem we value, hold attitudes on a range of subjects never previously considered, or perhaps attitudes which contradict those acquired from our parents. In such a situation we are more likely to accept attitudes expressed by friends whom we admire, rather than those of our parents. Thus if we wish to belong to, and be accepted by, a group we will tend to adopt the attitudes appropriate to, or commonly held by, that group.

3. *Personal experience* — a third source of attitude formation is our own experience, events which occur and which mould our view of the world. A positive attitude towards the British police being armed may result from being involved in a bank robbery; a negative attitude towards government intervention in business may result from the experience of being in business yourself. An attitude towards the appropriate size of a student grant is often formed in the first term of a course of study, by having to live on one.

Thus most of our attitude formation can be traced to our early socialisation, the groups to which we belong or have belonged, and our own personal experience of the world.

It may have occurred to you by now that in fact attitude formation and attitude change are inextricably linked in the lives of most people — attitude change is simply the formation of a new attitude in place of an old one. For most of us, then, attitude change occurs for one or more of the following three reasons:

(1) *Additional information* — the strength of information to change an attitude depends particularly on the *source* of the information and the *nature* of the information. Unfortunately some people consider the printed word to be an irrefutable source of information, and so the newspapers, for example, can possess enormous power over the attitudes of their readers. Similarly we have learned to distinguish experts, whom we tend to believe, from the lay person, whose information we may regard with some scepticism. If, for example, I go to the butcher's one morning and he tells me that I am not looking well and that I have got glandular fever, I will probably ignore him. If, however, my doctor tells me I have glandular fever, I am far more likely to believe him, as I consider him to be an expert in such matters. So the source of information is an important variable affecting attitude change.

The nature of the information is also important. A number of campaigns launched for road safety, dental care and such causes, have found that very frightening, shocking, or gruesome information tends to make people 'switch off' mentally, no doubt whilst convincing themselves that it could never happen to them. Instead it has been found that a more mildly toned 'message', indicating how accidents can happen to ordinary people, or how tooth decay can be avoided by a particular routine of dental care, is far more effective.

Another aspect of the nature of the information presented concerns the use of statistics and diagrams. The following graph is far more convincing than a simple statement that the consumption of beer went up last quarter:

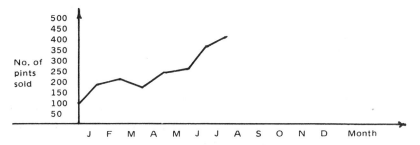

Figure 14 : Example of graphic representation

Similarly I am far more likely to be convinced by a statement that 98% of pubs are managed by men, compared to one which claims that there are more males than females in pub management.

Thus the likelihood of additional information leading to attitude change is significantly affected by the source and the nature of that information.

2. *Changes in group affiliation.* We saw in the section on attitude formation that group membership and the esteem of group members is an important influence on the attitudes we adopt. Similarly, if we change the groups of which we are members, some attitude change is involved. This can cause significant problems for the individual, as in the case of the shopfloor worker who is promoted to the job of foreman. He is required, by virtue of his new group affiliation, to adopt managerial or supervisory attitudes concerning punctuality, time wasting and so on, and to reject those of his shopfloor origins.

Obviously a change in group does not require a total change in all attitudes, but only those which are central to the group. Thus, while our newly promoted foreman may have to alter his attitude towards pilfering, he is free to continue to hold his attitude towards football hooliganism, modern art, and Americans. In other words, only attitudes which are highly relevant to the group, its interests, and its reason for existence are necessarily called into question through changes in group affiliation.

However, the foreman may have been promoted unwillingly; he may be aware that he is near to retirement and so unlikely to receive further promotion. In such a case, where acceptance by the new group is not of vital importance to the individual, attitude change might not result from a change of group. Similarly, if I want to join a particular squash club very badly, I will freely agree to abide by any rules or regulations they may require. If, on the other hand, there are a number of squash clubs in the vicinity, I may reject a new regulation introduced by my existing club, and consider leaving.

Thus attitude change as a result of changes in group affiliation is affected by both the centrality of the attitude to the group and the importance of group membership to the individual.

3. *Experience.* I may have unfavourable attitudes towards certain ethnic groups, but these may be changed by meeting members of those groups and becoming acquainted with them. My former, unfavourable attitude may have been formed on the basis of a small sample of behaviour, or on the basis of what other people had told me, but actual experience has led me to change my attitude.

A person who is quite willing to drink a lot of alcohol and drive a car may have his attitude changed by the experience of a friend being killed in an accident involving a drunk motorist.

Experience, then, can be a very powerful source of attitude change.

The apparent simplicity of attitude change hides the fact that people rarely change their attitudes, and that attitudes are very difficult to change. Let us now turn to a consideration of why this might be the case.

The first reason why attitudes are difficult to change is because, as we saw above, many of our attitudes are acquired from, or significantly influenced by, people whose affection, esteem, or respect we desire. In our section on learning theory we will see that rewarded behaviour is repeated, and so in this context of attitude formation and change, we can see that people derive 'rewards' in the form of love, approval, or agreement when they express attitudes which are in harmony with those of their parents, friends or teachers. It is highly improbable that an individual will change a piece of behaviour which leads to a reward without other, and probably greater, rewards being offered in its place. Thus an individual is unlikely to change an attitude which has brought approval in the past, without an assurance of greater approval following attitude change.

This is a point which managers, market researchers, and others concerned with attitude change must consider, and there are many examples of advertisements which offer 'rewards' in the form of better value for money, social approval, better quality, if you switch from your existing brand to another. In the same way, technological change, change in times or location of work, or in a remuneration package are 'sold' to a workforce by emphasising the improved rewards under the new scheme as compared with the old one.

To summarise, one reason why attitudes are difficult to change is because they elicit rewards, and we do not discard rewards without being assured of greater ones to come.

Another reason why attitudes are difficult to change is because they are useful to us. D. Katz (1960) claimed that attitudes may fulfil any one of four functions or purpose:

1. *Ego-defensive,* that is they help us to protect our image of ourselves. Negative attitudes concerning other races or groups of people are very often functional to the individual because they enable him to project feelings of inferiority in himself onto other groups, thereby enhancing his own self-image and self-esteem. Frequently those individuals who manifest extreme prejudice against a certain group are people who are insecure in their jobs, or who feel inferior in their educational attainments, and by 'blaming' another group, they can project their own shortcomings onto others, so protecting or defending themselves.

2. *Value-expressive,* that is attitudes may cause satisfaction by expressing the 'type' of person the individual believes himself to be. Attitudes may demonstrate who you are to other people. Some people pride themselves on being 'objective', on being able to see both sides of an argument, others pride themselves on being liberal or tolerant. Our set of attitudes provides a short-cut to explaining to others the sort of person we are.

3. *Instrumental,* that is that the expression of certain attitudes in particular social contexts has a utility in obtaining rewards or avoiding punishments. This purpose relates closely to the previous section, where we were looking at the link between attitudes and the groups to which we belong. In a group which believes that Queens Park Rangers are a magical football team, the expression of an attitude which supports this, which points out the vast improvement in the performance of the team and so on, is almost guaranteed to obtain praise and social rewards for the individual who is expressing it.

4. *Knowledge,* that is attitudes form a framework which enables us to structure our world, to assess new information and to make judgements in new settings. We receive vast quantities of information every day through what we see and hear, and it would take a considerable length of time to assess, from scratch, each new piece of data as we received it. Because we have an existing range of sorting categories in the form of attitudes, this task is significantly easier. Unfortunately, however, we sometimes, unknowingly, distort the information we receive to enable it to fit in more comfortably with our existing attitudes. A dramatic example of this was illustrated when a group of racially prejudiced white Americans were shown a picture of a white person stabbing a black person. They were only able to see the picture for a very short period, but most reported the picture to have depicted a black person stabbing a white person. In this case their anti-black attitudes had decoded the information received into information which could be accommodated into their existing frame of reference, their set of attitudes, and this led to the distortion.

Thus attitudes have a number of functions or uses, and just as you would not consider discarding something useful, like a tin-opener or a pair of scissors, unless you had found something *more* useful or *more* effective, so people are reluctant to change their attitude towards a specific object, person, or event until a more useful attitude is presented. The implication of this for managers and others is that attempts to change attitudes must focus on at least one of these major functions — it must be demonstrated that different attitudes may also fulfil important functions.

The final point we shall consider concerning why attitudes are difficult to change relates to the fact that our attitudes are not independent and isolated, but form clusters. These clusters are constructed over a period and in such a way as to avoid inherent conflict. It is not very comfortable or easy to heartily dislike any person who smokes cigarettes, and yet to fall in love with someone who smokes a hundred cigarettes a day. Where this does happen, the individual has to go through a period of readjustment until the attitudes are brought into line again. This type of situation frequently occurs with relationships between people, thus:

X	has a high regard for	Y
X	has a very low regard for	Z
Y	has a very high regard for	Z

In order to regain a balance, either X must change his attitude to Y or to Z or alternatively Y must change his attitude towards Z, probably through the persuasion of X.

We tend to have developed over time a set of attitudes which do not contradict each other, and which are balanced. We therefore tend to be reluctant to change any one attitude as it will probably upset this balance, and cause a conflict between the new and an existing attitude.

Let us take for example a person who has very liberal attitudes towards penal reform, who believes that a prison sentence is not a suitable punishment for people convicted of burglary. What happens when that same individual comes home to find the place wrecked and all his valuables stolen? He will be under severe pressure either to rationalise away his severe feelings of anger and desire for revenge against the individual who has caused him this grief and hardship, or to change his attitude towards the punishment of such offenders. This is an extreme case, and will cause the person concerned considerable heartsearching and readjustment of his values. It is hardly surprising that, in the majority of cases in everyday matters, we try to avoid such conflict.

In summary, attitudes are difficult to change because they are a source of reward, they are useful to us, and they exist in balanced clusters whereby changing one attitude may cause imbalance.

There are two types of attitude change, congruent, and incongruent. *Congruent* attitude change occurs when an individual changes the intensity of an attitude, for example when he changes from a mildly favourable attitude towards individual bonus payments to a very strong favourable attitude towards bonus systems. Alternatively he may change from having a strongly negative attitude towards capital punishment to a milder negative attitude. *Incongruent* attitude change, on the other hand, occurs when an individual changes from a positive to a negative attitude or vice versa. An example of incongruent attitude change would be the individual who was a strong supporter of capital punishment, but who changes his attitude for any reason to a negative one.

It may be apparent to you that congruent attitude change is far easier to bring about than incongruent attitude change.

We said at the beginning of this section that a variety of bodies (such as market researchers, managers, and politicians) are interested in discovering certain attitudes because they give an indication of how people are likely to react in particular situations. Some psychologists have cast doubt on such assumptions, however, claiming that there is a significant difference between what people *say* and what people do. S.M. Corey (1937) found a very low positive correlation (+ 0.02) between stated attitude towards cheating and actual behaviour in cheating. For example a great many people would say that cheating is wrong, that it is a bad thing, that it is unfair and so on. Yet those same people, according to Corey's study, when placed in a suitable situation were themselves quite prepared to cheat.

R.T. La Piere (1934) similarly found a huge difference between the written replies to a questionnaire on the attitudes of hotel and restaurant personnel towards racial minorities, and the actual behaviour of these same personnel towards a Chinese person who presented himself at their hotel or restaurant. Whilst the personnel were prepared to say that they would not serve a Chinese, when that person was actually there, they appeared to have little hesitation in helping him. La Piere does not suggest that we reject the concept of attitude because of these findings, but rather that we become aware of the nature of the data which purport to give evidence about people's attitudes, and that we should be wary of suggested relationships between verbal statements and actual behaviour. In the same way, M. Fishbein (1967) pointed out that attitude surveys tend to focus on general attitudes, whilst behaviour occurs in a particular context or set of circumstances. Hence while I may *say* on numerous occasions that I am opposed to violence of any kind, in a specific situation, when someone hits out at me, I may be perfectly prepared to fight back.

Thus the relationship between stated attitudes and actual behaviour may be a somewhat tenuous one, but the better the device for measuring attitudes, the stronger that relationship may become. It is to the subject of attitude measurement that we will now turn.

Attitude measurement

An attitude survey is a systematic investigation of people's attitudes. It may be concerned with a very general area — for example, the work environment — or a very specific area — perhaps the introduction of a new incentive bonus scheme. In the light of the problems raised, what can be done to improve the data acquired in an attitude survey? The way in which questions are worded is of critical importance and, apart from the obvious problems of leading questions (e.g. 'You don't believe capital punishment to be an effective deterrent, do you?'), other aspects of question wording have been the subject of serious study. References to stereotypes (e.g. Fascists, Communists) may alter a response, as they might evoke emotions. Similarly, vague questions, such as 'What kind of house do you live in?', tend to result in a very broad and often unusable set of responses, such as 'large', 'nice', 'semi-detached', 'it's painted red'.

The conditions under which a survey is conducted are also important, as respondents may be prepared to say one thing to an interviewer in a face-to-face situation, but be prepared to write something very different in an anonymous questionnaire. The characteristics of an interviewer may also have a significant effect on results. I may be prepared to talk to a female interviewer with far more frankness than to a male interviewer and respondents often give different replies to a black interviewer than a white one, particularly when the subject matter of the questionnaire involves racial issues.

Let us use a specific example of a company whose management wish to carry out an attitude survey to discover the level of morale among employees. The first step is to decide who is to conduct the survey — an outside consultant, who is likely to have significant experience in this area, who is likely to be perceived by the whole workforce as objective, but who knows little or nothing about the company and who is going to cost a large amount of money? The alternative is to mount the survey internally, using perhaps the Personnel Department, but in this case much depends on the credibility of the specific department, group, or individual, and whether the workforce has perceived them to have a vested interest in the outcome of the survey.

In these early stages management must realise that by commissioning an attitude survey it has declared that it wants to know about employees' thoughts and feelings. It must realise that once a survey has commenced, the situation has changed, and it is impossible to return to the pre-survey circumstances, as employee expectations and interest have been aroused. If management is not perceived as having responded to the survey results by actually doing something positive, employees will become increasingly cynical about management's intentions and may develop strong negative attitudes.

Having chosen the person or group to conduct the survey, and being aware of the above point, management should consult with the Trade Union, if there is one, to ensure cooperation and to prevent any false rumours concerning the purpose of the study. Frequently the researcher will also write to all staff concerned, both to inform them of the purpose and to stress that participation is on a voluntary basis.

Bearing in mind the advantages and disadvantages of interviews and questionnaires, the actual method of eliciting responses may be established and the question wording designed. The method by which responses will be analysed must be borne in mind at this stage, and questions must be phrased so that responses may be analysed by computer, put on to punched cards, or be processed manually with the least wastage of data.

Having constructed the questionnaire, or designed the interview schedule, and having decided whether the whole workforce or a sample of the workforce are to be questioned, the researcher can then 'try out' the survey by doing a *pilot survey*. This is done by administering the questionnaire or interview to a small number of people who will not be participating in the full survey. A pilot survey enables the researcher to establish whether:

a) the questions are sufficiently clear;
b) the interviewers have been adequately trained;
c) the responses can be easily coded;
d) the level of responses is likely to be adequate;
e) any question areas have been omitted, or whether any should be left out.

When the researcher is satisfied with the survey, it is administered to the workforce, and the responses analysed so that the final report can be written. Frequently the final report is accompanied by debriefing or feedback sessions with appropriate staff, e.g. management groups or shop stewards, and finally, as mentioned above, it is up to management to be seen to act on the findings.

This is a very general example of an attitude survey, but specific techniques known as *attitude scaling* are also used to measure attitudes. One of the most widely used is the L.L. Thurstone (1929) scale. To construct a Thurstone scale, for example on attitudes towards the cinema, a large number of statements concerning the cinema are collected, each one being written out on a separate slip of paper. The researcher will try to ensure that a full range of statements is included, from very favourable to very unfavourable. The final set of slips will probably number around one hundred. A large number of different individuals or 'judges' are asked to place each slip in any one of 11 piles, marked A to K, and each judge is instructed to place in pile A those statements which he believes to express the highest appreciation of the cinema, in pile F those in a neutral position, and in pile K those expressing strongest disapproval. The intervening piles are to be arranged according to the degree of approval or disapproval the statements express. It is important to note that the judges are not being asked to express their own attitudes towards the cinema, but only to classify the statements.

The piles onto which the various statements are placed are carefully noted, and statements which are placed by different judges on a variety of different piles are discarded as being ambiguous. The resulting attitude scale may consist of forty to fifty statements which have been proved to be unambiguous and which represent an even distribution between strongly favourable and strongly unfavourable. The respondent whose attitude is being measured then reads the final forty or fifty statements and simply marks all the statements with which he agrees.

An alternative form of attitude scale is the R.A. Likert (1932) scale. In this it is not the statements which are graded, as in the Thurstone scale, but the range of possible responses. Each statement is accompanied by a scale of responses ranging from 'strongly agree' to 'strongly disagree', and the respondent is required to indicate on the scale provided his particular level of agreement. An example is provided below:

'Cinemas today cater too much for the mass market and ignore specialist interests.'

strongly agree   agree   undecided   disagree   strongly disagree

To score such an attitude scale, numbers from one to five are allocated to each category of response — where 1 is strongly disagree and 5 is strongly agree.

Other specific attitude measures exist such as the E.S. Bogardus (1925) Social Distance scale, which is used to measure specifically the strength of positive or negative attitude towards racial groups. The respondent is asked which category would apply to a specific racial group:

1.   I would exclude them from our country;
2.   I would allow them into our country as visitors;
3.   I would permit them to become citizens;
4.   I would employ them;
5.   I would permit them to live in my street as neighbours;
6.   I would permit them entry to my club, as a friend;
7.   I would permit them kinship via marriage;

Recently 'hidden' techniques have been developed which elicit attitudes without appearing to do so. This is particularly useful when there is a possibility of attitudes violating group norms or cultural values. It was mentioned previously that people are frequently prepared to write things in an anonymous questionnaire which they might not be prepared to say to an interviewer. However it is possible that even direct questions in an anonymous questionnaire may not be answered honestly, and that overriding political, religious, or cultural views may emerge rather than the individual's personal attitudes.

One way of eliciting attitudes in a hidden way is to put forward an apparently factual question. For example, views about profits may be demonstrated by asking the respondent to ring the appropriate figure in the following statement:

'Financial reports show that out of every pound (30 pence) (15 pence) (5 pence) is profit.'

A gross overestimate might indicate negative attitudes towards profits and perhaps the capitalist mode of organisation. Similarly, a gross underestimate might indicate a strong support for capitalism, a right-wing viewpoint in industrial matters, and so on.

Other examples of hidden techniques include asking the respondent to write an essay or a story on a particular topic, sometimes using a picture or series of pictures as a stimulus. Asking people to complete half finished sentences is also a hidden way of eliciting attitudes.

In this section we have considered the sources of attitudes, the ways in which attitudes may be changed and how they may be measured. We have pointed out that one of the reasons why managers, politicians and market researchers wish to discover people's attitudes is because they may be a predictor of behaviour, although some doubt has been cast on this by Fishbein, La Piere and others.

Chapter 7

The Motivation To Work

Let us observe a number of people performing the same task in an office — typing or filing for example. One thing will become apparent, and that is they work at different speeds, different levels of interest, and with differing amounts of enthusiasm. Why does this happen? There could be many answers to this question of individual differences — perhaps they have different types or amounts of skill, perhaps the equipment used by some of the typists is better than that used by others, but one thing is almost certain and that is the fact that their motivation will be different. At any given point individual employees vary in the extent to which they are prepared to devote their energies toward the attainment of their employers' goals.

In our discussion of the work of Taylor in Chapter 2 we introduced the topic of motivation at work, for Taylor believed in an 'economic man' philosophy of motivation. This view, which considers man as essentially economically motivated and acting as a rational individual in the pursuit of these financial aims, was, and is, a widely held one. It certainly appears to be a very attractive view in terms of implementation, for it suggests that in order to make people work harder, management simply has to devise stimulating incentive schemes, and motivation problems will disappear. It was assumed that high productivity would inevitably follow from high morale which good motivation practice would provide. There was one problem which led to the development of further views of motivation, however, and that was the fact that this traditional view failed to deliver this raised productivity. The failure of many incentive schemes and productivity 'deals' led industrial psychologists to suggest that motivation to work is a very complex phenomenon, and attempts to simplify motivation to a single cause or single remedy are likely to be misleading and unhelpful.

Today we generally accept that an individual rarely behaves or responds in a situation as a result of a single motive, and that in many cases behaviour is unpredictable because of this. Motivation is frequently affected by the interaction of such variables as physiological needs and previous experience, such that many means may attain a single end. For example, the physiological state of being thirsty arouses in us a *need,* a need to drink. That need can be completely satisfied by drinking water, but, depending on the time of day, our surroundings and our past experience, we might decide that a glass of beer, a cup of tea or a coke would be far more attractive.

Let us look at another example of the different ways in which a goal might be achieved. Let us assume that you have an overwhelming desire to be rich. To achieve that you could:

a) Study hard to become successful in business;
b) Marry a very rich person;
c) Start filling in the football pools;
d) Play the stock-market.

It is possible to suggest therefore that motivation is a very complex phenomenon, which does not readily lend itself to simple explanations and theories, particularly as far as the motivation to work is concerned.

In this section we will outline some of the major theories which have had an impact on motivation at work in the last forty years, and the application of these theories will be discussed in later sections on payment systems.

Maslow's hierarchy of needs

A.H. Maslow (1943) believed that human needs form a type of hierarchy, such that normally a lower level need has to be at least partially satisfied before a higher level need is pursued.

Maslow placed human needs, as he perceived them, in the following order:

Figure 15 : Maslow's hierarchy of needs

Maslow would suggest that if you were starving or dying of thirst your first priority would be to obtain food and drink and these, together with other basic physical necessities, come under his category of *physiological* needs. Once these have been satisfied you might be concerned to have shelter, a home which was secure from danger, a way of life which was relatively hazard free. These he classified as *safety* needs. The satisfaction of these lower order needs, in part if not completely, allows the individual to develop his social nature. Maslow believed that human beings need to associate with other human beings, and we saw in Chapter 6 on attitude formation, for example, how significant our relationships with other people tend to be in our own personal development. So *belongingness* or *social* needs form the third level in Maslow's hierarchy. However, as these social needs are satisfied we find that it is no longer sufficient simply to be with other people, or to enjoy their company: instead we find that we need to be liked and respected. We frequently derive respect and esteem for ourselves from a perception that other people like, respect, and esteem us as individuals. Hence the fourth level in the hierarchy is termed *esteem* needs. Finally, Maslow suggested that self-esteem, derived from the esteem of others, would lead the individual to strive for self-fulfilment, or what he called *self-actualisation*. He believed that each individual has a need to fulfil his own potential, and that this formed the highest order need in the hierarchy. In many respects this ultimate need explains why individuals are always subject to motivating forces, for it is a very self-complacent individual who can honestly claim to have fulfilled his potential and thereby to be incapable of further development.

Maslow proposed that human needs may be ordered in a hierarchy, and that a lower order need must normally be satisfied before a higher order need is pursued. However there are examples of individuals deliberately sacrificing the satisfaction of lower order needs in preference for higher order needs. The individual who goes on hunger strike is giving up satisfaction of his physiological needs in favour of belongingness needs, if he is attempting to show solidarity with others, or perhaps he is pursuing esteem needs, by attempting to gain the respect and admiration of others for his cause. Similarly people who engage in dangerous sports are frequently denying safety needs in favour of esteem or self-actualisation needs.

Although Maslow did not develop his hierarchy of needs with the motivation of people at work in mind, the ramifications of his theory in this context are obvious. Maslow claimed, for example, that the only motivating need is an unfulfilled need. The logic behind this becomes apparent if the following example is considered. It is nine o'clock on a Saturday evening and you are due at a party. It has been a hectic day, so you haven't eaten anything since last night and you are very hungry. On the way to the party you spot a hamburger restaurant, so you stop and satisfy your hunger with a large hamburger and chips, a mixed salad and a huge banana split, washed down with a glass of lager. Feeling much happier, if decidedly bloated, you arrive at the party just in time for your hostess to be bringing out trays of sausages, bread and cheese, and pizzas. How would you feel? Would you tuck into the food with the same verve and enthusiasm as you might have done an hour or so previously? The answer is probably 'no', because the physiological need of hunger has already been satisfied, so you would probably rather talk to friends, thereby fulfilling social needs.

To a certain extent this applies to the motivation of people at work — they are motivated by unfulfilled needs, and so simply giving them more of something of which they already have enough is likely to be unproductive. To follow through Maslow's ideas, management must motivate the workforce by establishing the level at which unfulfilled needs are operating and gear their incentive schemes to that point. The development of autonomous work groups, job enrichment schemes, and even giving a job a new title to increase the prestige of the job holder, are examples of how this can be done.

Maslow also suggested that needs and motives were subject to change, particularly through change in environmental circumstances. Changes in the state of the economy, for example, may activate financial and security needs in the individual, and temporarily lessen the drive to satisfy some of the higher order needs.

Maslow's theory of motivation consists of three fundamental proposals:

1. Human needs are ordered in a hierarchy.

2. Lower order needs must normally be at least partially satisfied before a higher order need is pursued.

3. The only motivating need is an unfulfilled need.

Maslow's work was developed and modified by C.P. Alderfer (1972). He agreed with the basic idea of groups of needs motivating human behaviour, but instead of Maslow's five needs, he organised needs under three basic headings of:

      Existence
      Relatedness
      Growth

If we take the first letter from each of the headings we can see why Alderfer's theory is sometimes called the ERG theory of motivation. Very simply, Existence needs comprise Maslow's first two categories of physiological and safety needs, Relatedness corresponds to social and esteem needs and Growth is similar to Maslow's category of self-actualisation.

Alderfer did not entirely agree with Maslow's idea of hierarchy, as he believed that two or more categories of need could co-exist. This was linked to his belief that needs had two forms:

Chronic needs
Episodic needs

People who are unfortunate enough to have chronic back pain will tell you that this means that the pain is always there, and that they are almost always aware of it. A Chronic need, therefore, is almost always there motivating our behaviour towards the achievement of a long term goal, like success, wanting to be popular and so on. Episodic needs, on the other hand, come and go over time. If you think of episodes of Coronation Street, Brookside, East Enders or Dallas, they occur every week or every few days. In the same way Episodic needs occur at varying intervals, then when they have been satisfied they fade away until the next time. An urgent need for a cup of coffee will often disappear after drinking one or two cups, although it may reappear a few hours later.

These modifications render 'need' theories of motivation at work more comprehensible, and certainly suggest that an effective manager should attempt to appreciate the varying needs of subordinates.

The work of F. Herzberg

F. Herzberg (1966) surveyed a sample of two hundred accountants and engineers, who were asked to describe incidents or events at work which had brought them particular job satisfaction or job dissatisfaction. When he analysed these replies, Herzberg found that there was a noticeable difference between the type of event identified as causing job satisfaction and that causing job dissatisfaction.

Herzberg concluded from this that the opposite of job satisfaction is not dissatisfaction but a lack of job satisfaction. In other words, that there are two sets of variables to be considered, one set being related to job satisfaction and another, different, set being related to job dissatisfaction. Job satisfaction and job dissatisfaction are not opposite ends of a scale, but rather they must be considered to be different measurements. Let us turn to some examples of Herzberg's findings. If we take money as an example, poor wages caused many people to be dissatisfied with their current job, but very few people would say, 'Oh yes, I love my job because the pay is so good.' Similarly, with canteen facilities, a number of people cited examples of poor canteen facilities as incidents which annoyed them, but few talked about good canteen facilities as being a contributor to their job satisfaction.

Herzberg called the factors which tended to be associated with dissatisfaction *hygiene factors* and those associated with job satisfaction *motivators*.

In Figure 16 you can see examples of hygiene factors and motivators.

Herzberg's Hygiene-Motivator Theory

Hygiene factors	*Motivators*
DISSATISFACTION	SATISFACTION
Company policy and administration	Achievement
Supervision	Recognition
Work conditions	Work itself
Salary	Responsibility
Status	Advancement
Relationships with colleagues	Growth

Figure 16

There are some significant similarities between the work of Maslow and Herzberg. Herzberg's hygiene factors are preventive and environmental in nature, and they approximate to Maslow's lower-order needs. They prevent dissatisfaction, but do not lead to job satisfaction — in effect they bring motivation up to a theoretical zero level. By themselves hygiene factors do not motivate, this is left to the motivators, which are roughly equivalent to Maslow's higher-order needs.

Herzberg's two factor theory generated significant attention among managers to the problem of motivation at work. Managers became aware that they had tended to concentrate on the hygiene factors — when faced with a problem of motivation they had typically used a solution of higher pay or better fringe benefits. Herzberg had now provided them with an explanation of why this did not necessarily work — only a challenging job which provided opportunities for personal achievement, recognition, and responsibility would motivate personnel. Yet although this theory was widely accepted by managers from the mid 1960s onwards, it came under attack from academics, for example, V.H. Vroom (1964). Much of the controversy lay in the methodology used in the study. Other researchers, using the same method, known as the critical incident method, had discovered similar findings, but researchers who departed from this method were often unable to substantiate Herzberg's conclusions. Why might this happen? It has been suggested that many of the respondents who are asked to describe incidents which have caused them job satisfaction or dissatisfaction are influenced by what they feel they *ought* to say, rather than the 'truth'. If you were a professionally qualified accountant who had undergone perhaps five or six years training, would you talk about the delicious food in your canteen as a major source of job satisfaction? You might fear that the interviewer would form a poor impression of you as a person and as a professional accountant. Thus it is possible that this method of research actually pushed people into giving the answers which led to the formulation of Herzberg's two factor theory.

In spite of these criticisms, Herzberg's theory of motivation has continued to be of interest to managers in their shaping of policies concerning incentives and job enrichment.

Another fundamental criticism of both Maslow and Herzberg is that they ignore individual differences, and Vroom similarly built these into his theory.

V Vroom and Expectancy Theory

Unlike the majority of Herzberg's critics, V.H. Vroom (1964) proposed an alternative to his model. A number of assumptions underlie his theory:

1. People have preferences among various outcomes, for example I prefer to go out with John rather than Mark because I have a more enjoyable evening with him.

2. People have expectations (expectancies) about the likelihood or probability that an action on their part will lead to a particular outcome. For example, if I go to the Red Lion tonight it is very likely that John will be there, and he might ask me to go out with him tomorrow evening.

3. People do not behave, or take actions, at random, but try to achieve their preferred outcomes.

To summarise, expectancy theory assumes that people act in a rational manner; that people choose, from a range of plans, one that they expect will maximise their chances of achieving an attractive outcome.

Vroom uses a number of terms in a very specific way to describe his theory. His concept of *force* is basically equivalent of motivation and is shown to be the sum of the products of valances x expectancy.

$$F = V \times E$$

Valance is the strength of an individual's preference for a particular outcome. An important part of valence is the *instrumentality* or usefulness of a first level outcome in obtaining a desired second level outcome.

For example, I believe that there is a high instrumentality in the achievement of a high level of performance at work leading to promotion:

Superior performance	Promotion
1st level outcome	2nd level outcome

So, because I want promotion, I will also have a high preference to achieve a high level of performance, and I will therefore act in such a way as to achieve this. In Vroom's terms, the first level outcome of superior performance acquires a high positive valence by virtue of its expected relationship to the preferred second level outcome of promotion. *Expectancy* is the probability ranging from 0 to 1 that a particular action or effort will lead to a particular first level outcome, where a probability of 0 means that I believe there is no chance that an action will lead to a specific outcome, and a probability of 1 means I am virtually certain that an action *will* lead to a particular outcome.

Vroom's theory of motivation is different from that of Maslow and Herzberg in that it stresses the differences between individuals in their motivation. It suggests that people may be doing the same type of job for different reasons, and that they want different things out of work. The conclusion which we must draw, therefore, is that an incentive scheme applied to all workers may only appeal to some of them, and thus may lead to only some of them improving their performance in the desired direction. This may explain why output does not always increase when a productivity bonus is introduced. It may be the case, as in the Hawthorne experiments, that group loyalties and adherence to group norms is a preferable outcome to more money for the individual.

Vroom's model of motivation indicates only the conceptual determinants of motivation. It is saying that we should consider motivation as a personal and possibly unique process, which does not lend itself to generalisations such as those found in the work of Maslow and Herzberg. It does not provide, as Herzberg's work provided, a readily usable answer to managers — a set of answers to motivation problems. However it does pose a fundamental question to managers — how probable is it that in helping to achieve the goals of the organisation, the individual worker will be able to achieve his own goals? What can be done to improve the expectancy that worker behaviour which is desirable to the management of an organisation will be instrumental in achieving the desired second level outcomes of the workers? As you can see, this set of ideas is far less readily applicable in the work situation and for this reason it is perhaps not surprising that Vroom's work has not had the same managerial support that Herzberg's work has received. There are, however, some points which are of importance and which can be readily translated into action. If we take as an example the proposal that people tend to expend more effort toward reaching goals when both the probability of receiving a reward and the magnitude of that reward are known in advance, then it becomes apparent that relevant information, such as salary scales and promotion possibilities, should be widely disseminated, and also that feedback on performance (see Chapter 14 on Performance Appraisal) is vital.

Another form of expectancy theory was proposed by L.W. Porter and E.E. Lawler (1968). Their model, like Vroom's provides an alternative view to the simplistic traditional one concerning the positive relationship between job satisfaction and performance, particularly in the area of managerial performance. They suggest that satisfaction is derived from the extent to which actual rewards fall short of, meet, or exceed the individual's ideas of an equitable level. Thus, as we can see from Figure 17, the amount of effort an individual will put into a task is influenced by both the value of the reward he may obtain, and also his perception of the likelihood of his effort actually leading to this reward. It also indicates that effort is not the only factor leading to the effective performance of a task — the individual's abilities and personality and his interpretation of the job he is supposed to be doing are also important. Having completed the task, the individual will receive some intrinsic rewards, such as satisfaction from a job well done, and extrinsic rewards such as pay and, whether or not he is satisfied with these will depend, at least in part, on the rewards he thinks he *ought* to have received. Further, Porter and Lawler suggest that the overall satisfaction derived from the performance of task A will later influence the individual's calculations concerning his willingness to attempt task B.

D. McGregor — Assumptions about the motivation to work

D. McGregor (1960) discussed two sets of assumptions which managers might hold about the motivation of their work force.

The first set of assumptions, listed below, he called Theory X:

1. Work is inherently distasteful;
2. Most people at work try to avoid responsibility;
3. Most people have a very limited capacity for creativity at work;
4. Motivation of a work force should concentrate on the physiological and security levels of need satisfaction;
5. People must be closely controlled if the objectives of the organisation are to be achieved.

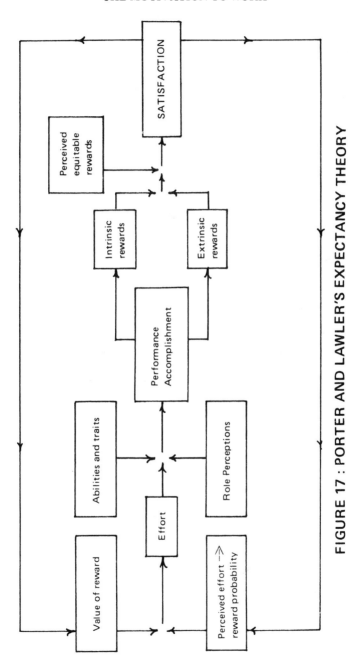

FIGURE 17 : PORTER AND LAWLER'S EXPECTANCY THEORY

You will notice that there are many similarities between these views and those proposed by Taylor and other Scientific Management theorists — you may have even heard managers saying very similar things about their subordinates. McGregor agrees that often workers' behaviour supports these assumptions, but he suggests that this is not because of their basic nature or attitudes, but rather that it happens as a result of the nature of industrial organisations and of management philosophy and practice. McGregor suggests that often workers appear to need close supervision because the nature of their jobs and their experience of organisational control is such that it encourages rule breaking and 'irresponsible behaviour'. If I simply told you to stand on your head 'or else ...' you would probably mutter to your neighbour that I must be mad, or that you could not see any good reason to follow this instruction and that you would not do it. On the other hand, if I explained to you in a rational manner that standing on your head led to a flow of blood to the brain and that this would improve your intellectual performance, you might be significantly more inclined to carry out this task.

McGregor invites managers to act on a different set of assumptions — Theory Y.

1. Work is not inherently distasteful, but excessive fragmentation and control has made it so;
2. People are self-directing, so the task of management should be coordination not control;
3. Motivation is needed at all levels, not just at the physiological and safety levels;
4. People seek responsibility at work, and are capable of creativity in conducive surroundings.

McGregor is suggesting that management is thus a process primarily of creating opportunities, releasing potential, removing obstacles to effective performance, and encouraging personal growth and development. He proposes that if management performs its task in an appropriate manner, as outlined above, the work force will react accordingly and will prove themselves to be capable of a much higher level of effectiveness than had previously been expected of them.

Having taken this overview of some of the theories put forward concerning individual motivation, what conclusions may we draw?

It should be apparent that motivation is a very complex phenomenon, and that any theory which suggests that motivation can be reduced to a single cause is likely to be simplistic at least. Thus the application of motivation theory to the workplace in such areas as job enrichment, payment systems, and bonus schemes must take account of the range of differences. It has been illustrated, by S.M. Nealey for example, that priorities change over the individual's life cycle, such that longer holidays are more attractive to the young worker, while more money added to their pensions is a strong preference of the older workers. Similarly we can see that, although money is an important element in the motivation to work, a fact that is given recognition in the area of salary administration, its role can easily be overstated, particularly in attempts to persuade people to work harder.

Thus motivation theories have made a significant contribution to our understanding of behaviour at work.

Chapter 8

Communication and Perception

In order to qualify for the title of 'social being' man has to be able to communicate, as indeed much evidence is provided to suggest that a very high proportion of other creatures are able to communicate with one another. It is possibly not too cynical to suggest that the very importance of this process predisposes it to a large variety of problems, and it is common to hear the majority of industrial problems being blamed on poor communications.

In this section we will look at what is meant by communication, some of the problems inherent in the process, and how to select the most appropriate means of communication in an organisation.

A very simple but accurate way of defining communication is that it is the transfer of a message from one party to another so that it can be understood and acted upon. This simple definition is described diagrammatically in Figure 18. The first component in the model is a sender. The sender may be a person, a number of people, for example 'The Board of Directors', or it could be a piece of machinery — my car sends me a message when the oil pressure is low. The information which the sender wishes to send out must then be put into a message or signal — the information has to be encoded so that it is in an appropriate form for the method or means of communication.

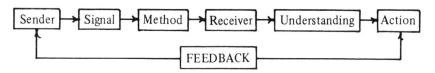

Figure 18 : A simple model of communication

This stage may involve putting our thoughts into words, or a message into the appropriate computer language, or even a more literal encoding, as for example in the case of a message being translated into Morse code before being sent. This is obviously dependent on which method of communication is to be used, so the sender's signal will vary according to whether a telephone call or a letter is the method to be used. The choice of method is a very important one, and we will consider it in greater depth later in this chapter. At the moment we will note that methods of communication subdivide into three main headings, thus:

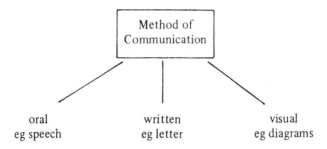

Figure 19 : Methods of communication

The fourth component in the model is the receiver — again this may be one person, a number of people, for example a committee, a piece of machinery and so on. Having received the words, or diagram, or whatever signal was transmitted, the receiver then has to make sense of it, in order to reach an understanding. This stage is sometimes known as 'decoding', as in the case of a spy who may receive a message consisting of a set of letters of the alphabet in front of him but, until he has decoded the message, it is meaningless and he is incapable of taking action on it. Many communications lead to or necessitate the receiver taking action, and this is very valuable in many cases as a way of telling the sender that the message *which he intended to send* has been received and understood, and, therefore, that there is no need to repeat the message. If you order 200 pairs of welder's gauntlets from my company, for which delivery is four to six weeks, I will send you an acknowledgement, which will confirm the number and precise items you have ordered, so that you know that the message (this particular order) has both been received and understood correctly, and also that you need take no further action for the time specified. Had I not sent you an acknowledgement, you might suspect that your order had got lost in the post, or on my desk, or that the message had been taken down incorrectly from a telephone call, and so you might 'phone up to find out what is going on, wasting your time and mine — or worse still, you might consider that I have so little regard for my customers that you should take your business elsewhere. Feedback is a vital part of the communication process, and its introduction into communication systems in organisations should be encouraged.

Problems of Communication

Given that the process of communication consists of these few, relatively simple steps, it may seem surprising that so many problems of communication emerge. It is to these problems, specifically that we will

85

now turn. Many of the problems of communication are the result of distortion of the intended message of the sender, and this distortion is sometimes called 'noise'. This term is used both literally and figuratively in communication. The literal use applies to crackling noise in the telephone which prevents the person on the other end from hearing your message. Similarly, it may refer to a poor public address system which distorts the sender's voice such that the message becomes incomprehensible. The figurative use of the term implies that noise may exist 'inside the head' of the receiver for example, blotting out the sender's intended message as effectively as a high speed train rushing by. Joe might be thinking of the great night out he had last night whilst his manager is briefing him on a new project, and his lack of concentration will prevent his hearing, understanding, and acting on that message. The sender will need feedback before he can be sure that no noise has interfered with the effective communication of his message.

The language used in the signal may also lead to problems. It is possible to be imprecise in the use of language, which permits a failure in communication to occur. Let us imagine that today is Tuesday, and I am asking you to come out with me for a drink next Sunday. When would you expect to go out for the drink, in five days' time, or in twelve days' time? To some people 'next Sunday' implies the 'very next one' to occur, while to others it means 'a week on Sunday', expecting me to say 'on Sunday' if I meant the very next one. It is unfortunate that so many ambiguities can occur in the English language, as they may hinder effective communication, and it is thus important that we check our signal for any such potential misunderstandings, as in this case, for example, by mentioning the date as well as the day of the week.

You are probably aware that in addition to the generally accepted range of English vocabulary, many sub-groups have their own particular form of vocabulary. A computer specialist will commonly use terms like VDU, bytes, chips and logging on, and to communicate effectively in such a context either the computer specialist must 'translate' or explain his terminology to the lay person, or the latter must learn this terminology beforehand. Such terminology or 'jargon' is often a sign of professionalised occupational groups, and it can be a very significant sign of membership of a group. It is not only occupational groups which employ jargon — drug users for example have a jargon which includes terms such as 'snow', 'grass', to 'OD', 'speed', and to 'mainline'. To the outsider these words have either no meaning, or one that is very different to that understood by a member of that group.

The important point about jargon is that where it is used in speech, or even in written communication, the sender must ensure that the receiver appreciates the intended meaning of all the message, which may include a special vocabulary or jargon. Some receivers will be very swift to tell you that they do not understand your message. A computer, when given an incorrect command, for example, will very quickly inform you that your command has not been understood, but a person may perceive it as a sign of inferiority or ignorance to admit that they do not know the meaning of a word in your signal. To avoid problems of communication arising from semantic or jargon problems, it is important that we are as precise as possible, providing as much back-up material as necessary to result in an unambiguous signal, and that, when using jargon, we can be confident that the receiver is aware of the meaning of our vocabulary.

Communication is easily distorted when the sender pays little attention to the motivation of the receiver. It is often tempting to believe that everyone is as interested in what we have to say as we are, and as this is obviously not the case, it can lead to difficulties. When the receiver is in a hurry, he is going to pay less attention to your long and detailed account than when he has more time. Someone who is motivated by a need for achievement is going to be relatively disinterested in your communication regarding the welfare policy of the organisation. For some people, first thing in the morning, or alternatively when they have just arrived home from work, may be very inappropriate for introducing a complex and lengthy discussion topic. Thus the motivation of the receiver, which will often include the time of the communication, will be carefully considered by the effective communicator.

Not only is the motivation of the receiver important, but also the attitudes held by the human receiver will affect his receptivity to the signal being transmitted. We do not receive each piece of information with a clear and unbiased mind — rather we have a set of attitudes and preconceived ideas which we will use to judge the signals we receive (see Chapter 6). If I have very negative attitudes towards Trade Unions, I am likely to disbelieve or even distort signals I receive from a shop steward, or alternatively information which is supportive of Trade Unions. Similarly, I am far more likely to accept the signal I receive from someone I like and believe to be honest, whilst I might reject without consideration a signal from someone I dislike. When we considered the knowledge function of attitudes it was pointed out that our attitudes form a type of sorting device which enables us to classify, accept, or reject the information we receive, and it is important to realise that the receiver's attitudes towards the sender himself, the content of the signal, and the method of communication, may all affect the success of the communication. Some people may claim to disbelieve anything said by a politician, for example, or alternatively to believe anything they see in print. Attitudes will significantly affect the receiver's receptivity to signals on the topic of race relations or nuclear disarmament, but they will also affect his reaction to the method of communication, so that some people tear up circulars which come through the post without ever opening them, or disbelieve everything said by their suppliers until they have seen it in writing.

While the effective communicator will take account of the attitudes of the receiver, he would also be wise to consider his own attitudes, for they can similarly affect the process of communication. The negative attitude of a sender to his 'audience' may be perceived in the way he talks down to his listeners, or in his manner of presentation. Some senders have negative attitudes towards certain methods of communication, which is made apparent by their use of an inappropriate method because they dislike writing letters, for example, which can result in long involved and expensive telephone calls, whereas others consider themselves to be ineffective on the telephone, which can lengthen the communication process if letters or memoranda are substituted.

Perception

So far we have suggested that communication problems may arise due to 'noise' in the communication system, to problems of semantics and jargon, and to the motivation and attitudes of both receiver and sender. However, we have assumed that the communication which the receiver picks up via his eyes or ears is the one which he will 'register' as having seen or heard. This process, which is so vital to effective communication, is known as *perception*. Very simply the process of perception consists of information being received through the sense organs, in this case particularly through the eyes and ears, and being sent to the brain. In fact vast quantities of such data are sent to the brain almost continually whilst we are awake, and so the brain selects information which it considers to be important at that time. You can try out this process any time you are at a party or in any crowded, noisy place.

Although you can *hear* that there are numerous other conversations going on around you, you will only be listening to the other person or people with whom you are sitting. However, if any of the other conversations suddenly includes your name, or perhaps the name of your firm or a car you particularly like, you will become aware of it, almost as if your brain is giving you a nudge, saying 'listen to this because it is of relevance to you.' Similarly if you quickly 'scan' a page of a newspaper, certain items will attract your attention, because again the brain has alerted you to the relevance of those words as against all the other words your eyes have 'seen'. What factors determine which items are perceived while other sights and sounds are apparently ignored? Again attitudes and motivation are important here, as in the example used above. Your name or an item of particular relevance, is noted above the rest of the 'noise'. Thus it is important to indicate the relevance or importance of a communication to the receiver, both to attract and to retain his attention. The impact of our attitudes is so strong that sometimes they cause the brain to misinterpret information sent to it by the senses. Someone who dislikes men with long hair may 'see' hair to be longer than it really is.

The context of the information received by our senses is particularly important. As a gimmick, an invitation to a party was once circulated to friends at work in the form of a memorandum, written on official looking stationery, and worded in a manner that was appropriate to a memo rather than a party invitation. Worried, a few day later, by the lack of response to the invitation, its author went round the various recipients to enquire about the event. Sadly, the majority of recipients had to admit that they had only glanced at the 'memo', considered it of no immediate relevance and discarded it! This suggests that the content of the signal and the method of communication should be carefully linked in order to avoid misperceptions.

Perceptual processes also operate to rationalise a signal which is only partially understood into one which is fully understandable. The old game of 'Chinese Whispers' can demonstrate how a message which is passed on unclearly, is distorted into one which makes sense to the receiver, and hence the famous, if undoubtedly apocryphal, story of the message 'Send reinforcements, we're going to advance' being finally delivered to headquarters as 'Send three and fourpence, we're going to a dance.'

To summarise, the process of perception is important in communication as it reminds us that we only receive communication in a selective manner, greatly influenced by our attitudes and motivation; that our perceptual processes may distort communication; and that the context of the signal must be considered.

Communication Media

It was stated above that communication methods could be classified under three main headings — oral, written and visual. We will now look at each of these in turn, to identify their strengths and weaknesses in the organisational context.

Oral communication concerns the spoken word, and it embraces face-to-face conversation, the telephone call, and such devices as the meeting, seminar, and lecture. Face-to-face conversation is particularly useful for general matters, as feedback can be instantaneous and any misperceptions may be cleared up immediately. However, it is a very inefficient way of transmitting information to a large number of people and can be very time consuming. Also it is not an effective method of transmitting large quantities of technical data, as the receiver is, in that case, being required to retain information in his memory when it could have been delivered to him in writing. The telephone call similarly has the advantage of speed and rapid feedback, although the latter is of a lower quality due to the absence of feedback obtained by being able to see the facial expression of the other party. This aspect of non-verbal communication will be covered in greater depth below. There are some major problems with communication by telephone which must be carefully considered. The first problem is that already mentioned above, notably the problem of noise or a 'bad line'.

Another weakness of the telephone call is that it is relatively insecure — few people would consider transmitting highly confidential material over the telephone, as there is a possibility of a telephonist on your switchboard, or that of the other party, listening in to your conversation, either intentionally or by accident; or a crossed line/wrong number dialling in on your conversation; and of course there is always the possibility of your line being tapped by official or unofficial bodies. Thus security is an important consideration. A third problem which is shared by all oral, as opposed to written, communication is that there is no record of the conversation, no document which can be referred to at a later date, in case of disagreement over what was said, or simply for information purposes.

Another very common form of oral communication is found in meetings. Here, provided that the numbers of people are small enough to enable them all to contribute, an interchange of information can occur relatively speedily and with each individual receiving feedback on his contribution. To a great extent the success of a meeting as a communication event rests with the Chairperson, in terms of controlling the length and timing of the meeting; the contributions of the various participants; and, in the case of formal meetings, the written record of the conversations, in the form of minutes, afterwards.

Some generalisations may be made about oral communication, namely that it is direct and provides rapid feedback, with a consequent lessening of the risk of misunderstanding, but, on the other hand, there may be the problem of the limited capacity of the receiver to take in large quantities of data, particularly technical data, and also the lack of any reference document.

Written communication, varying from a very short memorandum, through the longer letter, to a full report, may overcome some of the problems inherent in oral communication, although, in so doing, it generates additional problems of its own. Written communication provides a record of the signal, the receiver may absorb the information at his own rate, and security and confidentiality may be higher. The memorandum typifies some of the problems inherent in written communication. In the first place it is slower — a written message has to be delivered and this may take hours or even days. Once it has been delivered, there is little likelihood of the receiver immediately dropping his existing task to answer the question or act on the information contained in the memorandum, whereas the sender's 'presence' on the other end of a telephone may prompt him to do just that. Secondly, more thought and care has to go into the formulation of the signal, as the reduced possibility of feedback increases the pressure on the sender to make the signal as clear, comprehensible, and unambiguous as possible. Where the subject matter is particularly crucial, and the sender has any doubt about the clarity of his message, he may be well advised to phrase his signal in terms of a number of steps, with confirmation of correct interpretation and action taking place at the end of each step. Thus ambiguity over the most suitable content of a report can be checked by a superior at a draft stage, for example, rather than waiting until a final report to provide feedback as to whether or not the message has been understood. On the other hand, a memorandum may be distributed widely, thus ensuring that a relatively large number of people obtain exactly the same signal.

A letter, while involving many of the features mentioned above, is more likely to be used to communicate with a receiver outside your organisation. This introduces an additional point for consideration, and that is the impression which you are providing of you and your organisation to this 'outsider'. It is most uncommon for an organisation not to provide headed letter paper and some typing assistance so that correspondence will give a good impression.

Similar points may also be made of the report as a method of communication, in terms of the advantages of a reference document, and the receiver's ability to absorb the information at his own rate, together with the disadvantages of lack of feedback and associated need for clarity. An additional factor is introduced and that is the need to produce a report that is capable of satisfying the needs of a variety of receivers, with a variety of levels of skill in the appropriate specialism. To cater for this range of receivers, it is common to provide a summary, together with recommendations at the beginning of the report, and to keep the most detailed and technical information for Appendices towards the back of the document. There is also the temptation when writing a report, which will be a relatively lengthy method of communication anyway, to take advantage of the situation to include any information of relevance, rather than only the essential information. This is associated with a point which is relevant to all forms of written communication, but particularly with letters and reports, and that is the expense involved, when stationery, typist's time, reprographic facilities, and redrafting are taken into consideration.

The third form of communication is *visual*. In one sense this is a fairly limited method, consisting of the use of posters for such areas of communication as Health and Safety. However, widely interpreted, visual communication may also include charts, slides, or films which may be used to back up a lecture or presentation on a new product launch, for example, and perhaps, more importantly, it can also include non-verbal communication, which we have briefly referred to above. If we take each of these in turn, notices or posters on a notice board can be an effective way of communicating a limited quantity of material to a large number of people. Posters and notices have a rather limited impact, they have to be designed to catch the eye and impress the message on the individual, but having done so, they either have to be changed frequently to retain attention or it has to be accepted that the communication will be of little value in the long run.

Visual communication as an aid to a lecture or presentation can be important, but should be carefully designed to make the maximum impact and to avoid confusing the issue with an excessively complicated diagram, or too many words on a chart. Obviously where such aids are being used for presentation to an outside body, they need to be even more carefully planned, as they will be a very important influence on the customer's impression of your organisation.

Non-verbal communication is a vital part of the communication process, and takes a number of forms. It can completely alter the meaning of a signal, for instance. I can say to you with a grin on my face that you have made a dreadful mess of a piece of work and that you will be in serious trouble if you do anything like that again, and, in spite of the oral signal, the visual signal would take precedence. If I said exactly the same words with a frown on my face, you might well quake with fear. The sender can pick up a significant amount of feedback by looking at the expression on the receiver's face — it may register agreement, puzzlement, or total incomprehension. The sender may thus modify his signal as he goes along repeating in a different way a part which has been misunderstood, and so on. Many people use their hands to accompany oral communication, but this must be used with care as it can be very distracting, with more attention being paid to the hands than to the signal itself. Posture can similarly communicate feelings and attitudes, or provide feedback. If you sit back in your chair, your hands still and perhaps your legs crossed, you are telling me, without saying anything, that you are relaxed and confident. Non-verbal communication can have problems associated too, perhaps the most significant being the need for these visual ones to be interpreted, and thus the possibility of mistaken interpretation. If you catch someone's eye and observe that he or she has winked at you, how are you to interpret that information? It could be that the person has something in his or her eye, and is winking to expel it. It may be that he or she suffers from a twitch, and that the wink is involuntary. But perhaps it was intentional, does that mean it was a general, bland friendly wink, or an extremely personal sexual one? Thus a very simple gesture lends itself to a wide variety of interpretations, and this can be a problem in any form of communication. It is unfortunate that both shyness and dishonesty are characterised by a reluctance to look another person in the eye. Since non-verbal communication tends to override oral communication, this can provide significant problems for the shy manager in his dealings with subordinates.

Non-verbal communication is visual communication and it is, perhaps the most important form.

The choice of method of communication is governed by a variety of factors, as we have tried to indicate throughout the text, but they are summarised as follows:

a) The right use of the appropriate senses — a complex diagram is better described by use of eyes rather than by ears;

b) Speed — a telephone call is a far more rapid method of communication than written communication.

c) Impression — a formal letter on headed paper will provide a much more favourable image than a rapidly written note;

d) Feedback — face-to-face communication provides faster and more accurate feedback than written communication;

e) Confidential information — there may be a need for a written record of communication, which may influence the choice of communication method, or alternatively it may be undesirable to discuss confidential matters on the telephone due to its inherent insecurity;

f) Quantity of information to be retained — large quantities, or even small quantities, of very complex data is far better communicated in writing than orally;

g) Expense — it may be necessary to consider the cost of different forms of communication, investigating the relative costs of a typed letter as against a long distance telephone call, as against a telex message, and so on.

It is necessary to point out at this stage that communication in organisations may be regarded in terms of vertical and horizontal communications, as well as formal and informal. In this last part we will look at these four types of organisational communication, with a more detailed discussion of two forms, namely briefing groups and the 'grapevine'.

Traditionally, vertical communication downwards was the most widely, if not only, recognised direction of formal communication in organisations. The evolution of more democratic styles of management has meant that some upward vertical communication is encouraged, if not sought, and thus two-way vertical communication is now far more common. However, the traditional view is inaccurate in another respect, and that is in its emphasis on vertical communication, for the modern business can only function when there is unimpeded communication, not only between superior and subordinate (vertical), but also between individuals in different departments. This latter form is known as horizontal communication and is only effective when a large element of trust and cooperation exists in the organisation, for competitive departments are unlikely to share information, and a desire for empire building by a departmental head may easily block effective horizontal communication.

Vertical communication may also be impeded by a variety of factors. Long chains of command may mean that a signal is severely distorted in its transmission up or down the chain. Another problem exists because of the authority system which co-exists alongside the communication system. A subordinate may be very reluctant to pass on communication to a superior which might suggest that he, the subordinate, has been incompetent, as this would be perceived as likely to result in adverse effects on his career. Moreover, information which could be construed as a criticism of the superior will also be avoided, for exactly the same reason. Thus upward communication can be distorted due to the hierarchical authority system, resulting in bland or exclusively favourable communication passing upwards.

Similarly, although organisations will have a formal communication system, as discussed above, even though it may vary in strength, they also tend to have informal communication channels, centred around individuals who know each other, or based on gossip and rumour. Whilst such channels can be a menace, they will be ignored at management's peril — indeed some organisations go to considerable lengths to strengthen informal communication channels.

Communication in Organisations

Let us now turn to two specific forms of organisational communication, the first being briefing groups, which are an example of formal communication, usually of a vertical nature. *Briefing groups* consist of a manager or supervisor and some or all of his subordinates, in discussion over some matter relevant to work. This can be spread throughout the organisation, as Figure 20 indicates, subordinate B, having been briefed by superior A, can then go on to brief subordinate C, and so on.

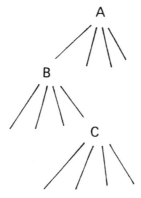

Figure 20 : Briefing groups

These groups may be brought into existence to discuss a specific topic — for example an office relocation plan, or they may be held on a regular basis to discuss day-to-day problems.

In contrast, the *grapevine* operates most strongly on the horizontal plane, and is an informal method of communication. The grapevine is infamous for the rapidity with which communication is spread, but sadly it suffers from distortion in much the same way as formal channels do. Perhaps the main reason why information spreads so quickly on the grapevine is that only spectacular pieces of gossip are used, and thus the motivation of each individual both to hear and pass on the information is high. Because the distortion of information found in this method of communication may be harmful or threatening to management, they may be most anxious to prevent its operation. One of the most effective means of doing this is to keep employees fully informed about all decisions likely to affect them. On the other hand, it has been known for managements, unwilling to make a formal announcement on a very sensitive subject, to drop a hint to a central figure in the informal communication network, so that initial employee reactions may be observed with management still preserving their apparent neutrality.

Chapter 9

Groups

A visit to any organisation will demonstrate the fact that we spend a relatively small proportion of working life as individuals, but rather we tend to belong to some kind of group. Similarly many leisure activities require, or are preferable in, the company of others. In this chapter we will look primarily at the group in a work context to examine its characteristics, its impact on the individual, and the influence individual members can exert on the group.

What is a group? It consists essentially of a number of people who share common goals or purposes. Yet it is more than that, for very few people would consider a number of people queueing at a bus stop to be a group — they are simply a number of people who happen to share the common goal of wishing to catch a bus. The additional element of interaction must be present, together with a psychological awareness that 'we' form a group. Ed Schein summarises these points in his definition of a group as:

> 'Any number of people who (1) interact with one another, (2) are psychologically aware of one another and (3) perceive themselves to be a group.'

So when we are talking about a group we are not simply referring to a random set of people, nor are we referring to departments of fifty or sixty people, since interaction and psychological awareness of one another are essential characteristics of a collection of people who form a group.

Types of Group

In the work context there are two main types of group — formal and informal. *Formal* groups are those which are officially designated as such by management and which have a specific organisational function to perform. Their membership, structure, and purpose may be clearly defined and stated. These groups may be relatively permanent, or they may be set up on a temporary, short-term basis. Management may divide the direct labour force into permanent work groups or might do the task of managing by means of a management team. The stability of such permanent groups will obviously depend on the stability of the workforce, since a high rate of labour turnover will inevitably mean that the membership of these groups will change from time to time. The basic characteristic of such groups is that one normally belongs to a formal group by virtue of the role played or the job performed in the organisation rather than because of any particular personal characteristics of the individual. Formal groups may also be temporary in nature, such as a project team concerned with the development of a new product, which will inevitably be disbanded when the product has been launched — or perhaps abandoned. Similarly a working party may be set up in order to organise a particular function, such as a Christmas party, or to arrange for the relocation of a company from one area to another. These groups have a specific and essentially short-term brief, which means that at the end of a particular period the group, as formally constituted, will cease to exist. It is perhaps worth noting that such temporary groups may be difficult to 'kill off', as sometimes people find working in a particular group so satisfying that they keep finding more work for their particular group to do, in order to prevent its demise.

The other type of group found in any organisation is the *informal* group. Such groups lack the management sanction and explicit organisational function of the formal group, and membership is usually on the basis of personal characteristics rather than organisational role. Friendship groups are a typical example of informal groups, or people who normally have lunch together, who have a common interest in football, bridge, or photography. In these examples the purpose of the group may have little or nothing to do with the organisation, although this is not always the case. In practice the dividing line between formal and informal groups may be less distinct than has so far been suggested. It is not uncommon for members of a formally constituted working party (a formal group) to meet up after work on a Friday for a drink as a friendship group (informal group).

Whilst formal groups have an explicit organisational purpose, they also have particular purposes as far as their individual members are concerned. As people join many groups voluntarily, they presumably do so because group membership is attractive to them, and it is to this question of the functions of group membership for the individual that we now turn.

The first reason why the individual may join a group is to increase his effectiveness. Thus I might join a group of people who are interested in playing squash because it is more exciting and challenging than playing squash on my own. I might join the Ducati Owners' Club because, being proud of my motorbike, I want to learn more about it, about the best places to buy spares, and about particular ways of tuning it. Being interested in local history, I might join up with a group of people with a similar interest because I believe that as a group we will be able to gain access to places normally closed to individuals and, by pooling our information, we will all learn more. Thus one reason why people join groups is to help them achieve a goal or accomplish a task which they could not do, or could only do less effectively, as an individual.

Another reason for group membership is security — the idea that there is safety in numbers. In pioneer days in America settlers would rarely travel as individuals, or even as a family, but would rather combine with other settlers to better protect themselves against the natural and human hazards which lay ahead. In a less picturesque way, workers may combine as an informal work group to agree a rate of output if they fear that a high rate of production might lead to redundancies or renegotiation downwards of their rate of pay.

Associated with this security function is the idea that a group may be more influential than an individual in attempting to affect the environment. We commonly talk of 'pressure groups' but rarely of 'pressure individuals'. A number of employers may band together to form an influential counter to Trade Union pressure or Government intervention, where an individual employer might never be heard. A Residents' Association has more sway in a Local Authority Planning inquiry than Mr Smith who lives at number 45. This point will be confirmed if you look at the list of people who provide evidence to a Royal Commission or similar body — almost invariably evidence is presented on behalf of some group or other, rather than by individuals speaking entirely for themselves.

A fourth function of group membership is that of facilitating comparison, often social comparison. We should not underestimate the amount of our behaviour that is learned, and this applies as much to the adult as it does in childhood. But how do we learn how to behave when faced with new problems and situations in adulthood? One way is through our group membership, since by sharing information or voicing attitudes groups can 'teach' their members appropriate behaviour. Thus, as a new member of an organisation, you may be troubled by a severe reprimand from your boss. A work group can reinforce your fears by comparing the man's behaviour to you with his behaviour to them and by assuring you that you are being victimised or treated unfairly. However, if the other members of your group tell you that he is 'always like that', and 'not to take any notice', then you can adjust your expectations and behaviour accordingly. Allied to this function is the fact that in comparing ourselves with other people we learn more about ourselves or, more precisely, our self-identity. I might have considered myself a generous person until I saw how much my friends donated to a leaving present. Similarly I might have considered myself to be very aware politically, but discussions with others in my group have shown me how ill-informed I really am. Thus we need other people to act as a focus of comparison so that we can learn more about ourselves.

Some people join groups because they anticipate that such groups might be useful to them for achieving their goals. Young people may join political clubs at college or university because they consider them useful for making contacts for later life. Some far-thinking people at school join a debating society because they believe it will look impressive on an application form for college or for a job. In these ways group membership may be instrumental in the achievement of a future goal.

To summarise, individuals join groups for various reasons, the most important of which are:

1. to improve their effectiveness in a task;

2. for security;

3. to facilitate learning through social comparison;

4. to exert greater influence over their environment;

5. because they believe that group membership will be useful to them in the achievement of some goal in the future.

Group Size

Now let us turn to the group itself, and initially to the impact of size on the structure, nature, and effectiveness of the group. If you arrive early at a party your host will probably be able to introduce you to all the other people there, who may be standing in one clump, discussing the same subject. As more and more people arrive, however, introductions are made on a small scale, newcomers being introduced to only a few people, and the original clump of people will split up into various different groupings, no longer discussing the same topic. This very commonplace example illustrates one fundamental aspect of group size that, after a certain size (often seven or eight people), the group begins to split up into subgroups, because it is very difficult to interact effectively with a large number of people. A psychologist, R.F. Bales (1950), found that as group size increases, so does the gap between the most involved and least involved member. For example, in a group of four even someone who is very shy and retiring will be involved in the conversation, and will make a contribution from time to time. In a gathering of twelve, however, there will be less 'air-time' available; in other words, there will be insufficient time for each individual to say all he would wish, so the more retiring members will probably remain silent, and the group will lose the benefit of their points of view.

In part the relationship between group size and task effectiveness is dependent on the nature of the task. If our group has the task of clearing a stretch of canal bank then, to a great extent, the more the merrier, or more people will mean a faster job. Similarly the experience of six travellers is likely to be more useful than the experience of two travellers in deciding on the most exciting place for a foreign holiday, as six people are likely to have more information amongst them than two people. However, if the task requires a high level of agreement among participants or a significant amount of precise coordination of members, then a large number of group members is likely to be a liability rather than an asset. One of the factors in operation in this situation is group structure. Like an organisation, a group will usually have a structure and its members will adopt specific roles. We will examine this latter aspect below, but as far as structure is concerned it appears to be the case that an increase in group size leads to a need for greater coordination and control of member activities. This may lead to a significant diminishing of group member satisfaction, and there is a clear inverse relationship between group size and individual satisfaction. Studies of work groups, for example, suggest that absenteeism and labour turnover increase as work group size increases, both of these being sensitive indicators of low satisfaction. Even accident rates appear to be related to group size. An effective management will attempt to ascertain the optimum size of a work group in their specific context to maximise member satisfaction, and thus minimise avoidable absenteeism and labour turnover.

Group Dynamics

The effectiveness of a group is influenced not only by its size, but also by its composition. If group membership is relatively homogeneous, or in other words if the group members are very similar in important characteristics, then the group is likely to be stable, needing little organisation and coordination, whereas a group whose membership differs widely will experience significant instability and will require a high level of coordination and organisation to function effectively. If we take a group of people involved in the game of squash as an example, we can see that if they have joined the group for different reasons, then a much wider variety of activities will need to be provided, and this will require more organisation than if the membership was homogeneous in its reasons.

Social activities might have to be provided for some, a competition for others with the competitive instinct, coaching for those who have joined the group to improve their game and so on, whereas life is much simpler if the members have joined the group to play competitive squash. Even if there is commonality of purpose, other characteristics may be important. Thus our group may be homogeneous in relation to purpose (competitive squash), but greater organisation will still be required if the membership possesses a variety of levels of competence for, in that case, to preserve member satisfaction and thus stability of membership, some form of 'ladder' or handicap system will have to be devised.

The perception of homogeneity also increases the morale and motivation of group members. We are more inclined to throw ourselves into the organisation of a Christmas party if we believe everyone wants one, and even wants the same kind of party, whereas it is most demotivating to be in a group which is split between a variety of goals or strategies. In most groups there is an underlying assumption that there are certain values or attitudes or ways of behaving which are central to membership of the group, and there are significant pressures to conform, which maybe exerted by group members on the deviant. These group 'norms' may be formally embodied in a written set of rules or may be implicitly understood, but they set the limits on permissible variation in behaviour. A golf-club may have an explicit rule which states that gentlemen may not appear in the bar after 7 p.m. unless they are wearing a tie; a work group may have an implicit understanding that if someone is feeling a bit under the weather, the rest of the group will help him reach the required level of output; and a group of children at school may have a norm of behaviour which frowns on 'telling tales'. Such norms are effective because most people have a need to belong and not to be different from other members of their group, and so are very susceptible to pressures to conform.

If a group is to survive it must ensure that a certain degree of cohesion exists, and so it requires that its members act and believe in the same way concerning issues vital to its existence. For example, a football supporters' club requires that its members claim that 'their' team is the best, particularly when talking to supporters of other teams, but it does not indicate where their political affiliations should lie. However, the end result of group influence is that an individual member's beliefs and actions will become more similar to those of others in the group, particularly in matters central to the group's existence. It is important to note here that the *extent* of its attempted influence varies from group to group, and that the *strength* of this influence varies with the importance of the item to the group's existence. Thus, for example, a football supporters' club will be less extensive in its attempted influence than a church organisation, and it will be more concerned about its members' team loyalty than their religious beliefs.

Each member, then, influences others and is influenced himself, and consequently the members become more and more like each other in attitudes and action. In many groups one of its members may feel pressure on him to change his attitudes and actions to be more like those of the others, and overall the group then becomes more uniform in belief and behaviour. However, there are two types of degree of conformity which this individual member might adopt in the face of group pressure — namely *compliance* and *private acceptance*.

When an individual conforms through compliance, he does so because he feels that it is important to be seen to hold group norms, either because he fears or dislikes group disapproval; or because he wants to be accepted by the group; or, again, because he feels that the group goal is important and that his conformity will help towards the attainment of this goal. However, the fact that he *complies,* i.e. agrees outwardly with the group, does not mean that he necessarily believes in their norms and values. It is only when an individual complies through private acceptance of the group's norms and values that he fully *internalises* them, and really believes as the group does.

Whilst it is obviously difficult to separate out in practice conformity through compliance and private acceptance, the distinction does have important implications for questions of attitude change and change in group membership. If an individual only complies with the norms of a group, it will be much easier for him to admit to change of attitude and more likely that he would change his group membership than if he privately accepted these norms.

So far we have noted that pressures towards conformity exist in all groups, but in fact they are not usually in evidence. Because of this most psychological studies of conformity involve unusual situations. Examples of this involve situations in which a 'new' group is formed by the experimenter. This new group may have no norms to begin with, or more often, a situation is manufactured whereby an individual is in conflict with this group. Alternatively, we may have a situation in which the norm is questioned and potentially breaks down. Studies of conformity, therefore, tend to be rather artificial, not just because they are laboratory studies, but also because they aim to bring to light processes which are normally hidden.

Bearing these points in mind, we will now turn to one of the best known studies of conformity, namely that carried out by J. Asch (1952).

A number of 'confederates', after being told what to do beforehand, participate with a naive subject who believes that he is part of a group taking part in an experiment on perception. The experimenter tells the group that they will make judgments of a series of lines. They are to compare one line with three others and choose the one of the same length. An example is given below.

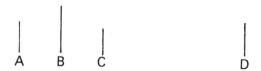

Which line out of A, B and C is the same length as D?

Figure 21 : Asch's experiments on group conformity

Which line out of A,B and C is the same length as D?

After a few tries the confederates, instead of choosing the line which obviously matches the comparison line choose one of a different length. The subject is then in a dilemma — should he identify what he knows to be the correct line or yield to social pressure and pick the line which the others have chosen?

Asch repeated this experiment a number of times, varying such things as the number of 'naive' subjects, the status of the confederates *vis à vis* the naive subject, and the similarity of length between the lines.

It is interesting to note that in the first experiment around 40% of the naive subjects conformed with the group, yet the existence of another naive subject reduced significantly the likelihood of conformity.

Notable examples of conformity in an industrial context may be found in studies of restriction of output, such as T. Lupton (1963) and D. Roy, and in reports on work done in the Hawthorne Plant (F.J. Roethlisberger & W.J. Dickson, 1939).

Reference Groups

So far in our discussions of groups we have talked about a goup to which an individual belongs, or a membership group. However we must also be aware of the existence of *reference groups,* that is to say groups of which an individual is not a member, but the norms and values of which significantly affect his behaviour. Such reference groups, or groups to which we refer, may have two purposes or functions — they may have a normative function, in that they provide a set of norms and values which we may adopt, or they may have an evaluative function, in that they provide a standard or benchmark against which we may compare our own behaviour. Some young children use older children as a reference group, and instead of adopting the norms and modes of behaviour of their peers, they imitate those of their reference group, the older children. This may have some impact on their future, as, for example, it has been suggested that school children who use prefects as their reference group are more likely to themselves become prefects than those children whose membership group and reference group are identical. Similarly, we may use a reference group as a standard against which we measure our own performance or values, the evaluative function. I might compare my standard of living, not with people in a similar job to me, but with other people with whom I am friendly. The important point about this evaluative function of reference groups is that the group against which I choose to compare myself may significantly affect my motivation and satisfaction. If I choose a group which has a lower standard of living than I have, I may well feel satisfied, and not particularly inclined to strive to improve my standard of living. If, on the other hand, the chosen group has a much higher standard of living than I have, I may feel highly dissatisfied, and motivated to strive harder to obtain this goal. The application of reference group theory to wage-bargaining becomes clear if one considers the importance of relativities as opposed to absolute levels of pay.

It was mentioned above that groups have not only a structure, but also roles which their members adopt. These roles may be concerned with task effectiveness, such as a coordinator; or with the maintenance of the group morale, such as a mediator or comic; and some roles are solely self-centred ones, where the individual uses the group solely as a means of achieving his own purposes without giving anything or helping the group in turn. Such roles may be those played by the person who uses the group to show off his own abilities, or the person who continually seeks help advice, or clarification from the group without contributing anything to its success.

It has been pointed out above that obviously people join groups to achieve a particular goal, and thus some aspects of these self-centred roles must be expected. Indeed J. Thibaut & H.H. Kelley (1959) formalised this in their statement that people begin and continue interacting as long as their rewards exceed those expected from individual action or alternative social relationships. On the other hand, for a group to be effective it is vital that roles pertaining to task effectiveness and group maintenance predominate. One of the most important and widely researched of such roles is that of the leader as shown in the following chapter.

Chapter 10

Leadership

One of the best known roles in a group, and possibly one of the most important of those roles, is that of a leader. Perhaps because of the importance of this role, and the implications of role performance for group success, numerous psychologists and management theorists have put forward advice and research evidence suggesting how an individual might perform as an effective leader. This chapter aims to provide an overview of some of the main themes running through the history of leadership studies, and as such it should not be considered a comprehensive coverage of the material available.

As has already been suggested, definitions of 'the leader' abound. We will define a leader as 'any member who influences the group'. The attractions of this definition are two-fold. Firstly it suggests that the leadership role may pass from person to person in the group, and is not always occupied by one incumbent. Secondly, it allows for the distinction, often only too visible in real life, between the person who is supposed to be in charge of a group — the official leader — and the person who, in reality, is the most influential — the unofficial leader. While these two roles, that of official leader and most influential member, may often be occupied by the same person, it can happen that two (or more) individuals are concerned and the definition of leader given above can cope with this discrepancy.

The first attempts to study leaders and leadership in a systematic manner concentrated on characteristics of the leader himself — the so-called trait theory of leadership. It is possible to trace this theory of leadership back to the ancient Greeks and Romans, for they believed that people are born leaders, in that they have the necessary characteristics for effective leadership from birth. If an individual does not demonstrate possession of these essential characteristics from an early age, it may be assumed that he is not a natural leader, and that there is no real point in trying to train him to become one.

What are these essential characteristics which a leader must possess? Numerous studies have been undertaken to provide a definitive list, among the more modern being that of Keith Davis (1972) who offered the following four traits which seemed to indicate successful organisational leadership:-

1. Intelligence — the leader has a slightly higher intelligence than the average of his followers.

2. Social maturity and breadth — the leader is emotionally stable and mature and tends to have broad interests.

3. Inner motivation and achievement drives — the leader strives for intrinsic rather than extrinsic rewards.

4. Human relations attitudes — the successful leader is employee, rather than production, centred.

R.M. Stogdill (1948) suggested that research findings pointed to intelligence, scholarship, dependability and social participation as being characteristics which leaders possessed to a greater extent than non-leaders. Here, however, we begin to see the problems which emerged from the adoption of the trait approach to leadership, for, with the exception of intelligence, there was little or no agreement between the theorists on what the essential characteristics of a leader might be.

C. Bird (1940) examined a large number of studies of leadership and drew up lists of the traits they described. He found only 5% of the traits were mentioned in more than four studies, which might suggest that the essential characteristics of one leader were not the same as the essential characteristics of another leader, which is highly dubious.

This lack of agreement among researchers was not the only problem associated with the trait approach, for it was also difficult to apply in an organisational context. Since we assume, according to this theory, that leaders have a certain set of characteristics which followers do not possess, at selection we must be careful to identify the person who possesses these characteristics, or who possesses them to the greatest extent. Unfortunately, however, our sophistication in the measurement of such traits is relatively low, and therefore the utility of the theory becomes somewhat questionable.

A different perspective on leadership was taken by K. Lewin, R. Lippitt, & R.K. White. Instead of looking at the characteristics of a leader in isolation from the group, they studied the impact of different styles of leadership on group members. They trained four people to be able to exhibit any of three leadership styles. These styles were as follows:-

1. Authoritarian — leader determines what will be done, by whom, at what time and in what way. Only one step at a time is described, so that there is uncertainty as to the future. He is personal in his allocation of praise and blame, and he remains aloof and apart from the group.

2. Democratic — tasks, techniques and time scales are all a matter for group discussion and group decision with guidance and encouragement from the leader. He acts as a regular group member and is very objective in praise or criticism — for example, 'that piece of work is beautifully decorated' rather than 'Mary, you have decorated that beautifully'.

LEADERSHIP

3. Laissez-faire — the leader participates to the least extent possible both in planning or work activity. He gives no feedback.

Each leader worked with each of four groups of young people, adopting a different style of leadership with each new group. Thus, each group experienced working with three different leadership styles. The behaviour of the group members under each of the different leadership styles was observed.

It was found that leadership style caused significant variations in member behaviour. For example, under authoritarian leadership aggression was expressed through using other group members as scapegoats, while democratically led groups were more friendly. Constructiveness of work decreased sharply when the authoritarian leader was absent, but hardly any decrease was observed under the other two leadership styles. Most (but not all) group members were most satisfied with the democratic style of leadership, and most individuals worked hardest and most effectively under this style. These findings were supported by D. Katz & R.L. Kahn (1966) who suggested that foremen of groups which had a high level of output behaved in more democratic ways than foremen of groups who produced a low level of output.

These findings which might lead us to propose that democratic leaders are the most effective leaders, have been questioned by a number of more recent researchers, who suggest that the effectiveness of a leadership style depends on the demands of the situation. In a highly structured situation such as an operating theatre, or in an emergency, such as an accident, a more authoritarian leader would not only be tolerated, but would probably be preferred, while in a loosely structured situation a more democratic style might be most useful.

Lewin, Lippitt & White *trained* their leaders in three different leadership styles they wished them to adopt, and the implication of Katz & Kahn's work is that supervisors should be trained to adopt a more democratic style of leadership. A number of other writers have developed theories of leadership which they have then embodied in training programmes which they have designed and marketed with a view to improving the quality of leadership in managers. John Adair (1979), for example, suggests that every group operates on three levels:-

The Group Task level: most groups have some task to complete, and may exist primarily to effect that task.

The Group Maintenance level: a group needs to have an awareness of itself as a group, and of the need to manage the constantly changing pattern of interaction and relationships.

The Individual Needs level: each individual joins a group to satisfy one or many needs.

A mature, effective group will operate to balance these three levels, and so, according to Adair, the function of the leader in a group is to ensure that these three levels are dealt with. This leadership task can be illustrated by three overlapping circles, as in Figure 22. If you look at Figure 22, you will see that the three circles overlap. This suggests that the three needs are not, in fact, independent, but are interrelated, so if the leader acts in such a way as to strengthen the team, it will probably make each individual more confident, and facilitate the effective completion of the task. Conversely, however, if the leader ignores one of the three components of the leadership task, for example the individual needs one, he will be inadequately meeting the other two needs. This can be demonstrated by covering over the whole of the individual needs circle. You will see that there is a segment missing from both the task need and group needs circle, suggesting that these are not being completely met either.

Task Needs — Clarification of Task
Demonstration of how it fits into the objectives of firm
Definition and provision of resources needed
Ensuring that structure allows task to be achieved effectively
Control of progress towards goal by monitoring the operation
Evaluating results and comparing them to plan

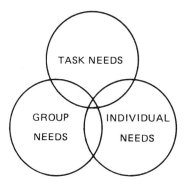

Individual Needs — Need to contribute
— Challenge and
responsibility

Group Needs — Sets and maintains group
objectives
— Recognition

— Involves whole group in
achievement of objectives
— Authority to carry out
delegated tasks

— Maintains unity and minimises
disruptive activity
— Opportunity to develop
in experience and ability

Figure 22 : Adair's Model of Leadership

108

Adair is not suggesting that the three components have to be constant-ly in balance since cyclical work like the Christmas rush in the retail trade, or end of year accounts, will probably push task needs to the front for a period of time. However, he would suggest that these needs must be balanced over time, so that the end of a busy period should signal the time to 'recharge' the individual and group 'batteries' by paying specific attention to these areas.

Action centred leadership is the name frequently given to Adair's view of leadership, and training schemes associated with his ideas are designed to develop skills in each of the three areas of need satisfaction, namely Task, Group and Individual.

Another theory which is associated with a range of training packages is R. Blake & J Mouton's (1964) managerial grid. This can be used as the basis of an Organisation Development programme (see Chapter 21) but it is also used in management development. The grid, which is illustrated in Figure 23, is a 9x9 matrix which plots scores of concern for people and concern for production, as measured by responses to a questionnaire.

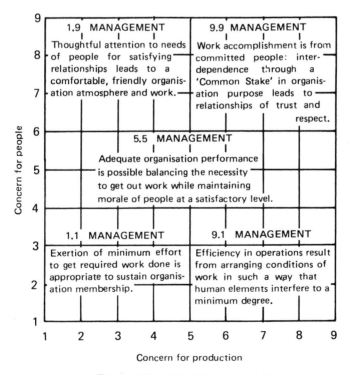

Figure 23 : The Managerial Grid

Descriptions of five different managerial styles are given on the diagram to illustrate the implications of different 'scores'. Thus an individual manager, or group of trainees will each be given a questionnaire to complete; their answers will provide two scores, one of concern for people one of concern for production and the combination of these will 'locate' the individual on the grid. A training programme may then be required to shift the individual to a preferable location on the grid.

Blake and Mouton's two dimensions were added to by W.J. Reddin (1970), who postulated a third dimension of effectiveness, in addition to concern for people or relationships orientation and concern for production or task orientation. He believed that managerial effectiveness is the result of adopting the appropriate style for the current situation, and it is measured by the extent to which the manager achieves the results required of his position. This three-dimensional grid, or 3D theory of leadership is illustrated in Figure 24.

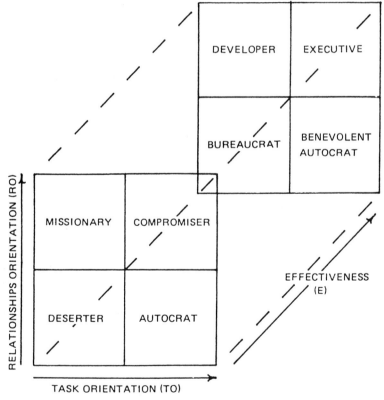

Figure 24 : Reddin's Theory of Leadership

The 3D Grid is thus an eight-style typology of management behaviour. These eight styles result from the eight possible combinations of Task Orientation, Relationships Orientation and Effectiveness. Four styles are less effective and four are more effective:-

Less Effective Styles	*More Effective Styles*
Deserter	Bureaucrat
Missionary	Developer
Autocrat	Benevolent Autocrat
Compromiser	Executive

The eight styles may be briefly described as follows:-

DESERTER

One who often displays his lack of interest in both task and relationships. He is ineffective, not only because of his lack of interest, but also because of his effect on morale. He may not only desert, but may also hinder the performance of others through intervention or by withholding information.

MISSIONARY

One who puts harmony and relationships above other considerations. He is ineffective because his desire to see himself and be seen as a 'good person' prevents him from risking a disruption of relationships in order to get production.

AUTOCRAT

One who puts the immediate task before all other considerations. He is ineffective in that he makes it obvious that he has no concern for relationships and has little confidence in others. Whilst many may fear him, they also dislike him and are thus motivated to work only when he applies direct pressure.

COMPROMISER

One who recognises the advantages of being oriented to both task and relationships but who is incapable or unwilling to make sound decisions.

Ambivalence and compromise are his stock-in-trade. The strongest influence on his decision making is the most recent or heaviest pressure. He tries to minimise immediate problems rather than maximise long term production. He attempts to keep those people who can influence his career as happy as possible.

BUREAUCRAT

One who is not really interested in either task or relationships but who, by simply following the rules, does not make this too obvious and thus does not let it affect morale. He is effective in that he follows the rules and maintains a mask of interest.

DEVELOPER

One who places implicit trust in people. He sees his job as primarily concerned with developing the talents of others and of providing a work atmosphere conducive to maximising individual satisfaction and motivation. He is effective in that the work environment he creates is conducive to his subordinates developing commitment to both himself and the job. While successful in obtaining high production, his high relationships orientation would on occasions lead him to put the personal development of others before short or long run production, even though his personal development may be unrelated to the job and the development of successors to his position.

BENEVOLENT AUTOCRAT

One who places implicit trust in himself and is concerned with both the immediate and long run task. He is effective in that he has a skill in inducing others to do what he wants them to do without creating resentment so that production might drop. He creates, with some skill, an environment which minimises aggression toward him and which maximises obedience to his commands.

EXECUTIVE

One who sees his job as effectively maximising the effort of others in relationship to the short and long run task. He sets high standards for production and performance and recognises because of individual differences and expectations that he will have to treat everyone differently. He is effective in that his commitment to both task and relationship is evident to all. This acts as a powerful motivator. His effectiveness in obtaining results with both of these dimensions also leads naturally to optimum production.

This idea of range of management styles was also put forward by R. Tannenbaum & W.H. Schmidt in 1958. They described a continuum of managerial styles ranging from more conservative styles at the left hand side to more liberal styles at the right hand side. This is represented diagrammatically in Figure 25.

In 1973, however, Tannenbaum & Schmidt modified their view to incorporate the influence of the prevailing organisation climate. In other words they adopted a contingency approach to leadership. This modified version of their theory indicates that the leadership style that emerges is influenced by the relationship between the manager and non-managerial employees, and that this relationship is in turn influenced by the climate of the organisation (which is in turn probably influenced by the values of the larger society in which the organisation is located). Thus the attitudes and values of society influence those of the organisation, resulting in a certain 'climate', whilst this climate then influences the relationship between manager and non-managers. Having indicated that the choice of leadership style is dependent on the manager, the non-managers and the situation, Tannenbaum & Schmidt suggest guidelines for this choice. For example, the greater the leader's confidence in the non-managers' competence, the more likely he is to adopt a more liberal style; the more the non-managers identify with the objectives of the organisation, the more likely is the adoption of a more liberal style; the greater the time pressure to make decisions, the more probable is the adoption of a more conservative style. Complexity of problems, work group size and cohesiveness and geographical dispersion are also situational variables which Tannenbaum & Schmidt suggest as being significant influences on the choice of managerial style.

This consideration of choice of style and of situational variables brings us to the last theory of leadership to be outlined, namely the contingency theory of leadership put forward by F. Fiedler (1967). His examination of previous research concerning leadership style led him to the view that the effectiveness of a particular style of leadership, for example authoritarian or democratic, is contingent upon the situation. He then picked out characteristics of 'the situation' which he considered to be most important, and these were the relationship between the leader and group members, the source of power of the leader, and the degree of structure of the task. Fiedler then developed this broad view into a specific hypothesis, namely that more autocratic leadership styles are more effective in situations (as defined above) which are either very

INDIVIDUAL AND GROUP BEHAVIOUR

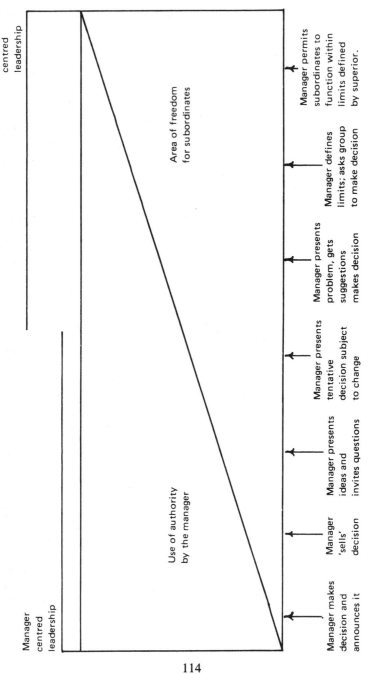

FIGURE 25 : CONTINUUM OF LEADERSHIP BEHAVIOUR (TANNENBAUM & SCHMIDT)

favourable or very unfavourable to the leader. Conversely, a more democratic leadership style is more effective in situations which are moderately or intermediately favourable.

Let us now examine the variables which Fiedler considered to be so influential in the situation. Fiedler measured the relationship between the leader and group members by means of a questionnaire which the leader completed concerning how he got on with the group members. The power of the leader was similarly assessed by means of a questionnaire, but this time it concerned the extent of the leader's power to hire and fire, use 'punishments' or sanctions against group members and so on.

The task structure was determined by the extent to which an empirically verifiable 'right answer' was obtainable, by how many routes this solution could be achieved, and the extent to which goals were clearly definable. Thus, performing a surgical operation in a hospital is a fairly highly structured task whilst designing a collection of *haute couture* fashions is relatively unstructured.

Fiedler tested his theory in a wide range of contexts, and most of these and other similar studies tend to confirm this contingency model of leadership. One of the reasons for any variation in results that does exist might lie in the lack of precision of the measuring instruments. The instruments for measuring situational variables have been outlined above, but perhaps more debate has occurred over the measurement of leadership style itself. For this Fiedler used what he called the LPC score or least preferred co-worker score. This is determined by asking the leader to describe the person with whom he has least enjoyed working. A description of such a person in relatively favourable terms gains a high LPC score and Fiedler claims this tends to be found among leaders who are relatively democratic. A low LPC score is obtained by leaders who use relatively harsh, unfavourable descriptions, and Fiedler similarly claims a high correlation between low LPC scores and more autocratic, directive leadership styles. It is argued that these scores do not highlight leadership styles other than the two mentioned, or combinations of styles, and thus that it may be considered to be a relatively 'blunt' instrument.

In conclusion, it appears to be accepted by most current writers on leadership that no one leadership style can be applicable to all situations, and also that today's leader must be trained both to be flexible in his style and approach and also to be able to analyse a situation so as to make an effective choice of style. Thus in addition to the training programmes in leadership mentioned above, Fiedler has also produced a programmed text which is designed to teach managers how to assess their leadership style and the situation with a view to optimising the match between the two.

Section 3

Assessing and Monitoring Employees

CHAPTER 11 : ACQUIRING NEW EMPLOYEES

CHAPTER 12 : PSYCHOLOGICAL TESTING

CHAPTER 13 : THE INTERVIEW

CHAPTER 14 : HUMAN RESOURCE PLANNING AND CONTROL
TECHNIQUES

After looking at the sources of the individual differences in personality, attitudes, and motivation we now turn to the question of how the organisation assesses and monitors such differences in characteristics and performance among its actual and potential employees. Chapter 11 examines methods of recruitment and selection, including person specification, methods of attracting employees, and assessment of candidates. A more detailed study of psychological testing follows in Chapter 12 with an emphasis on its reliability and validity. The selection interview is covered in Chapter 11, but other types of interview, which are important vehicles for monitoring and assessing personnel, are described in Chapter 13. Chapter 14 deals with some techniques used in organisations to monitor performance, such as performance appraisal and Management by Objectives, and to monitor certain trends, by means of personnel records and data relating to labour turnover. The various techniques for human resource planning are then outlined, including extrapolation and work study based methods.

Chapter 11

Acquiring New Employees

This is an activity in which many organisations invest a great deal of time and money. People are recruited either to replace employees, who for some reason have ceased to work for the organisation, or as additional new employees. Whatever the reason for the need to recruit extra staff, it should have been anticipated as a result of human resource planning. The marketing and production plans will determine the type of job to be filled and its starting date, and will equally have been specified in the human resource plan. When the need to recruit results from an employee leaving, the exact time that a replacement will be required is often difficult to anticipate, for other than a short period ahead of the event. The only common exception to this is where the employee being replaced has retired. Most other forms of termination are less easily predicted. We will consider the question of labour wastage in more detail in Chapter 14.

Even though the recruitment needs will have been anticipated in the human resource plan, the wise manager will check that recruitment is in fact the best course of action. Before it is considered the following questions should be asked. Why does the job exist, what is its purpose? Is the job necessary now and, if so, will it be necessary in the foreseeable future? Could the job be amalgamated with other jobs? Are there any existing employees who would be suitable for the job? There are a number of circumstances in which an existing employee may move into the job. The move may be a promotion for another employee; it may be a transfer, on a job rotation basis, providing an existing employee with broader experience. The job may be suitable as a training position for an employee who is moving up through the organisation. Is there any other employee who may be suitable, whose current job has or will cease to exist in the near future, and could such an employee by redeployed? Could the vacancy be used as a run down job for someone approaching retirement? It is appropriate that these questions are asked since the vacancy provides the organisation with a little room for manoeuvre, which it would be foolish not to take advantage of.

Assessing the Job and drawing up a Person Specification

If the managers of the organisation have considered all the possibilities noted above, and the decision is to recruit a new employee to fill the job, then this should be approached in a systematic way.

ASSESSING AND MONITORING EMPLOYEES

If you are running a business yourself, let us suppose it is a restaurant and you need to recruit a new chef, the most important first step is that you should know what you want. This sounds obvious, and indeed is obvious, however that does not mean that actually specifying in detail what you mean is easily done. You want someone who can do the job, but how do you know who could or could not do the job? Firstly you must determine what the job is. In order to do this you will look at the job description and job specification. (We will assume that you are a very progressive restaurant owner who has these documents readily available. In the case of the job specification it will, on this occasion, be expressed in terms of the *knowledge, skills* and *attitudes* required to perform the tasks, duties and responsibilities noted in the job description.) You will check that these documents accurately describe the job and specify what is needed to do the job. Can you learn anything about it when you consider the record of the last job holder? Is there any absence pattern? Why is he leaving? You may learn a great deal by looking into this. For instance, your menu may offer a full range of French cuisine, and this fact may be reflected in the job description and specification for the chef. Indeed your previous chef may have been experienced in such cooking, and this may be the reason for his leaving. Whilst your menu offers continental cuisine, perhaps your customers are nearly all ordering steak and chips. The result is that the chef's work does not actually match what is written in the job description, and, indeed, the knowledge and skill which are probably called for in the job specification are rarely, if ever, used by the job holder. It may be that this is the very reason that your chef is leaving, i.e. he does not find the work exciting, challenging, and creative. You must update your job description and specification (and possibly your menu) to take account of this information.

We can say, therefore, that before an organisation does anything about recruitment, the job description and specification must be checked to ensure they are up-to-date and accurate. A job description merely tells us what is involved in a job whilst, broadly speaking, a job specification details what is needed in order for the job to be performed. Neither a job description nor a job specification describe the kind of person who can do the job and clearly we want to recruit a person who can do so. It is reasonable that we should be able to describe and specify the kind of person wanted. We know we are not going to be describing some actual person (this would probably be impossible, bearing in mind individual differences amongst people), but we should be describing the features we would look for in a person whom we believe could do the job. We normally refer to the document that we draw up for this purpose as the *person specification*.

ACQUIRING NEW EMPLOYEES

Drawing up a person specification

When we are drawing up a person specification we are defining the attributes a person would require, not only to be effective in the job but to be satisfied in doing the work. If we think back to the chef in the previous example, he may well have been effective in the job in so far as he produced good steak and chips, but he was not satisfied in doing the work. His satisfaction was just as important since his lack of it led to his resignation. When drawing up a person specification we are concerned with identifying the attributes of a person who would not only have the abilities required to do the job but would also be motivated to do it. Underpinning this is the belief that performance is a consequence of a combination of ability and motivation and that if either is absent then performance will be adversely affected.

The list of attributes we draw up for our person specification should all be relevant and assessable. By relevant we mean that the attribute should be either *essential* or *desirable*. We should keep to a minimum those attributes that we specify as essential, since we are saying that they must be satisfied. There may also be attributes which constitute contra-indications, these are attributes which rule out any person who possesses them. An example would be if we were drawing up a person specification for an electrician, then colour blindness would be a contra-indication. In this case no matter how well suited an individual might be for the job, if he was colour blind he would be automatically ruled out. By relevant we mean a list of attributes that we would like to, or feel we must, see in a candidate, if he is to be effective and satisfied.

However, there is no point in producing a list of attributes which are essential, desirable, or contra-indications unless we can assess them or measure them. We must therefore concentrate on attributes, the presence, absence, or degree of development of which we can identify or assess, using the tools and devices we will have available to use in the selection process. What we mean by the tools and devices of selection is how we will carry out the selection, the techniques we will use. We would need to know whether, in addition to application forms, we would interview all applicants, give them tests, medical examinations, and take up references. So, for every attribute that we list, we should be able to say how we would assess whether any given applicant possesses the attribute or, if we are looking for some degree of development of an attribute, how we would measure the extent of its presence in an applicant. To take an example, if the attribute we are looking for is *height,* let us say the applicant must be at least 5 feet 8 inches tall, then we know the devices we will use to determine the degree of development of this attribute (i.e. whether any applicant is in fact at least 5 feet 8 inches tall). The device will be the application form, where we will require the applicant to state his height and, if necessary, a medical examination where we will measure his height. This particular factor, which may be essential or desirable, is clearly assessable and we know exactly how we will assess it. Unfortunately not all attributes are either so clearly defined or so easily assessed.

The seven point plan person specification

A number of different schemes have been drawn up for compiling person specifications. The one we will use is based upon what is known as the *seven point plan,* developed by Professor A Rodger. The method we will describe is not presented in exactly its original form, but in the slightly modified form.

The scheme considers what is required of a person who:

a) Could do the job — i.e. what physical make-up, attainments and skills would be possessed by any person who could do the job;

b) Would want to do the job, i.e. what work interests and work attitudes should any person have who would want to do the job;

c) Would be prevented from doing the job satisfactorily — i.e. the kind of personality or personal background factors which would make it difficult for any person possessing them to fit into the job or the environment of the job.

The headings used for each factor in the seven point plan are:

1. Physical Make-up
2. Attainments   'Could do the job' factors
3. Skills

4. Work Interests   'Would want to do the job'
5. Work Attitudes   factors

6. Personality   'Could be prevented from doing the
7. Personal Background   job' factors

We will now consider each of these factors in turn, define what we mean by them, and what we would be looking for when we apply them. Before we do so, however, we should remind ourselves that what we are trying to do is to specify the type of person we feel would be capable of doing the job and also would be satisfied in doing it. We have no particular individual in mind. We are describing our acceptable and, if possible, ideal candidate. When we are drawing up a person specification we must ensure that we do not break the law. The main points of the most relevant legislation are noted in the last part of this chapter.

Physical Make-up

When deciding what we will include under the heading of physical make-up requirements, we should ask ourselves, firstly, if there are any underlying physical qualities important to the performance of the job, and secondly, whether the first impression that the person makes is important in determining how effective he will be in the job.

We should confine our physical requirements to those which we can specifically justify. So if the job calls for specific height, say like that of a policeman, then this is fine. We should avoid general expressions concerning physical fitness and strength, unless we can be specific. Some jobs may call for excellent sensory abilities, eyesight or hearing, but many do not. In fact there are many jobs which can be perfectly well performed by the physically handicapped person. If the job for which we are drawing up a person specification does call for specific physical attributes, then the devices we will use to determine whether an applicant possesses them will be the application form and/or the medical examination.

The second aspect of physical make-up, the first impression that a person makes, is clearly a very subjective matter. People who make a good first impression on us may not make such an impression on other people. We must decide what features or characteristics will cause someone to give a good or bad first impression in the context of the job we are considering. It may be any or all of the following: speech, manner, bearing, dress. We must remember that these attributes often only apply to first impressions, but in some jobs, for instance a sales person, this is probably very important. The only way we will be able to decide whether applicants match up to the requirements of the person specification will be to meet them and note what first impressions they make on us. This will normally be achieved in an interview.

Attainments

Much of what we are looking for under the heading of attainments, when we are drawing up a person specification, will be directly available from the job specification. Certainly most job specifications will include information on the knowledge and experience required for the job to be adequately performed. For the purposes of drawing up a person specification we would normally classify attainments under the following sub-headings:

a) Academic — to include GCSE, 'A' levels and degrees;

b) Vocational — trade and professional qualifications, apprenticeships;

c)   Functional Experience — experience in a specific function, e.g. work study, sales;

d)   Products and Services — what expert knowledge might we expect any successful candidate to have of particular machinery and equipment for instance;

e)   Geographical — would we expect knowledge and/or experience of working in various parts of the country or overseas.

With respect to (a) and (b) appropriate questions on the application form will probably be sufficient. If it is felt necessary, a sight of copies of certificates and qualifications may be requested. With respect to (c), (d) and (e) basic information may be obtainable from the application form, but some assessment of the quality of depth of experience will need to be obtained at the interview. But how are we to express the quality or depth of experience that we require and how are we to assess it at an interview? Both are difficult, but the very process of attempting, when drawing up the person specification, to express what standards will be required, may clarify our thinking.

Skills

When we are specifying skills we must first set some basic standards. We will generally set standards by reference to the group of people who meet our attainments criteria. So, for instance, if our attainments criteria included a craft apprenticeship in engineering, then the skills we would expect from a person who has successfully completed such an apprenticeship would form the basis for comparison. If we need no extra skills than those normally found in a person so qualified, we could assume that anyone achieving this level of attainment would also automatically have obtained the required level of skill. When specifying skill requirements we will therefore only note those which we would consider as exeptional, over and above what might normally be expected from the reference group. The main skills areas we would look at would be as noted below, remembering that we would not necessarily expect to specify skill requirements in all areas for any one job:

a)   Administrative skills — this includes the skills required of anyone doing the job in collecting information; dealing with and recording ideas, facts, and figures, with care and attention for the purpose of implementing policies;

b)   The skills of flexibility — the skills required in dealing with problems and unexpected situations;

c)   Fluency — the requirement of the job for the job holder to be able to communicate quickly, clearly, and precisely when speaking;

d)   Practical skills — Does the job call for a person who is good at constructing or repairing things, working with materials, machinery and equipment?

e)   Social skills — Does the job call for a person who has highly developed social skills — for instance the ability to get on with other people, to motivate them or to persuade them?

f)   Verbal skills — Does the job call for someone who has exceptional abilities of grasping and expressing ideas through the written word?

We should note here the difference between fluency and the physical make-up requirement of clear voice. Whilst perhaps in most circumstances fluency will be impaired by the absence of a clear speaking voice, the converse is not necessarily true. Take the example of a telephonist where a clear speaking voice is an essential attribute, the need for fluency may only be a desirable attribute.

Setting standards for the skills requirements of the job specification will not be easy. We will probably think we know what we want, but how we will specify it, in advance of seeing or experiencing any applicant, is difficult. Wherever we can we should state on the person specification definite standards that we are seeking and how we would expect to be able to determine whether anyone had reached those standards. For some skills we may decide that we can test them. We may, for example, use a verbal reasoning test and set a minimum acceptable score. Other skills we may feel we can assess during an interview; these may include social and fluency skills. Still others we may feel we can assess by examining achievements in school, college work, or leisure activities. Whichever methods we decide to use, we must specify the standards and the basis on which we will evaluate against those standards when we are drawing up the person specification.

Work interests

Here we are not only looking for attributes in a prospective employee that would satisfy our needs for the effective performance of the job, we are also trying to state what aspects of the job may provide satisfaction for a prospective employee. We recognise that each person has a pattern of interests and that it is important to ensure that their major interests, both likes and dislikes, are compatible with the work. In this sense we are not only specifying what we think would make a person suited to the job but also what would suit the job to a person. We will therefore note in our person specification those attributes which we consider a person should possess to suit them to the job, those which help them to be effective in the job, and also those aspects of the job which may make it appealing to an individual. We will consider these interests under the following headings:

a) Active/outdoor interests — Does the job call for someone who enjoys being physically active and spending a lot of time outside?

b) Artistic interests — Does the job require someone who enjoys creating or dealing with beautiful things?

c) Ideas, words and figures — Does the job provide scope for and/or require someone capable of carrying out research; theorising; problem solving and communicating facts, figures, and concepts?

d) People interests — Does any successful job holder have to be interested in people and deal with people? Do they have to have a sympathetic and understanding nature?

e) Interests in things — Will the successful candidate enjoy working with machinery and equipment?

Setting realistic standards in the person specification for this factor is particularly difficult. How do you for instance set a standard for the interest any applicant might have in people? It is more likely that you will specify in general terms that the person should, through things they have done in the past or do in the present, show some voluntary interest and enjoyment in dealing with people, both in work and leisure time. Clearly any individual himself is best able to know what his interests are, so it is essential that he is adequately informed about the scope of the job.

Work attitudes

In *work interests* we are concerned with what in the job could bring satisfaction. Here we are concerned with the satisfactions of the work situation or organisation as a whole, and, conversely, the dissatisfactions inherent in the job, and or, organisation, that must be accepted by any person if they are to be reasonably happy doing the job. Many, if not all, of these factors should emerge from the job description.

a) The working situation — this includes the physical working conditions of the job, the social contacts within the job and those which are required outside and the type of person who will be the job holder's boss, his personality and management style.

b)   The organisation itself — whether the organisation structure is very *mechanistic* or *organic,* what is the general ethos of the organisation?

c)   What might be called external factors — what does the job offer in terms of rewards, both financial and non financial? (See Chapter 17.) How easy is it to travel to and from the organisation? What are the hours of work, shift arrangements etc. What social and leisure facilities does the organisation offer?

All of these are significant factors which would help to determine whether any individual would want to do the job.

Personality

In the sixth factor of *personality,* when we are drawing up a person specification we should be looking for those identifiable aspects of personality which will prevent a person being successful in the job. What we are saying is that it will be difficult, if not impossible, to specify what type of personality would make for a successful job holder, but that we must try to identify the type of personality which would definitely be unsuited to the job. We must take care, not only how we define personality, but also how we identify unsuitable personalities. We are not going to talk here about specific theories of personality, but to define some general characteristics in layman's terms and attempt to show how they may be identified in prospective candidates.

a)   Acceptability — Is it important that the person who does the job is able to quickly fit in with a variety of other employees, clients, and customers?

Warning signs with respect to an applicant's acceptability may include: if the person seems to be highly selective in his choice of friends, or the people with whom he happily associates, or if the person complains about personality clashes or difficulties with people in previous jobs.

b)   Flexibility — Is it important for the person to be able to cope with new and changing problems and demands?

Warning signs may be if an applicant has experienced difficulties when faced with unexpected problems in the past, or perhaps, seems ultra conservative.

c)   Emotional stability — This will be important if the job involves unpredictable elements that can create stress and tension.

Warning signs may be lack of persistence when faced with difficult and trying situations; putting the blame on other people, or bad luck.

d) Self reliance — This will be of significance where the job calls for someone who can act independently, identifying and exploiting new opportunities.

If this is a requirement of the job, warning signs in applicants may be that they always take a passive rather than an active role in activities in which they are involved. Another sign may be an absence of well-defined ideas about their intentions for themselves for the future.

A note of warning must be sounded with respect to these personality factors within the person specification. It is dangerous to draw conclusions about anyone's personality on the basis of scant information. However, the fact remains that the decision of whether to appoint a person will almost certainly have to be made using imperfect information. This makes it doubly important that we should identify in advance those personality characteristics which constitute contra-indications for the job. We must be certain that we can justify, at least to ourselves why we are including them and how we intend to identify or assess them in candidates.

Personal background

This factor, which is sometimes known as 'circumstances', is concerned with all the influences that act on a person which may tend to prevent them from being able to cope adequately with the job. In many jobs the importance of some of these factors will be very limited. In others notably some demanding management jobs, they may take on much greater significance. Personal circumstances will include domestic situation, whether the person is married with family commitments, dependent relatives etc. These relationships could affect an individual's willingness to work overtime or away from home, which may be important in the job. Local ties may result in the person being reluctantly geographically mobile. When considering this factor we must be certain that we are staying within the spirit of the anti-discrimination legislation. We must beware of stereotyping by for example making assumptions about the domestic circumstances of married women.

We must remember when we are drawing up a person specification that we are trying to specify the type of person who would be both capable of doing the job and satisfied in doing it. There is a large element of mutual interest in obtaining the right person. To use the well worn analogy of fitting pegs into holes, if we consider that the hole is the job and the peg is the person, then the job description and specification relate to the hole, which may or may not be adaptable, but can probably only have its shape modified a little. The person specification relates to the definition of the requirements of the peg which will fit into the hole. However, people are fairly adaptable within limits, so we should beware of over-specifying the peg. We must remember all the time that our objective is to fit the right-shaped pegs into the right shaped holes.

In Chapter 4 we presented a job description and specification for a personnel officer. In Figure 26 we present a person specification for the same job:

Figure 26

PERSON SPECIFICATION FOR JOB OF PERSONNEL OFFICER

Factor		Essential	Desirable
1.	*Physical Make-up*	Clear speaking voice for interviewing	Good first impression since dealing with the public. Smart but not over-dressy
2.	*Attainments*		
a)	Academic	Nil	Degree in Social Sciences Business Studies
b)	Vocational	Sound knowledge of employment legislation	Membership at least to graduate level of the IPM
c)	Functional Experience	Interviewing experience	Experience of personnel work preferably in manufacturing company
d)	Products & Services	Nil	Nil
e)	Geographical	Nil	Nil
3.	*Skills*		
a)	Administrative	Nil	Nil
b)	Flexibility	Dealing with Trades Union representatives, members of the public	
c)	Fluency		Required for interviewing in many circumstances
d)	Practical	Nil	
e)	Social	Supervising staff, dealing with personnel in difficult circumstances	
f)	Verbal		Interpreting personnel policies and practices
4.	*Work Interests*		
a)	Active Outdoor	Nil scope	
b)	Artistic	Nil scope	

127

c)	Ideas Words Figures	Some scope in relating performance to human resource plan
d)	People Interest	Great deal of scope dealing with people under variety of circumstances
e)	Interest in things	Nil scope

5. *Work Attitudes*

a)	Work Situation	Small office, noisy, people passing through
b)	The Organisation	Tendency to be a little bureaucratic, personnel department is exceptional in organic type structure
c)	External Factors	Salary — £x000 per annum Sick Pay — See Company policy document Status — 1 level below management status monthly paid Holidays — see Company policy document Prospects — After 2 to 3 years, if successful, can expect to be appointed to Assistant Personnel Manager on large site Hours of work — 37½ hours per week Leisure Facilities — Sports & Social Club

6. *Personality*

a)	Acceptability	Must be acceptable at all levels of the organisation	
b)	Flexibility	Must be able to see the other person's point of view	
c)	Emotional Stability	Must be able to accept criticism which sometimes seems unreasonable	Can assist others in stressful situations, e.g. counselling
d)	Self Reliance		Pro-active personality

7. *Personal Background* — Prepared to come into work on night shift at short notice on occasions

Attracting the Candidate

Having drawn up a person specification, we now need to attract suitable applicants. There are a number of methods available to us. Our decision on what methods to employ will be on the basis of how cost effective each of them is. We would be wise to consider the cheapest methods first. When deciding whether a method is cheap or not we must not ignore the aspect of how long it is likely to take before it can be expected to yield results. The importance of this will be determined largely by the amount of time we have available. If there is no particular urgency in attracting applicants, we will be more inclined to use methods that are cheap but involve quite long lead times. If a speedy appointment is essential, we may be forced to immediately use more expensive methods of attracting candidates. This is not to say that more expensive methods are necessarily quicker, indeed they will often take longer. Here then we have another instance where a carefully drawn up human resource plan can save the organisation money, since the more notice we have of the need to recruit an employee, the greater scope we have in the selection of methods for attracting applicants.

When deciding how long we have available to us to attract applicants, we should work backwards from the time that we require the appointed applicant to be in the job and working effectively. Let us take an example to show what we mean by this, suppose our existing Personnel Officer is due to be promoted to another site of the Company as an Assistant Personnel Manager and that this is scheduled to take place on the 1st July. We need to have the new Personnel Officer ready and able to fully take over the duties of the job on that day. Working backwards then from this date we must:

i)   Allow, say, one month for the new employee to pick up the job and familiarise himself with the tasks that will be currently in hand in June. This will be done by the existing Personnel Officer, working in tandem with the new appointee for one month.

ii)   We must allow, say, two weeks formal induction programme for the new appointee. This will be used for familiarising the new person in the products, manufacturing methods, and structure of the organisation. He will need to be introduced to the personnel with whom he will be dealing when he takes over the job.

iii) We must allow time for the new appointee to give notice to his existing employer. Assume one month.

iv)   We must allow time to assess the various candidates who apply for the job and to select the best one. Bearing in mind the difficulties in arranging mutually convenient times for interviews and other assessment techniques, we should allow six weeks for this process. This may seem an excessively long time, but we should allow for the possibility of there being a large number of applicants and the fact that those people within the organisation who will be involved in the assessment procedures will have other commitments on their time which may cause delays. It means that in this example we must allow approximately 4 months selection and placement lead time. If it is now the 2nd January, that means we have two months available to us for the purposes of attracting candidates. However, as we shall see, the actual process of attracting candidates has within itself certain built-in delays. For example it may take us a week to get an advertisement placed in a newspaper if we choose this method of attracting applicants.

Methods of attracting applicants

When we are deciding on methods of attracting candidates we must remember that our objective is to get a sufficiently large number of suitable applicants whilst minimising the number of unsuitable applicants, and to achieve this at the minimum reasonable cost. If we get a reasonable number of suitable applicants we give ourselves a wide choice, and if we minimise the number of unsuitable applicants we waste as little of our time as possible in unproductive work. The way we go about attracting candidates can significantly affect our performance against these objectives, this will become apparent as we look at the various methods.

Nowadays many organisations make the claim that they are equal opportunity employers. The pursuit of this objective may have an influence on the way thay go about attracting candidates. This will be particularly the case if the organisation wishes to attract candidates from groups which it feels are currently under-represented within its workforce. Employers pursuing a policy of equal opportunities may therefore be reluctant to use either of the first two methods mentioned below, because they may tend to re-inforce what is perceived as being an already unsatisfactory situation. Moreover in an attempt to redress a perceived imbalance within the workforce an employer may for example choose to advertise vacancies in publications aimed at specific groups in the hope that this will lead to applications from individuals who are members of the groups which it is felt are under-represented in the workforce.

Contacting ex-employees

This can be the cheapest method of recruiting, particularly if the organisation has a few specific vacancies, and ex-employees who did those specific jobs in the past are contacted. For example, if a company only employs three telephonists and a vacancy occurs, then contacting previously employed telephonists whose ability and competence in the job is proven would seem to be a sound approach. The situation is less easy if the organisation has fifty vacancies for assembly operators, and the decision is made to write to employees who have left in the last couple of years and notify them of the vacancies, encouraging them to re-apply. There are two aspects which differ from the case of the telephonist. Firstly, because of the numbers involved, the cost of contact will be increased significantly. Secondly, there is a need to check on the suitability of all those who may be contacted. The organisation would not want to encourage an ex-employee, whose performance they had previously been dissatisfied with, to re-apply. The records of all ex-employees to be considered for contact, must be checked before contact is made. This can be a lengthy, and therefore costly, business. The cost of this method should be compared with other methods of contacting and informing prospective applicants of the vacancies. It must not be overlooked that ex-employees differ from the public at large in at least one significant way. Ex-employees know something of the organisation and, therefore, are much better able to judge whether they will like and want to do the job. This means there is an element of self selection by ex-employees, which cannot occur from members of the public at large. If we think back to the seven-point plan for drawing up person specifications, we can see that ex-employees would have knowledge of points four and five, *work interest* and *work attitude,* which we called the 'would want to do the job' factors. In this respect, applicants who respond as a result of being contacted as ex-employees may have a head start over other applicants.

Word-of-mouth using existing employees

This method of attracting and contacting applicants can be very successful. Take, for instance, the example of an organisation which has a specialist high level vacancy for an engineer. It is quite possible, if not likely, that existing engineers within the organisation will know, personally, other engineers doing the same kind of work. They may know one another through membership of professional engineering bodies, or because they have studied together at some time in the past. It would be worthwhile for the organisation to inform its existing engineers of the vacancy and elicit their support in finding prospective applicants.

Another approach, using this method, is to offer some form of 'bounty' payment to any existing employee who introduces a subsequently successfully-appointed applicant. This approach is more appropriate where there are a fairly large number of vacancies and the management inform all existing employees that they will pay a sum of money to any employee who introduces an applicant who is subsequently appointed and stays with the organisation for a specified period of time (say 6 months). In this way the organisation involves its existing employees in the recruitment process. There are some potential problems associated with this approach. The biggest problem concerns applicants who are introduced by existing employees, who are either rejected at the selection stage, or who prove unsatisfactory after appointment. In both cases the employee who introduced the applicant may be upset if the applicant is unsuccessful. The employee may be upset at both not receiving the bounty and the embarrassment of having introduced a friend or relative who is rejected. Further the cost of operating and administering the 'bounty' system must be taken into account.

Using the services of the Department of Employment

There may be legal reasons why an organisation should notify the Department of Employment of any vacancies which it wishes to fill. We will discuss this later in the chapter, when we deal briefly with employment legislation.

The Training Commission (TC) has as its main purpose to help secure a skilled, flexible and adaptable workforce by: providing training for all school leavers; improving the skills and employability of the unemployed; improving the training system; and protecting access for disadvantaged groups to vocational education and training. The TC has two operating divisions: the Vocational Education and Training Group and the Skills Training Agency. The Department of Employment has responsibility for running the Employment Service which consists of Jobcentres and Local Employment Offices and Professional and Executive Recruitment (PER).

The employer notifies the *Jobcentre* of the vacancy giving details of the job. The details provided should include a brief description of the main duties involved in the job, the skills or qualifications that would need to be held by a successful applicant, the hours of work, shifts, holidays etc, and the rate of pay. Most of this information will be obtained from the job description and specification. If the employer chooses he may limit the information to that noted above and inform the Jobcentre that he would like the details of the vacancy displayed on the 'self service' notice boards within the Jobcentre. In this way any member of the public, whether currently employed or unemployed, who sees the vacancy displayed in the Jobcentre, can contact the organisation. The organisation effectively obtains free advertising of its vacancy in the Jobcentre, which will probably be situated in a prominent place within the town or city, with ready access to all members of the public. Alternatively the organisation may decide that it wants to have all applicants screened by employment advisers in the Jobcentre. In this case it will need to send details of the person specification to the Jobcentre so that the employment advisers are able effectively to interview prospective candidates. In this case the vacancy is still advertised but interested parties are referred to an employment adviser, who, if he or she feels the applicant is appropriate, will contact the organisation concerned and arrange a second interview for the applicant at a convenient time. This service is free to both the applicant and the employer. When an organisation makes regular use of a Jobcentre it is not uncommon for employment advisers from the Jobcentre to visit the organisation to familiarise themselves with it, so that they can more effectively perform their task of screening applicants. Clearly this can be of enormous assistance, since it combines both the process of notifying potential applicants of the existence of the vacancy and the first stage in the selection process. Moreover, if the organisation wishes to advertise its vacancy outside its own immediate locality, then the Department of Employment with its nationwide network of Jobcentres will advertise in selected areas of the country through the Jobcentres in these areas. In addition to this the Jobcentre keeps records of people who are seeking employment and may therefore be immediately available for employment.

A second service offered by the Employment Service is Professional and Executive Recruitment (PER) which is operated on a commercial basis, charging employers for its recruitment and selection services.

Private Agencies and Consultants

Private Agencies and Consultants offer a variety of services to employers and potential employees.

Some keep registers of individuals who are seeking employment of a particular type, say scientists. The individual compiles a detailed *curriculum vitae* (CV) and/or is interviewed by the consultant. There is normally no charge to the individual seeking employment. Consultants make their money by different methods of charging employers who are seeking new employees. We will look at the 2 main ways employers are charged by means of examples. Firstly, let us suppose an organisation wishes to recruit a Work Study Manager. The Personnel Manager provides details of the job and the kind of person they are looking for. The recruitment consultant looks through the details of individuals he holds on register to see if any seem to meet the needs of the client organisation. If the consultant has a suitable person on file he contacts them to enquire whether they are interested in the position being offered by the client organisation, in this case Work Study Manager. If the individual is interested, the consultant will either send the client organisation details or arrange for him to be interviewed. Alternatively, the consultant may have no suitable candidates on his register and may advertise for someone to fill the vacancy. The consultant then interviews applicants and recommends those suitable to the client. In this way he will also obtain applications from people who may not be suitable for this client, but may meet the needs of some other client seeking a Work Study Manager. It is common for consultants to ask permission of unsuccessful applicants to keep their names on file should some other suitable vacancy arise. In this way the consultant increases the size of his register.

The method of charging may be a fixed fee or a certain percentage of the annual salary of the appointed applicant. So, for instance, if the annual salary of the Work Study Manager was £18,000 and the consultant's charge was 15% of the annual salary, then he would charge the client £2,700 for the appointment, out of which he would have to meet all his expenses, including any advertising. It is in the consultant's interest to fill vacancies from his register.

Some other agencies offer a different kind of service. They maintain registers in the same way, but their method of operation is to advertise themselves, usually in the press and professional and trade journals. Applicants to the agency fill in an application form giving their personal particulars, qualifications, experience etc. and these are then held on a register which is kept up-to-date. If an organisation wishes to use the agency's services they provide them with details of their vacancy. The agency then sells them copies of the information about individuals registered with them who meet the requirements. If we take again the example of the organisation wishing to recruit a Work Study Manager, then they would notify the agency of the details of the vacant job and the kind of person they are looking for. A price will be agreed, which the organisation will pay the agency. In return the agency will furnish the names and full details of any individuals on their register whom they feel could fill the job. They will continue to send this information for a specified time. So the organisation can expect to receive, having made their payment, information on all those individuals registered with the agency at the time, who appear to meet the requirements of the job, plus any new registrations for, say, the next three months, if this is the time agreed and paid for. The charge for this service may be £900 for three months. This method is of course cheaper than the kind offered by the other kind of agencies. The difference is that it is more speculative in that there is no guarantee that the organisation will appoint anyone submitted by the agency. On the other hand, if the organisation has a number of vacancies of the same kind, say ten vacancies for mechanical engineers, then the *per capita* cost of recruitment could be reduced using this service. So, for example, if ten engineers were recruited at salaries of £15,000 each, using the first kind of agency. Then with a 15% of annual salary fee basis of charges the cost would be 15% of £15,000 ten times, i.e. £22,500. The same ten engineers may be obtained from the second system, over a twelve month period (at a charge of £300 per month), for £3,600.

ACQUIRING NEW EMPLOYEES

A third type of service offered by agencies is where the organisation informs the agency of their need, who then advertise and draw up short lists. The basis of charges in these cases include the costs of advertising, administration, screening, and short listing.

Advertising the vacancy

Many of the methods we have discussed for attracting candidates have already involved some form of advertising. Advertising can vary from a postcard in a shop window, which attempts to attract applicants for the job of newspaper delivery person for the local newsagent, to advertising at peak times on the television for operators to work at a well-known motor manufacturer. Whatever kind of advertising and media is used, the aims should always be the same:

(i) To ensure an adequate number of suitable applicants are made aware of the existence of the vacancy;

(ii) To ensure an adequate number of suitable applicants respond to the advertisement;

(iii) To minimise the number of unsuitable applicants who respond to the advertisement;

(iv) To balance the coverage obtained by the advertisement with the cost involved in obtaining it;

(v) To facilitate further recruitment in the future by, for example, maintaining a good image of the organisation in the eyes of the public;

(vi) To ensure that the effectiveness of the advertising can be evaluated.

Let us first consider the question of the choice of media. That is the decision of *where* we are going to advertise. One factor which will be of great importance when considering media will be the cost. Certain forms of media, like television and the national press, may be prohibitively expensive. However, they are not necessarily the most appropriate media for all jobs. If, for instance, we wished to recruit sewing machine operators and, for some reason, we feel the need to advertise the vacancies, then a small advertisement in the local newspaper may provide us with an ample supply of applicants. Similarly, if we wished to recruit a plumber, the *Financial Times* newspaper would not be an appropriate medium, whilst again the local newspaper or a Trade journal which plumbers read would be more appropriate. If, on the other hand, we need to advertise for a financial director then probably the *Financial*

Times will be the best bet. The criterion to be adopted will be to use the medium which gives us adequate results within a reasonable time at minimum cost. Therefore, if there is one particular medium which is likely to be seen by more of our prospective candidates than any other, we should consider the cost of using it and, if it is too expensive, we must reject it and look at the second most likely medium, and so on, until we come to the one which will meet our needs, but is cheapest. Other factors that will affect our choice of media will be the numbers of people we require and their availability, both in terms of the numbers available and their geographical location or dispersion. If we intend to recruit two hundred graduate engineers for various parts of our organisation all over the country we will probably choose national media like the *Daily Telegraph* or some professional journal. Whereas, if we wish to recruit just one graduate engineer, in a particular location, we are likely to use the local press. However, if we wanted to recruit one very specialised chemist and we believe that there are perhaps only twenty people in the country who could do the job, assuming that we cannot locate them personally, we may be forced to advertise either nationally or internationally.

We must now ensure that our advertisement is noticed. Since most recruitment advertising appears in the press, we will concentrate upon this type. Many devices are used by advertisers to ensure they gain the attention of their potential applicants given that they are advertising in the appropriate medium. We have all, for example, seen the advertisements which employ the use of pictures to draw our eye to them. Probably the most commonly used device is the bold printed headline, which attempts to immediately identify the potential candidate by the use of a job title or a work subject.

Having gained the attention of all our prospectively suitable candidates, and probably some who are not suitable, by the use of our headline, we must hold their attention and provide them with some more details of the job. All the time we must remember that our advertisement probably appears on a page full of other advertisements all of which are trying to gain the reader's attention, therefore the details we provide must be interesting to prospectively suitable candidates, to convince them that it is worth reading on further. Many advertisements provide brief general details about the organisation, usually stressing the opportunities available.

Having gained and held the attention of our readers (only some of whom will be suitable prospective candidates), we will start to do some pre-selection, by providing details of the job. In this way we hope to eliminate the readers who are not suited to the job and also to make it clear to potentially suitable applicants that we wish to communicate with them as individuals.

Finally, having whetted the appetite of all the prospectively suitable applicants, we must spur them into action. We must state as simply as possible, what they should do to make an application.

Having gained a response to our advertisement, we must ensure that we keep the interest of the suitable applicants, whilst at the same time noting how many suitable applicants respond to each advertisement. We must do this to evaluate the effectiveness of the advertising. This may sound obvious and indeed quite simple. This is the case if only one method of recruitment is being employed at any given time or only one advertisement is being used. The most common device is to ask the question on the application form: 'Where did you hear about the vacancy?' In this way we can determine the effectiveness of various recruitment efforts.

The normal way of comparing and evaluating all recruitment methods is to divide the total cost of recruitment effort for each method by the number of successfully appointed candidates. This will yield a *per capita* cost of 'conversion' for each method of recruitment used. Another method, which under certain circumstances is more appropriate, is to divide the total cost of the recruitment effort by one method (or one advertisement) by the total number of suitable candidates who applied for the job. This second method may be more appropriate if, for instance, the organisation is not able to offer a particularly attractive salary or wage for the kind of job which it is seeking to fill.

Initial Contact with Applicants

The selection process begins once we have made initial contact with applicants. Before we look at the devices available for the purpose of selection, we must make one important point.

This is something we have noted previously when discussing person specifications. Selection should be a two-way process, where the organisation selects the individual and vice versa. We will call this the mutuality of selection. Even before we see applicants, we have the opportunity to enhance this aspect of mutuality of selection, whilst at the same time keeping the interest of suitable candidates. We can achieve this by providing as much information as is reasonable about the job, the organisation in which the job is located, and the circumstances relating to the offer that may be made to applicants considered suitable.

Information about the job should be readily available in the form of job description and specification, and this should be sent to applicants. Information about the organisation, which could include reports to shareholders and employees, and general background information, should also be sent to applicants. Finally, if, for instance, there is the possibility of relocation expenses for successful applicants, then general details of these should also be provided. In this way we will not only prepare candidates for the selection procedure, but also afford them the opportunity to decide whether they wish to pursue their application further.

Assessing the Candidates

This is the selection stage of the recruitment and selection process. We have seen how we drew up a person specification and attracted applicants who felt themselves to be suitable for the job and had at least some interest in it. We must now consider how we decide whether applicants are in fact suitable for the job by comparing and evaluating them against the yardstick of the person specification. An organisation can choose to use some or all of a number of selection devices for this purpose. The devices used will be determined mainly by the type of job that is to be filled. The order in which the devices are used will also vary from job to job but may follow the pattern as shown in Figure 27.

The Application Form

Rarely, if ever, will the application form be used as the sole device for selecting a candidate for a job. It will normally be used as a screening device for identifying unsuitable candidates. This is one of the three functions that are performed by application forms. However in order that the function of screening applicants can be done effectively it is essential that the application form invites information of a useful kind about the applicant. Here we run into our first small problem, namely the information we are going to request on the application form. Clearly the sort of information we would want to know about candidates for one job will be different than for another. For example, one job may be suited only to people of a certain height, whilst another may require applicants to be fluent in a foreign language, and their height may be of no interest whatsoever. So what information is to be sought on the application form? Most organisations compromise and ask for basic information corresponding roughly to those aspects of the person specification covered by 'physical make-up', 'attainments', 'skills', and 'personal background': often there is some limited opportunity for the applicants to make comments associated with 'would want to do the job factors'. There is no reason why we should not supplement our standard application form with an additional questionnaire seeking information which will not be revealed on the application form. This would assist us in using these documents as screening devices for identifying unsuitable candidates.

Stages	Selection Activity	Reason for Rejection
1.	Candidates express an interest in the job	
2.	Candidates sent application forms + other information on job orientation etc.	Some candidates self-select out on the basis of negative 'would want to do the job factors'.
3.	Candidates return application forms	Some candidates rejected on negative 'could do the job factors'.
4.	Candidates attend initial screening interview	Some candidates self-select out on the basis of negative 'would want to do the job factors'. Some candidates rejected on negative 'could do the job factors'. A few candidates rejected on 'could be prevented from doing the job factors'.
5.	Candidates take tests	Some candidates rejected on negative 'could do the job factors'.
6.	Candidates attend 2nd interview with line manager &/or panel/board interview &/or group interview	Some candidates self-select out on the basis of negative 'would want to do the job factors'. Some candidates rejected on 'could be prevented from doing the job factors'. A few candidates rejected on 'could do the job factors'.
7.	Candidates given medical	A few candidates rejected on negative 'could do the job factors'.
8.	References taken up	Very few candidates rejected on negative 'could do the job factors' & 'could be prevented from doing the job factors'.
9.	Candidate/s made offer of job	Hopefully very few candidates reject the offer.
10.	Candidate/s accept(s) job offer	
11.	Placement & follow up procedure to include evaluation of selection techniques used.	

Figure 27

STAGES IN THE SELECTION PROCESS — DEVICES USED

The second function of the application form is to provide information as a starting point for an interview. In other words it provides some basic data about the candidate so the interviewer knows at least a little about him before the interview starts.

The third function of the application form is to provide a record of the candidates who applied for the job. In the case of applicants who are rejected, it will constitute the only information the organisation has on them. If we decide to reject a candidate on the basis of the information obtained from the application form we must note, either on the form or on a document attached to the form, our reason. It is also good practice to attach a copy of the letter we sent informing him that he has been rejected. Whilst it is not often the normal practice to tell rejected candidates why they have been rejected, it is essential that they are sent a courteously written letter, thanking them for their application and the interest they have shown in the job and the organisation. Remember, courtesy costs nothing at all.

Tests

Tests of all sorts are in fairly widespread use in UK organisations nowadays. Selection tests can and do provide useful supplementary information on candidates applying for jobs. It is essential that tests, like other devices, meet the criterion requirements, which we shall discuss later, that they are valid and reliable, and that they are administered and interpreted by trained people.

Reasons for using tests

There are five main reasons for using tests:

(i)   Since most tests are objectively scored, they can act as checking devices on interviews, which are highly subjective selection devices.

(ii)   Where specific requirements in terms of skill, intelligence, and aptitude for a job have been identified in the job and person specifications, tests can be used to determine whether candidates possess these characteristics, and whether these characteristics are developed, within the candidate, to the extent required for successful performance of the job.

(iii) When there are a large number of applicants for the job, then tests, particularly if they can be administered to a number of applicants at the same time, can eliminate some of the candidates, thus reducing the amount of time spent on interviews.

(iv)   Some candidates may find it difficult to communicate in interviews, though they may be well suited to the job for which they have applied. In these cases tests can provide such candidates with the opportunity to display their abilities.

(v)   By using tests organisations get a little more information about applicants to assist in the process of selection.

140

Types of tests

Achievement tests are probably the most commonly used type, the candidate being given either a practical or theoretical task or set of tasks to perform. A practical test would be useful where there is a vacancy for a shorthand typist. Candidates are asked to take shorthand notes of a test piece, which is read at a pre-determined speed (normally equal to the speed of shorthand writing which is required for the job). They are then required to type from their shorthand notes, thus to reproduce the text which has been dictated. The time spent typing is recorded (to establish their typing speeds). Finally the typing is checked for errors to establish the applicant's accuracy. In this way it can be established whether any given applicant can perform shorthand and typing tasks to the standards required in the job.

Some jobs, for which the requirements in terms of 'attainments' may be very limited, may however call for some *special aptitude*. This special aptitude may be in no way related to intelligence or academic ability. Such factors could be identified when considering candidates' attainments. Sometimes we refer to these special aptitudes as gifts that an individual possesses. We hear of, for instance, some outstanding sportsmen and women having a gift in their particular field. When the presence of the aptitude is not quite so dramatic we say that someone has the knack to do something easily, which most people find difficult to do. It is possible to use tests to identify whether a candidate has such a knack or gift. We ourselves may be all fingers and thumbs and unable to perform well in a test which requires us to assemble some intricate mechanism, whilst other people with a special aptitude for manual dexterity may find the task perfectly simple.

Tests of *intelligence* have been used by some organisations for particular types of recruitment for many years now. Most intelligence tests used for selection purposes are of the pencil and paper type, where candidates answer questions or solve problems that involve the use of words, figures, symbols, and abstract concepts.

Tests of *personality* are not as common as tests of intelligence, but are nonetheless used by some organisations. (For psychological testing, see Chapter 12.)

Medical Examinations

There is a legal requirement for any organisation employing a person under the age of eighteen years to ensure that they are able to perform the duties.

Generally the medical examination has three purposes, only the first two of which are truly related to the selection process.

(i)   The person specification will, under the factor of physical make-up have noted any particular physical requirements of the tasks in the job. The medical examination will, in some cases, be used to check these requirements. An example would be colour blindness tests for potential electricians.

(ii)   The person specification may not have noted any particular physical deficiencies which would preclude someone from being able to adequately perform the tasks involved in the job. There may, however, be candidates who suffer from some disability or disease which rules them out for certain types of work. Care must be taken when ruling people out, on this basis, that the decision is a valid one. For example, there are very competent telephonists who suffer from a hearing deficiency in one ear.

(iii)   The third function of the medical examination is in relation to the successfully appointed candidate. In this case the reason is that the organisation may require a record of the state of the individual's health on joining.

In virtually every situation it is imperative that a medical examination is given, and the results are made known before the offer of employment is made. It seems wholly unfair to make the offer of employment conditional upon a successful medical examination, if the candidate is not able to undergo this examination before he gives notice of intention to leave his existing employer. Very often, what purports to be a medical examination is little more than a self-declaration of the health of the candidate, and in many cases this will be perfectly adequate.

References

In Figure 27 references are shown as the last selection device used. Only very few candidates are rejected on 'could do the job' and 'could be prevented from doing the job' factors as a result of references. The taking up of references on candidates can rarely be anything more than a check on other devices used. As a device for actually making a positive selection it is virtually superfluous. If we remember that the object of the exercise is to compare candidates with, and evaluate them against, a person specification drawn up by members of the employing organisation, it is unreasonable to expect that third parties (i.e. the referees) will be in a position to judge, except very superficially, the appropriateness of an applicant for a job, since they will know very little about the job. There are three other features of references for consideration. Firstly, an applicant asked to furnish the names of referees is unlikely to give the name of anyone they would not expect to speak highly of them. Secondly, if references are sought from existing employers, they may be reluctant to say anything critical about applicants. The existing employer may be concerned about the confidentiality of any comments that he may make (will it ever get back to the applicant?) and, in any case, they may be pleased to see the back of that particular employee. In the last case, it is not unknown for employers to give deliberately ambiguous references, of the type 'Anyone who gets Mr Brown to work for them will be very lucky'. The final consideration with respect to references from existing employers is the fact that the applicant may not want his existing employer to know that he is seeking new employment elsewhere. Where this situation arises, organisations often try and overcome the problem by telling applicants that they will only take up references, if they intend to make an offer of employment, thus giving the applicant the chance to notify his existing employer that he is considering taking up a new appointment.

If an organisation decides to take up references on applicants, then probably the best method of operation is to seek the applicant's permission immediately prior to making contact with the referees. Having obtained the applicant's approval, a telephone call to the referee will almost certainly prove more useful than written enquiries.

Interviews

The interview in its many forms is the most commonly used selection device after the application form. We shall define an interview as *a conversation with a purpose*. Selection is only one of the areas in which interviews are used. For this reason, we will look at the various types of interview and consider the conduct of interviews generally in more detail in Chapter 13.

The screening interview

In many organisations, particularly large organisations, the screening interview may be conducted by a member of the Personnel Department. Sometimes this stage is dispensed with and just one main interview is carried out, either on a one-to-one basis (i.e. one interviewer and one interviewee), or by a panel or board (still just the one candidate, but a number of interviewers).

Since the screening interview is intended more to determine who is not suitable than to select the most suitable candidate, it is likely to be conducted in a slightly different way to the main interview. The interviewer must study the job description and specification, to ensure that he is fully familiar with the job and its duties. He must then fully familiarise himself with the person specification. Finally, with the person specification firmly in his mind, he must study the candidate's application form. By comparing the information called for in the person specification and the information already provided on the application form, he must decide what areas need clarification and what areas must be probed for further information to determine whether the candidate meets the requirements of the person specification. The benefit of a well-designed application form will become immediately apparent at this stage. Having decided upon the extra information required from the interview the interviewer must then determine how he intends to obtain it. Let us take a fairly simple case. If we go back to the example of the job of personnel officer for which we have drawn up a person specification, we can see that under the factor of skills we had the heading *flexibility*. It states on the person specification that it is essential that the candidate appointed must be flexible when dealing with trade union representatives and members of the public. Let us take the case of the requirement of flexibility when dealing with trade union representatives. The interviewer will not have information on the application form which will show whether the candidate possesses such flexibility. He must therefore find this out at the interview. How is he to do this? Should he just ask the applicant, 'Are you flexible when it comes to dealing with trade union representatives?' This would not be a very useful approach, since the candidate will probably merely answer 'yes', and the interviewer will be no wiser at all.

The fact is that the interviewer must prepare beforehand how he is going to elicit this particular information. This will involve preparing some questions intended to obtain the required information. This is not all, for he must give some thought as to how he is to evaluate the candidate's answers to his questions. So, for instance, the interviewer may decide on a general line of questioning concerning trades unions. He will probably ask whether the applicant has any experience of dealing with trade union representatives and to describe and comment upon the dealings he had. In this way he is likely to find out a lot more about the applicant's flexibility in this area. So, for instance, if the candidate were to affirm that he had experience with trade union representatives and that in his experience they were unreasonable people who had to be kept in their place, then the interviewer may be justified in concluding that the applicant is somewhat deficient in this area. However he cannot come to this conclusion with any certainty. He must then ask the applicant why he holds this opinion and probe him further along these lines. The interviewer should think along these lines even before he meets the candidate.

He should not only know what it is he wants to find out, but also how he intends to find it out. This takes very careful preparation.

When preparing for the screening interview the interviewer must remember that the selection process is a mutual one. With this in mind he will prepare as much information as he is able, of the kind that he feels the applicant may wish to know about the job, the organisation and so on. Having thoroughly prepared for the interview, he will then conduct it, ensuring that he has allowed adequate time and that it will be held in suitable surroundings. When the interview is completed and the interviewee has left, having been paid his travelling and other out-of-pocket expenses, and having been thanked for attending and informed when and how he will hear the outcome, the interviewer must make his decision on the candidate. In a screening interview the decision to be made is whether the candidate is to be rejected or is to progress to the next stage of the selection process. After the interview the interviewer must firstly check that he obtained information on all the areas he intended to. For each area he must evaluate the performance of the candidate and if he fails to meet the required standards on any of the points noted in the person specification as *essential,* he must be rejected. If the candidate fails to meet the standards specified as *desirable* in the person specification, then unless he fails to do so, badly, in a number of areas, he should not be rejected. Whatever the outcome of the interview, the interviewer must make full and comprehensive notes, detailing what information was sought and found and evaluating that information. A useful method is for the interviewer to run through the seven-point plan person specification, noting the performance of the applicant against each point. In this way a full and clear record of the interview can be made. Irrespective of the outcome, the candidate should be promptly and politely informed of his success or failure.

The main interview

The main interview will normally be conducted by the manager of the department in which the vacancy exists, or by the supervisor for the job. Some organisations, however, still rely on the personnel department to carry out this selection function. By the time candidates reach the stage of the main interview many, if not all, of the unsuitable ones on the basis of 'could do the job factors' should have either been eliminated from the reckoning or withdrawn themselves. In terms of their performance against the requirements of the person specification, all candidates at this stage should certainly appear to meet all factors which are noted as essential in the person specification and most factors that are noted as desirable. The main interview will almost certainly centre on those areas we have referred to as 'would want to do the job' factors and 'could be prevented from doing the job' factors. In terms of the 'would want to do the job factors' the presence of the line manager or the immediate supervisor is of some significance, since candidates can meet potential supervisors and form some opinion of them and their styles of management.

The main interview should be prepared for in the same way as the screening interview. If we consider the example of the job of personnel officer, we could expect the main interview to be the time when serious consideration is given to the factor of work attitudes. We may recall that in the person specification under the heading of personality it states that it is essential that the successful candidate is acceptable at all levels of the organisation. The interviewer may plan to probe this by giving the candidate a number of hypothetical situations to deal with and asking him to role play them out in the interview, with the interviewer playing the parts of different people at different levels in the organisation. For example, the interviewer may ask candidates how they would approach a senior manager who has repeatedly misinterpreted a piece of the organisation's personnel policy with repect to holiday entitlements. The interviewer would be looking for how tactfully candidates could approach a senior person on a delicate matter, but at the same time ensure that, at the end of the discussion, the manager would realise that he would have to revise his interpretation of the policy concerned. In another situation the candidates may be asked how they would inform an employee that his wife has just been rushed into hospital after a road accident. By using these types of questions the interviewer would hope to gain an appreciation of how candidates would deal with colleagues, both at higher and lower levels.

At the end of the main interview the same procedure described for the screening interview should be followed. On this occasion, the final or near final decision will be made on the suitability of the candidates. It may be that the organisation is fortunate enough to have a number of applicants who are suitable to fill the vacancy and so a choice must be made. It would now seem appropriate to look further than the immediate vacancy which is to be filled. So, to go back again to our example of the personnel officer vacancy, if the organisation was fortunate enough to have three comparable applicants for the job at the end of the selection process, then a choice would need to be made. In this case the basis may be the perceived long-term potential of the candidates. So probably the candidate who would seem to make the best potential assistant personnel manager would be selected.

Panel or board interviews

These types of interviews are conducted with one candidate or interviewee at a time and a number of interviewers. Normally one of the interviewers will play the main role with others acting in support. This kind of interview requires very careful planning and preparation. Each interviewer should know clearly what part he is to play in the process. One of the criticisms levelled at this type of interview is that it may be more difficult to establish and maintain rapport between the candidate and the interviewers (see Chapter 13). On the other hand, a number of different people can evaluate the candidate, thus reducing the degree of subjectivity in the decision making. Any bias that one interviewer may have should be moderated by the opinions of the others. These types of interview also allow for a number of assessors, from different disciplines, with different outlooks and priorities, to judge the candidate. Another advantage is that whilst one interviewer is asking questions, his colleagues can each independently assess the quality of answers given by the candidate. So, for example, when interviewing an applicant for the position of development engineer, each member of a panel consisting of the Personnel Manager, the Quality Control Manager, the Chief Development Engineer, and the section leader of the area in which the vacancy exists, may assess the candidate from their own particular point of interest. The Chief Development Engineer may ask the candidate how he would deal with a technical problem, to assess the technical quality of the answer. At the same time, the section leader may be considering the candidate's answer in terms of how his suggested method of dealing with the problem might affect potential colleagues and their method of working. In answer to the same question, the Quality Control Manager will consider the applicant's answer in terms of quality department considerations: does the candidate show any awareness of the problems of quality in manufacture and so on? The Personnel Manager may be more concerned with the candidate's ability to communicate and deal with other people.

At the end of the interview, when the applicant has left, each member of the panel or board should make an independent assessment. Then members discuss their assessments with each other and a joint decision is reached.

The group interview

In this type of interview there are a number of candidates assessed and evaluated simultaneously. The intention is to see how candidates perform in what is inevitably a competitive situation. A commonly-used approach is to set the applicants, of whom there will be between six and eight in number, a topic of general interest to discuss. Having defined the topic for discussion, the interviewers pass it over to the candidates, assessing the contribution and conduct of each. The interviewers judge the quality of contribution of the candidates in terms of how well they express themselves, how they adapt to the behaviour of other candidates, how persuasive they are, and so on. The interviewers perform this function as discreetly as they can, only contributing to the discussion if absolutely essential, to keep it on the rails.

Another method of group interview used, which has been highly developed in the armed services, is for the candidates to be set a particular problem and to be allocated roles for working towards a solution. Again the interviewers play no active part in the discussion, but assess the performance of the contributing candidates.

It is claimed that such interviews are useful devices for assessing how candidates perform as members of groups and for evaluating leadership potential. It is acknowledged that the process of evaluation by the interviewers, of which there are usually three or four, is a highly skilled technique. The main criticism of this selection method is the lack of control, in a highly subjective situation. In any interview the performance and behaviour of the interviewee is affected by the interviewer. In the usual one interviewee to one interviewer situation, where the same interviewer is used for all candidates, then at least half the factors are partially controlled. That is, given that for each interview the interviewer does not change, the personality of one of the parties is relatively constant. Most differences that are noted can then be attributed to differences within the candidates themselves. So, for instance, if Mr. Smith interviews first Mr. Brown and them Mr. Jones and, of the two, Mr. Jones seems the more lucid, persuasive, and forceful then, since Mr. Smith is a common factor to both interviews it is valid to assume that Mr. Jones is indeed more lucid, persuasive, and forceful. In the case of the group interviews Mr. Jones may be in a group of six people, the other five of whom are all highly aggressive and forceful. By comparison Mr. Jones may come across as quiet and reserved. In the case of Mr. Brown he may be a member of a group of six people, the other five of whom are rather shy and retiring types. In this company Mr. Brown may appear as the dominant personality. After the two group interviews it is quite likely that the assessments of Messrs. Brown and Jones would be quite the opposite than those obtained in a more traditional interview and, almost certainly, the opposite to the conclusions that would have been drawn had Mr. Brown been a member of Mr. Smith's group and vice versa. We must therefore conclude that the reliability of the group interview, and indeed, to some extent its validity, are open to question.

The Choice of Selection Devices

The choice of selection devices used will be determined by the type of job. For some jobs, where applicants may be expected to have very little experience (perhaps school-leavers) and very limited knowledge of what the job involves and requires, tests may be very useful. The determination of whether a device should or should not be used must be on the basis that the device provides a method of evaluating some feature of candidates which needs evaluating according to the person specification. Within this general rule, the decision to use various devices will be based upon time available and cost of operating or administering the device.

Selecting and Rejecting Candidates

At the end of the selection process the decision must be made for each candidate, whether he or she is to be offered the job, or rejected. Normally, if a candidate is to be rejected, then a short but courteous letter should be sent as soon as possible. Sometimes the applicant may have come close to acceptability, but another applicant was considered to be slightly better suited. In this case the organisation may anticipate that it could have other similar vacancies arising in the future and may want to reconsider the applicant for them. It is perfectly legitimate to tell the applicant of the situation and to ask his permission to reconsider him at a later date.

Whatever the circumstances of an applicant's rejection, full details of the application, interview notes, and reasons for rejection should be kept on record. There are two reasons for this record being kept. Firstly, as noted above, the organisation may wish to reconsider the applicant for some future vacancy. Secondly, the organisation needs such records, including records of the reason for rejection, in case the applicant feels that in some way he has been unfairly treated or discriminated against on the basis of sex, race, marital status, or trade union membership.

When a candidate is considered as suitable and an offer of employment is to be made, it will be useful if, at the final stages of the selection process, he has been given some hint of this possibility and, just as important, an idea of the expectations the organisation would have of the candidate appointed. So, for example, if we are seeking a Personnel Officer and an applicant is not taking a course for the Institute of Personnel Management (an essential qualification for the post), then such information should be provided to the applicant at the interview. Moreover, when the offer of employment is made this fact should be restated with any pertinent ancillary information; like, for instance, preparedness to pay tuition fees and/or give paid time off for study. Other information which should be included in an offer of employment, which should also be discussed at the interview includes:

(i)   Job title;
(ii)   Salary information related to the job;

(iii)   Holiday entitlement;

(iv)   Hours of work and location of work;

(v)   Relevant details about the pension scheme;

(vi)   General details about conditions of service, including information on any probationary period, if appropriate;

(vii)   Information on any agreements that would affect the new employee (e.g. the existence of a Union Membership Agreement);

(viii)   Starting date (taking into account the requirement to give notice of termination to his existing employer);

(ix)   The requirement for the new employee to furnish any appropriate documentation (e.g. P45 tax form);

(x)   The place and time to report on the first day of employment.

Just as it is important to keep full records on candidates who are rejected for employment, it is essential to keep records of the selection process for those who are selected. In selecting a candidate we are in fact predicting that his future performance will satisfactorily meet the organisation's requirements in the job to which he is appointed. It is possible that the decision has been made with some reservations about the candidate's suitability in terms of some desirable aspects noted in the person specification or indeed that the candidate is expected to be exceptional in some area of performance. It is essential that this information is recorded so that at a later date a check can be made on the accuracy of all aspects of the prediction.

Placement, Follow Up, and Induction

When anyone starts a new job there is a great deal of information they need to absorb, some of it in the very early stages of employment. The problem is that however receptive the new employee is, there is a limit to the amount of information he can be expected to absorb and assimilate in a limited time. For this reason it is essential that a new employee's induction programme is carefully planned.

The first step in planning an induction programme is to make a comprehensive list of what the new employee needs to know or do. Many different items will be included and the list noted below should not be considered as comprehensive:

(i)   General information about the organisation, its products and/or services;

(ii)   General information on the organisation's methods of operation;

(iii)   General information on the organisation's structure;

(iv)   Specific information on the location of toilets, washrooms, cloakroom facilities etc;

(v)   Specific information on eating arrangements and restaurant facilities;

(vi)   Information on the organisation's policy and practices regarding health and safety;

(vii)   Information on the organisation's policy and procedure on security, in as far as it affects the new employee;

(viii)   Specific information and instruction regarding evacuation in the event of fire;

(ix)   Information on any agreements between the organisation and Trades Unions, in so far as they affect the new employee;

(x)   Information on organisation operated schemes, like employee suggestion schemes;

(xi)   Information on rules and procedures related to sickness and absence;

(xii)   Information on rules and procedures related to holidays;

(xiii)   Information on the operation of disciplinary and grievance procedures;

(xiv)   Information on procedures associated with promotion and transfer;

(xv)   Information on the organisation's sports and social facilities;

(xvi)   Specific information on salary payment procedures;

(xvii)   Information on where the new employee's own job fits into the organisation;

(xviii)   Information on the general rules of the organisation covering employee behaviour and conduct;

(xix)   Familiarisation and instruction as necessary in the job to which the new employee is appointed;

(xx)   Introduction to colleagues with whom he will work;

(xxi)   Introduction to the Trade Union representative for the area in which he works.

Having drawn up a list of what the new employee should know, other questions are: when and how the new employee should be made aware of these things? To some extent the question of how the new employee will be informed is dictated by the time scales and practicalities. It is obvious that the new employee must be shown the washroom and cloakroom facilities very early on, in the first day of employment, whilst information on promotion and transfer procedures are unlikely to be of such immediate interest to him. Given that there is clearly going to be too much information for anyone to absorb properly in the first day or even the first week of employment, some form of priorities must be established. There is no reason why the induction process cannot start before the first day of employment. Any information that can be written can be provided to the new employee before he arrives. This will serve two purposes; it reduces the amount of information the new employee is expected to absorb in the first few days of a new job and it means that the new employee can start with some useful background knowledge.

There are certain pieces of information which must be provided to the new employee at a very early stage which cannot be given in written form. An example is an explanation of the evacuation procedures, showing exit and assembly points. It is normal for a short induction programme providing this kind of information to be arranged for the first day of employment.

Other information, instruction, and experience can be provided over a period, which takes account of the new employee's ability to learn. This information may be spread over the first week, month, or even three months of employment.

Follow up to the selection process

The selection process involves assessing and evaluating candidates against the specification and description of the adequate or ideal applicant, as noted in the person specification. When a candidate is offered and accepts employment, it must be assumed that at the time it was felt that he adequately measured up to the requirements of the person specification and that the selection devices used adequately identified the factors required for subsequently successful performance in the job. To see whether this is the case the criteria for success must be set. Criteria may be defined as the goodness of the employee. In short this means, after appointment, does the employee adequately perform the tasks required of him in the job for which he is employed? For an organisation to do this it must operate some form of performance appraisal. (We discuss performance appraisal as a subject in its own right in Chapter 14.) Our interest here is in seeing whether the person specification is correct and if so whether the selection devices used are effective in identifying suitable candidates. If the person specification is incorrect good staff will only be selected by chance. If however the person specification is correct then the performance appraisal process can act as a feedback loop or evaluation of the selection devices used (see Figure 28). The easiest way to discuss this is to return to the example of the selection devices used for the job of personnel officer.

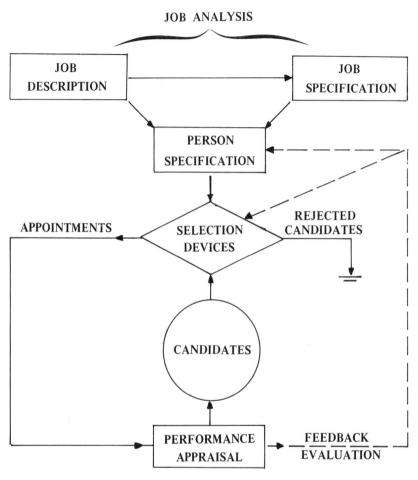

ACQUIRING NEW EMPLOYEES

JOB ANALYSIS

JOB DESCRIPTION

JOB SPECIFICATION

PERSON SPECIFICATION

APPOINTMENTS

SELECTION DEVICES

REJECTED CANDIDATES

CANDIDATES

PERFORMANCE APPRAISAL

FEEDBACK EVALUATION

FIGURE 28: THE EMPLOYEE ACQUISITION SYSTEM

Let us assume that we appointed a Miss Andrews to the position of Personnel Officer. At the time we appointed her we were perfectly happy that as far as we were able to tell she adequately met all the requirements stated in the person specification. After ten months, through the process of performance appraisal, it becomes quite clear that in one important respect Miss Andrews does not perform the job in the way required in her dealings with Trades Union representatives, with whom she has notoriously bad relations. On a further investigation it is found that the main reason for this bad relationship is because Miss Andrews is very inflexible in her dealings with shop stewards. We may be able to overcome this deficiency in Miss Andrews by some form of training, but that is not our main interest here. We are concerned here with how it is that during the selection process we came to the wrong conclusion that Miss Andrews would be a flexible person when dealing with Trades Union representatives. We must refer back to our records on the selection of Miss Andrews. What methods did we employ to try to measure Miss Andrews' flexibility in this respect? We will recall that we asked questions about her experience in dealing with TU representatives and asked her to describe and comment upon her previous dealings. At the time we were obviously happy with her answers. The problem we have can be related to one or both of two causes. Either the questions we asked were inadequate, in that they did not probe Miss Andrews deeply enough on the subject. Alternatively the questions were deep enough, but our evaluation of her answers was incorrect. The fact remains that for whatever reason we failed to correctly identify or predict this skill deficiency. There is a lesson to be learned, that the device we are using (the questions in the interviews), or our operation of that device, is inadequate and must be changed. What we are doing is evaluating both our selection devices and our own efficiency in using them. It is essential that we do this, otherwise we will continue to make the same mistakes repeatedly. The only way that this can be done is to regularly appraise the performance of our employees and consider in detail the results of those appraisals with respect to the selection process we used when appointing individuals to their jobs.

Recruitment and Selection and the Law

The laws relating generally to employment, and specifically to matters affecting recruitment and selection, change with new legislation and are interpreted through the Courts and Tribunals in which cases are heard. There is no real substitute for studying the Acts of Parliament and the decisions of the courts if one wishes to keep abreast of the law in this field. All that can be provided here is an outline of what we consider to be the main legislation affecting recruitment and selection.

The Contract of Employment Act 1972

The Contract of Employment Act 1972 gives most employees in Great Britain the right to a minimum period of notice of termination of their employment according to length of service, and the right to receive from their employer a written statement of the main terms and conditions of employment along with certain other information. The Act has from time to time been amended by other Acts, including notably the Employment Protection Act 1975. The Act is now embodied in the Employment Protection (Consolidation) Act 1978.

Rights to notice of termination of employment

An employer is required to give an employee at least one week's notice if the employee has been employed by him for at least four or more weeks continuously. After the employee has been employed for two years continuously, then the employer must give him at least two weeks' notice. When an employee has worked for an organisation for more than two years he is entitled to one week's notice for every complete year of employment, up to a maximum of twelve weeks. For example, an employee who has been continuously employed on a full time basis (i.e. 16 hours per week or more) by an organisation for seven and a half years is entitled to seven weeks' notice from his employer. An employee who has worked for an employer for seventeen years is entitled to twelve weeks' notice. Special arrangements apply to part-time employees who work more than eight hours each week, but less than sixteen hours.

An employee is required to give his employer at least one week's notice if he has been employed by him for four weeks or more. This does not increase with longer service.

Written statement of main terms of employment

An employer must give each employee a written statement which contains information about the main terms of his employment, not later than thirteen weeks after his employment has begun, unless he leaves before the thirteen weeks are up.

The written statement must include information on: the job title; the pay for the job; the hours of work; the holidays and basis of holiday payment; sickness and sick pay; pensions and pension schemes; and notice provided for termination of employment. The statement must also contain an additional note to inform the employee of any disciplinary rules applicable to him and to indicate the person to whom he should apply if he is dissatisfied with any disciplinary decision relating to him, or if he has any grievance concerning his employment. The additional note must also state whether a contracting-out certificate, under the Social Security Pension Act, is in force for the employment in which the employee is engaged. The employer must also bring to the employee's attention the written statement of the organisation's safety policy.

155

Sex and race discrimination

The legislation covering these areas is embodied in the Sex Discrimination Act 1975 and the Race Relations Act 1976. We will deal with them together here, since the two Acts are framed in very similar ways.

The two Acts make it unlawful for an employer to discriminate on grounds of sex, or against married persons, or on grounds of race, colour, nationality, or ethnic or national origins. Both Acts make it unlawful to practice: direct discrimination, indirect discrimination, and victimisation. Both Acts cover discrimination by employers in recruitment and selection, as well as in relation to existing employees.

Direct discrimination means treating someone less favourably, on the grounds of their race or sex, than anyone else would be treated under similar circumstances.

Indirect discrimination is applying a condition or requirement (for instance to job applicants) which, although it is equally applied to all applicants, is such that a considerably smaller proportion of women, or members of one particular racial group could comply with it, than could men or members of other racial groups.

Victimisation means treating a person less favourably, either because they have asserted their rights under one of the Acts, or they have helped another person to do so.

With respect to advertising, the Acts make it unlawful to publish or have published an advertisement which indicates, or could reasonably be understood to be indicating, an intention to discriminate unlawfully.

The Disabled Persons (Employment) Act 1958

The purpose of this Act is to enable people handicapped by disablement to secure employment or work on their own account.

The Department of Employment is required to maintain a register of disabled persons who register with them. The Act requires every employer, who employs twenty or more people, to employ a quota of at least three per cent registered disabled persons amongst his workforce. The Act also requires employers to keep records showing the percentage of registered disabled people they employ.

The Act empowers the Minister concerned to designate certain types of jobs for registered disabled persons.

The Act establishes the job of Disablement Resettlement Officers with the Department of Employment who have the duty to advise disabled persons and to help them obtain suitable jobs.

If an employer, who has not obtained an exemption certificate and is not employing his quota of disabled persons, has a vacancy, then he must notify the Disablement Resettlement Officer at the Department of Employment so that a disabled person may be given the opportunity of employment.

The Rehabilitation of Offenders Act 1974

The purpose of this Act is to rehabilitate offenders who have not been reconvicted of any serious offence for a period of years and to penalise the unauthorised disclosure of their previous convictions.

The Act introduces the concept of a 'spent' conviction. A conviction will become 'spent' if within a stated number of years (the number varies depending upon a number of factors) from the date of conviction, the person does not commit a serious offence during the rehabilitation period.

An employer may not ask any prospective employee whether he has a spent conviction. The employer may ask if the prospective employee has any convictions, but the prospective employee is under no obligation to reveal a spent conviction and can therefore say that he has no convictions.

An employer should not disclose information about any spent conviction, of which he happens to be aware, of employees for whom he gives references.

Chapter 12

Psychological Testing

In earlier chapters we have considered the concepts of motivation, attitudes, and personality and, only in the case of attitudes, have we considered how such attributes may be assessed. In this chapter we look at the characteristics and variants of psychological testing, and discover how confident one ought to be in the use of such devices.

The fundamental purpose of psychological tests is to measure differences between individuals in their possession of a specific attribute, or alternatively to measure differences in the same individual at different times. If we use a physical rather than psychological example, we can measure the difference in height between Richard, John, and Benjamin, or alternatively, we can measure Richard's height today and compare it to his height at this time last year.

Psychological testing is used in a variety of areas. Its application in selection at work is considered in Chapter 11, but other applications include the detection of educational subnormality, the examination of emotional disturbance, and vocational guidance.

You have probably seen 'tests' in Sunday newspapers or magazines which purport to measure your personality, sociability, or your performance as a husband, wife or lover. They normally consist of a number of questions, often descriptions of a situation, and you are asked to indicate whether you would act in way (a), (b) or (c).

On the surface there appears to be a high degree of similarity between the fictitious example above, and the following, which is taken from a frequently used test of personality:

> 'If someone tells me something which I know is wrong, I am more likely to say to myself:
>
> > (a) he is a liar
> > (b) in between
> > (c) apparently he is misinformed.'

A psychological test is not simply a collection of questions, but is aimed at measuring a standardised sample of human behaviour. To do this, psychological tests have a certain number of essential prerequisites:

1. The sample of behaviour should be large enough to enable the tester to generalise and predict from the test results.

2. The test should be standardised, that is the series of questions (or

tasks) should be administered in exactly the same way whenever the test is used.

3.   There should be a set of 'norms' against which the test results can be compared. If we were designing a test which was aimed to predict the performance of our sample on passing examinations, we would need a set of norms or characteristics of excellent 'examination passers' against which we would compare our results.

4.   Psychological tests should have a high level of validity and reliability, which is published, and thus known by the users of the test. It is on this particular characteristic that we will now concentrate our attention.

Reliability and Validity

If we assume that the purpose of a psychological test is to discriminate between respondents with respect to a certain characteristic, or between characteristics of the respondents at different times, then two vital questions emerge:

1.   Does the test always discriminate in the same way? Does it always test the same characteristic? Is the test *reliable*?

2.   Does the test discriminate in the way it is intended to? How well does the test measure what it is supposed to measure? Is the test *valid*?

When we are administering a published test we want to be sure that we are measuring the same characteristic the person who designed the test was measuring — i.e. that it is *reliable*. However, if we look at the range of different scores obtained by respondents, we must be aware that the differences are attributable to two causes. The first cause of these differences lies in the 'true' differences between our respondents in the variable measured by the test, but there will also be a second cause, that of temporary differences between them in such variables as motivation, state of health and so on. These latter causes of differences are called *errors in measurement,* and they change from time to time. The more these errors affect the results obtained in the test, the less reliable the test becomes, as the less will a respondent's score reflect his 'true' score on the variable measured by the test.

There are three main methods of measuring the reliability of a test:

1.   *Test-retest reliability.* In this method, the same group of respondents is given the same test on two different occasions. The correlation bet-

ween their scores on these two occasions is called the *coefficient of stability*. The closer this coefficient is to +1.00, the more reliable the test. There are a number of disadvantages associated with this form of assessment. For example, a short interval of time between the two tests, resulting in a very high coefficient of stability, may in fact indicate that respondents have remembered their previous answers. This is sometimes known as the practice effect. Alternatively, the fatigue effect may be present, when a low coefficient of stability emerges, as the group is tired due to the two consecutive tests. It has been found that test-retest reliability decreases as the interval between the tests increases, which suggests that there is a greater likelihood of 'error in measurement' variation contributing to these differences in scores.

2. *Equivalent form reliability*. This form of assessing reliability involves the use of equivalent forms of the same test with the same individuals at more or less the same time. The Stanford-Binet test has two forms (L and M) which have a correlation of 0.91 between them. We saw with the previous method that time to time differences were treated as error, but in this case we have a two-fold or compound measurement of error. In the first place error may be caused, as before, through the time factor — the tests being administered too close together, or too far apart, affecting the coefficient of stability. Secondly, however, error in this method may be caused by differences in the forms of the test.

3. *Split-half reliability*. We noted above that equivalent forms of a test cannot be administered to the same individuals at exactly the same time so that the procedure cannot rule out the possibility of including variations in the 'true' score from time to time as part of the error score. The split-half procedure attempts to eliminate this variation by correlating the scores of the same individuals on one half of the test with their scores on the other half. The correlation obtained by this method is sometimes known as the coefficient of equivalence.

Split-half reliability differs from the other reliability measures in that it is mainly concerned with the internal consistency of the test, rather than differences in score over time. As such, it is frequently used in the construction of a test, when selecting items to be included or excluded.

Much research has been carried out to discover the possible sources of variation in test scores. It has been discovered, for example, that one can improve performance on tests by practice, as one's confidence in the test situation increases, and stress of the respondent can have a significant effect on results, and, as every examination candidate knows, luck often makes an important contribution to the final score. We will return to some of these causes of score variation later, but it is important at this stage to appreciate the range of variables, other than 'true' differences in the measured characteristic which may account for such score variations.

Even if we are confident that the test we are using is reliable, we still have to be assured of its *validity,* for a test may give highly reliable scores which are not measures of the characteristic we are supposed to be measuring. Thus validity is a measure of how well a test measures what it is supposed to measure. There are five main types of validity:

1. *Predictive validity* — how accurately does the test predict future performance in a specific task? For example, how accurately does a reading test administered at the age of six predict reading ability at the age of ten?

2. *Concurrent validity* — how accurately does the test estimate *present* performance? How accurately does a test of reading administered at the age of six estimate performance in writing at the age of six?

3. *Content validity* — how well is the full range of the specific ability measured by the test? Does the test only discriminate between those with a great amount of the ability and those with hardly any, thus failing to discriminate between the 'average' people in the middle?

4. *Face validity* — does the test 'look' right to those who are taking it? If you were asked to do a test on car maintenance, and the questions were about flour, eggs, and margarine, you might complain that the test appeared to have little relation to what it was supposed to measure. Low face validity can cause poor test performance due to a lessening in motivation on the part of the respondent.

5. *Construct validity* — how well does an intelligence test measure 'intelligence'? How well does a beauty contest measure 'beauty'? These are the issues which are tackled in construct validity. It is appropriate when a general dimension of individual difference is to be measured, and depends on the tester having a theory about appropriate measures of such a dimension. If you were to design a test of intelligence, it would be determined by your ideas about and definition of the construct 'intelligence'.

So much for the different types of validity, but how do we assess the validity coefficient of our test? One way is to correlate test scores with a variety of other, external criteria, and this applies to all forms of validity except face validity. With predictive validity, for example, we can correlate test scores with other apparent predictors — spelling tests, to use our previous example of reading ability — as well as engaging in a longer term research project which would involve testing the children again at the age of ten. Alternatively, if it has been proved to our satisfaction that the AH5 is a valid test of intelligence, we may decide to compare the results obtained on our test with those obtained in the AH5 so that a high correlation between the two sets of scores may be taken to be indicative of high validity. We may seek the advice of others who are knowledgeable in the field of testing particularly if we are concerned about face validity.

Thus the validity and reliability of published tests, or of any test which you wish to use, are essential information, for only with these will you know how much confidence to have in the test results.

Types of Test

Having examined these two areas, let us now turn to the different methods of testing, and to a consideration of their advantages and disadvantages.

There are three main methods of testing:

1) Paper and pencil tests
2) Situational tests
3) Projective techniques

Paper and Pencil tests are the ones most commonly associated with psychological testing, and most of the examples we have used so far are taken from this type of test. A printed booklet of questions, often with a set of multiple choice answers, is provided for each respondent, and in many cases he is asked to indicate on a printed answer sheet which response he considers appropriate, or the response he would give in the particular circumstances.

Such a test is very easy to administer. A large number of respondents may be tested at the same time with minimal extra cost, as one tester can supervise a great number of respondents. Some tests even provide an answer guide which is placed over the top of the respondent's answer sheet so that the correct answers show through, but incorrect answers are masked. By this method it is possible to mark large numbers of answers in a very short time. On the other hand, there are some notable shortcomings associated with this method of testing. The first is that it is possible for the repondent to 'cheat', in that he may be able to guess the appropriate response instead of saying what he really thinks. A rather simplistic example of this would be a personality test administered to candidates for the job of a salesman.

Imagine a question was posed along the following lines:

'Which of the following do you prefer doing at work? (a) Talking to people and persuading them to accept your viewpoint. (b) Working in a quiet room on your own.'

If you wanted the job of salesman, how would you answer that question?

A disadvantage of paper and pencil tests is the possibility of respondents saying what they think is appropriate rather than what they really believe. A second problem is that paper and pencil tests can look, and be administered, like an examination, which immediately puts anyone who suffers from examination nerves at a disadvantage. In such a case the test may discriminate more effectively between people on the basis of their ability to do examinations rather than the intended variable. A third problem of this type lies in the notion of there being right and wrong answers to questions. Intelligence tests suffer particularly badly from this problem and A. Heim (1970) gives a number of examples of items from tests which have a number of possible correct answers. Unfortunately, the respondent who does not think in the same way as the person who set the test will be marked 'wrong', if his answer does not correspond to the one laid down by the tester. The respondent is very rarely given an opportunity to explain why he chose one particular answer rather than another, and this may certainly put the creative or lateral thinker at a disadvantage.

Some paper and pencil tests are designed to overcome some of these shortcomings. Some tests include 'trick' questions, such as putting the same type of question in a variety of different ways in the same test so that the consistency of responses may be analysed. Testers are trained to administer the tests in a non-threatening way and specific tests are designed to assess creative thinking. However, such a format remains popular because of its administrative convenience and in spite of many of the problems we have noted.

Situational tests represent a sample of activities which might be present in a job or task, and as such they frequently have a high face validity. Their predictive validity is usually good, as we can assess how an individual actually responds in certain situations. Thus a potential salesman may be required to 'sell' something, in the presence of a tester, under carefully controlled conditions; a potential army officer may be asked to lead his men on a 'mission', with a certain set of objectives in mind and a particular issue of equipment; or a management trainee may take part in a group discussion so that, not only the content of his contribution, but also his style in controlling the group or facilitating its work can be assessed.

The major advantages of this method are its high face and predictive validity, and the difficulties it presents to respondents in terms of 'cheating', since they actually have to behave in appropriate ways rather than simply indicate what *ought* to happen. This type of test may also avoid the problem of appearing to resemble an examination, since it is an active and involving method of discriminating between individuals.

However, situational tests also have significant disadvantages. The first is the selection of an appropriate sample of behaviour to assess. This sample must be large enough to give an indication of the range of potential responses, and sufficiently representative of the behaviour expected in a job or task to enable an accurate prediction to be made. Hence, in the case of the potential salesman mentioned above, he may be very skilled in the art of selling, but we know nothing about his organisational abilities, his ability to handle the appropriate paperwork, or his stamina and driving skills, and many managers would argue that these are vital parts of a salesman's job. On the other hand, it is tempting to err in the opposite direction, including a vast range of behaviours in a situational test which would render the test unwieldy, time consuming and very expensive to administer. A second disadvantage is that the situational tests are, by their very nature, expensive to administer, relative to paper and pencil tests. A far higher level of skill is demanded of the tester, who needs a significant awareness of the task content, as well as abilities in processing or perceiving what is happening in such a task. Obviously there are limits to the number of candidates or individuals who can be tested at the same time and this, too, adds to the cost. Another problem area concerns whether we are testing for *aptitude* or 'potential' in an individual, or *achievement,* a level of performance already obtained. The distinction between these two types of test has to be borne in mind in test construction and administration, or we run the danger of assessing too highly the individual with some past experience as opposed to the complete newcomer who may have enormous potential. If we return to our previous example of the salesman, it is possible that candidate A has already had some experience of selling, and knows some 'tricks of the trade'. He might be assessed highly. Yet we are using the test in this case, virtually as a test of *achievement,* and it is quite possible that candidate A has in fact reached the height of his possible or potential performance. Candidate B may have had no experience of selling whatsoever, and the test is, for him, one of aptitude. Even if he scores lower than candidate A, it is possible that his potential is significantly greater. Thus designers of situational tests must take into account this distinction between achievement and aptitude tests, and endeavour to design tests which discriminate in the same way between different respondents.

This problem of discrimination between individuals in the same way is indicative of a further problem associated with situational tests, that of standardisation. In a paper and pencil test it is possible to achieve a high level of standardisation of conditions in that an identical test is used for all candidates. They will probably all experience the same physical conditions in terms of the room, level of illumination, temperature etc., and the test will be administered by the same person. A very objective system of marking and subsequent comparison is possible, as responses to all questions can be compared, probably without the marker knowing the identity of the respondents. In a situational test the same level of standardisation and objectivity is difficult to achieve. The tester may find one candidate more likeable or attractive than another and be unconsciously influenced by this. Unless each test is videotaped, and carefully compared to each other test, the full range of responses may not be recalled and an overall 'impression' used instead. Similarly the test itself may not be exactly the same for all candidates. Because the majority of these tests are interactive in nature, in that they involve two or more people in some sort of dialogue, the exact sequence of events or pattern of speech cannot be laid down in advance, again only the overall pattern of events. Thus lack of standardisation may lead to problems of comparability between the different testees.

The third method of psychological testing is the use of *projective techniques*. This method is based on the assumptions of psychoanalytic techniques, and is sometimes known as a 'hidden' method of testing. There is a wide range of different projective techniques, but all are based on an assumption that a more accurate assessment may be made of an individual when he is asked 'safe' questions which do not apparently involve him. A very simple example is the use of a Thematic Apperception Test (TAT). This involves the use of a set of pictures which are presented to the respondent, who is then asked to construct a story, often with the additional instruction that he is to imagine himself as the central character. As this is a relatively impersonal, and therefore safe or non-threatening situation, the respondent may put far more of himself into the story than he is probably aware, thereby giving the tester richer insights into his personality, attitudes and so on than he might do if directly questioned on such matters.

The psychoanalytic assumptions behind projective techniques may be clearly observed in the use of word association. This is a simple method with the tester saying a word, and the respondent quickly replying with the first word that comes into his head. It is assumed that this gives a greater degree of freedom to the unconscious mind, as the reply is given without the censorship of the superego coming into force. By starting with very neutral words, this phenomenon is strengthened, as again the perceived 'threat' of the situation is very low. A more structured form of this example may be found in sentence completion exercises, where respondents are required to complete sentences such as the following, again very rapidly, so that the 'uncensored' first response may be captured:

> All women are . . . .
> Selling cars is like . . . .
> My favourite people are . . .

A well known projective technique, although one which is rarely used in a work context, is the Rorschach Ink Blot test. A number of symmetrical impressions, similar to that achieved by a splodge of ink on one side of a piece of paper, which is then folded over, are provided, and the respondent is required to say what they represent. His replies are compared to a set of replies which are published and normalised for certain sections of the population. Again this technique allows the unconscious mind to display its workings in a more unfettered manner than normal, and greater insights may be gained from the respondent than in more conventional methods, such as paper and pencil tests.

The advantages of projective techniques are that they provide a greater depth of information about the respondent, and information about the whole person, rather than specifically his intelligence or personality, as a paper and pencil test might do. Because of the oblique or 'hidden' form the test takes, it is significantly more difficult for the respondent to 'cheat' by guessing at an appropriate or favourable response.

There are, however some formidable disadvantages concerning the use of such methods, particularly in a work context. The first is that such methods are costly, since the testing is not only done on a one-to-one basis, but also requires test administration to be carried out by a qualified psychologist. Many organisations cannot afford the full-time services of such an individual, and so consultants have to be brought in periodically to administer this part of the selection process. A second disadvantage is an ethical one, as it involves the extent to which a *prospective* employer, let alone an actual employer, has a right to the insights into an employee which projective techniques provide. It might be argued that an employer should content himself with overt behaviour, without requiring access to the unconscious mind of his employees and prospective employees.

This ethical aspect of projective techniques leads us to consider the ethical implications of psychological testing in general. Most people would argue that tests, like any part of a selection procedure, should be 'fair', and in the preceding sections the importance of the administration of tests and the standardisation of procedures has been discussed. Yet it is possible that certain tests and certain conditions discriminate unfairly against certain groups. Let us be quite clear, however, psychological tests are *designed* to discriminate between individuals, and so discrimination, far from being undesirable, is the *raison d'etre* of tests. But psychological tests should be designed to discriminate along clearly laid out lines, such that 'irrelevant' characteristics do not interfere with what is being measured. Thus in giving a personality test such as the 16PF to a number of people, we should be wishing to discriminate between them on the grounds of certain specific personality attributes. Yet it is known that the manner of the tester can have a significant effect on the results of such a test, and thus an 'irrelevant' characteristic may emerge concerning the mood or temperament of the tester on different occasions. Thus standardisation of conditions is vital in psychological testing.

There is some body of evidence which supports the following:

1. Young people tend to be better at paper and pencil tests than older people;

2. Older people tend to be better at situational tests than young people;

3. An aloof tester tends to be associated with lower test scores than a friendly tester;

4. Cheerful respondents tend to score more highly than miserable respondents.

This last example was demonstrated by two groups, with similar characteristics, one of which was asked to write an essay on 'The Best Thing That Has Ever Happened To Me', while the other group's title was 'The Worst Thing That Has Ever Happened To Me'. When the two groups had finished writing their essays, they were asked to take an intelligence test, and the members of the group with the cheerful title consistently scored 4 or 5 points above the members of the group with the depressing title.

It may be, of course, that performance in a cheerful or miserable environment may be a relevant factor to take into account, as may be age, when we are dealing with selection, but in many cases these aspects are acting as discriminators, without the intention or, perhaps, even the knowledge of the tester. Not only is this a waste of time, effort, and potentially valuable employees, it is also, in some situations, illegal. In law it is fair and allowable to assess individuals on their capacity to perform a particular job or to benefit from training in a particular job, but it is unfair and illegal to use assessment methods which are significantly influenced by factors unrelated to the job or training, such as a person's sex or race.

Unfortunately many tests have been devised with a specific population in mind, so much so that there is evidence to suggest that the same test may need to be used in different ways in the North of England and the South of England. If this is so, how can we expect a test to be 'fair' to groups with different ethnic as well as cultural backgrounds? There are a number of tests on the market which claim to be 'culture fair', that is they claim not to give white, middle class respondents a better chance of scoring highly in the test than black respondents. Sadly however, this is not always the end of the dilemma for the conscientious tester, since even where the claim to culture fairness is justified, there is a variety of other ways in which a test may unfairly discriminate among respondents. One such example is in differing levels of 'test-sophistication'. It has been demonstrated that people improve their performance in psychological tests as they become more familiar with them — as they get to 'know the ropes'. This very fact raises the question among testers as to whether high results necessarily reflect a high ability or aptitude in the area being tested, or whether they reflect a high ability, possibly brought about by extensive practice, in doing tests. If the latter should be the case, we are again questioning the validity of such a test.

In the last resort perhaps the only solution, and certainly the most fruitful solution currently available for all concerned with the fair assessment of individuals (be it because of their fear of prosecution or their desire for validity in assessment), is for a thorough analysis of the job or task to be undertaken, such that very clear guidelines are provided concerning the attributes required for an effective performance of such a task. Although this particular aspect is dealt with in greater depth elsewhere, it should be apparent at this stage that any attempt to use a psychological test *without* such a specification of the characteristics of interest and relevance to the tester, would be, at best, futile and, at worst, open to accusations of discrimination of an unfair kind.

Chapter 13

The Interview

The interview has been defined as a *conversation with a purpose*. Not all purposeful conversations between people within organisations are interviews, though many are. In Chapter 8 we look at communication of all kinds. Let us recap briefly the main advantages and weaknesses of the interview as an example of face-to-face communication.

Any face-to-face communication makes immediate feedback possible. One advantage of this is that it allows us to adjust our behaviour when we see the effect it is having upon the person we are communicating with. For example, if we say something that the listener does not fully comprehend, this will be apparent by the words or other behaviour (e.g. puckering of the brow) of the listener. This feedback encourages us to explain the point more fully. Similarly, the speaker may say something which the listener appears not to like. This matter can also be clarified at the time, avoiding the situation where the listener goes away and broods over it.

The human voice is capable of expressing great intensity of feeling, laying emphasis on certain words and phrases. In short, the spoken word, well delivered, is usually far more persuasive than equivalent statements made in writing. Not only can the spoken word be more persuasive, it can also convey more subtle shades of meaning, which most ordinary people find much more difficult to put across in writing.

There is no doubt that, if the matter to be communicated is a delicate or difficult one, oral communication is more effective than the alternative bald written statement. It is possible in an interview to show understanding, support and, perhaps, even sympathy far more effectively than in a form of communication that is not face-to-face.

There are two areas where the interview as a form of face-to-face communication has limitations, which are overcome by written forms of communication. The interview does not allow either party to study at leisure the messages passed between them or to go over them again at a later date. It can be argued that the participants can recall what was said but memories can be notoriously unreliable. In the same vein neither party to an interview has a permanent record of the communication. Both these difficulties are overcome when using written communication. When we look at specific types of interview we acknowledge these limitations and try to minimise their effects during our preparations for, and follow up to, the interview. Before we look at the various types used in organisations, let us consider the conduct of interviews which, irrespective of their purpose, can be broken down into five stages.

The Five Stages of the Effective Interview

The five stages are:

(a) The preparation;
(b) The beginning;
(c) The middle or main body;
(d) The close;
(e) The post-interview.

The importance of preparation cannot be overstated since, if this stage is inadequately done, the chances of an interview being successful are very slender. There are two key points to be noted, which, although apparently obvious, are often forgotten by interviewers.

(i) The interview is a two-way process involving at least two people. The purpose of the interview is the concern of both interviewer and interviewee.

(ii) Although the purpose of the interview is of interest to both parties, the responsibility for achieving what is sought rests mainly with the interviewer. To put it another way, there is no such thing as a bad interviewee. There are interviewees who either intentionally or unintentionally, make the job of the interviewer more difficult. It is up to the interviewer to adapt his behaviour to the interviewee so that the purpose is achieved.

In the preparation stage these two key points mean taking account of the aims, objectives and needs of both parties.

The interviewer must be sure that he is clear about what is to be achieved. Not all interviews have the same purpose or seek to achieve similar objectives. Some are intended primarily for the interviewer to get something across to the interviewee, so that the latter modifies his behaviour in the future. Others have the intention of an exchange of views so that interviewer and interviewee can more fully understand one another's position. Yet another may be set up so that the interviewer can elicit information and opinions. Whatever the purpose, not only must the interviewer be fully aware of it, he must also ensure that the interviewee is equally aware. To do this it is essential for the interviewer to inform the interviewee well in advance of the interview taking place, of the objectives. We are often, as interviewers, prone to assume that the interviewee is equally clear about what we hope to achieve. There is very often no reason at all to believe this. He is not clairvoyant, so why should we expect him to know our intentions unless we tell him? If we give him enough notice of our intentions or objectives then he can prepare himself, and thus be able to contribute more. We will look at this aspect of preparation in more detail with respect to each of the different types of interview.

Once the objectives have been made clear to the interviewee, the interviewer still has some preparatory work to do. Since he is the person who has to be the most adaptive, he should prepare himself. This will be easier when he already knows the interviewee through direct and personal contact. From his previous experience, he can make certain general predictions about expected behaviour at the interview. Where he has never previously met the interviewee, he should obtain all the information he can about him, from application forms and so on. The last part of the preparation stage concerns the physical arrangements. He must ensure that the interview is taking place at a time which is suitable for both the interviewee and himself. Enough time must be allowed. The physical arrangements for the place where the interview is to be held must be conducive to the conduct of a purposeful conversation. Seating and lighting arrangements must be checked, the room should be free from disturbance from noise, such as telephones.

After introductions have been made and the interviewee is seated comfortably, the interviewer must confirm the purpose of the interview and check that this purpose is understood. Where he has never previously met the interviewee he must establish what is known as rapport. In simple terms this means that he must make the interviewee feel comfortable enough to contribute in a fairly relaxed way to the conversation. He must therefore avoid exhibiting any behaviour which will arouse anxiety or hostility. This can be very difficult with certain types of interview. In the process of establishing rapport it is common for the interviewer to explain his own role. He will also often ask the interviewee to confirm or run through certain factual, uncontentious information. In this way he gets the interviewee to speak on a subject that is quite neutral and unthreatening. The physical action of speaking usually 'loosens up' the interviewee.

In the main body section he will guide the interviewee through the areas to be covered. The responsibility for keeping to the point rests squarely with him. This may be relatively easily achieved where he is doing most of the talking, for example in a disciplinary interview. It is more difficult where one is trying to obtain information or opinion from the interviewee, who should thus be doing most of the talking.

Some general comments can be made about the fourth stage of the process, that is the end of the interview itself. Firstly, the interviewer must make it clear that the conversation is drawing to a close. He must also ensure that the interviewee feels he has had a good chance to express himself and must give him the opportunity to raise any relevant matter which he considers outstanding or inadequately covered. He will often summarise what has been said and seek confirmation as to the accuracy and completeness of the summary (this will rarely happen in the selection interview). Finally, in all types of interview at this stage in the process, he must inform the interviewee what is to happen next; when this action is to take place; and, where necessary, how the interviewee will be contacted or informed. It is essential that when the interviewee leaves he knows what arrangements have been made.

The post-interview stage, which is the fifth stage in the process, is unfortunately often dealt with in a very cursory manner, and yet it is the part which provides the end results. It is at this stage that the contents of the interview are evaluated. The interviewer considers what was said and determines what form the subsequent action will take. In the case of a selection interview this may be to proceed or not with the candidate's application, whilst, in the case of the exit interview, it may mean putting into operation some remedial action to try to reduce labour turnover.

Since we defined an interview as a conversation with a purpose, it is at the fifth stage that the conversation is evaluated to establish whether the purpose has been achieved. Very often this will require some subsequent action, which we also include in this stage. The follow-up action may take place over a long period, as in the case of evaluating the effectiveness of the selection interview. Alternatively, the follow-up action may take place quite quickly, as in the case of a disciplinary hearing, where a note of the interview may be recorded.

Types of Interview

The seven most common types of interview are:

1. The selection for employment interview;
2. The performance appraisal interview;
3. The interview used for seeking information about jobs, i.e. job analysis interviews;
4. The counselling interview;
5. The grievance interview;
6. The disciplinary interview;
7. The exit interview, in which the interviewee is an employee who is about to leave.

THE INTERVIEW

The selection for employment interview

There are three aspects to the preparation stage of the selection for employment interview; the candidate preparation, setting preparation, and interviewer preparation. (We have considered these in Chapter 11.)

The second stage of the selection interview process is the beginning of the interview itself. Firstly, the interviewer must introduce himself and welcome the interviewee. Secondly, the interviewer must set the scene for the interview, confirming the arrangements, (especially where the selection process is to include more than just the interview), restating its objectives, noting the mutual nature of the exercise. He must also check that the interviewee understands what is required for the job, from what he has read in the job description. Thirdly, during this stage, he is attempting to establish rapport between the interviewee and himself. Different interviewers use a variety of techniques for establishing rapport. Using the information provided on the application form as a starting point, it is quite common for him to ask the candidate to talk about some fairly uncontentious, factual matters about himself, like his job history to date. Whilst this confirms the information on the application form, its main function is in getting the interviewee to talk, and, in so doing, starting to make him feel more relaxed.

The interviewer will seem interested in what the interviewee is saying, which aids the establishment of rapport. As rapport is developed he starts to move the interview from the second stage to the third stage of the process, i.e. to the main body of the interview.

The main body is characterised by his probing the interviewee in an attempt to find out whether he could do the job, would want to do the job, and is not prevented from doing the job. He will be following through the lines of questioning he planned in the first stage of the interview; he will also be evaluating the answers the interviewee gives on the basis he decided upon in the first stage. In the main he will be asking the interviewee to give opinion rather than providing factual information, most of which should have been obtained from the application form. To obtain these opinions he will ask what are termed *open-ended questions*. Open-ended questions are the kind that give the interviewee the chance to give a full and comprehensive answer, expounding his views or opinions. Examples of this type of question are: 'How would you deal with this sort of situation?' or 'What is your opinion on this subject?' There is experimental evidence to show that the interviewer, by his reactions to the interviewee's statement of opinion, can significantly affect the amount of comment the interviewee is prepared to make. If he seems to agree with what the candidate is saying, this encourages the latter to give more opinions or 'value judgement' comments. Conversely, where he shows no reaction or disagrees with the stated opinion of the interviewee, the number of opinions given declines significantly. Since he normally wishes to gain some insight into the personality and attitudes of the applicant, through the opinions and views he expresses, he should generally react positively to the views expressed.

It is not easy, for the interviewer must guide the interview so that the areas of interest to him are covered, and prevent the conversation digressing into areas which he sees as of little or no relevance. At the same time he is attempting to evaluate the answers, comments, opinions, and apparent disposition of the interviewee, within a limited time.

The fourth stage of the selection interview is when the concept of mutuality should be realised. The interviewee should be invited to ask any questions he may have, or to bring up any subjects or aspects of subjects which he feels should be discussed. Having satisfied the enquiries of the candidate, the interviewer must draw the conversation to a conclusion. He will do this by thanking the applicant for attending, and informing him about the subsequent stages of the selection process, and at what time and by what means he will be informed of the outcome of the process.

The post-interview stage has two components, assessment and evaluation. *Assessment* takes place immediately after the interview has been concluded, and whilst recollections of what has just transpired are still fresh in the interviewer's memory. He reviews the interview, drawing up notes of what was said and what was deduced or inferred. Interviewers will very often use the seven point plan as the basis for this assessment. This is logical, since the decision to be made is not whether the interviewer liked, or even approved of the applicant, but whether he is a suitable person to perform the job to be filled. He will compare his assessment of the candidate characteristic by characteristic with the personnel specification. We can use the analogy of the personnel specification as a 'photofit' picture of the type of candidate being sought, whilst the interviewee is compared with this picture, feature by feature. The interviewee who most closely fits the requirements of the person specification, provided he is successful in respect of any other selection devices used, should be offered the job.

Evaluation takes place both immediately after the interview is concluded and over a longer period, in the case of successfully-appointed applicants. As soon as the interview is over the interviewer should consider how well it went. In other words, he should evaluate his own performance. The part of evaluation that takes place over a longer period is confined only to the instances where the interviewee is appointed. By appointing the applicant it is implied that the interviewer, through the process of the interview has made a prediction that he will be a successful employee. This prediction may be made with some slight reservations. For instance, the interviewer may feel the applicant is slightly deficient in one area, when compared with the person specification. This point will have been noted in the assessment. The evaluation process involves checking how accurate the interviewer's assessment was at the time of the interview, compared with the actual performance of the individual as an employee. This can only be achieved after the employee has worked for long enough for his performance to be appraised. When the employee has been appraised, the interviewer's notes should be checked to see whether he was able to predict future performance accurately. If his predictions are consistently inaccurate, this may be for one or both of two main reasons, which should be investigated. Either he is working against an inappropriate yardstick, i.e. the person specification does not accurately specify the type of applicant who should be sought, or he lacks competence (see Figure 28).

The performance appraisal interview

The exact form of the preparation stage for an appraisal interview will vary with the different systems of appraisal used, though, like the selection for employment interview, it will involve preparation of the interviewee, the interviewer, and the setting.

The preparation of the setting will be the same as that for the selection interview. The preparation of the interviewee, however, will be different. In this case the interviewer and the interviewee will be known to each other, although they may have different perceptions of the objective of the interview. It is the responsibility of the interviewer to be sure that not only is he himself clear on the objectives but that the interviewee has the same understanding. Since the interview will inevitably be based on the performance appraisal document and the job description and specification, it is essential that these are clearly understood by both participants. The responsibility for this again rests with the interviewer.

In his preparation the interviewer will plan the way in which he:

(a)   intends to check that the appraisee understands the objectives, intentions, and consequences of the appraisal interview;

(b)   will communicate his review of the appraisee's performance;

(c)   will discuss areas of weakness in the appraisee's performance, without demotivating his future performance;

(d)   will obtain the appraisee's view of his strengths and weaknesses so that the strengths can be built upon in the future and the weaknesses can be objectively analysed and improved.

175

The beginning of the appraisal interview will almost always take the form of confirming the purpose of the interview and explaining the documentation used. The interviewer must appreciate that the appraisee may be apprehensive and should do all he can to relieve his tension. In this state of mind, he will not be receptive to what is being said.

The middle or main body of the interview will take the form of a discussion of the appraisee's performance in specific areas. The interviewer will review specific areas of performance, explaining how each has been asssessed. To do this he must outline the criteria used to assess performance, should avoid 'fudging' issues, particularly those which may be criticisms. Every criticism should be followed by some diagnosis of the circumstances that resulted in the deficient performance, and some agreement between the parties of how the problem could be remedied, or at least ameliorated. If the appraisee feels that the interview is a positive conversation in which genuine attempts are being made to resolve difficulties, he is less likely to become defensive about his performance, and more likely to be receptive to suggestions of change. If, alternatively, he views the conversation as being primarily unconstructive criticism, he will psychologically avoid the situation.

The responsibility for creating and maintaining a positive approach to the appraisal rests with the interviewer. A method sometimes used to achieve this is to sum up the discussion in a positive way after each performance area has been discussed. In the case of an area of performance in which the appraisee is strong, the interviewer will confirm the strength and congratulate the appraisee. For an area of weakness he will sum up by confirming what positive steps will be taken to remedy the weakness, after the problem has been identified and discussed.

At the close, the interviewer ensures that there is nothing that the appraisee feels is still outstanding and in need of discussion, and then sums up actions agreed.

As with the selection for employment interview, the post interview stage is of critical importance. If the process of appraisal is to have any credibility, it is essential that whatever is agreed during the course of the interview is implemented afterwards. This may take the form of training, development, transfer, or promotion for the appraisee.

The job analysis interview

Increasingly, in large organisations, this type of interview is conducted by specialist job analysts. The interview, which is just one of the techniques used in job analysis, may take place between the analyst/interviewer and either a job incumbent or a job incumbent's immediate supervisor, or any other person who may throw light upon the duties and responsibilities involved in the job to be analysed.

The preparation stage will involve referral to any other job analysis data available for the job in question. Whether this is available will depend upon whether any other techniques have already been employed. The formal relationship between the job and others should be checked, although it must be recognised that such formal organisation structures often do not represent accurately the way the organisation actually functions.

The analyst will inform the interviewee of the purpose of the interview, there being many reasons for conducting job analysis; including reasons associated with recruitment and selection, training, and job evaluation. Arrangements must be made for conducting the interview, which will sometimes be arranged to take place in the work place itself. This is sometimes helpful, since it enables explanations of duties to be demonstrated or supported by reference documents or equipment which are readily available in the work place. The disadvantage is that the environment may not be conducive to conversation, particularly in a workshop or noisy office.

To begin, the interviewer/analyst confirms the purpose. It is usual for the interviewer to stress that it is primarily the job that is being considered and not the job incumbent, particularly in the case of job analysis interviews conducted for the purpose of job evaluation.

The main body of the interview will take the form of questions about the job. This will normally follow a description of the duties and responsibilities of the job provided by the interviewer. He may use the method of *critical incident* to get the interviewee to concentrate on certain aspects of the job. His role is relatively passive, merely prompting the interviewee or seeking clarification of points which are unclear to him. He will always be taking note of what is said.

The analyst will close by running through the main points of the job, as he has recorded them, and confirming that he will be drawing up a more detailed report, the contents of which he will confirm with the interviewee. When the analyst returns to discuss his full report, it will provide the interviewee with an opportunity to add any other points which he may have recollected or which may have been omitted.

The post-interview stage involves drawing up a full description and/or specification for the job concerned. As noted above, the accuracy of these documents must be confirmed with the interviewee.

The counselling interview

The counselling interview may be defined as helping the interviewee to help himself. Counselling interviews may be carried out by all types of employee but are most commonly conducted by supervisors, welfare officers, and personnel specialists. They were brought to the attention of management through the Hawthorne studies, referred to in Chapter 2. They may not be confined exclusively to problems the employee is experiencing at work. The essence of the interview is that the employee who perceives himself as having a problem can discuss it in confidence. It is important that he has confidence in the counsellor as a fellow human being, and that whatever is discussed will be treated as confidential.

By its very nature, it will often be impossible for the counsellor to do much preparation, save obtaining what information he can about the general circumstances, both at work and outside, of the employee. Even this will only be possible if he has some prior warning.

The beginning of the counselling interview is critical. The counsellor must encourage the employee to feel that he is dealing with a sympathetic person so that he will start to relax and feel free to speak.

The middle or main body of the interview is essentially non-directive with the counsellor neither agreeing nor disagreeing with what the employee says, but listening and asking neutral questions which seek to encourage an analysis of the problems. His skill is to establish empathy, encouraging the employee to look clearly at what he sees as the problem and to come up with his own form of solution to it. He should very gently guide the employee towards solutions, or at least a perspective of the problem, which are both practicable and satisfying.

The close may occur fairly naturally with the employee summing up what he has said and how he perceives the situation. In these circumstances, this may be an indication that the purpose has been achieved. Alternatively, the counsellor may have to sum up what has been said and suggest some lines of thought for the employee, rather than suggesting specific courses of action. The counsellor should give the clear impression that further conversations on the same, or on any other subject, would be welcomed.

Whether there is a formal follow-up stage to the interview will depend, at least in part, on the relationship established during the interview between the employee and the counsellor. The counsellor should avoid taking any action, or even raising the matter again, if there is an appreciable chance of the employee misinterpreting this as interference in what is essentially his own problem.

The grievance interview

There is a requirement, stated in the Employment Protection (Consolidation) Act 1978, that when individual employees are given the statement of their main terms and conditions of employment, they should also be made aware of the *grievance procedure* arrangements within the organisation. The grievance procedure is the mechanism through which an individual employee raises with his employer matters where he feels personally aggrieved or improperly treated. The procedure for dealing with these matters will usually state that in the first instance the employee should bring the matter to the attention of his immediate supervisor. If the outcome of this interview does not satisfy the employee, mechanisms usually exist for further interviews to take place with other members of management in attempts to resolve the grievance. These interviews are generally known as *grievance interviews* and must be considered separately from counselling interviews, since they form a part of formal arrangements within the organisation which have often been the subject of agreements between management and the employees' representatives.

The preparation stage from the point of view of the interviewer will involve obtaining as much background knowledge as possible about the particular grievance being raised. Both the interviewer and the employee who feels he has a grievance should ensure that they have checked through agreements, both procedural and substantive between the organisation and its employees, to ensure that none of these covers, or significantly affects, the matter under discussion.

The interviewer usually begins by giving a brief resumé of the organisation's procedure for dealing with grievances. The employee, who may be accompanied by his representative or shop steward, then states the nature and details of his grievance.

The main body of the interview is a discussion of the problem and consideration of possible methods of resolving it, to the satisfaction of all parties concerned. All parties to the discussion will be aware that the manner in which the problem is resolved may have implications and precedents for employees other than just the individual concerned. If the matter to be resolved could have such implications, the decision has to be jointly made whether this particular problem should be resolved on a once-off, ad hoc basis, in which case both parties will agree that it does not bind their future conduct, or whether they wish to embody the arrangements in a formal agreement, which will affect their future conduct.

At the close, the interviewer confirms what has been agreed and how it will be put into operation. In the event of the interview not resulting in agreement, he outlines the next stage of the grievance procedure and how the employee should avail himself of it, if he wishes.

The follow-up stage may simply implement the decision made during the interview, and, in some cases, make arrangements for a formal agreement (oral or written) to be established.

ASSESSING AND MONITORING EMPLOYEES

The disciplinary interview

Just as there is a legal requirement for a grievance procedure, so there is a similar requirement for a *disciplinary procedure.* Moreover, like the grievance procedure, the disciplinary procedure will involve a number of stages, most of which will themselves require an interview to take place between some member of management (the interviewer) and the employee in connection with whom disciplinary action is being considered (the interviewee). Once again, the employee is likely to be accompanied by his representative or shop steward.

To prepare for a disciplinary interview the manager should acquaint himself with the circumstances which led to the alleged contravention of organisation rules. He must satisfy himself that he has no doubt, on the information available to him that the employee concerned is in breach of organisational rules or procedures, to such an extent as to justify the contemplation of disciplinary action. Where the interview pending is a second or subsequent stage of the disciplinary procedure, the manager must satisfy himself that earlier stages were properly conducted and properly recorded. Finally, in preparation the manager must ensure that the employee is fully aware of the nature of, and reason for, the forthcoming interview and has been encouraged to seek the representation of his shop steward. The manager will be responsible for arranging an appropriate time and place and for informing the employee.

To begin, the manager will explain the purpose of the interview and the disciplinary procedure as a whole, noting the stage at which the current interview occurs. Details of the alleged breach of discipline will be explained and also that the interview is the opportunity for the employee to state his point of view and raise any matters which he, or his representative, consider pertinent. By this stage sufficient investigations should have been made for the facts of the incident to be established.

The main body of the interview will be concerned with providing the employee with the opportunity to state his position and introduce any factors which he considers should be taken into account in mitigation. The manager should note what is said by the employee, or his representative; seek further information or clarification, where he feels this is useful or necessary; and finally, take account of what has been said, to reach a decision on the disciplinary action. (The sanctions available to the interviewer should be clearly stated in the disciplinary procedure.)

At the close, the manager should restate the disciplinary procedure and explain the stage currently in operation. He will then inform the employee of the disciplinary action which is to be taken. He must then go on to advise the employee of his right to appeal and the way in which he should go about exercising that right, if he so wishes.

The follow-up stage to a disciplinary interview requires that the manager make a detailed record of what occurred and the decision reached. Secondly, the manager must carry out the disciplinary measures to be imposed, provided no appeal is pending.

The exit interview

Exit interviews take place when management wish to find out employees' reasons for leaving.

As usual the interviewer prepares by arranging an appropriate setting. He should also find out all he can about the employee: how long he has worked for the organisation; the kind of jobs he has done; his pay rates; his performance record; and any other data which will help to provide a detailed picture.

The interviewer begins by explaining clearly the purpose of the interview and requesting the assistance of the employee, stressing that anything discussed will be confidential.

The main body of the interview will probably be fairly highly structured, at least to start with. He will ask open-ended questions, attempting to elicit not only the employee's reasons for leaving, but also his feelings towards procedures and methods of working in the organisation.

In the follow-up stage the interviewer makes a detailed record of what has been said, and relates this to what is known of the employee's experience. So, for instance, if the interviewee has made critical comments on the payment system, the details of the system which have been applied to him should be recorded, along with his comments.

Since each exit interview is made up essentially of the opinions of one employee, it will be subject to individual bias. Enough should be conducted for a general, 'unbiased' picture to be obtained. The information should then be analysed to see whether action to change any aspects of the organisation's structure, procedures, or operations should be considered. In short, the management are asking employees who are leaving, 'What is it that you like and, more particularly, dislike, about this organisation?' Only when management have found out what it is that leaving employees do not like, can they even consider whether they wish to change anything.

Chapter 14

Human Resource Planning and Control Techniques

PERFORMANCE APPRAISAL

Performance appraisal is defined as *the judgment of an employee's performance in his job. Whilst this will include the evaluation of the output of work of the employee in quantitative and qualitative terms, it will not be confined solely to this.*

The Objectives of Performance Appraisal

The main general objective of performance appraisal is to maximise the efficiency of the organisation by trying to get the best out of all the employees who work within it. The achievement of this objective is assisted by the following action being taken for each employee:

(i)   Communication to each employee the way his performance is judged by his superiors;

(ii)   Discussing with the employee his strengths and weaknesses in the performance of his existing job;

(iii)   Identifying training and development needs of an employee which would make him more effective in his existing job;

(iv)   Identifying an employee who is either ready for promotion, or has potential for promotion within the organisation;

(v)   In some cases, identifying the performance or level of performance for which the employee may be further financially rewarded (i.e. for determining salary reviews).

We can see from these points that performance appraisal is an important personnel practice which can be used for many types of employee, not only for those who are paid on a time rated basis, although the technique is most commonly used for such employees.

Methods of Performance Appraisal

There are a number of methods of performance appraisal, but here we will consider only the most commonly used method, which is known as *rating*.

In the rating method, performance is assessed against specific factors which are considered essential to the efficient performance of the job. The individual's performance is rated against each of these factors in turn, using a scale of performance (say a five point scale ranging from 1 — signifying unsatisfactory performance, to 5 — signifying excellent performance). An overall composite rating for the performance in the job as a whole may be derived. When compiling the factors to be assessed for any job it is essential to:

(i)   Avoid overlap between factors;

(ii)   Avoid using factors which cannot be assessed objectively;

(iii)   Ensure that the whole job is covered by the factors;

(iv)   Ensure that the factors can be used to discriminate between various levels of performance, i.e. can the factor discriminate between good and bad performance?

(v)   Ensure that the factors can be uniformly understood;

(vi)   Ensure that the relative weightings of the factors are clear.

The kind of factors which are often included are:

(i)   Knowledge of the job — How well does the worker know all the aspects of the job he is employed to do?

(ii)   Judgment — If the job calls upon the worker to make judgments and decisions in the course of his work, how good is his judgment? Does he usually make the right decision?

(iii)   Initiative — If the job requires that the worker show initiative, how well does he do this? Is he prepared to take the initiative or does he always have to be told what to do and how to do it?

(iv)   Accuracy — Some jobs call for a high degree of accuracy, for instance an accounts clerk who is making out invoices. This factor is used to assess how accurate the employee is in his work — does he make mistakes?

(v)   Reliabililty — This factor is used to assess how dependable the worker is;

(vi)   Management or supervision — This factor is used only where the employee supervises other workers. It is used to assess how effective he is as a supervisor; to measure whether he is able to motivate and control his subordinates so that they achieve their objectives;

(vii)   Output — This factor is designed to assess the quality and quantity of actual work produced by the individual. This may be difficult to quantify;

(viii)   Communication — This factor is used to assess the capability of the worker in communicating with subordinates, colleagues, superiors, customers, suppliers, etc. It attempts to measure how able he is in getting himself understood by others, using the spoken and written word;

(ix)   Relations with others — How well does the worker get on with other people? Is he an asset to the workforce or is he a disruptive person?

By just looking at these factors we can see that their importance (or weighting) will vary between jobs. For instance the factor of communication will be critically important in the job of teacher, but of far less importance in the case of a bus driver.

The strengths of this method of appraisal are:

(i)   It identifies the separate job performance elements which make up the whole job;

(ii)   Performance is expressed in a quantitative and standardised form which should help consistent rating amongst assessors;

(iii)   It is seen as practical and related to the job by the appraisee;

(iv)   It should be fairly easy to administer.

The weaknesses of this method of appraisal are:

(i)   It may be difficult to determine the relative weightings of factors within the job;

(ii)   The relative weightings of factors will vary from job to job, thus making overall comparisons difficult;

(iii)   The terminology used with respect to each factor must be well defined so that different appraisers understand that they are evaluating the same features;

(iv)   To ensure (iii) above, appraisers must be given exhaustive training in the system to attempt to ensure consistent standards;

(v)   Despite training, appraisers tend to bunch their results, often avoiding extremes of scales;

(vi)   The method is highly subjective.

The Procedure for Conducting Performance Appraisal

There are three main stages to the procedure for conducting performance appraisal. These are: report, communication, and follow-up. Each stage may be subdivided into parts.

(a) *Report Stage.* The report stage will always be undertaken by the appraiser. In some cases the appraisee may also draw up a report. These reports will then probably be exchanged before the communication stage so that each party to the appraisal is aware of the other's thinking.

The report stage involves:

(i) The compilation of details relating to the appraisee, to include:

name

age

qualifications

training received to date in the job

time that the appraisee has been in the job (there must be some minimum time before which appraisal will not be conducted)

time that the appraisee has worked for the organisation;

(ii) The compilation of details relating to the appraiser(s), to include:

name

position (i.e. job title)

training received in appraisal system

time that the appraiser has been the manager or supervisor of the appraisee (there must be some minimum time before which appraisal will not be conducted)

details of other superiors involved in appraisal;

(iii) Consideration of the job description and job specification with note taken of any changes that have occurred since the last appraisal;

(iv) The collection of data and information relating to the appraisal.Wherever possible this information should be specific rather than general;

(v) The assessment of performance to include an overall assessment where individual factors are being considered. The assessment of performance must relate to the information collected in (iv) above;

(vi) Specific notes on strengths and weaknesses of appraisee;

(vii) Notes on action to be considered to fulfil potential and/or correct weaknesses of the appraisee;

(viii) Notes on promotability of appraisee (when applicable) to include details of when he will be ready for promotion and any action required to prepare him;

(ix)   Notes on any salary revision considered as a result of performance during preceding period.

(b) *The Communication Stage.* The communication will take the form of an interview. It is important in the case of this interview that both parties are aware of, and agree on, the objectives. In broad terms they are to discuss the performance of the appraisee, to review that performance, and agree, where possible, ways in which that performance may be improved for the benefit of the organisation and the appraisee. To achieve these objectives it is essential that the interview is carefully prepared and planned, the responsibility for this rests mainly with the appraiser. To maximise the chances of the objectives of the interview being achieved the appraiser must ensure that:

(i)   Both parties have adequate time to prepare for the interview;
(ii)   The interview setting and timing is appropriate;
(iii)   Both parties know what form the interview will take and its objectives;
(iv)   Both parties are familiar with the details of the appraisal system being used;
(v)   Both parties should understand the affect upon career, training, salary etc. that the appraisal will have.

Only in this way will both parties be able to make useful contributions.
In respect of the conduct of the interview, the appraiser must ensure that the appraisee is relaxed and appreciates that the interview is to be conducted in a positive way, encouraging mutual exchange of views. (Under no circumstances should the interview be associated with any disciplinary procedure.) The appraiser should build the interview on the strengths of the appraisee, but avoid glossing over the weaknesses and thus misleading the subordinate. No deficiency should be referred to vaguely, the appraiser should be able to provide concrete examples. No weakness should be noted without being discussed and some form of action agreed. As agreements are reached, the appraiser should record them point by point throughout the interview, with a summary at the end. Any specific outcomes of the appraisal should be made clear to the subordinate and the appraiser must check to ensure that these are understood before the interview is brought to a close.

(c) *The Follow-Up Stage.* Only through effective follow-up (promotion, training, salary review etc.) will the appraisal system have any credibility. Follow-up actions may be outside the direct area of control of the appraiser, in which case he should make tentative arrangements prior to the appraisal interview so that the agreed action can be confirmed at the interview. The onus is upon the appraiser to monitor the follow-up action and ensure that it occurs.

MANAGEMENT BY OBJECTIVES (MbO)

Definition. The Phrase Management by Objectives has been used to mean two different concepts. Firstly, it is used to describe a particular approach to the running of a business; secondly, it is used to describe a particular method of performance appraisal (used mainly for management performance appraisal). Whilst it may be argued that the first concept should inevitably embrace the second, the use of the approach merely for performance appraisal purposes has rarely, if ever, been successful.

A definition put forward by J.W. Humble (1972) is: *'Management by Objectives is a dynamic system which seeks to integrate the company's need to clarify and achieve its profit and growth goals with the manager's need to contribute and develop himself'.*

Management by Objectives may be viewed as four progressive stages:

(i)   Preparation of objectives;
(ii)   Agreement of objectives;
(iii) Performance of organisation and individuals;
(iv)   Review of performance against agreed objectives.

As noted in the definition above, business organisations are dynamic by nature; it is essential that the 4 stages are not seen as discrete events taking place at particular points in time, but rather that they are viewed as ongoing and developing activities.

Preparation of objectives

The directors of the organisation determine and clearly state the objectives of the organisation as a whole. From this it is suggested that directors should establish objectives for every area which directly affects the survival and prosperity of the organisation. The central objectives must be to maximise the long term return on resources employed, and to this end corporate strategies and plans will be directed.

Once a strategic plan is established, supporting tactical plans can be derived in such areas as organisation changes, product/market developments, allocation of financial and physical resources, and operational tasks (see Chapter 4). These plans will be formulated in terms of objectives. It is from these objectives that individual objectives will be derived. Therefore, for example, the *general tactical plan objective* may be to increase the organisation's market share by x% in the next year. This will be translated into individual objectives for different senior managers; so the Production Manager will be required to manufacture more; the Marketing Manager to sell more; and specific *targets* will be set to meet the objectives.

Agreement of individuals' objectives

The formulation of individual objectives may be considered in 6 steps:

(a)   The Superior communicates the *objectives of his own job* to his subordinates. Ideally this should be done at a single meeting of the superior and all subordinates so that each can understand where his own job fits into the overall arrangement of jobs and objectives. Moreover, it is implied that the objectives of each subordinate will be derived from those of the superior and that the total of all subordinates' objectives will be a major contribution to the achievement by the superior of his own.

(b)   The superior and subordinate confirm that they both have the same understanding of the contents of the subordinate's *job description*. This may seem to be an unnecessary step, but there is plenty of evidence to show that very often superiors and subordinates have quite different perceptions of what the individual (i.e. subordinate's) job is. This, in turn, leads to unrealistic expectations and unwelcome misunderstandings regarding the individual's performance.

(c)   The individual subordinate should identify the *key results areas* in his job, usually between 5 and 8, and agree with his superior that these do in fact constitute the key results areas for the job. *(A key results area is one where excellence of performance by the individual would have an extraordinary impact on the economic results of the organisation, or, conversely, where poor performance would significantly threaten the economic well-being of the organisation.)* The individual subordinate should then suggest targets for himself in each of the key results areas, such that he will maximise his contribution to the fulfilment of the superior's objectives. These targets should be discussed, modified if necessary, and agreed between the individual subordinate and his superior. In these discussions it is the responsibility of the superior to ensure that account is taken of factors like the resources that will be available to the subordinate; the objectives agreed with colleagues of the subordinate; and external factors which may affect the attainability of targets. This discussion between superior and subordinate, during which the individual subordinate's targets are confirmed is a vital part of the whole process, since no individual can be expected to be committed absolutely to a set of objectives unless he has had some part in their determination.

(d) Having agreed targets for each key results area it is next necessary to specify *standards of performance*. This is essential since the targets will be generally unquantified. For example, suppose a key results area for a personnel officer is recruitment advertising, then a target might be 'To choose the best media for regular advertising to achieve optimum results.' This is a general statement of intent, but there are no specified standards of performance against which it will be possible to judge whether the intention has been fully achieved. Each key results target will normally require more than one standard by which performance can be judged; these will probably refer to quantity and quality of performance. The standards set should not be so easy as to require no effort nor so difficult as to be unattainable. They should 'stretch' the individual. Whenever possible, standards of performance should be accurately measurable in terms of ratio, figures, percentages, time etc., and care should be taken that imprecise terminology like 'reasonable' or 'adequate' is not used. To take the example of recruitment advertising, the standards of performance might relate to the average number of insertions for each vacancy and the conversion rate (*number of people employed for every pound spent in the particular medium*) for particular types of job.

(e) Having agreed standards of performance, the next step is for the superior and subordinate to establish a means of *measuring performance*. This will sometimes be apparent from the standards of performance specified, but in some cases it will be necessary to set up a control mechanism to measure performance. The important features of a control mechanism are that it is accurate and provides information in the right form, at the right time. The provision of such a control mechanism must not itself be more costly than the savings resulting from the achievement the control is set up to measure. In the example of recruitment, the control for measuring performance will be obtained from records of expenditure on advertising, records of responses to advertisements, and records of new employees recruited.

(f) The final step in formulating individual objectives is that of establishing *improvement plans*. These specify how the results will be obtained and therefore represent short term objectives. The improvement plans are statements of the action the subordinate is going to take to achieve the objectives already agreed. The subordinate should specify what he is going to do, and how and when he is going to do it. The superior, when agreeing these improvement plans, must satisfy himself that the individual subordinate has adequate resources (human, physical, and financial); appropriate authority to decide on and initiate action; is adequately trained in the methods and techniques he will need to employ; and will be supplied with adequate control information to monitor his own performance. To take the example of the Personnel Officer again, one particular improvement plan, related to the objective already considered, may be to carry out a survey of the media not currently used (TV, radio, posters, direct mail) and produce a report for the Personnel Manager, by a specified date.

Having agreed specific objectives and how their achievement will be measured, the superior and subordinate should agree when reviews will take place. There are no hard and fast rules for this, except to say that 12 months would seem the maximum time any subordinate should go without formal review of his achievement against objectives, and review and reconsideration of objectives and improvement plans. Some areas will require review earlier than this, other objectives may be planned for achievement over a longer period than 12 months and, of course, since the organisation itself is dynamic, factors outside the control of the subordinate and his superior may make review desirable at other times.

Review of performance against agreed objectives

At the end of this period (having met during the preceding 12 months to discuss the progress of the subordinate against his objectives, when appropriate), the superior and subordinate should formally review the latter's performance against the agreed objectives.

Each objective should be considered in turn by reference to the agreed standards and methods of measuring performance, including the short term objectives of the improvement plan, which have not been considered in progress reviews.

When considering objectives that have been fully achieved, the superior and subordinate should discuss whether there was anything to be learned from the methods by which the objective was achieved.

When considering objectives that were not achieved, the superior and subordinate should agree whether this was due to failure on the part of the subordinate; failure caused by the superior providing inadequate support in some way (e.g. failure to give the subordinate sufficient authority or financial resources); or failure due to unforeseen circumstances. In the cases where objectives have not been achieved the discussions should centre on how the objective can be achieved, assuming its achievement is still appropriate (i.e. circumstances have not changed to the extent that objectives need to be significantly modified). In this way the appraisal becomes a constructive assessment, and gives the opportunity for fresh targets to be agreed for the next period. Whilst encouraging an atmosphere of joint decision making on the part of the superior and the subordinate, including decision on the subordinate's progress within the organisation (perhaps the type of training that may be necessary; the readiness for promotion of the subordinate; identification, by reference to specific activities, of the subordinate's strengths and weaknesses), MbO avoids the appearance of being merely a critical judgment of the subordinate by his boss.

PERSONNEL RECORDS

Personnel records provide a picture of the human resources of the organisation, past and present, in quantitative and qualitative terms. They also provide information on how changes in the human assets have occurred.

We use the term human assets intentionally, since clearly employees are just as much assets of an organisation as are buildings and plant and equipment. The main difference between human and other assets is in respect of their disposability, i.e. the employees of the organisation are not owned in the way that other assets are, and cannot be bought and sold in the same way. This does not mean that they are any less important.

Considering employees as assets is most clearly illustrated by the example of professional soccer clubs. Here players are 'owned' in as far as they are bound by contract to a club and are bought and sold. They are just as much assets of the clubs as its stadium. In fact one could argue that they are the most important assets, since the success of the club is almost completely dependent upon their ability, as reflected in their performance. Unlike employees in most other organisations, soccer players can be valued in financial terms, as much as they cost the club to buy or could be converted to cash by being sold. In these days of multi-million pound transfer deals, such human assets are probably of greater financial value than the non-human assets of the club.

The reason for keeping personnel records is to provide the necessary information upon which decision about the use of human resources can be soundly based. There are three main ways in which personnel records provide the information necessary for this decision making:

(i)   by the provision of historical information from which trends can be derived;

(ii)   by the provision of information for computing statistics, in the form of ratios and indices which can be used for future plans;

(iii)   by the provision of control information, which can be used to check whether human resource objectives are being met.

Information provided in this way will assist in the process of human resource planning, which we have previously defined as *the strategy for acquiring, using, improving and preserving the organisation's human resources.*

Personnel Records and Statistics

We should distinguish between personal records and personnel records. Personal records are those *which relate to one specific employee and provide information which is unique or personal to him.* Thus the personal records of an employee would include:

(i)   Name
(ii)   Address
(iii)   Date of Birth
(iv)   Marital Status
(v)   Family details, including next of kin
(vi)   General health and features of health of relevance to his job
(vii)   Date of joining the organisation
(viii) Job title and job grade
(ix)   Job history, both in the organisation and in any previous employment
(x)   The individual's performance appraisal history
(xi)   Individual's rate of pay and pay history
(xii)   The individual's accident history
(xiii)   A record of the training and development the individual has received within the organisation and in any previous employment
(xiv)   The qualifications the individual possesses
(xv)   Any special skills the individual possesses
(xvi)   The individual's expected potential
(xvii) The individual's timekeeping record
(xviii) The individual's attendance record
(xix)   Details of how the individual was recruited
(xx)   The date on which the individual left
(xxi)   The reason for the individual leaving
(xxii) Details of any reference given for the individual.

HUMAN RESOURCE PLANNING AND CONTROL TECHNIQUES

Personnel records are the *total* of all this information *for all the employees.*

To be useful tools for decision making, these records must be kept so that they can be readily analysed, to provide an overall view of the organisation's human resources. Useful headings are:

(i)   Human resource statistics
(ii)   Labour turnover
(iii)   Absence and timekeeping
(iv)   Safety records
(v)   Medical records
(vi)   Pay records
(vii)   Training and development records
(viii) Recruitment records

(i) Human resource statistics

This is the type of information all organisations need and includes the numbers of workers employed; their age structure and length of service structure; and the proportion of men to women in various departments and jobs. Much of the information has to be provided on a regular basis to various government agencies. We can see that information of this sort can be used to assist in decision making in all three ways listed previously. Let us consider an example of each way such information can be used. An example of historical information from which trends can be derived is the record kept of apprentice craftsmen's career patterns. Over a period this will reveal some interesting features — see page 194.

We can derive certain trends from this information; the number of craft apprentices entering craft areas, on completion of their apprenticeship, has steadily declined as the number entering technician areas has increased. This information, in itself, should prompt an investigation into the cause. Moreover, account must be taken of these trends when the organisation considers future needs for craftsmen and technicians, and the sources from which they expect to obtain them.

Human resource statistics are essential for the computation of ratios and statistics for future plans. Ratios can be kept on, for instance, the sales revenue compared to the number of employees. Given a reliable sales forecast for the future, certain labour requirements may be inferred. We will look at the types of correlation and regression and their uses later in this chapter when we consider human resource planning techniques.

Finally, in the provision of control information which can be used to check whether objectives are being met, human resource statistics are essential. Consider the case of an organisation which has to keep a tight control on the size of its indirect labour force (i.e. those workers who are not directly associated with the manufacture of the products). A monthly statistic, provided to management, showing the proportion of indirect to direct workers employed, will be an essential piece of information for control purposes.

Year of completion of apprenticeship	Percentage of craft apprentices on completion of their apprenticeship entering jobs in:		
	(a) Craft Areas	(b) Technician Areas	(c) Other Areas
1969	92	0	8
1970	90	2	8
1971	96	0	4
1972	85	5	10
1973	88	4	8
1974	70	16	14
1975	86	4	10
1976	80	10	10
1977	78	15	7
1978	66	28	6
1979	56	30	14
1980	60	34	6
1981	51	42	7
1982	42	48	10
1983	32	56	12
1984	28	62	10
1985	25	60	15
1986	20	65	15
1987	20	70	10
1988	18	66	16

(ii)   Labour turnover and its measurement

Traditionally, labour turnover is defined as the *severance of employment of workers from the organisation*. There are a number of ways in which workers cease to be employed by organisations:

(a)   The worker's employment may be terminated by the management; i.e. he may be dismissed. (This will include dismissals due to redundancy);

(b)   The worker may retire on attaining the normal age of retirement;

(c)   The worker may die;

(d)   The worker may leave of his own accord.

The first two reasons noted above can be reasonably anticipated by the management. Normally interest in labour turnover centres on the last reason and it is that which we will concentrate upon.

Partly because of the ways that labour turnover is measured, it is easy to fall into the trap of thinking about it in terms of a discrete event, i.e. the worker actually leaving the organisation. To deal with the problem we must take a longer term view of the process which leads up to the worker leaving.

Imagine that you work for an organisation. It is unlikely that you will wake up one morning and suddenly decide that you will leave your job, and that this is the first thought that you have given to the subject. What is much more likely is that you have been considering leaving for some time and something happens, or some combination of events occurs, which finally result in your taking the decision to leave. Let us consider what factors may have led you to think about leaving. You may be unhappy in your work, or you may dislike certain features of the organisation's policies as they affect you. Perhaps you feel you could earn more elsewhere, or that you are disappointed in your career prospects. Possibly your journey to work is an unpleasant one. You may dislike your supervisor or manager. You could have to move your home due to family or domestic circumstances. You might have inherited a fortune, or won the football pools and be about to embark on the life of the idle rich. One thing is almost certain, you will weigh up the situation before you make the decision, and doing this will take some time. Indeed, you may mention to friends and colleagues at work that you are considering leaving. We can conclude that the actual act of leaving is merely the culmination of the process. It is fair to say that the same would apply to most workers who leave their job of their own accord. To put it in general terms we can say that any employee who leaves does so because the desire to stay within the employment of the organisation is not strong enough to overcome the factors which tend to pull him away from it. From the point of view of the management, there is rarely very much they can do to affect the strength of the pull from outside the organisation. Therefore, if they wish to reduce the number of people leaving (i.e. their labour turnover), they can only do so by changing internal features to make the alternative of staying more attractive to their employees. We will return to this theme later when we have considered how labour turnover is measured.

The traditional measure of labour turnover

This is a rather crude method of calculation and is sometimes referred to as the 'crude measure of labour turnover'. It is also the most commonly-used means of expressing labour turnover, and takes the form of the number of leavers expressed as a proportion (normally in terms of percentage) of the average employee strength during a given period, say twelve months. We can express this by the formula:

Rate of Labour Turnover =

$$\frac{\text{Number of leavers during 12 months period}}{\text{Average number of employees during 12 months period}} \times 100$$

To take an example, suppose an organisation employs 240 people at the beginning of the year, and that during the year 50 people leave. The fifty leavers are replaced and an additional twenty people are recruited, giving a workforce at the end of the year which numbers 260. The number of leavers during the 12 months = 50. The average number of employees during the 12 months is the average of the number employed at the beginning (240), and the number employed at the end (260)

i.e. $\dfrac{240 + 260}{2} = \dfrac{500}{2} = 250$

Therefore, the rate of labour turnover = $\dfrac{50}{250} \times 100 = 20\%$

Whilst giving us some information about the labour turnover within an organisation, the traditional measure can be very misleading. To prove this point let us take another example. Let us consider three organisations, each employing 200 workers. They are all in the same area and all have a rate of labour turnover of 52% per annum. If they were all engaged in the same kind of manufacture, we might be forgiven for thinking that they all had the same labour turnover problem. In fact, all they have in common is the same rate of labour turnover, using the traditional method of calculation. Firstly let us look at all three:

Organisations	A	B	C
Number employed at beginning of the year	200	200	200
Number employed at the end of the year	200	200	200
Number of employees leaving during the year	104	104	104

We need to investigate the leavers in each organisation in more detail.

In organisation A, throughout the course of the year, 104 of the employees who were working at the beginning of the year left, and were replaced by 104 new employees who were all still employed at the end of the year.

HUMAN RESOURCE PLANNING AND CONTROL TECHNIQUES

In the case of organisation B, in the course of the first 6 months, 52 people left. As each person left he was replaced by a new employee, but before the end of the year, these 52 new employees had themselves left and been replaced. Therefore, the total number of leavers in the course of the year was 52 (the original leavers) + 52 (their replacements who also left) making a total of 104.

Finally, in organisation C, in the first week of the year two people left and were immediately replaced. Unfortunately, these replacement employees only stayed one week and themselves left, to be immediately replaced by two more new employees. This process continued every week throughout the year, with each new pair of employees staying just 1 week. Therefore, the total number of leavers from organisation C is:

2 in week number 1
2 in week number 2
2 in week number 3
2 in week number 4
2 in week number 5
2 in week number 6
2 in week number 52

making a total of 104 leavers in all.

The three organisations clearly have different problems, and it is reasonable to assume they will probably require different solutions. The first step is to identify that they have different problems in a quick and easy way. One way of achieving this is to use a second calculation in combination with the traditional measure, probably that known as the *labour stability index*. One such index is calculated as follows:

Skill Wastage Rate =

Number of employees with more than 12 months service now   x 100

Total number employed one year ago

Let us apply this formula to each of our three organisations:

Organisation A: $\frac{96}{200}$ x 100 = 48%

Organisation B: $\frac{148}{200}$ x 100 = 74%

Organisation C: $\frac{198}{200}$ x 100 = 99%

197

ASSESSING AND MONITORING EMPLOYEES

By using this labour stability index (Skills Wastage Rate), we can see that the three situations are very different, with C having a very stable workforce, while A's is highly unstable.

By using the two calculations together, i.e. labour turnover and labour stability, a fuller picture emerges. However, these measures merely tell us *what* is happening, they do not tell us *why*. If we wish to take remedial action we must find out why people are leaving. There are four stages to this process:

(a)   Objective Analysis
(b)   Causal Identification
(c)   Review of Personnel Practices
(d)   Investigation of the Local Employment Situation

By keeping personnel records and calculating labour turnover and labour stability, some objective analysis has been done. In addition, it is wise to look at a breakdown of the details of people who have left, looking for common features. For instance, were the leavers all doing similar kinds of jobs? Did they all work in one department, on one shift and so on? We do this so that, if the problem is peculiar to one type of worker, we can home in on that area for further and more detailed investigation. Only through having comprehensive personnel records, which are easily analysed, can we carry out this exercise. Not surprisingly, turnover decreases as length of service increases or, to put it another way, the longer individuals work for an organisation, the less likely they are to leave.

Having carried out an objective analysis of labour turnover and identified the main problem areas, the next step is to attempt to identify the cause or causes (assuming that there will be common causes) for workers in this department, or of this type. The most common way of trying to find out why people leave is to ask them. This is often done at what is known as an exit interview, when a trained interviewer, usually from the personnel department, attempts to find out from employees why they have decided to leave. Contrary to what we might expect, people are often very reluctant to give their real reason for leaving and will often be very evasive. Another approach is to conduct an attitude survey of all employees in the problem area, to find out what it is that they like and dislike about the job, organisation, general environment, etc. In this way it is hoped that a more representative view may be found. It could be argued that the attitude survey will include people who, at the time, have no intentions of leaving. One thing is certain, at some time in the future, one way or another, they will all leave the organisations' employment.

By conducting such interviews and surveys, we hope to be able to identify the organisational practices that need to be improved if labour turnover is to be reduced. The changes may be needed in many areas. Organisations often look very carefully at their recruitment and training, especially their induction training, to see whether improvements will lead to a reduction in labour turnover. Induction training is often given a high priority, mainly because it is during the first few weeks of employment that the new worker is most likely to leave, i.e. before he is socialised into the norms of the organisation.

Finally, although there may be very little that management can do to affect it directly, they should investigate the local employment situation and general environment. This is necessary, since labour turnover is likely to be affected by external, as well as internal factors. So, for instance, if another new employer has moved into the area, he may be attracting away workers from our organisation. As well as maintaining a good level of knowledge about the local labour market, through contact with various agencies (e.g. branches and divisions of the Training Commission), the management of the organisation should keep themselves abreast of other developments which may affect their workers and result in labour turnover. To give a simple example, if the local bus service was reduced, it might make the journey to work for many employees far more difficult, which could lead to some of them thinking about leaving. The management may be able to do something about this, either by approaching the public bus service, or by the provision of their own transport service for their workers.

(iii) Absence and timekeeping records

These are some of the most important and useful records kept on manpower utilisation. If there is work to fully occupy a workforce of 100, but absenteeism of 9% and losses due to poor timekeeping, equivalent to 1% of the total employee hours, occur, to achieve the required levels of output without working overtime, 110 workers will need to be employed. This could push up labour costs by as much as 10% (though it may be less, depending upon payment arrangements). It is important that levels of absence and timekeeping are monitored over time, not only because of the direct expense involved, but also because absence and poor timekeeping may be indicative of a form of industrial malaise within the workforce, which may also show itself in increasingly higher levels of labour turnover.

The normal way or recording absence and poor timekeeping is to express the total employee hours lost through each cause as a percentage of the total employee hours available. Analysis will normally be carried out on the basis of sex, age, department, shift, and frequency and duration of absence.

(iv)   Safety records

Safety records are mainly concerned with the recording of accidents. The information is kept for analysis so that trends or tendencies can be identified and remedial action planned. Once again, it is essential that as many variables as possible should be capable of being analysed. For records of accidents it is not just the personal details of the employee who has the accident which are considered, but also the time of the accident, and its nature. There is an obligation under the Health and Safety at Work Act 1974 for accidents to be recorded and investigated. To give an example, if there is an increase in the number of accidents involving eye injuries and, on further analysis, it is found that these injuries rarely occur to new employees, one conclusion that may be drawn is that new employees are wearing eye protection, whereas longer-serving employees are not. From this it may be concluded that new employees wear the eye protection because great stress is laid upon the use of this equipment, during the induction programme to which they have been recently subjected. A solution may be to reinforce with longer-serving employees the need to wear this form of protection, and may involve some training specifically designed for them.

(v)   Medical records

It is common for medical records to be related to absence and sickness records although, in one significant respect, they are different. Medical records put greater stress on classifying illnesses, particularly those which may be categorised as industrial diseases. Medical records deal with long-term trends in the health of employees as a whole, and of sub-groups of the workforce, like women or men working on particular jobs. These records are also very important in the short-term. Say, for instance, there is a sudden increase in the incidence of skin irritation in a factory. If this is identified soon enough the cause may be traced (it could, for example, be contaminated oil), and remedial action taken, before large numbers of employees contract dermatitis.

(vi)   Pay records

Since the pay structure of any organisation has such important implications on recruitment, industrial relations, costs, and profitability, it is essential that comprehensive records are kept.

The record system, as well as providing the basis for dealing with payroll queries, should be maintained in such a way that it can give a variety of different types of information. It should be possible, through the record system, to monitor the performance of incentive schemes and to analyse what proportion of earnings are being paid as a result of the incentive element. Relative pay rates for groups of workers can be compared over time to detect any changes in differentials. The cost of overtime working should be evaluated through interrogation of the pay record system. Labour costs by department should be available, as well as any variance from budget.

(vii) Recruitment records

Records should be kept of the whole recruitment and selection process starting with records of the number and types of vacancies outstanding. Records of vacancies that have been filled, noting the lead time to fill them, the media used, the cost of filling them, and the selection technique used, will also be kept. It is only by building up these records over a period that the various stages of the recruitment and selection procedure can be evaluated.

The Use of the Computer in Personnel Records

If a personnel record system is to be of any use, the information stored in it must:

(i)   be accurate and up to date;
(ii)   be clear and easily understandable;
(iii)   be capable of quick retrieval and updating;
(iv)   be easily analysed — i.e. the information must be stored in such a way that it can be sorted and compared very quickly.

The last point is probably the one which most clearly shows the superiority of computerised, over manual, systems of records. To demonstrate this point, let us consider a few examples.

Suppose an organisation employs 1000 people in a great variety of jobs, and that their personal details are coded and held on computer records. If management wishes to know the names of all those employees who are due to retire before the year 1995, and the policy is that all employees retire at age 60, the procedure is simple. The computer is merely asked to produce a listing of all employees whose date of birth is prior to 31st December, 1935. This is the simplest type of search operation, where sorting is with respect to one variable only (in this case date of birth). However, more complex sorting is equally easy. Suppose we require a list of all employees under the age of 45 years who had attended a particular training course, who spoke French, and who had worked for the organisation for at least 5 years then, provided that the computer was programmed to do the operation, a list of those who met all 4 criteria would be just as easily and quickly provided. Another type of task, which is easily performed when personnel records are computerised, is the provision of regular management reports, on the state of the human assets of the organisation. For instance, monthly reports on labour turnover and stability by department, or by job type, or any other variable selected, could be readily supplied. The other great strength of computerised systems is that information can be provided on an exception only basis. So, in the previous example, to avoid producing data on departments which are performing satisfactorily, the computer could be programmed merely to produce information for those departments where the rate of labour turnover is above a specified level. To carry out these types of task with manual records would be a significant and time-consuming clerical exercise, which would always have a higher risk of error or omission attached to it.

Because of the nature of the information held on them, most personnel records are treated as confidential. Security is more easily obtained with a computerised system than one based upon manual record systems, which may be scattered. Finally, given a good data base of personnel records, a computerised system can, provided it is correctly programmed, provide human resource planning information in the form of forecasts.

The Data Protection Act 1984 introduced certain principles which are of significance to computerised personnel records. It should be stressed that this law refers only to computerised records, though it may suggest good practice for all personnel records in organisations.

The main principles as applied to personnel records are that personnel data should only be held for lawful purposes, should be relevant but not excessive for those purposes, should be accurate and not kept longer than necessary, and be secure against unauthorised access or alteration.

Potentially one of the most significant principles is that an individual employee should at reasonable intervals and without undue delay or expense, have access to any data held about him and where appropriate have that data corrected or erased.

Having put the case for computerised records, we should not imagine that there is no room for manual systems. Computers work on the principle of the information being input in some coded form, to facilitate sorting. Some information concerning human assets is of such a qualitative type that it does not lend itself to being coded. Such information may be best kept in a manual form. An example is the record of disciplinary actions and the detailed reasons for the action having been taken.

Human Resource Planning Techniques

In this section we will look at some of the simpler human resource planning techniques, concentrating on those which we may call quantitative rather than qualitative in nature. These methods are primarily of the forecasting type and we will consider them under the following headings:

(i)   Work-study based techniques;
(ii)   Techniques based upon extrapolation;
(iii)   Techniques based upon correlation and regression.

Work-study based techniques of manpower planning

When we look at payment by results systems in Chapter 17 we see how a standard time is computed for a job. We can also use this information when trying to forecast the number of employees we will need in the future. Let us consider an example. An organisation makes wooden boxes, which are assembled by hand. Suppose the standard time for assembling one box is five minutes for one operator working alone. Therefore, the rate of assembly is 12 boxes per worker hour. Now, let us assume that the boxes are used to pack products X and Y and that the sales forecast for the year for these two products is 10,000 and 14,000 respectively. To meet this sales forecast the organisation will need to assemble 24,000 boxes. According to our work study data, 12 boxes can be assembled per worker hour, and assuming the normal working week is 40 hours, one worker may be expected to assemble 480 boxes per week. If 24,000 boxes are required, the total labour force needed for this particular operation is 24,000 ÷ 480 = 50 worker weeks. This provides a statement, albeit a rather simplistic one, of the labour required for box assembly. To obtain a comprehensive forecast of the labour needs for the year a similar exercise would have to be carried out for all operations undertaken.

This method of forecasting, which we have described in a very oversimplified form, is dependent upon the availability of a reliable sales forecast, which can be converted to a production forecast. Moreover, this technique can only be applied to jobs where work measurement techniques can be employed or, in the strictest sense, have already been employed.

Techniques based upon extrapolation

Forecasting methods using simple extrapolation predict the growth or decline of a single variable (or set of variables such as ratio) over time. Take a simple example of an organisation manufacturing a single product at a constant annual level of output, over a number of years. If we record the worker hours employed each year, we may be able to extend the graph to forecast the number of worker hours that will be required in future years. (See Figure 29.)

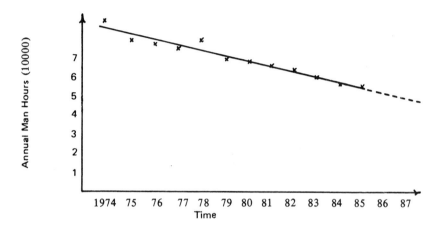

Figure 29 : Example of forecasting by sample extrapolation

We can see that the worker hours used in 1988 were 55,000 and, if we extend the graph, we may expect them to be 52,000 in 1989. From this we can detect that there has been a steady increase in labour productivity over the ten-year period. By extrapolating (i.e. continuing the graph) into the future, we are assuming that the productivity will continue to improve at the same rate. Before we took any action based upon that assumption, we would be wise to check whether anything else has been happening over the last ten years which has caused this steady improvement in productivity. The organisation may have been investing regularly in new plant and equipment, which has facilitated the improved labour productivity. Provided this purchase of new equipment is to be continued in the same way, and at the same rate, then the extrapolation of labour needs could be quite sound. If, alternatively, no more plant and equipment is to be purchased from 1988 onwards, then the probability of the productivity trend continuing is questionable.

204

HUMAN RESOURCE PLANNING AND CONTROL TECHNIQUES

Techniques based upon correlation and regression

Correlation provides a measure of the extent to which the movement in one variable is related to change in another. So, for instance, there may be a strong positive correlation between the number of people employed and the value of the organisation's sales. That is to say that when the sales go up so, historically, has the number of people employed. Equally, as sales have fallen in the past, so the number of employees has fallen. When we say there is a good correlation (a perfect correlation is denoted by a correlation coefficient of 1) we are not saying that a change in one variable causes the change in the other. To take our example, we are not saying that more people are employed because sales have risen, nor are we saying sales have risen because more people have been employed. We are merely noting that the changes in the variables seem to be consistently related. The way we define the nature of the relationship, not merely its strength, is known a *regression*. We will consider here only simple linear regression, by means of an example.

Suppose we are interested in the lead time on recruitment of maintenance electricians from the local labour market. From our records, we may have found that if we plot the time it has taken us to recruit electricians in the past against the level of unemployment in the country as a whole, there is a strong relationship. (See Figure 30.)

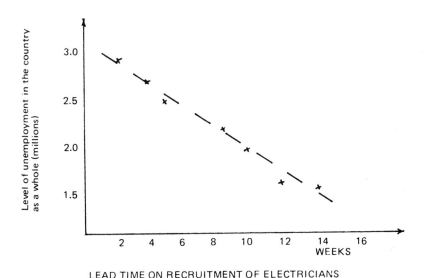

LEAD TIME ON RECRUITMENT OF ELECTRICIANS

Figure 30 : Example of simple linear regression

205

From the graph we can see that, when the level of unemployment was 2 million people, it took us ten weeks to recruit an electrician.

Also there seems to be a *negative* correlation (i.e. as the level of unemployment rises the lead time reduces). The relationship seems to be quite a strong one (i.e. a good correlation). We could check this by calculation, by drawing in a line of *best fit,* (shown as the dotted line). This second calculation is known as *linear regression.* Armed with this information, provided we can obtain some fairly reliable forecasts of umemployment in the economy as a whole, then we will be able to predict how long it will take us to recruit electricians. Let us suppose that we expect to have a number of electricians retiring in 6 months' time and that the level of umemployment is forecast to be 2.5 million. By reference to the line of best fit we could expect the recruitment lead time to be 5 weeks. Therefore, we could start our efforts to recruit some 5 weeks before the need actually arises. This is a gross oversimplification of what would actually be done, but it serves to illustrate the use of regression analysis in forecasting.

For all these simple methods of forecasting it is obvious that a comprehensive data base is required and the ability to analyse and look for possible relationship is essential. These needs are more likely to be met by a comprehensive computerised system of personnel records.

Section 4

Developing Employees

CHAPTER 15 : LEARNING

CHAPTER 16 : TRAINING

So far we have considered some of the devices and techniques used in organisations to assess the differences between individuals and to monitor and plan the effective utilisation of the human resource. Now we will consider the development of the individual's capabilities in ways which meet organisational needs. Chapter 15 provides a background by outlining some of the major theories of learning which underpin traditional techniques, including the concepts of drive, stimulus, response, and reinforcer, and the work of Pavlov, Skinner, and Kohler. Chapter 16 views training as an investment and examines a systematic approach to training, including training methods and the evaluation of training. The Section ends with an overview of management development (which will be further developed in Chapter 22 on organisational change) and of legislation which applies to training.

Chapter 15

Learning

Although it is tempting to relegate the activity of 'learning' to the classroom or the library, learning starts at the moment the normal child is born, and continues throughout adolescence and adulthood until the last days of life. Let us try to imagine ourselves with our past learning wiped out. We would not be able to walk or talk, read or write, use a knife and fork, or drink from a cup, let alone drive a car, or cook, or use a calculator. In other words, we would be like adult-sized babies. So from birth we have been learning — we have found out for ourselves, or someone else has told us, or shown us how to perform an enormous variety of tasks and behaviours.

In order to account for all the different forms and varieties of learning we will use the following definition:

Learning is a relatively permanent change in behaviour that occurs as the result of practice and/or experience

Let us look at some of the implications of this definition. We learn to talk — how to communicate using recognisable and commonly accepted sounds. This is a process which is dependent on practice and experience, so that the language we learn initially depends on the language used by those who have the greatest influence on us. However, the change in the pitch of a boy's voice when he reaches puberty, when his voice 'breaks', is not a learned characteristic — it is inevitable with the process of growing up or 'maturation'. So changes in behaviour which are attributable to maturation are not included in our definition of learning. Similarly changes of behaviour brought about by drugs, or fatigue, or illness, are excluded — it is not accurate to say that someone has learned how to relax since he has been taking a tranquilising drug — again, the process is inevitable.

This definition of learning also alerts us to another major area of interest, and that is the assessment of learning — how do we know that learning has taken place. If you look around a college library you can be fooled quite easily into believing that learning is taking place — people look as if they are concentrating furiously, with deep frown-lines on foreheads, writing vast quantities of notes from books which are piled up around them. However these clues *can* be very misleading — it is often the case that an individual, who *appears* to be concentrating on a knotty problem outlined in the book open in front of him, is in fact just staring at the book unseeingly and is actually working out tactics for Saturday's football match. Perhaps someone who is writing vast quantities of what appear to be notes is in fact writing letters, shopping lists or poetry. So the basic problem concerned with the assessment of learning is that we can never be certain that someone is learning, we can only *infer* that learning has taken place by observing subsequent behaviour change — we can only say that learning has taken place by observing the behaviour changes it produces.

Learning Curves

One way in which we can infer that the learning process is taking place is by testing the learner's level of performance over a particular period. If the learner is engaged in a very simple task, the graph of his performance over time will look something like this:

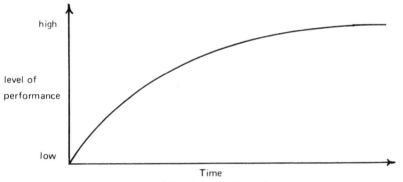

Figure 31 : Simple task-learning curve

As we might have expected, the level of performance appears to be related to learning time, but, possibly contrary to our expectations, this relationship is not a simple, linear one — performance is not improved by equal amounts for each successive equal increase in the length of time spent learning. In other words, you will probably not learn twice as much in two one-hour periods as in one.

There are several reasons why we tend to observe this rapid initial improvement in performance, followed by a flattening of the curve as target performance is approached. Motivation is one very important factor — very often we are more keen and interested in learning something new rather than learning a bit more about something we have done before. Secondly, we often bring some knowledge from our past experience to the new task, but this is usually 'used up' quite early in the learning process, so again we see the sharp initial rise followed by the flattening of the curve as this stock of previous experience is used up.

When we move on to observe more difficult tasks being learned, a different curve may be plotted as indicated in Figure 32:

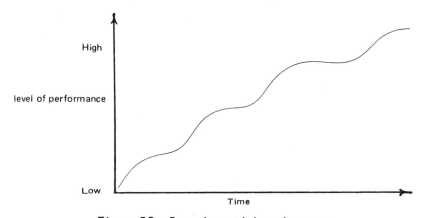

Figure 32 : Complex task-learning curve

We can see that in learning a complex task, the learner is likely to go through several *plateaux* — times when the improvement of the level of performance slows right down. You have probably experienced these plateaux as a student — a time when no matter how hard you tried to work, you felt that you were getting nowhere at all. These are times when a teacher has to be particularly wary and supportive, since the learner is probably feeling anxious about this levelling off of performance and is likely to be low in motivation. The teacher can help by general encouragement, by explaining what is happening and, perhaps, by varying the method of learning until an up-turn in level of performance is reached.

Four Basic Analytical Concepts

When we are looking at any kind of learning process there are four basic concepts which can help us:

Drive

   Stimulus

      Response

         Reinforcer

LEARNING

Drive

We have already mentioned this in connection with learning curves, as drive is the motivation for learning. A drive may be *primary* — unlearned — such as hunger, or *secondary* — learned — such as desire for social status. Our motivation to learn may be based on the primary drive of hunger, such that we are motivated to learn about sources of food to satisfy hunger pangs, or we may be motivated to obtain a particular qualification to satisfy the learned or secondary drive of acquiring social status.

Stimulus

A stimulus is something that evokes a reaction, it is the occasion for a response. The rumbling noise in your stomach is a stimulus to start thinking about food. A speaker turning to you and saying, 'What do you think of this argument?', is a stimulus for you to start speaking.

Response

A response is the behavioural reaction to a stimulus or the behavioural result of stimulation. For example, the alarm clock bell going off is a stimulus, and your response should be to turn it off and get out of bed.

Reinforcer

A reinforcer is any object or event that serves to increase or maintain the strength of a response. Reinforcers, like drives, may be primary or secondary. Food is an example of a primary reinforcer, because we 'know' without learning that food reduces hunger, and that the particular response of looking for food was an effective one — in other words, that response will be maintained or used again. In the same way, secondary reinforcers can be used — if you tell a joke once, and your audience roars with laughter, you are likely to tell it again. We learn that laughter may be a sign of social approval, and thus something we learn to value, and so a response which elicits laughter will be strengthened or maintained.

It is also possible to use negative reinforcement — a discomforting, annoying, or punishing state of affairs which is commonly avoided by the learner. We may avoid certain foods, for example, because we know they cause indigestion.

Receptor processes

If you think about learning to speak, it is a process which is made very much easier by the use of appropriate equipment. Most people are born with a set of apparatus to assist in this learning process — and many others. In learning the word 'cat', a child normally has to combine the - *sound* of the word cat with an object or picture which he can *see*. Similarly the work 'hot' is normally learned by associating a *sound* with *touching* something which is hot. Receptor processes are the various senses which give us information through which we may learn.

There are *seven* receptor processes:

Sight   Smell   Touch   Taste

Hearing   Balance   Kinaesthesis

Let us look at some examples of these receptor processes:-

We can use *sight* in learning by reading, by looking at a picture, or by watching a demonstration.

We can use *smell* in learning to cook, when learning about engines, as it can provide a danger signal.

We can use *touch* in learning the feel of tools, fabrics, of heat and cold.

We can use *taste* in learning to distinguish sweet from savoury, in learning to distinguish Real Ale from the rest.

We can use *hearing* in learning by listening to instructions or answers to questions, or by recognising different sounds in an engine as symptoms of possible engine faults.

We can use *balance* in learning to ride a bicycle, or walk a tight rope, or carry a laden tray.

Probably the only one of these receptor processes you have not already heard of is *kinaesthesis* — this is a muscular sense — muscle tone — which is particularly important in learning a physical skill. If you have ever tried to drive a car when you have 'pins and needles' in your foot, or to drink a cup of tea when you have had your mouth 'frozen' by a dentist — then these are examples of occasions on which your muscle sense or kinaesthesis is impaired.

Thus, the seven receptor processes form the basic equipment needed for effective learning. Now let us turn to an example of learning which illustrates the concepts of drive, stimulus, response, and reinforcer, together with the receptor processes.

Classical Conditioning

Have you ever noticed that if someone is describing a particularly delicious meal, you can often both 'see' it in your imagination and 'taste' it — in other words, your hearing, sight, and taste may combine — often with the result that you salivate at the very thought of it?

I.P. Pavlov (1927), whilst experimenting with the digestive systems of dogs, noticed that they certainly salivated at the *sight* of food, and not necessarily only at the *taste* of food.

Pavlov used this as the foundation of his work to teach a dog to salivate at the *sound* of a bell, and not even at the sight, let alone the taste, of food. The type of learning involved in the process is called *classical conditioning,* and it can be explained by the following steps:

1. A dog 'naturally' salivates at the sight of food. We call this natural or unlearned stimulus of the sight of food the *unconditioned stimulus* (UCS). We call this natural, unlearned or instinctive response of salivation the *unconditioned response* (UCR).
    Diagrammatically Step 1 is UCS $\longrightarrow$ UCR

2. During the learning process a neutral stimulus — a bell — was presented at the same time as the food, and the same response was obtained.

3. After a while the dog learned to associate the sound of the bell with the sight of food, and so it salivated at the sound of the bell alone. The bell had become the *conditioned stimulus* (CS) — it had been learned as the occasion for the response of salivation, and we call this response a *conditioned response* (CR).
    Thus Step 3 may be stated as

    CS $\longrightarrow$ CR.

    Thus classical conditioning is based on learning responses to neutral stimuli, and may be illustrated in three steps.

    1.   UCS $\longrightarrow$ UCR
    2.   NS + UCR $\longrightarrow$ UCS
    3.   CS $\longrightarrow$ CR

There are a number of interesting features which emerge from this simple learning situation:

1. *Timing.* It is vital that the two stimuli which are to be associated occur close together in time. There will be very little learning if the bell is rung two hours before the food is tasted. Similarly, you would not learn to associate drinking too much with a hangover if a hangover occurred a month after you had over-indulged in drink!

2. *Extinction.* When the ringing of the bell is consistently separate from the appearance of food — that is, when there is no reinforcement — the learned response gradually disappears. It is interesting that this lack of reinforcement does not actually destroy the conditioned response, since it often recovers spontaneously after an interval.

4. *Generalisation.* This refers to the process whereby the learner responds in the conditioned manner not only to stimulus of an identical form, but to broadly similar stimuli too. Thus if Pavlov had conditioned his dog to respond to a bell which was similar to an alarm clock bell, generalisation would refer to the process whereby the dog learned to respond to front door bells, Swiss cow bells, and church bells too! This is sometimes referred to as *transfer of learning.*

4. *Discrimination.* This is the opposite of generalisation. Discrimination is a reaction to difference in stimuli — thus in discrimination, Pavlov's dog would react to one very specific sort of alarm clock bell — not any old alarm clock bell.

Classical conditioning is a form of learning which is particularly relevant in early childhood learning and early language learning.

Operant Conditioning

Another form of simple learning is called operant conditioning or instrumental conditioning. It is based on a simple principle — rewarded behaviour is repeated. If, every time you tried to answer a question in class, you were rewarded with sweets, a drink, or money, you would probably try much harder to answer questions in class. Then you might find that rewards were being given not simply for *trying* to answer questions in class, but for giving the correct answer, or a very original answer, for example. If these rewards were very appealing to you, you might be prepared to change your behaviour in such a way as to obtain as many rewards as possible. Thus your behaviour is 'shaped' by the application of rewards.

B.F. Skinner (1938) is the most notable researcher in this area. He used a specially designed cage, a Skinner Box, at one end of which was a lever. Skinner put a rat in this cage and shaped its behaviour by means of food. First of all the rat was rewarded for being near the lever, then it was rewarded when it accidentally knocked into the lever. Eventually the rat learned that there was a connection between the lever and the appearance of the reward and, in time, the rat learned to pull the lever in order to obtain the reward. Thus the rat's behaviour was shaped by careful use of reward or reinforcement.

Animals, as well as human beings have learned to perform very intricate tasks by the application of this method of learning.

LEARNING

Cognitive Learning

So far we have looked at learning in terms of responses to stimuli — and we have conveniently left out any ideas about 'thinking' and 'understanding'. Most of the learning you are concerned with may seem to have little to do with rats in cages, and everything to do with understanding.

Insight learning — or the 'aha!' experience — looks at this very process where everything seems to click into place. Since there is relatively little evidence concerning this sort of learning — remember you can only infer that learning has taken place by observing behaviour change — we can only make a few generalisations.

W. Kohler (1925) studied insight in chimpanzees by placing a short stick within reach of a caged chimp and a bunch of bananas well out of reach. There was long stick a short way from the chimp, but out of his reach. The chimp tried stretching out his arm further and further — but he could not get hold of the bananas. He tried to reach the bananas with the short stick — but still no satisfaction. The chimp sat in his cage, folded his arms, frowned and appeared to be deep in thought. He then suddenly leapt to his feet, grabbed the short stick and used it to drag the long stick closer to him. He then took hold of the long stick and used that to obtain the bananas.

As we said before, the variables which influence this phenomenon of insight are not fully understood, but we can make a few general comments:

1. Insight depends on the *arrangement* of the problem — e.g. where the two sticks and bananas are placed, or whether the problem looks like one you may have tackled before.

2. Once a problem is solved the solution is readily repeatable.

3. A solution achieved with insight is easily applied to new situations.

Thus we can conclude that an effective learner is a person who is adaptable, able to use his past experience in new situations, and who can discover for himself solutions to the problems he has not previously faced.

Chapter 16

Training

In the last chapter we talked about learning which we defined as *a relatively permanent change in behaviour occurring as a result of practice and/or experience.* From this definition we can see that for training to be worthwhile it is imperative that learning takes place. It is important that the outcome of learning results in the individual's improved performance and ability to meet organisational goals. This is more likely to be achieved if the learner's goals are compatible with those of the organisation. In the previous chapter we looked at learner motivation as an important feature in effective learning, let us now turn to the needs of the organisation.

Training as an Investment

Training which we will define as *the purposeful development of the required skills, knowledge, and attitudes in the employees,* should be seen as an *investment* by an organisation in its human resources. In simple terms an investment is money spent now in the expectation of future rewards resulting from the expenditure. An investment is sound if the discounted rewards are sufficiently greater than the original money spent. In such cases there is an adequate return on investment. So, if we consider training as an investment, we would expect to get returns as a result of initial expenditure. To maximise the chance of this happening we should approach systematically the decision of whether or not to train.

Since training is to be considered as an investment, it is necessary for us to specify and quantify the elements of cost involved and the returns expected. The costs fall into three categories; the costs of learning, the costs of training, and the costs of not training.

The costs of learning

There are five main components to the costs of learning:

(a) the cost of wages paid to the trainee during the training period, whilst his performance is ineffective. The trainee may produce some useful work whilst learning, but he will produce less than an experienced

216

worker would in the same time. Therefore, it is necessary to reduce the element of cost associated with the trainee's wages by the value of the work he produces.

(b)   the cost of materials used during training, if the output produced from these materials is not saleable or usable. (If the output is usable or saleable in the normal way, then this element of cost should be disregarded).

(c)   the cost of rectifying mistakes made by the trainee during training, where this means that other employees carry out the rectification, or where the error or mistake has caused a direct loss.

(d)   the repair or replacement costs of equipment and tools broken by the trainee whilst he is learning. (Only the cost of excessive repair or replacement should be considered). The cost of extra repairs etc. should be obtained by reducing the total by the amount of the cost that would have been incurred by an experienced employee producing the same amount of work as the trainee. Clearly, if no useful work is produced by the trainee, then all elements of cost associated with repair and replacement should be included.

(e)   the replacement cost of trainees who leave before completing their training because of their inability to reach the standards required. This involves the costs of recruitment and selection of new trainees. (See Chapter 11.)

The costs of training

The costs of training may be considered in terms of *direct* and *indirect* costs:

(a)   direct costs of training include: the cost of courses; cost of wages for training staff; expenses incurred by trainees which are reimbursed by the employer, for example, travelling expenses; costs of depreciation of plant and equipment used by the trainee.

(b)   indirect costs of training include: the costs of office accommodation for training staff and for the training area, in addition to an apportionment of the overhead costs associated with the provision of the training facility.

The costs of not training

The costs of not training can be readily quantified in some respects, but not so easily in others. The costs of not training are:

(a)   the cost of levy to the Industry Training Board which covers the organisation, where this applies.

(b)   the costs incurred in appointing new employees who already possess the skills/knowledge/attitudes in which the employer would otherwise have trained existing employees. (This assumes that such potential employees exist). An example of recruiting ready-made skills, as opposed to training within the organisation, is to recruit a craftperson rather than to train an apprentice. The main elements associated with not training in this case be the costs of recruiting the craftperson, which may be an expensive and lengthy business (assuming a shortage of craftpersons). Moreover, there is a large element of uncertainty about how long it will take to recruit such an employee, since, unlike training, this is an activity over which the organisation does not have direct control. From time to time there may be an unfilled vacancy for a craftpersons, the cost of which may be considerable, but is likely to be difficult to calculate, involving the concept of *opportunity cost.*

(c)   similarly to (b), if new employees are recruited rather than existing employees being trained, then there are the costs of disposing of those existing employees who would be surplus to requirements as a result of recruiting already proficient new employees to take their jobs. The costs associated with this approach may be readily quantifiable in some respects, like redundancy payments, but difficult to quantify in others, for instance, the costs of the effect on morale and/or industrial relations of such a 'hire and fire' policy.

The returns expected from training

The returns expected from training are:

(a)   a reduction in trainees' learning time and, therefore, reduced costs of learning.

(b)   a reduction in breakdowns or stoppages and, therefore, reduced down times for plant and equipment, leading to higher output.

(c)   a reduction in wasted and scrapped materials.

(d)   a reduction in accidents, both to trainees and to other employees, resulting directly in savings in sick pay, and indirectly in the reduction of excess costs of employees replacing those injured.

(e)   a reduction in the failure to meet targets of production, which leads to increased customer satisfaction and, consequently, potentially greater profitability.

(f)   an improvement in quality standards.

(g) an improvement in the morale of employees, which may result in improved labour retention.

(h) levy exemption or grant from the Industry Training Board.

Pay-back period

The time horizon over which returns are expected will depend upon a number of factors including:

(a) the magnitude of the costs involved, which will relate to the type of training;

(b) the time period over which the costs are incurred;

(c) the possibility of the returns never being realised because the trained person leaves.

So, for instance, different pay-back periods may be considered when evaluating the investments involved in training a manager, or training a machine operator.

The problems of quantification of costs and benefits

Clearly, many of the costs and benefits associated with the training investment are very difficult to quantify. Indeed some of the more significant costs may not only be difficult to quantify in money terms, but also difficult to quantify in respect of the probability of their occurrence (notably the opportunity cost of a labour deficiency). This is still a poor reason for not carrying out the exercise.

A Systematic Approach to Training

There are four stages to a systematic approach to training. Diagnosis — Analysis — Implementation — Evaluation. These four stages are consistent with viewing training as an investment.

1. Diagnosis

The Board of Directors or Managers of an organisation have a mix of resources to meet corporate objectives. These are: capital resources; buildings; plant and equipment; and human resources. These resources should never be considered as separate, but must be seen as interrelated and interdependent. Moreover, all investment decisions should be subjected to the same process of evaluation, taking account of the fact that a change in one resource will almost inevitably have an impact on the others. Investment made in one resource will also probably require investment to be made in another. So, for example, the purchase of a new piece of equipment will almost invariably result in the need for some training investment. The costs and benefits of both investments should be appraised together.

It is the responsibility of the Board of Directors in their corporate planning activities to make decisions between alternative total investments, since financial resources are limited.

When assessing organisational training needs (i.e. the diagnostic stage of the systematic approach to training), some fairly broad questions need to be raised. These concern the present and the predicted future; aims and objectives of the organisation; its policies; the effectiveness of its major work areas (finance, production, marketing, etc.); its location, plant and equipment; manufacturing techniques; products; and the external environment (to include such matters as legislation), in which it does or will find itself. In parallel, thought must be given to the existing human resources (i.e. employees) and their ability to meet the requirements of the present situation and future plans. This should be covered in a human resource inventory considering both the numbers, types, and qualities of existing personnel and any succession plans that may be made.

Any changes required may not best be met through the process of training. The major alternative to training may be recruitment, but if this is not the case, change will have to be sought in other ways. These may be organisational and involve changing the content of jobs; or they may be personal concerning relationships between employees, or the type of people employed; or they may be associated with the work process itself, the design of equipment and machinery.

Training and human resource planning

The recognition that a training need exists is likely to come as a result of a human resource planning exercise. Clearly human resource planning must be an integral part of corporate planning, and not merely a derived statement of requirements in terms of human resources. The process of human resource planning may reveal the need for training in five situations:

(a) to improve performance in existing jobs where it is not satisfactory;
(b) to provide for future changes in the content of existing jobs;

(c)   to provide training for new recruits;
(d)   to provide for actual, or intended, staff promotions;
(e)   to provide for the creation of totally new jobs.

2. *Analysis*

At this, the second stage of the systematic approach to training, the people who are responsible for arranging training should establish clearly: who needs to be trained; in what order of priority; how many need to be trained in each category of labour; and to what standards of performance.

The most important element of this stage is to establish individual training needs, in other words, what does the trainee need to learn? More formally, we may define a training need as *that gap which exists between the skills, knowledge and attitudes necessary for effective performance in the job and the skills, knowledge and attitudes already possessed by the person who is or will be doing the job.* The training/learning need may be expressed in the equation:

'TRAINING/LEARNING NEED = REQUIRED BEHAVIOUR — CURRENT BEHAVIOUR'

The required behaviour (i.e. how the organisation wants the worker to do his job after he has been trained) may be determined through the process of job analysis, or the consideration of job descriptions and specifications, if these are available. (These are discussed in Chapter 4). Special problems exist where the job to be trained for does not yet exist.

The initial behaviour may have been identified as deficient through a process of performance appraisal (see Chapter 14), but it is likely to be necessary to clearly establish, through observation or interview, some details of initial behaviour (i.e. the state of development of the trainee's skills/knowledge/attitudes now).

It is important that training/learning needs are expressed in terms of skills/knowledge/attitudes, since in this way the most appropriate training methods can be identified.

3. *Implementation*

Before training methods are selected the objectives of training must be set and the content of training planned. These will probably affect the type of training method used.

DEVELOPING EMPLOYEES

Setting objectives and planning the content of training

Setting objectives involves identifying the performance expected to a specified standard, within a specified time. So, for example, in the case of a trainee machine operator, this could mean specifying the hourly rate of output that he will be able to achieve, on certain machines, within agreed production quality standards, after receiving one day's training. When setting these objectives it is important not to include items which are unteachable, because of either the trainee's incapacity to learn (this may in some cases be determined by his basic educational level of attainment), or the lack of internal or external resources.

When it comes to planning the content of the training, the most important factor is likely to be facilities available, including finance. Within these constraints, account should be taken of the needs of the individual trainees; the times that the training will take place (will the trainees be fresh and active or tired?), the sequence of material presented; and the pace at which the training will be conducted.

On and off-the-job training

Training methods can be conveniently divided into two types, those taking place on-the-job (i.e. where the training takes place within the actual work environment) and those taking place off-the-job (i.e. taking place away from the work environment). Among the on-the-job training methods are: coaching, delegation, job rotation, personal assistants, projects, junior boards, and demonstration. Off-the-job training methods include: lectures, group discussions, case studies, programmed learning, projects, business games, simulations, demonstrations, and role playing. As just noted, some training methods, like demonstration, can be used both on or off-the-job.

The two types of training have associated advantages and disadvantages. In general the advantages claimed for on-the-job training methods are: with this type of training there are no transfer problems (remember what we said about generalisation and transfer of learning in the previous chapter) and the learning is adapted to real needs. Because of its nature, valid learning is reinforced, whilst invalid learning is corrected (though there may be a time lag). An advantage that can be overlooked is that on-the-job learning is very natural, so natural in fact that sometimes it is not even identified as training. This may also constitute a disadvantage, because it is so natural it may not be treated seriously or approached in a systematic way. To be successful, this type of training is very dependent upon full management support.

The advantages claimed for off-the-job training are that this type of training can provide knowledge and skills to trainees which are not available within the organisation on-the-job. Moreover, trainees can be taught more effectively and often more quickly and economically through the use of professional trainers. Another advantage is that this type of training can provide an experimental atmosphere and environment which aids learning. This contrasts with the tensions that may exist on-the-job. The disadvantages of off-the-job training methods are that they can be unrealistic and, even when they are realistic, there may be transfer problems. Because of the nature of off-the-job training trainees are likely to experience less immediate achievement and possibly less immediate reinforcement or correction.

Training Methods

Each training method has its advantages and disadvantages, some are better suited to imparting knowledge to trainees, some for imparting skills, and others for changing and developing attitudes. Equally, the various methods may be more or less appropriate for different types of trainee (e.g. managers or craftpersons).

The lecture, which is a talk by the trainer/instructor, with or without illustrations, which is given relatively independently of the trainees' reactions or active participation, is of use mainly for imparting knowledge. As a training method its advantages are that it is cheap and can be used for a large number of trainees at one time, for the purpose of presenting completely fresh material, or introducing a new subject, or for summarising material presented by other training methods. It can be used for all types of trainees where facts have to be put across, but the length of the lecture should be limited (to about 40 minutes) since, because the trainee is passive, his attention is difficult to hold for long periods. Similarly, it is difficult for the trainer to tell during a lecture whether the trainees are actually absorbing and understanding the information presented. In industrial training, notes, of the main points of the lecture, will often be provided to the trainees.

In the *demonstration* training method the trainer performs an operation or task so that the trainee can see what to do and how to do it. Normally the trainer describes what he is doing as he is doing it and explains why he is doing it in that way. Usually the trainee repeats the operation or task after the demonstration. As has been noted, demonstrations are given both on and off-the-job, so sometimes they are conducted by professional instructors and sometimes by experienced workers, who may train other workers as part of their job. The demonstration is used mainly in the area of skills training, particularly manual skills, involving training in manipulative operations or explaining the use of equipment and materials, although it can be used for the purpose of clarifying some principle or theory. The demonstration is probably the most commonly-used method of skills training, because it can clearly focus the trainee's attention on the important steps of the task and provide him with practice. It also has the advantage that the pace of the demonstration can be readily altered for individual trainees, slowing down where they have difficulty and speeding up on points they grasp readily. This is related to plateaux on the complex learning curve. Additionally, while the skill is being learnt by the trainee, performance standards can be established in the trainee's mind by the trainer. Since much demonstration training, particularly the on-the-job type, will be carried out with very small numbers of trainees at any one time (necessarily since they must all be able to see what is going on), it can be an expensive method.

The group discussion method may be used for the development, through practice, of oral skills, but is most useful and powerful in the area of attitudes. The group discussion centres on a subject of interest to trainees and is carefully guided by the trainer, mainly through the use of questions. Thus trainees examine by argument, implying an interchange of ideas, opinions, knowledge, and experience on the subject under discussion. This method can be used to prepare the ground for further teaching and learning by establishing the existing levels of knowledge, comprehension, interest, and motivation of trainees. It encourages trainees to think for themselves and to consider the implications of what they have learned. The group discussion may not be a very effective way of teaching new facts, but it is very useful for consolidating knowledge already provided through other training methods. As a training method it is costly and requires a high level of competence by the trainer, but is used widely in management and supervisory training.

In *the project* training method, the analysis of practical problems and the preparation of conclusions in report form is undertaken by the trainee. The project usually involves some research and can be carried out on individual or a group basis. The project is normally based on a real or realistic problem, which the organisation actually wants solved. The learning obtained can be in terms of knowledge discovered by the trainee himself in the course of his researches, or in terms of skills involved in information handling and processing and inter-personal skills, where the trainee is required to elicit the support of other employees in order to obtain information from them. This method is used mainly for supervisory and management training and is popular for training graduates who have recently started work.

In *the simulation* training method the trainer provides a model or game, on anything which attempts to imitate reality, so that the trainee can use this device for learning purposes. The more realistic the simulation, the greater the potential for learning and the smaller the problem of transfer. Simulations require the trainee to follow procedures and make responses similar to those he would be expected to make in the real job. In the process of doing this, the trainee receives rapid feed-back or reinforcement so he can quickly see the relevance of what he is learning and practice the skills involved, whether they are manual or intellectual. Simulations have the advantage that the trainee can experiment in a safe environment. For example, a trainee pilot, using a flight simulator, can learn how to fly and if he 'crashes' the simulator, no-one is hurt. Simulations vary in complexity from those used for training astronauts in space flight, to fairly simple in-tray exercises where a trainee is provided with information that would come to a manager and has to react and decide what action he will take. Even though in most simulation exercises the trainee is actually learning whilst he is involved with the simulation, it is often useful after the exercise to analyse what happened to confirm and reinforce the learning. This method of training can be used for all types of trainee. Machine operators can learn how to use the controls of a machine on a simulator rather than on the real machine; senior managers can use sophisticated computerised models of business organisations to gain experience of decision-making in fields with which they may be unfamiliar.

In *the Case Study* method trainees examine at secondhand a real or contrived event or problem. They analyse the factors leading to the problem and propose remedies for solving it. This method gives the trainee the opportunity to practice problem solving and, through discussion, attitude development. Although used for intellectual skills training, the area of knowledge learning may be covered in the course of the case. The aim of the case study method is to provoke clear thinking about a set of facts which are presented to the trainees, who are then required to work out the underlying principles. This method makes use of many of the principles of cognitive learning. It is not important to arrive at an agreed solution to the case. The idea is that trainees learn to isolate and study the significant facts and to delay judgment rather than to hasten to solutions which may be wrong, when subjected to more intensive questioning and testing. In a case study the trainer provides all the necessary information, then leaves the trainees to discuss the facts and to arrive at a point of view without guidance or direction. Case studies, which are expensive training methods, are used mainly for management training.

Programmed learning is a self-instructional method where the trainee is presented with the subject matter broken down into small elements, usually with one element on a page or frame. The information is provided in a carefully arranged step-by-step form. At each step the employee is given just enough information to enable him to make a satisfactory response to the question posed. He progresses on to the next page if he has the correct answer, or back through remedial stages if he has an incorrect answer. You can see that this method makes use of the idea of shaping behaviour, as in operant conditioning. The trainee gets immediate confirmation of a correct response, since he is directed to the next step. This method is suitable only for the presentation of knowledge and intellectual skills although, as technological developments provide more sophisticated systems of presentation, the potential uses increase. The difficulty with this method is in the development and provision of texts, however they are presented. The advantages are that the trainer can supervise a large number of trainees, each working independently, and at his own pace, on his own programmed learning text.

Role playing is a method where trainees act out the roles for which they are training or the roles of the people with whom they will interact when doing their own job. This method is used largely for interpersonal skills training, but can be effective in the realm of attitude development by exposing trainees to 'the other man's situation'. Closed circuit television is often used with role playing so the trainees can review their performance and analyse their behaviour and the effect of their behaviour on others. It is then that the trainer makes his major contribution. The difficulty is that trainees may over-act or 'ham'. Role playing is widely used in training for social skills, including industrial relations negotiation training.

Coaching is the most commonly used, and abused, method of on-the-job training. In its best form the trainer, often a manager or supervisor, explains the various facets of the job to the trainee progressively, over a period, and ensures that the trainee learns. The trainer questions and counsels the trainee to ensure that he is progressing. As a training method it is highly dependent upon the personality and management style of the trainer, who should develop a relationship with the trainee so that he feels able to improve his performance in a relatively secure and supportive environment. Too often this form of training amounts to nothing more than the trainee 'sitting by Nellie', and can be counterproductive, since the trainer has little or no expertise in training, may have even less motivation, and may have been selected to fulfil this particular role for reasons which have nothing to do with meeting the needs of the trainee. Coaching is a method used for all types of trainees. In fact it might be considered as a responsibility of all supervisors towards their subordinates, and, as such covers all three areas of knowledge, skills, and attitudes.

In the method known as *delegation* the supervisor, who acts as trainer, places the final responsibility for certain decisions, and for the consequent results, in the hands of the trainee. The theory of delegation is that the supervisor chooses which decisions he himself makes and which he delegates to the trainee. Thus the trainee is held accountable for the results and not merely for developing solutions designed to obtain the approval of his superior. He can see the results of his actions and can correct his mistakes. This feedback is an important element in the learning process. The method permits the trainee to work out the details of the operation himself in order to meet the goals, within the limits set by the supervisor.

Job rotation provides the trainee with a series of assignments or different jobs. The job rotation is planned so that he faces successively more advanced learning opportunities. At the same time he receives coaching from his immediate superior in each of the different job assignments. He acquires valuable perceptions and knowledge of interrelationships from the varied situations he faces. The method provides for learning in the areas of knowledge, skills, and attitudes for many types of trainee and is commonly used for clerical and administrative jobs.

There are two different objectives which may be sought by the training method of *Personal Assistants*. The first is where a fairly junior employee, often a management trainee, acts as an aide to a senior manager, performing certain limited tasks (perhaps acting as minutes secretary at meetings), whilst observing the work of his trainer. The second objective is where the trainee is being specifically developed to take up the appointment to which he is acting as personal assistant. In the latter case a large element of delegation is involved. Like job rotation, delegation and coaching, the personal assistants method aims at developing knowledge, skills and attitudes, but, in this case, is used almost exclusively for management training.

The junior board method of training is a special assignment often used to supplement coaching. The trainee is asked to serve on a junior board to investigate a number of top management problems on a sustained basis. Possible solutions are offered, which are examined and evaluated by senior management. The problems assigned to the junior board cut across departmental lines and often require long-term planning. This method is intended to give management trainees top level experience, both as individuals and as members of a committee. In this way it is hoped that trainees will see problems in a wider perspective than would be possible if they were just confined to one job. Not only will the trainees acquire knowledge and develop skills, they may also appreciate higher-level management which in itself may develop and change their own attitudes.

4. Evaluation

This is the fourth stage of the systematic approach to training and includes validation.

Evaluation is defined as *the measurement of the total value of a training course or programme, in the context of improving effective performance towards company objectives.* Evaluation differs from validation in that it endeavours to measure the total overall costs and benefits of the course or programme, and not just the achievements of its laid-down objectives.

Validation is an important part of evaluation, in fact, if a piece of training is not valid, then attempts at evaluating it will be pointless. Validation may be defined as *a series of control tests carried out on the trainees, designed to ascertain whether the training has achieved its aim* (i.e. has been successful in teaching what it set out to teach) *and, judged on the basis of its effectiveness measured against specific yardsticks* (e.g. improvements in quantity of production), *whether the aim itself was realistically based on training needs.*

The importance of validation cannot be overstressed for the following reasons.

(a)   there are many reasons why something learned may not be put into practice after training. It is essential to establish whether, if something is not being done correctly, it is a result of inadequate training.

(b)   it is easier, particularly for management training, to establish what has been learned than it is to establish exactly the effects of the training in terms of the behaviour and performance of the trainee when he gets back to his normal work.

(c)   it demonstrates, for the trainers and instructors formally responsible for the training, whether their part of the learning process has been successfully carried out, and whether they are effective and proficient providers of learning.

The problem facing the trainer is how to validate particular pieces of training. It must be remembered that we can only infer that learning has taken place by observing changes in behaviour. Normally, one or more of three methods are used. The first is *pre and post training achievement tests.* The trainee's performance is assessed before training is given and then, again, afterwards. This method of validation lends itself to the type of training given for a job where output can be readily measured. Such jobs may include machine operators, assembly workers, and typists. In these cases it may be appropriate to give the post training test fairly soon after training has been completed.

The second method of validation is known as *achievement against objectives.* Here performance objectives are stated before training is started. These objectives will constitute the required behaviour and may be expressed in terms of the trainee's ability to undertake some type of work satisfactorily. The trainee may have been unable to perform this work before training, or may have performed it inadequately. An example of this method of validation is where a machine tool setter has been trained in the setting and operation of a new machine tool, or a supervisor has been taught how to compile and interpret departmental performance statistics. In both these cases it will become apparent after the training, whether the trainee can in fact perform the new tasks. An assessment of how well he performs them may be more difficult to ascertain and, in any case, his performance is likely to improve with practice.

The third method of validation is based upon *reports*. Reports may be of the kind given by the trainee in which he assesses the usefulness and effectiveness of the training he has received. Reports may also be provided by the trainee's superior, or the trainee himself after he has performed his job for some time. These reports should note the improvements in performance that are attributed to the training received. This method is commonly used to attempt to validate management of interpersonal skills training.

In viewing training as an investment, evaluation becomes the process of quantifying and comparing the benefits (i.e. the return on investment) with the magnitude of the investment made (i.e. the cost of the investment in training). The difficulty resides in the requirement to quantify results, which may often be qualitative in nature (i.e. the trainee has become better at doing some task as a result of training received). How can this be converted into money terms? This may involve the concept of opportunity costs. Alternatively, it may be that an organisation just embarks upon training as an act of faith.

MANAGEMENT DEVELOPMENT

So far, in this chapter, we have looked at the way organisations view training and a systematic approach to training. We have noted, when we have looked at various training methods, that different types of trainees have different learning requirements. Why then should we pay special attention to one group of workers — that is managers? There is one main reason and a number of subsequently derived reasons.

The main reason is because of the type of work the managers perform, compared with most other types of workers. Most employees are paid for the work that they do, whilst managers are generally paid for their efforts in getting others to actually do the work. It is the manager who determines what will be done and, to a greater or lesser extent, how others will do it, managers are therefore expected to initiate and organise the work of others, normally their subordinates.

This implies a need for a high degree of knowledge or skill in the particular specialist area in which the manager works, whether he is an accountant or an engineer, which will require a long period of learning. Moreover, having acquired this knowledge and skill the manager's success in the job will be measured in terms of how able he is in getting his subordinates to execute decisions. Managers, through their leadership, ensure that organisations are dynamic and adapt appropriately to their environments.

Management training may be singled out for special consideration for the following reasons: Firstly, the degree of skill, knowledge and expertise required to perform this type of job is difficult to achieve and likely to take a long time, thus proving expensive. Secondly, managers operate at the frontiers of the organisation, in its interface with the external environment. The organisation will stand or fall dependent upon their success in the job. Thirdly, managers are in the position of getting others to do work for them, which requires special skills, so not only must they be capable of being adaptive to the external environment, but also to the internal environment of the organisation. (We will look at this in more detail later, and also why nowadays this poses particular problems.) The further reason is a consequence of the demands of the first three reasons, that is the growth of professional managers. You, the reader of this book, are likely to be following a course in business studies which you expect eventually to lead to some position of professional management. This is relatively new.

Changes in Science, Technology and Knowledge

We can all observe changes that are taking place in society as a result of technological progress. Many of us own calculators, which we can slip into our pockets, and which were relatively cheap to buy. Some may own watches that act as calculators, or vice versa. The impact of the silicon chip is well publicised and known to all. We can only wonder whether there will be any products or processes which will not be significantly affected by this new technology. This is, of course, just one example of how technology touches all our lives. The manager not only has to cope with these aspects of a rapidly changing environment, but his management tools are changing too. For instance, a problem which might previously have been identified as within the domain of the accountant to solve, may now be claimed as a problem to be solved by the skills of the operations research specialist. This all helps to make the environment in which the manager is required to operate less stable.

Much of the work that managers perform is concerned with decision making, and the ability to provide information for decision making at high speed poses new challenges. Traditionally a manager needing information to solve a problem could expect a delay of several days before answers were available. This time delay allowed an opportunity for 'mulling' the problem over, and perhaps a discussion with colleagues, considering possibilities, and weighing them up, even before he got the information. In other words, there was built into the system of data collection and presentation a long enough period to ease the problem of the manager being rushed into a decision. Clearly these same delays can on occasion have made the manager's job significantly more difficult, because sometimes he may have been unable to wait for data collection and presentation and have been forced to take the decision with inadequate information. The speed of communication certainly puts pressure on managers to make decisions with less time to reflect upon the problems.

Economic Changes

An increasingly affluent society may lead to more competitive marketing. A natural consequences of this is that each organisation is less sure of how it will be required to perform. Every organisation will be operating in an increasingly dynamic economic environment, presenting a more difficult task for managers. Another economic feature which makes the manager's task more demanding, particularly for managers in certain functions, is the variable rate of exchange between currencies.

Political and Social Change

In the post-war period, the consequence of the government's management of the economy has often posed particular managerial problems. This government activity has made both the internal and external environments of the organisation more difficult to manage, often reducing the options available to managers whilst, at the same time, creating difficult situations in themselves.

The most significant change in society which has affected the demands of the manager's job is related to the question of authority. In the post-war period there has been an ever-increasing tendency for 'authority' to be questioned at all levels. This is of great significance to a group of employees whose work is primarily concerned with directing others. The questioning of authority is something which is occurring throughout the western world. For example, if a Prime Minister of this country makes any major policy statement, then one can almost guarantee that on the same night he/she will be grilled by a television inquisitor/interviewer on the reason for the policy, exactly how it is to be applied etc. Whilst not implying that people in positions of authority should not be held accountable, we note that this presents a new and demanding situation for such people. In terms of management this goes hand-in-hand with what has come to be known as management by consent or consensus. This may be a sign of a mature and civilized industrial society, but does not alter the fact that it makes the process of management more demanding, particularly where there are a large number of interest groups with different and sometimes conflicting desires to be taken into account. Indeed some managers still pine for the good old days when 'what they said went with no argument'.

Professional Management

Whilst there are a number of features which may be considered under this heading, including the degrees of specialisation within management, we will concentrate upon managerial obsolescence. This problem may be highlighted by the fact that managers seem to be attaining managerial positions earlier in life. This poses the problem of what to do with all these managers. If the normal age of appointment is fifty years of age and retirement is sixty, then the average manager holds a management position for ten years. If, alternatively, the normal age of appointment is thirty years of age and retirement is still sixty, then the average manager holds a management position for thirty years, which either means he is blocking the opportunities of all those younger men and women coming up behind him for thirty years, or a vast increase in managerial jobs will have to occur to absorb the supply of potential candidates. There are signs of just such a managerial explosion, but there must be some limit to how long it can continue.

The Philosophy and Aims of Management Development

Any organisation embarking upon a programme of management development should recognise some fundamental points, which are prerequisites for success.

Firstly, management development is a long term process and it is unrealistic to expect quick results. This means that top management must be prepared to invest a lot of time and money in a programme, the returns from which will not often be visible in the short term.

Secondly, management development is essentially providing opportunities for managers to develop themselves. This is somewhat different from many other forms of training, which are often instructional. On the face of it, this statement on self-development may seem absurd. Does the individual know in what areas he is lacking and, if so, is he necessarily able to achieve the required improvement through self-development? Given the nature of the work of a manager, the probability of being able to identify shortfalls may be quite high (particularly if one believes in the adage, there are no such things as bad soldiers, only bad officers). In other words, the manager should be able to tell if he is successful by the results achieved by his subordinates since, through them, his success is measured. The manager will receive assistance in this process of appraisal (maybe formally through a system of management by objectives — see Chapter 14). The person who is likely to be most influential in this process, and who is generally likely to be the most powerful influence on the manager, is his immediate superior. It is the recognition of this which is the third prerequisite to a successful programme.

The fourth requirement is that the climate of the organisation is favourable to managerial development. This will only ever be achieved if the most senior management are not only completely committed to a policy of management development, but are seen to be so, both in their words and deeds. Even this will not guarantee success. The climate must also be such that individual managers feel able to experiment and take chances without fear of the consequences if results are imperfect. Such an atmosphere is unlikely to be found where there is a managerial style of the autocratic type. This is likely to result in a climate of risk minimisation or 'keeping one's nose clean' on the part of employees, including managers and to suppress initiative and risk taking. The converse, a more democratic style, resulting in a more supportive climate is more likely to encourage the operation of successful management development.

The final prerequisite for successful management development is the acceptance that all development and training programmes should be geared to the needs of the individual and the organisation. To achieve this the needs of the individual and the organisation must be harmonised, which may be easier said than done.

Management development will normally be the responsibility of a senior executive, assisted by a committee, who will formulate policy and ensure that it is implemented, and assess future managerial needs and ensure that management appraisal takes place. Let us look at the aims of management development and how they may be formulated into a policy, and how future managerial requirements may be assessed. The question of performance appraisal is dealt with in Chapter 14.

Management Development Policy

The policy should start by defining what is mean by management development — something like the following: *'Management develop-*

233

ment is a systematic and continuous process which starts with an analysis of present managerial resources, estimates future needs, and operates policies of recruitment, training, transfer, and promotion to secure and make the most of these resources.'

Not surprisingly, given the definition above, aims of the policy might be stated as:

(i)   To ensure an adequate supply of trained managers to meet the future needs of the organisation;

(ii) To provide every manager with the opportunity to develop and fulfil his potential so that he does his existing job to maximum effectiveness.

Having defined the aims, the policy statement must then elaborate on the conditions required for their achievement and how their achievement will be secured. Thus the statement may continue: 'In order to achieve the aims of the management development programme it is essential that:

(a)   the organisational climate is conducive to managers maximising their contribution;

(b)   scope is given for managers to exercise initiative and they are encouraged by their superiors to do so;

(c)   every manager fully understands the purpose of his job;

(d)   every manager's performance is regularly and satisfactorily appraised;

(e)   every manager's medium and long term potential is regularly appraised and reviewed;

(f)   every manager is encouraged to treat his subordinates in a way that promotes the achievement of the aims of management development.'

Assessing Future Managerial Requirements

Determining the future managerial requirements or the managerial human resource plan of an organisation involves four successive steps. These steps are: firstly, a study of the existing organisation, or an audit, secondly, planning the future organisation structure; thirdly, the job and person specifications which are, and will be, required to fulfil present and future organisational needs; and, finally, planning management succession.

When those responsible for management development first look at the existing organisation structure and how it functions, they will almost certainly find that it does not function in the way that it is intended to (i.e. by reference to the formal organisation chart). Job titles often seem to be poor designations for what the incumbents actually do. This may be simply explained by the *person-job relationship*. Because of the nature of managerial jobs, there is often scope for the actual job holder or incumbent to mould the job to suit himself, his strengths, his interests etc. This may occur to the extent that the job becomes virtually personality-dependent. By this we mean that one chief engineer may mould the whole of the engineering activity to such an extent that, should he be replaced, then the engineering arrangements may lose all cohesiveness or purpose. Similarly, a chief executive may lead an organisation in a particular way which another person in the same job would do entirely differently. This is a feature, the relationship between the job and the job holder, which is different for management than for most other jobs, because the prescribed or 'determined from above' element is much smaller. For those studying the existing organisation structure, the reality of how it functions, taking into account the person job relationships, is what is really required. Taking these relationships into account, the following questions should then be asked. Are the responsibilities within the whole organisation sensibly grouped? Can the existing organisation structure be simplified? Are the lines of authority clear? Any weaknesses noted in the answers to these questions should have remedial action planned.

The next step in assessing future managerial requirements is to plan the future organisational structure. This may mean a totally new structure, as determined by the corporate plan (see Chapter 4), or it may be largely dependent on changes in job holders due to transfers, promotions or retirements. Whether it involves minor or major re-organisations, it is best to draw up ideal or prospective organisation charts for, say, three and five years in the future.

In the light of the existing and planned organisation structure, those involved in management development must ensure that job specifications are drawn up. From these it will be necessary to derive person specifications for all management jobs. The job specifications will be used for performance appraisal and training needs analysis, and the person specifications, in conjunction with job descriptions and specifications, will be used for planning management succession.

The final step in the assessment of future managerial requirements is to plan management succession. There are two common ways of carrying this out. The first method is to draw up a series of organisation charts, perhaps representing the envisaged organisation structure for, say, three and five years ahead, and then, against each position or job, noting the names of existing or intended job holder and replacements.

In Figure 33, page 237, which represents a part of an organisation's current structure, details of each person are recorded beside his name, using symbols. The top name refers in each case to the existing job holder.

The second method uses a managerial replacement table. On this table each management position is recorded with the name and age of the existing job holder, plus the same details for an immediate and long-term replacement. It is quite possible that the person designated as immediate replacement may not be the same as the long-term replacement. The immediate replacement would be the person expected to fill the job in the event of the current holder leaving or falling under a bus. The longer-term replacement may presently be unsuitable to fill the vacancy, due to deficiencies in his experience or training. Conversely, the immediate replacement may not be considered as the best long-term replacement.

Figure 34, page 238, shows an example of part of a managerial replacement table.

We can see, by looking at the two charts, that these methods highlight weak areas in succession planning. For example, succession planning looks particularly weak in production, with J. Brown nearing retirement and no long-term replacement having been identified.

If these charts are to fulfil their purpose, then it is essential that they are kept up to date.

Development Programmes

Since, as we stated earlier, successful management development must be based upon self-development, then an individual manager's development programme will only succeed if it is based upon his own awareness of his needs and an agreement between him and his boss on how to meet those needs. Methods that may be used for management development will include, coaching, special assignments and projects, junior boards, job rotation, and personal assistants. These methods may be supplemented by off-the-job training, to cover specific deficiencies in knowledge or skill, and may include case study work and sensitivity training methods.

TRAINING LEGISLATION

There have been two major pieces of legislation affecting training: the Industrial Training Act 1964 and the Employment and Training Act 1973.

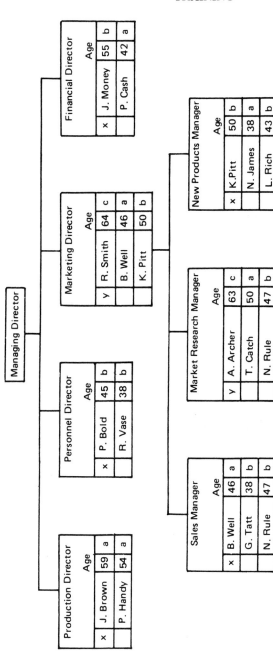

FIGURE 33 : MANAGEMENT SUCCESSION CHART

Key to Symbols

Number against each name represents age

Current Performance: x = Good, y = Average, z = Poor

Promotional Potential : a = Readily available within 6 months

b = Further development needed, available in 18 months

c = Doubtful potential, not available within 18 months

POSITION	Present Incumbent	Age	Immediate Replacement	Age	Long Term Replacement	Age
Production Dir.	J Brown	59	P Handy	54	—	
Marketing Dir.	R Smith	64	B Well	46	K Pitt	50
Financial Dir.	J Money	55	P Cash	42		
Sales Manager	B Well	46	G Tatt	38	N Rule	47
Market Res. Mgr.	A Archer	63	T Catch	50	N Rule	50
New Product Mgr.	K Pitt	50	N James	38	L Rich	43

FIGURE 34 : MANAGERIAL REPLACEMENT TABLE

TRAINING

The Need for the Industrial Training Act 1964

The need was felt for some form of training legislation in the early 1960s, mainly because of the shortage of skilled manpower in the economy as a whole. This shortage was causing bottlenecks in production within industry at a time of economic expansion. Though training was being undertaken, the burden was falling on the shoulders of a relatively few organisations and companies, who were effectively meeting the cost for all the training taking place in the economy as a whole. More importantly, there seemed little incentive for other organisations to train and, in any case, training efforts throughout the country were largely uncoordinated.

The Objectives of the 1964 Industrial Training Act

The objectives of the 1964 Act were: to ensure an adequate supply of properly trained men and women at all levels of industry throughout the country; to secure and maintain an improvement in the quality and efficiency of industrial training; and to share the cost of training more evenly amongst organisations. These objectives were to be met through the activities of the Training Boards, which the Act established.

The Training Boards

The Training Boards were established on an industry basis. They were composed of a chairman, with industrial or commercial experience, members from the field of education, and an equal number of employer and trade union members. The Boards themselves employed professional training officers to carry out their functions.

The main functions of the Training Board were to ensure that sufficient training was undertaken within their own industry and to give advice on how such training should be carried out. They had specific functions of providing, securing, and approving training courses. They were to make recommendations about the nature and length of specific kinds of training, to recommend standards and test proficiency. In addition to giving grants and travelling expenses, they assisted people in finding training facilities and devised and applied selection tests for new entrants to training programmes. Each Board provided careers literature for their industry and conducted training research. They were able to enter into contracts of apprenticeship with trainees and to train training officers for organisations.

With the Industry Training Boards came the *levy-grant system,* the aims of which were to spread the costs of training fairly amongst organisations within the industry for which the Board had responsibility, and to provide an incentive to carry out training. The basis of the levy was a percentage of the payroll costs of each organisation. In the case of the Engineering Industry Training Board, the levy was 2½ per cent of the annual payroll for each organisation. A grant was awarded on the basis of the quantity, quality, and type of training undertaken. The training provided by each organisation was assessed by Training Officers of the Training Board who determined the amount of grant paid. Those providing good training could receive grant back from the Board to an amount in excess of the amount of the levy they had paid. Organisations that provided no training received no grant.

The Central Training Council

The Central Training Council, which advised the Minister on the running of industrial training services, also reviewed the progress of established Boards, considered proposals for, and advised him on, the establishment of Boards. The Central Training Council also carried out research and considered matters of general interest to training and related areas.

The Success of the 1964 Industrial Training Act

It can be fairly stated that the 1964 Act encouraged the development of the training profession and improved the quality of training provided within industry as a whole. It increased the number of places in Government Training Centres and increased the liaison between government, industry, and education in matters concerning manpower. Another consequence of the Act was that the information available nationally about manpower was improved. The Act however was not without deficiencies, mainly that it did not cover the whole labour force and the needs of small firms were not adequately met. As a result of the Boards being organised on an industry basis, there was duplicated effort amongst them, but at the same time they failed to resolve national or regional training problems, with the field of redeployment being largely neglected. The levy grant system was seen to be deficient.

The Employment and Training Act 1973

This Act established the Manpower Services Commission (MSC) the Employment Services Agency, and the Training Services Agency as statutory bodies, and modified the Industrial Training Act with the introduction of the *levy grant exemption* scheme. Through this Act the Youth Employment Service became the Careers Service.

The Training Services Agency, renamed Training Services Division, was given responsibility for this levy-grant exemption scheme, which replaced the levy-grant system. The new scheme had a one per cent ceiling on the levy Training Boards were able to exact. Organisations showing that they carried out adequate training could obtain exemption from levy for one year at a time. Small firms became completely exempt from levy and specific grants could be claimed for particular types of training. The Division had three main programmes. The first related to the needs of industry and concerned the roles and relationships between the TSD and ITBs and the development of important training areas, for example, safety. The second related to the needs of the individual and concerned the operation of the Training Opportunities Programme Scheme (TOPS). The third programme was concerned with improving the efficiency and effectiveness of training, which covered the development and dissemination of fresh knowledge about training methods, along with research, and strengthening the competence of training staff.

The MSC (now the Training Commission (TC)) provides several adult training schemes in two main programmes; the Job Training Programme and the Wider Opportunities Programme.

In November 1981, the number of Industry Training Boards was reduced from 23 to 7. Where ITBs were abolished, the industries concerned were expected to develop their own voluntary arrangements.

The government, through the divisions of the TC has been active in the development of the country's manpower resources, in ways which relate significantly to the field of training. Notable amongst the initiatives that have been taken are the Youth Opportunities Programmes (YOP) and the Youth Training Scheme (YTS) which replaced YOP. The YTS guarantees a year's foundation training for all those leaving school at 16 to 18 with no job. Much of this training will be undertaken within private and public organisations as well as educational establishments. Given the large numbers of young people concerned, the effect upon the training activity in the economy as a whole is likely to be considerable.

Section 5

Rewarding Employees

CHAPTER 17 : REWARDS

The chapter on rewards opens with the aims of payment systems and a description of the various components of the rewards package. The techniques of job evaluation are described, together with their role in determining levels of pay. We then consider several types of payment system — for example, time related systems, merit and incremental systems, and output related schemes such as piecework and group bonus payments. The chapter concludes with an overview of added value schemes of payment and profit sharing.

Chapter 17

Rewards

Why do organisations pay people? Our immediate answer may be that if organisations did not pay people then no-one would work for them. But if we think of all those people who do unpaid voluntary work we have to reconsider this initial answer.

In this chapter we are going to look at the subject of pay in general and some specific types of payment system.

Why Organisations pay people — the Aims of Payments

Organisations have aims and objectives which people are employed to achieve. The pay these employees receive is often a major cause (if not *the* major cause) of their interest, and hence employment. It is important that the pay employees receive and the basis of the payment system are such that they are encouraged to work to maximise the achievement of the organisation's aims and objectives. Remember though that these aims may be many and varied, and a payment system which tends to encourage work behaviour by employees which promotes the achievement of one aim may reduce the likelihood of another aim being met. Similarly, the employees are individuals and a payment system which is attractive to, and motivates, one employee may have the opposite effect upon another.

There will probably never be a perfect payment system that works for all people in all situations. But there are a range of payment systems for rewarding employees. The choice of payment system must be made in the light not only of the organisation's aims but also its circumstances.

Professor Tom Lupton (1972) defined a payment system as *'a way of so influencing the behaviour of workers that the purposes of the organisation (as the manager interprets them) are efficiently served'*. Given this objective of a payment system, it should be considered by reference to a number of features:

(i) It should be suited to the organisation, and its structure. Remember that organisations are dynamic, not static, and therefore a good system will be one which is flexible and adaptable to different situations.

(ii) Our choice of systems should be sufficiently flexible that account can be taken of changes in the market rate. So, for instance, we may have a payment system for engineers and accountants which results in them both receiving the same amount of pay. If the demand for engineers increases significantly (throughout the whole economy) and there is no commensurate increase in the supply of engineers (i.e. no extra engineers are being trained within organisations or educated in colleges and universities), then we may expect the price of engineers (i.e. the pay they can command) to rise, since the demand for engineers exceeds the supply. However, if there is no change in the demand for and supply of accountants, then no change in price (i.e. pay) should be expected for them. The consequence is that these two jobs, which were previously rewarded at the same level, are no longer likely to be paid the same amount. A good payment system should be adaptable to such circumstances. Clearly a payment system that could not adjust to the new circumstances would be deficient, since, unless the pay for engineers can be increased, we will probably lose many of our engineers to competitors who are prepared to pay them more. Moreover, we would be unlikely to be successful in attempts to recruit engineers to replace those leaving, since we would be offering less pay than other organisations. Similarly a payment system which, whilst able to increase the pay of engineers, because of the new circumstances, but unable to do so without also increasing the pay to accountants, would be deficient and the result would be that accountants were paid more than necessary.

(iii)   The system should be one that encourages the right sort of people to apply for jobs with the organisation, whilst at the same time ensuring that existing good employees feel sufficiently well rewarded not to want to leave.

(iv)   The system should encourage high performance by the workers. To ensure that it meets this requirement it is essential that we understand what constitutes high performance. If a company is manufacturing and selling a product in a particularly competitive market, for instance motor cars, then a given manufacturer, say Rolls Royce, may specialise in very high quality products. In a company like this, high performance is likely to be defined in terms of quality of work done rather than quantity of work produced. In this case the payment system should encourage high quality workmanship.

(v)   The system should encourage workers to be flexible in the way they are deployed. If, as a result of factors completely outside the control of the worker, his job needs to be changed or he needs to be moved to another job, then the payment system should be one which will encourage such flexibility. At the same time, this should be achieved without upsetting all the other workers. For example, there are two jobs in an organisation, paid at different rates, and there are normally four workers on each job. If, for some reason, there is a shortage of work on one job (say the higher paid job) and an excess or work on the lower paid job, a good payment system would be one where, not only would a worker willingly transfer for a temporary period, but also where all the other workers on both jobs felt the arrangement to be fair and reasonable.

(vi)   As well as serving organisational aims and being seen as both fair and consistent by employees, a good payment system should achieve these at minimum possible cost. Many of the preceding features of a good system could be easily achieved if this feature was ignored. To do so would be absurd though, since payment systems have a considerable effect upon the *amount* of pay and the payments made to workers constitute a cost of production which no organisation can afford to ignore.

The Rewards Package

So far in this chapter we have used the term pay rather than wage or salary. We have done this as the alternative terms wage and salary suggest money only. Whilst money is, in the case of most workers, one of (if not *the* most important) rewards they receive for working, it is rarely the only one. Let us consider other rewards that people gain from work.

Some people gain what might be termed psychological and/or social rewards from doing a job. We mentioned at the beginning of the chapter 'unpaid voluntary workers'. This is perhaps something of a misnomer, for what we mean when we use this term is that workers receive no money for their time and effort. It is reasonable to assume that, even though they receive no money, they do receive something of value to them as individuals. They may receive some sense of fulfilment through doing something which they consider worthwhile, some sense of personal satisfaction from what they do. This is not to suggest that it is only people who do work for no money payment who receive these rewards of satisfaction. Take the case of an artist commissioned to paint a picture. He will be paid in money for the output of his labours (the picture), but he will also probably achieve the personal satisfaction of creating a work of art. We are all familiar with the sense of satisfaction achieved through doing a good job well; few of us, however, can afford to have this as our only reward, since such a sense of satisfaction does not pay the rent or buy us food and clothes. Unfortunately many jobs are of such a type as to provide the worker with little or no sense of satisfaction in their completion. People engaged in such work may develop an entirely instrumental attitude towards their jobs (see Chapter 21).

245

REWARDING EMPLOYEES

As well as the rewards of work satisfaction, many jobs provide benefits and rewards which do not take the form of direct money payments. These rewards have often in the past been referred to, both by employers and employees, as 'perks' of the job, or fringe benefits. Since in certain occupations they form such a significant part of the total rewards received by the employees, it is misleading to think of them in this way. It is more accurate to think of them as a form of indirect financial payment. The reason for using this term is that, although the rewards do not constitute direct cash payments from the employer to the worker, the employee usually receives some goods or services, free of charge, or at a reduced price, which he would otherwise have had to pay the full price for. Any list of such rewards or benefits would have to include the following:

> Company car
> Clothing allowances
> Non-contributory pension scheme
> Free life assurance
> School fees for children
> Interest-free loans for season tickets, house purchase etc.
> Free or subsidised meals
> Discount on company goods or services

There are three aspects to these indirect financial payments. These are most easily shown by considering the case of a company car, where such a car is not an essential requirement for doing the job. Let us assume that your company gives you a Ford Sierra for your private use as part of the rewards it pays you. The first aspect is that you may not want a car of any sort, perhaps you do not like cars, or you cannot drive. How would you determine the value of this car to you? Secondly, perhaps you are a single person with an interest in sports cars, one of which you own. What value would you put on a Sierra, which you do not particularly want, but which would provide virtually free motoring compared with your sports car? Thirdly, you are not normally in a position to cash in this indirect financial payment. In this example you could hardly return from a fortnight's holiday in the Bahamas and when your boss asks you how the car is running, you reply that you no longer own it since you sold it to pay for the holiday.

This means that when you try to put a value on these indirect financial payments, you must discount their market value by some factor depending on what they are worth to you. So, though the car may be worth £9,000 on the open market, its value to you could range from nothing, if you did not drive and had no desire to, to £9,000 if you had been intending to buy such a Ford Sierra yourself.

REWARDS

The Importance of Rewards to Employees

Suppose you earn £8,000 per annum. You may feel either well paid or poorly paid, depending at least in part on your expectations. One feature affecting your expectations would be what you had to do to earn that £8,000. If you had to work just twenty weeks a year, for twenty hours a week, you might feel that your rate of pay was good. Alternatively, if you had to work fifty weeks a year, ten hours a night, six nights a week, you would probably feel your rate of pay was less than satisfactory. There are two aspects to these examples. The first is related to the rate of pay which, in the first instance, works out to £20 an hour for day work; in the second instance is £2.66 an hour for night work. The second aspect though related to the first, is different. In the first example you would have a considerable amount of time to enjoy your income, whilst in the second example you would have very little. Not only then is the *rate* of payment important, but also the amount of time you have to give up in order to earn the money. When working we normally give up our freedom of choice about how we spend our time. In one sense then the payment, or the rate of payment, may be viewed by the employee as compensation for the time over which he personally gives control to his employer (i.e. he does what his employer wants him to do, rather than what he, as an individual, wants to do).

If asked, many employees would not say that they saw themselves being compensated for the time they give up, but rather being rewarded for their efforts and output. The reasons for individuals holding one view or another (i.e. compensation for time given up or reward for efforts made) are interesting to consider. It may be that workers would say that they believe they are rewarded for effort, because this is what managements say they pay them for and, on the face of it, appear to pay them for. However, the actions of the workers may be interpreted as suggesting that their underlying belief is that they ought to be compensated for their loss of freedom for the time that they are employed. We will refer back to this point again when we look at the significance of employees' rewards to employers and the different payment systems used.

In Chapter 7 we noted that payments not only provide employees with money, which they can spend firstly on things they need to survive, like food, clothing, and shelter, but also satisfy the individual's social and status needs. Some of the indirect financial benefits may particularly satisfy the individual's needs for status or to be held in esteem by his fellow man. For instance, the man who buys himself a Rolls Royce may be telling his neighbours how wealthy he is. How much better though if the organisation that employs him provides him with a Rolls Royce and chauffeur. In this case it not only shows that he is wealthy, but also indicates that he is an important man. Pay not only gives the individual status in the community, it also provides status within the organisation, which can be just as, if not more, important. The manager who is given a company Jaguar car might, on the face of it, be expected to be pleased but if all his colleagues are given Bentleys, it may make him unhappy.

We come to the conclusion then that after some certain minimum level of pay is achieved, it is not the amount received in absolute terms which becomes important to the individual, but the amount he receives relative to others. This is not a phenomenon confined only to the very highly paid, it seems to apply to workers at all levels.

We find the situation where the worker is most concerned if his differential, of perhaps as little as one penny per hour, is threatened. He will seem to fight tooth and nail to avoid losing this differential over his fellow workers. This is not, presumably, because he is concerned about the forty pence extra it yields in his gross pay at the end of the week, compared with those earning a penny an hour less, but that the thing that sets him apart from the other workers is to be removed, and with it his own sense of importance. Those other workers, who newly receive the extra penny an hour, may, from their point of view, be receiving something far more valuable than forty pence per week. They are obtaining some acknowledgement that they have achieved the same level of standing in the organisation as the employee who is now unhappy about them joining his previously exclusive group. Their satisfaction will probably be greater if not all those who were previously earning the same hourly rate receive the one penny increase.

We may conclude that the importance of the total rewards package to employees has at least three distinct aspects. Firstly, the employee may perceive what he receives as pay not only as a reward for output or effort but also as a compensation for giving up his free time. What is more likely is that, if he thinks about it at all in these terms, he sees it as some combination of both. Secondly, the worker will be interested in obtaining enough pay in absolute terms to allow him to secure some standard of living. What amount of pay this is will depend upon his expectations. These will be a product of the socialisation processes the worker has been through and is experiencing and will, by implication, not be static. Thirdly, having achieved his expectations in terms of the absolute amount he is paid, the worker will be concerned with his pay relative to others, i.e. his relativities and differentials.

The Significance of Pay to the Employer

The first point to note is that payments made to employees are costs incurred by the organisation. The second point is that employers realise that pay is a major factor in determining their ability to attract and retain employees as well as to induce them to perform their jobs in a way beneficial to the organisation.

Pay as an element of cost

Let us take an example of two organisations, Companies A and B. Company A produces a product that may be termed labour intensive. The cost of producing the product can be split into three parts:

—direct labour costs
—direct material costs
—overheads (including depreciation of plant and equipment)

If the total cost to manufacture and sell one item which Company A produces is £100, then the costs may be split as follows:

direct labour costs per unit	£70
direct material costs per unit	£15
overheads apportioned per unit	£15
Total cost per unit	£100

If, on the other hand, the product that Company B produces has a very high material cost content, then the breakdown of its product costs may be:

direct labour costs per unit	£10
direct material costs per unit	£60
overheads apportioned per unit	£30
Total cost per unit	£100

Whilst both companies will want to keep all costs to the minimum, it is immediately apparent that the importance they attach to labour costs compared with others will vary. Suppose that the employees of both companies put in pay claims for a 20% increase in their wages. As far as the companies are concerned, if they agree to these increases, then the effect upon their product costs will be that in both cases the direct labour element of cost will rise by 20%. In the case of Company A this will mean that the direct labour cost per unit will rise from £70 to £84, an increase of £14 per unit. The same percentage change in direct labour costs per unit for Company B will be an increase from £10 to £12. Now let us assume that each company sells its respective products for £110 per unit. Therefore, the profit for each company expressed as a percentage of its costs is 10%. Now let us assume that both companies operate in competitive (but different) product markets and that, because of the selling prices of their competitors, they are only able to increase their selling price by 5% (i.e. new selling prices of £115.50), still maintaining the volume of sales. When each company receives the claim from their employees for a 20% pay rise they will look at the effect that conceding such a claim would have upon their profitability.

If Company A were to give their employees the 20% increase, and were not to raise their selling price, the effect would be:

Selling price per unit		£110
Direct labour costs per unit	£84	
Direct material costs per unit	£15	
Overheads apportioned per unit	£15	
Total cost per unit		£114
Loss per unit	£4	

Increase in labour cost as a percentage of total cost = 14%

If Company A were to give the 20% increase to their workers and to increase their selling price by 5%, the effect would be:

Selling price per unit		£115.50
Direct labour costs per unit	£84	
Direct material cost per unit	£15	
Overheads apportioned per unit	£15	
Total cost per unit		£114

Profit per unit expressed as a percentage of total costs
$$\frac{1.5}{114} \times 100 = 1.32\%$$

whereas their profit per unit before (expressed as a percentage of total costs) was 10%. Therefore, if Company A were to concede the pay claim to their employees and increase their selling price, their profits as a percentage of their total costs would fall by 8.68% (i.e. 10% − 1.32%).

Let us now look at the effect upon Company B. If Company B were to give their employees the 20% pay increase asked for, and not to raise the selling price the effect would be:-

Selling price per unit		£110
Direct labour costs per unit	£12	
Direct material costs per unit	£60	
Overheads apportioned per unit	£30	
Total cost per unit		£102
Profit per unit	£8	

Increase in labour costs as a percentage of total costs = 2%

If Company B were to give the 20% pay increase to their workers and to increase the selling price by 5% the effect would be:

Selling price per unit		£115.50
Direct labour cost per unit	£12	
Direct material cost per unit	£60	
Overheads apportioned per unit	£30	
Total cost per unit		£102
Profit per unit	£13.50	

Profit per unit expressed as a percentage of total costs

$$\frac{13.5}{102} \times 100 = 13.24\%$$

whereas their profit per unit before (expressed as a percentage of total costs) was 10%.

Therefore, if Company B were to concede the pay claim to their employees and increase their selling price, their profits as a percentage of their total costs would rise by 3.24% (i.e. 13.24% − 10%).

It is not difficult to imagine that, when presented with similar pay claims, the managers of Companies A and B will react rather differently. The Managers of Company B are far more likely to be prepared to concede the pay claim than their counterparts in Company A. Indeed the Managers of Company A will probably feel unable to concede the claim (even given their ability to increase the selling price) because of the effect upon the profitability of the Company.

The only circumstances under which the managers of Company A would be prepared to entertain the pay claim would be if they felt there was some way of reducing the element of direct labour costs per unit. To achieve such a reduction would require an increase in labour productivity.

The general point we can conclude is that labour constitutes an element of cost within all organisations, and that most are concerned with keeping costs as low as possible. The significance of labour costs as a part of total costs varies amongst organisations, and, therefore, so does the significance of changes in pay.

Pay as a motivating force on employees

Pay can be considered as a motivating force which attracts employees and retains them whilst inducing them to perform their jobs in a way that is beneficial to the organisation. There are two aspects to pay. The first is the amount of pay, both in money and indirect financial payments. The organisation must pay enough to attract new workers and retain existing workers. In this respect the organisation will want to pay enough, but no more than is necessary, to achieve this objective. We will look at how this level of payment is arrived at later. The second is more concerned with the aims of inducing the workers to perform in ways which are of maximum benefit to the organisation. Given the first aspect of the absolute level of pay required to attract and retain employees, the second is concerned with the basis on which the payment is made (usually referred to as the payment system or system of payment). Let us take an example. An organisation may have to pay a particular type of worker £150 a week in order to attract and retain him. Having obtained and retained the services of the required number of employees of this type, the organisation must now motivate them to achieve the goals. In other words, the decision must be made, on what basis the £150 per week is to be paid. There are two main variables which the organisation considers:

(i)   payments which vary according to the output of the worker;
(ii)   payments which vary with the amount of time the employee spends at work.

Most frequently some combination of these two variables is used. The choice of specific systems of payment which relate to these two variables is discussed later. At this stage we merely note that those systems which are based on the principle of payments varying according to output seem to exhibit certain features. In general terms, payment systems which are based exclusively on output seem to encourage the greatest effort on the part of the workers, but also seem to encourage the lowest levels of cooperation between workers and managers. Conversely, those systems of payment that are less directly and exclusively related to volume of output seem to encourage greater cooperation between the workers and the management.

General Determinants of Levels of Pay in Organisations

In this part we look at the factors which determine how much workers in organisations are paid. The importance of any or each of the factors we look at will vary amongst organisations and within any given organisation from time to time. Further, the factors themselves should not be seen as discrete and isolated from one another, since they tend to interact.

One factor is the organisation's pay policy, if it has one, which will include the payment systems used. There may be some form of job evaluation linked to salary/wage administration; it may simply follow the prevailing market rates for jobs; it may operate some form of payment by results system or some method of rewarding employees using performance appraisal techniques. Whichever system is used, it will be affected by a particular organisation's policy, which in itself will be influenced by its financial position.

Another factor which will affect the level of payments made to particular employees will be the state of the labour market, for that type of employee. If the demand for a certain type of worker significantly exceeds the total supply to all organisations, then the price (pay) for that worker will rise. The converse is rarely true in absolute terms — employees are rarely paid less (i.e. have their pay reduced). More often they will increase their pay less rapidly than other groups over time.

A third factor determining levels of pay of workers is the process of collective bargaining. The results of collective bargaining will be affected by a number of variables, including the strength of the trade unions concerned, which itself may be influenced by the state of the labour market amongst other things. (See Chapter 18.)

The cost of living may indirectly affect the level of pay, mainly through the collective bargaining process. Employee aspirations, which are affected by the cost of living, amongst other things, may either influence their individual levels of pay (by going to management and negotiating individual pay rises), or their collective earnings (through the process or collective bargaining).

Finally, the activity of governments, through incomes policy (whether statutory or voluntary), is a determinant of the levels of pay received by employees. Legislation on Equal Pay has also been influential.

Payment Systems Generally

One of the features we noted earlier of a good pay policy was that it would be seen to be fair by employees. Whether employees view a payment system as fair or not will depend on a number of things. We suggest if the payment system in some way acknowledges that jobs are different, some being more difficult than others, and that the more difficult jobs are better rewarded, then it is more likely to be seen as a fair system. The technique we use to do this is known as job evaluation.

Job evaluation

Job evaluation can be defined as the technique of comparing jobs, not of assessing a single job in isolation. The purpose of job evaluation is to assess the relative difficulty or responsibility of a number of jobs so as to put them into ordered ranks on which a pay structure can be based.

It must be clearly understood that in job evaluation it is the *job* we are assessing, not the person who does the job. We are concerned with evaluating the demands of the job and what these require of any worker tackling it, not just one particular worker. Job evaluation is not in itself a technique for determining rates of pay. Once all the jobs in an organisation have been analysed (for methods of job analysis, see Chapter 4) and ranked in order of their difficulty and responsibility, they are usually grouped into grades or categories. Then, by either unilateral management decisions, or by negotiation between management and unions, rates of pay are attached to these grades. Very often the rates of pay established for a particular grade or level of jobs will only constitute the base rate to which will be added bonus payments, resulting from payment by results schemes. Alternatively, each grade or level may have associated with it a range of rates of pay, through which individual job holders may progress. The basis for progression may be length of service of the employee, or the quality of performance of the employee in the job, as determined through performance appraisal. (Performance appraisal techniques are dealt with separately in Chapter 14.)

Although job evaluation cannot be said to be an exact science, since it relies upon peoples' judgments, it is an attempt to compare jobs in a systematic and objective way. If we have gone to the trouble of evaluating jobs and then providing rates of pay for each grade, we must ensure that the relative rates are maintained. If the basic rates reflect what is considered the proper pay relationship between grades, we must not allow bonus payments to distort this. To take an example, let us say we have evaluated three jobs X, Y and Z and have decided that jobs X and Y should be in the same grade, (grade 3) and job Z should have a higher grade (let us say grade 5). The basic rate of pay for grade 3 jobs should be £200 per week and the basic rate of pay for grade 5 jobs should be £240 per week. (The implication is that job Z is worth a fifth as much again in terms of pay as jobs X and Y.) However, this is merely basic pay, each job being of the type where workers can earn bonus payments in addition. If we have three workers, one in each of the jobs, each working equally hard, then we would hope that the relationships between earnings would be maintained. If the worker in job X earns £80 bonus making his total earnins £280, the worker in job Y earns £20 bonus making his total pay £220 and the worker in job Z also earns £20 bonus making his total pay £260, we see that the differentials we took such care to establish through job evaluation have been completely destroyed when total pay is compared amongst the jobs:

REWARDS

	Grade3		Grade 5
	Job X	Job Y	Job Z
Basic	£200	£200	£240
	Originally the same		Originally 1.2 times Grade 3 jobs.
Bonus	£80	£20	£20
Total	£280	£220	£260
	No longer equal		No longer same differential over Grade 3 jobs.

From this example, we can see that the original attempt to introduce some equitable relationship between the rates of pay for the three jobs, through the process of job evaluation, has been completely negated by the effects of the bonus on total pay.

The lesson to be learnt is that the pay relationships derived from job evaluation should ideally apply to the final, total pay levels. This may be easier said than done.

Methods of job evaluation

There are two main ways of assessing a series of different jobs — by non-analytical and analytical approaches.

The two most commonly-used non-analytical approaches to job evaluation are known as 'Ranking' and 'Grading or Classification' methods.

Ranking methods of job evaluation

In this method we write a description of each job (job description), defining its duties, responsibilities and the qualifications and qualities required in any job holder to perform the job successfully. The second stage is to identify what are known as 'key jobs'. Key jobs are those which are considered as the most and least important, i.e. those expected to be ranked as top and bottom of the list of jobs. Other key jobs will be those that we believe should be ranked at say roughly a quarter, half and three quarters of the way down the rank listing of jobs. Having identified our key jobs, we then look at all those remaining and, by the process of first comparing them with the key jobs and then with one another, we slot them into positions in the rank order. This gives a list of all the jobs ranging from the top to the bottom. The final stage is to divide the ranked jobs into grades and to fix a pay level for each grade. For example, we may have forty jobs to evaluate. Having gone through the process of identifying key jobs and making comparisons between jobs, we will end up with the forty jobs listed in descending order of importance. We then decide how many grades we want, let us say 5. We would then decide that the top eight jobs are to be in the highest grade (grade 5), the ninth to sixteenth ranked jobs in grade 4, and so on, with the bottom eight jobs (i.e. jobs thirty-three to forty in the rank order) being graded 1. Each grade would have its associated level of pay. Alternatively, we may feel that the total list of jobs break into five fairly natural groupings. In this case each grade may not contain the same number of jobs. Therefore the distribution of jobs in grades may end up as:

Grade	Number of jobs in the grade
5	5
4	6
3	10
2	14
1	5

Whilst the ranking method is simple to apply and can be introduced and operated fairly quickly (and therefore quite cheaply), in terms of the employee-hours spent on the exercise, it has some serious limitations. The main disadvantages of this method are threefold:

(i) It can only indicate that one job is more difficult than another — not how much more difficult. So, for instance, the job ranked thirty-eight in the example may be nearly twice as demanding as the job ranked forty, though they may still end up in the same grade and, therefore, with the same levels of pay.

(ii) It is highly subjective, since assessors have no real means of justifying why they have ranked a series of jobs in a certain order.

(iii) The decision of where to draw the line between one grade and another is highly subjective and quite arbitrary.

The grading or classification method of job evaluation

This is not unlike the ranking method, except that we approach the task from the opposite direction. Firstly, we decide how many grades we will have. Secondly, we draw up general descriptions for each grade. Each job is then examined, and considered against each of the grade descriptions, being slotted into the grade into which it fits most easily. We may, for example, decide that the lowest grade will include all jobs where the work is simple, repetitive, and performed under close supervision, with each successive grade recognising a higher level of skill and responsibility.

Like the ranking method, this is easy to apply and is quickly and cheaply operated, but is also highly dependent upon the subjective judgments of the assessors.

The points rating method of job evaluation

This is the most widely used method of job evaluation, each job is analysed under a number of headings and the requirements for the job are drawn up under these headings or factors in a document known as a job specification. (An example of a job specification for the job of Personnel Officer is given in Figure 13 of Chapter 4.) All jobs are analysed by reference to the same factors so, using the job specification for the Personnel Officer as an example, we can see that all jobs would have the factor 'Educational requirements'. The factor Educational requirements will have a range of points attached to it. The points available may be distributed as follows:

Description of Educational Level	Points
GCSE or 'O' level passes	75
'A' level, ONC or OND passes	150
HND/HNC or Pass Degree	300
Honours Degree or relevant professional qualification	325
Master's Degree	375
Doctorate	500

Thus for any job to be evaluated, this factor will be considered and a points score obtained. For the job of Personnel Officer points scored would be 300. The factors chosen by organisations for evaluation will vary, but many will include factors like:

Factor	Possible points range
Educational Requirements	0 – 500
Skills Requirements	0 – 300
Experience Requirements	0 – 300
Initiative	0 – 200
Judgments	0 – 200
Planning and Coordinating	0 – 250
Cooperation and Contact	0 – 250
Decision Making Affecting Costs	0 – 500
Mental and Physical Fatigue	0 – 150

Each factor will have a range of points associated with it in much the same way as the factor Educational Requirements. Each factor will not necessarily have the same range available, so, for instance, 'Mental and Physical Fatigue' may have a range of points from 0 to 150. The implication here is that this factor is considered less important than 'Educational Requirements'.

When we have drawn up a job specification, having considered each factor and awarded points, we can add up and arrive at a total score for the job. This process can be repeated for all jobs. It is normal to start the process with key jobs, known often in the method as 'bench mark' jobs. Bench mark jobs are often selected on the basis that they are considered as representative of a certain level or grade of job. The divisions between one grade and the next are determined by drawing arbitrary, but generally fair, lines between total scores. So, for example, using the possible points range for the factors noted earlier, the minimum possible score is zero, the maximum 2650. We may decide to have eight grades of jobs, in which the division points may be as follows:

Points range	Grade
0 – 300	1
301 – 600	2
601 – 900	3
901 – 1200	4
1201 – 1500	5
1501 – 1800	6
1801 – 2100	7
2101 – 2650	8

If the total score for any particular job is 1,000 points, then it will become a grade 4 job, which will have a particular rate of pay associated with it.

This method of job evaluation has certain advantages over the previous two methods described. The advantages are:

(i)   This approach is more objective;

(ii)   This method can be used in a variety of situations, is very adaptable and is easily explained to those affected (i.e. employees doing jobs which are evaluated);

(iii)   Assessors or job evaluators are able to explain why a particular grade has been arrived at for any specific job;

(iv)   When the contents of jobs change, they can be reassessed and, if necessary, the job specification changed accordingly. The job can then be re-evaluated. If the new total score moves the job into a new grade, then the necessary adjustments in pay can be made.

On the other hand, it is fairly slow, and therefore expensive, to administer. Moreover, because the system is fairly formal, it may become undesirably inflexible.

The strengths and weaknesses of job evaluation

We must remember that job evaluation does not itself determine rates of pay, it merely provides a basis upon which jobs can be compared with one another. When we have evaluated all the jobs in an organisation, and assigned rates of pay to the various grades, we can expect the result to be a more equitable pay structure. The term equitable is based on the assumption that rewards for work should be equated to job content. An effect of this structure should be that the chaotic jungle of different rates of pay, where individuals and groups continually haggle about their rewards, should be replaced by a more ordered situation. This provides a firmer base from which to make changes, if necessary, in the payment structure. Another desirable consequence of job evaluation, is that it encourages the development of defined promotion and upgrading policies. Job evaluation should help to remove any suspicions the employees may have about favouritism. If it is considered desirable by all the parties concerned, job evaluation can provide an area for trade union involvement in the joint regulation of workplace conditions. This can be achieved by trades union representatives participating in the process of evaluating jobs. The greatest weakness of job evaluation based pay structures is that what is internally equitable within an organisation, is not always externally essential. If we recall our earlier example of the accountants and engineers, both paid the same, but a shortage of engineers occurring (thus requiring the organisation to increase the pay of engineers in order to recruit and retain them), we have the problem in a nutshell. If the jobs had been evaluated and found to be of the same grade, how could we justify paying engineers more? The alternative of paying all the jobs in that grade the amount we would need to pay engineers, would result in many workers being paid more than they need be, an unattractive proposition from the organisation's viewpoint.

Payment Systems: Pay varies with time

In this type of payment system an amount of money is negotiated or agreed individually between workers and management (on behalf of the organisation) and paid, by the hour or week or month, to the worker for attendance at the place of work. This constitutes the employee's basic rate of pay. For example if Mr. Brown is employed by a company, on the basis of a forty hour week at a basic rate of pay of £3 an hour, and he attends work for five days at eight hours a day, his pay will be £120. If this is the sole basis of payment for Mr. Brown, he will receive his £120 irrespective of the amount of work he does during that week. Similarly, if Mr. Brown attends work for 32 hours a week, he will be paid £96, even if in that time he produces as much as he would have done in forty hours. In other words, Mr. Brown's pay varies only in relation to the time he spends at work and not with the amount he produces during that time. Many jobs are paid on this basis. The employee is thus certain of the amount of his total pay and he can control this, within limits, by the amount of time he spends at work. The employer normally states in precise terms the time he expects the worker to attend and he can predict his labour costs fairly accurately. The employer has a strong incentive to ensure that the workers are gainfully employed all the time they are at work, since they will be paid the same amount irrespective of the amount they produce. He will see pay to employees as a fixed cost of production. Many so-called staff jobs have this system of payment applied to them.

Time-rated payment systems apply to situations other than the basic hours of employees. Let us look at some of these, but, before we do so, note that a time-rated basis of payment in these circumstances may be used in conjunction with other payment systems, notably those which are based upon the output and effort of the worker.

Payment for overtime

To return to our example of Mr. Brown, suppose the organisation employing Mr. Brown has an abnormally heavy workload in one week. Mr. Brown may be asked to work overtime to do the tasks which he is unable to do during his normal working week, because of lack of time. It is common nowadays for such overtime to be paid at what is known as *premium rates*. If Mr. Brown is required to work overtime on any weekday (i.e. Monday to Friday), he may be paid at a premium rate of time-and-a-quarter for all such overtime. Therefore, every hour of overtime that he works on a week day is paid at a rate of £3.75 per hour (£3 x 1.25). If Mr. Brown works his normal forty hours in a week, plus two hours overtime each night Monday to Friday, his pay will be:

Basic pay for 40 hours at normal rate	£120.00
Overtime pay for 10 hours at time-and-a-quarter	£37.50
Total pay for week	£157.50

The premium rates for overtime worked on Saturdays may be time-and-a-half, whilst for Sundays they may be double-time. We can see that if Mr. Brown is required to work on a Sunday, all work on that day will be paid at the rate of £6 an hour.

Shift or unsocial hours payments

Suppose that the job Mr. Brown does during the day also has to be done at night. To do this work at night the organisation employs Mr. Smith. Since Mr. Smith does the same work as Mr. Brown, it is reasonable to assume that he will be paid at the same basic rate. In this case the organisation will pay Mr. Smith a premium rate for working shift work. In doing so they are recognising that to have to work at night is less agreeable than working during the day, hence the term 'unsocial hours'. The premium rate for night work may well be time-and-a-third. If Mr. Smith works 40 hours in a week, all of which are at night, his pay will be:

Basic pay	£120
Shift pay	£40
Total pay	£160

Time-rated systems and incentives

If we recall Professor Lupton's definition of payment system as *'a way of so influencing the behaviour of workers that the purposes of the organisation are efficiently served',* we may feel that, provided the rate of pay is high enough, we will be able to recruit and retain employees. However, we went on to say that a good payment system is one which encourages high performance by the workers to whom it is applied. So far as we have described it, there is nothing in a time-rated system of payment which in itself encourages, or provides an incentive for, high performance.

There are two main methods that are used for this purpose, the first known as *service increments* and the second as *merit payments.* Both are compatible with a pay system based upon job evaluation. Some organisations use both methods. We will deal with each in turn but, before doing so, we will look in more detail at our pay arrangements in connection with job evaluation.

Suppose we have an organisation in which each job has been evaluated and allocated to one of five grades. If we have decided to have a system of payment which involves either service increments or merit payments, or both, instead of establishing a single rate of pay for each grade of job we must establish a *range* of rates. In the process of job evaluation we assessed the value of the job to the organisation, not the worker doing the job. Our intention now is to reward the individual workers doing each job. Suppose our pay structure for the five grades of job in the organisation is:

Grade Number	Minimum pay for grade £/annum	Maximum pay for grade £/annum	Range of pay for for grade £
1	8,000	10,000	2,000
2	12,000	15,000	3,000
3	16,000	20,000	4,000
4	20,000	25,000	5,000
5	24,000	30,000	6,000

The first point to note is that someone earning the maximum in a grade 4 job will be paid more than another person earning the minimum in a grade 5 job. Such an overlap is not essential, but is quite common in organisations, being known as *overlapping wage or salary bands*. From the figures shown above, the range of pay for each grade is 25% of the minimum pay level for the grade. If the organisation decided it did not want overlapping wage or salary bands it could reduce this proportion to 20%.

Service increments

These are increases paid to employees for service in the organisation, or in a particular grade of job, or for some combination of both. Such increments are usually automatic increases in pay on an annual basis. The number of incremental steps in the pay range varies, but most organisations settle on about five. If, in our example, the organisation uses five annual incremental steps, based upon the service of the employee in a job in a grade, then a worker with three years service in a job, which is grade 4 level, will be paid £23,000 per annum.

Merit payments

These are payments which are related to the performance of the worker in the job, as assessed on a regular and systematic basis. Before looking at the methods used to assess employee performance, let us see how the results of such assessment may be used for pay determination.

Let us assume that in an organisation all employees have their performance assessed annually and are given a rating on that performance. The ratings being: satisfactory, good, very good and excellent. An employee obtaining a satisfactory rating may be given an increase equal to 10% of the range of pay for his grade. Similarly, a good rating may result in an increase of 12½% of the range, a very good rating in 16.6%, and an excellent rating in 25%.

If, in our example, the range of pay is solely for rewarding merit and we consider an employee doing a grade 4 job who has held the job for three years then, if we know how well he has performed in those three years, we can work out how much he will be paid. Let us assume that he started in the job at the minimum pay for the grade (£20,000 per annum) and that his performance in the first year was assessed as satisfactory. He would receive a pay rise of 10% of the range, i.e. £500. If, in the second year, his performance was rated as good he would receive an increase of £625 (i.e. 12.5% of £5,000). If in the third year his performance was rated as excellent, he would receive and increase of £1,250 (i.e. 25% of £5,000). Therefore, the employee's pay after three years is:

Original starting pay	£20,000
Increase after 1st year	£500
Increase after 2nd year	£625
Increase after 3rd year	£1,250
Pay after 3 years	£22,375

Clearly, if this employee continues to perform excellently for the next three years, he will have reached the maximum pay for the grade (indeed, if it were possible, he would exceed it).

Assessing the performance of employees in their jobs is a process which is mainly employed for non-manual jobs and is of use where the achievement of the employee may be expressed more easily in qualitative rather than quantitative terms. (See Chapter 14.)

Payment Systems: Pay varies with Output

There are a number of payment systems which are based upon the idea that pay varies with the output produced by the worker. The strength of the relationship (i.e. between amount of pay related to amount of output) varies amongst different systems. In the most extreme form, known as piecework, the relationship is absolute (i.e. there is a perfect correlation), whilst, in other systems, the relationship is weaker and less direct. Before looking at some of the main payment systems based on this approach, we note that there are certain pre-requisites for the successful operation of this type of payment system. Firstly, the amount of work produced, by any particular worker, must be measurable in some clear way. Secondly, there must be an opportunity for the worker to influence the amount of measurable output by his own efforts. In other words, if the worker puts more effort in and thereby works harder, then the amount he produces must increase. If this is not the case, then the incentive to work harder (i.e. harder work results in more output, which results in more pay) will not exist. Thirdly, quantity of output should generally be more important than quality.

Piecework

In piecework, the crudest and simplest form of this type of payment system, the amount the worker is paid depends exclusively on the amount of work he does, as measured by the quantity of his output. In the piecework system the employee effectively acts as a labour only sub-contractor to the organisation employing him. Two examples of piecework are fruit picking and making Christmas crackers. In the case of fruit picking, the employee's pay will be directly proportional to the weight of fruit he picks. Therefore if he worked as an apple picker, paid on a piecework basis, where the rate of pay was two pence per pound, he would earn £6.50 if he picked 325lbs weight of apples. If it took him one week to pick this weight of apples, his pay for the week would be £6.50. If, alternatively, he was able to pick this much in one day, then that would be his pay for that day. If we consider the example of making Christmas crackers, the employer will provide the worker with the materials for making the crackers and undertake to pay a fixed amount for each box of crackers made. The organisation may provide enough materials to make 500 boxes of crackers and agree to pay him, say, five pence per box. The organisation will also probably stipulate some deadline by which it requires him to provide the crackers, at which time it will pay him the sum of £25. The speed at which he works, within very broad limits, is up to him. Further the method that he chooses to make crackers is up to him as well, provided that he actually produces the required results. He can do this work in his own home, and indeed this is the most common form of payment used for homeworkers. From the point of view of the workers it is an attractive method of payment, if they are unable for instance to work during the normal working day, perhaps because of other commitments. Equally, if the worker can only do the odd hour or so of work each day, this method of payment is quite attractive. From the point of view of the organisation it is an attractive system of payment, where for instance the work is highly seasonal, as in the two examples given. It is only a suitable method of payment where there is a virtually unlimited supply of work, and where output is not restricted by production requirements.

Individual payment by results systems

We have seen that piecework is a method of payment based upon the output of the worker, virtually irrespective of the time it takes him to do the work. Most payment by results systems do take account of the time it takes for the job to be performed, indeed this is normally the basis. So, whilst piecework is concerned with the quantity produced, payment by results (PBR) systems are more concerned with the rate of production, i.e. the number produced in a given time. On piecework the worker is rewarded for the weight of apples picked, in a PBR system he would be paid according to the weight of apples he picked per hour.

Where this type of payment system is used the employer is normally interested in maximising the rate of production. For this reason he will provide equipment and instructions for its use so that the worker can do the task as quickly as possible. This contrasts with piecework, where the worker is usually left to decide entirely by himself how he will perform the task.

Let us look in more detail at individual payment by results systems. Let us assume that the task to be performed is to attach one piece of metal to another, by means of four nuts.

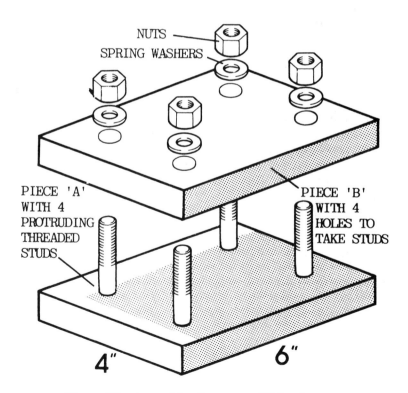

Figure 35 : Assembly diagram — PBR scheme

The worker will be provided with the appropriate tools and equipment, which, in this case, will be:

(i)   a bench to work on with a clamp to hold piece 'A' when it is being worked on;

(ii)   a torque wrench for tightening the nuts. (A torque wrench is a type of spanner which, when used, tells the worker whether he has tightened the nut down hard enough);

(iii)   a place to put the assembled components.

A work study engineer will look at the task and decide the most efficient, i.e. quickest, way it can be satisfactorily performed. He will ensure that the components are located in convenient positions for picking up, the tools are most readily to hand and so on. The instructions given may be quite detailed, so, for example, they may read as follows:

(i)   Pick up piece A with your left hand from the box in front of you.

(ii)   Locate piece A in the clamp on the bench and tighten the clamp using right hand.

(iii)   Pick up piece B with your right hand from the box in front of you, and locate piece B on piece A by means of the studs through the holes.

(iv)   Take two washers in each hand from the box in front of you and locate them on the protruding pegs.

(v)   Take one nut in each hand from the box in front of you and finger tighten on two back studs.

(vi)   Repeat operation (v) finger tightening nuts on the two front studs.

(vii)   Pick up torque wrench from location on the right hand side of bench and tighten down nuts to required torque. Replace torque wrench.

(viii) Loosen clamp on piece A using right hand.

(ix)   Remove assembled component with left hand and place aside in box provided on the left of the bench.

Having been instructed in the job, the worker will then do it for a while, until he reaches what might be called 'experienced worker standard'. At this stage the Work Study Engineer will return and time and rate the worker performing the operation. The task of timing and rating is itself a highly skilled one. The Work Study Engineer will observe the worker performing the task and ensure that the instructions provided are being followed. He will time and rate each element of the task a number of times. So, for instance, with the first two elements of the task, the Work Study Engineer will start his stop watch at the precise moment that the worker picks up piece 'A' with his left hand, and will stop the watch at the moment the worker finishes tightening the clamp with his right hand and is about to move his right hand across to pick up piece 'B'. Whilst the worker is performing these elements, the Work Study Engineer will observe him very closely and rate his performance to obtain an observed rating. That is, he will rate the performance of the worker compared with what is known as standard rating, where standard rating is given the value of 100 on the British Standard Scale. Standard rating corresponds to the 'average rate at which qualified workers will naturally work at a job, provided they know and adhere to the specified method, and provided they are motivated to apply themselves to their work' (BS 3138). This is done so that the observed time (i.e. that which is noted from the stop watch) can be converted into a basic time. The formula used is:

$$\text{Basic Time} = \frac{\text{Observed Time x Observed Rating}}{\text{Standard Rating}}$$

Therefore to go back to our example, the Work Study Engineer times the first two elements, using his stop watch, and obtains an observed time of 5.555 seconds whilst, at the same time, rating the effort of the worker at 90 on the British standard scale. He can then obtain a basic time by applying these figures to the formula as follows:

$$\text{Basic Time} = \frac{5.555 \times 90}{100}$$

Basic Time = 5 seconds

This process is repeated for all the elements of the task. These basic times are then totalled for the whole task.

The next step is for the Work Study Engineer to convert this total basic time into what is known as *standard time*. The standard time for a job must include a factor to compensate for necessary rest and relaxation, delays and interruptions in the normal job cycle. These are known as allowances.

Allowances are usually given as a percentage of the basic time and may include factors for relaxation and contingencies given for time required to perform additional activities which, because of their intermittent and irregular nature, are not included in the basic time. There are other factors which are often built into the allowances.

If we return to our example, and assume that the basic time to perform the whole job is 40 seconds, and that allowances are calculated at 20% then the standard time will be:

Standard time = Basic Time + allowances
$$= 40 + \frac{20 \times 40}{100}$$
$$= 40 + 8$$
$$= 48 \text{ seconds}$$

The standard time will form the basis of the payment system and it is important that this time is agreed with the worker and/or his representative as being a reasonable time allowed for the job.

If the standard time for this job is accepted as 48 seconds, then we can see that someone working at a standard rate (i.e. effort rating of 100) and using up the normal allowances for relaxation etc., might be expected to complete 75 assemblies in the course of one hour (since 75 x 48 sec. = 3600 seconds = 1 hour).

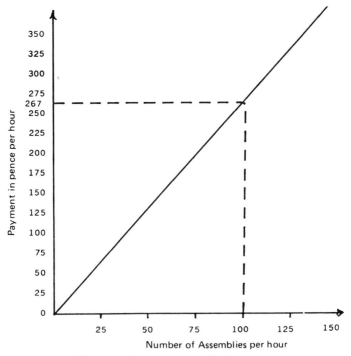

Figure 36 : Individual PBR scheme

REWARDS

The intention of the payment by results system may be to maximise the amount that the worker produces per hour. With this in mind, a scheme of payments will be devised, which is intended to encourage the worker to produce as much as possible, whilst recognising what is reasonably achievable. The simplest way of doing this would be by the use of a simple, single, straight-line graph. So, for example, if the rate of pay for producing 75 assemblies in an hour was set at £2 per hour, the rate for producing 100 assemblies in an hour would be £2.67 and there would be no payment if no assemblies were produced.

It may be decided to give extra incentive for the worker to produce at a higher rate than 75 assemblies per hour. This could be achieved by steepening the line of the graph for rates of production higher than 75 assemblies per hour. See Figure 37.

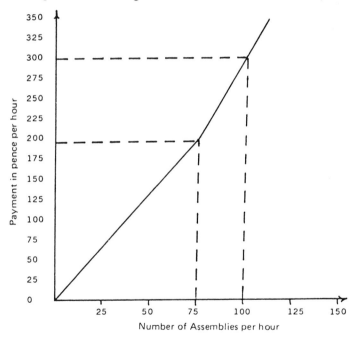

Figure 37 : PBR scheme — steepened graph

With this payment system there is a significant rate of improvement for hourly output in excess of 75 assemblies. Compared with the first scheme (where a 33.3% improvement in the rate of output, from a rate of 75 assemblies per hour to 100 assemblies, yields a 33.3% increase in rate of pay from £2 to £2.67 per hour), an equivalent improvement in

269

output on the new scheme (at the same position) yields a 50% improvement in the rate of pay (from £2 per hour to £3 per hour). This encourages the worker to put in the extra effort to produce at a higher than standard rate.

Let us assume that the organisation decides to operate the second scheme of payment, and that the workers work for 40 hours per week. If the worker engaged in making the assemblies produces 3500 assemblies in a week, then his hourly rate of production is 3500 ÷ 40 = 87.5 assemblies. His rate of pay per hour will therefore be £2.50, making his gross wage for the week £100 (i.e. 40 x £2.50).

In this example we can see that the whole of the worker's pay is based upon the PBR system. It is very common for workers to be given some sort of basic payment, related to time, with an additional bonus payment founded upon a payment by results system. So, for example, in the case of the payment system for the assembly operation described, the time rate element may be set at £1.60 pence per hour and the rates of pay for output (now known as bonus payments) reduced to one fifth of their previous levels — see Figure 38.

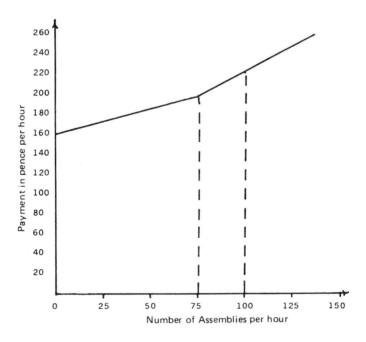

Figure 38 : PBR Scheme — basic + bonus

REWARDS

From Figure 39, we can see that earnings are set at a minimum of £1.60 pence per hour, even if no output is achieved. Let us consider the pay at the two levels of output considered previously, i.e. 75 and 100 assemblies per hour.

Rate of output per worker	75 assemblies/hour	100 assemblies/hour
Basic rate per hour	£1.60	£1.60
Bonus rate per hour	£0.40	£0.60
Total pay per hour	£2.00	£2.20
Total pay for 40 hours per week	£80.00	£88.00

Similarly, if the worker produces 3500 assemblies in a forty hour week, his hourly rate of production is, as before, 87.5 assemblies. His hourly rate of pay will be a basic of £1.60 plus a bonus of £0.50, giving a total of £2.20, yielding a gross wage of £84, compared with £100 when the payment was based entirely upon the rate of output. Let us briefly compare these two payment systems from the point of view of the employer and employee.

From the point of view of the employer, at rates of output that are higher than 75 assemblies per hour, the basic plus bonus method of payment is better, since wages, and therefore costs, are lower for the same rate of output. For rates of output lower than 75 assemblies per hour, the effect of the basic element of pay means that payments are higher for this method of payment than they would be for the method based solely on PBR. Therefore, from the employer's point of view, provided he can ensure rates of output in excess of 75 asemblies per hour, he will prefer this method. He must recognise, however, that the incentive for the worker to put in more effort is significantly less. The employer may need to provide close supervision of the worker to ensure that he maintains his effort.

From the viewpoint of the employee, the basic pay plus bonus method of payment provides him with security of earnings, since his gross income for a forty hour week cannot fall below £64. On the other hand, he is unlikely to be able to earn very large amounts of bonus and, in fact, may in practical terms never be able to achieve the £100 per week level which was obtainable on the other payment method. (To obtain gross pay of £100 on the basic plus bonus method of payment, the worker would have to produce 5500 assemblies in 40 hours.)

From this simple comparison we can see that the attractiveness of one method of payment compared with another, for both the employer and the worker, will be affected by a number of factors. Some of these factors may be considered generally to be related to the desires and aspiration of the parties, others to practical considerations related to the job of work.

From this very brief look at individual payment by results systems we can see that the business of designing payment systems can be very complicated.

Group payment by results systems

Some methods of payment are based, not upon the individual, but upon a group of employees and include group schemes of PBR, Measured Daywork schemes (which may also be applied on an individual basis), Added Value schemes of payment, and Profit Sharing schemes.

Group schemes of PBR

In their simplest form, in which we shall consider them, group schemes of PBR are an extension of the individual method of PBR, designed to cover a group of employees working together. Let us consider an example of a group of workers who have a number of tasks to perform, some of which are the same, some different, but which have some degree of interdependence. Let us assume that we have three workers performing assembly operations similar to that described earlier, one etching the part number of the assemblies on each, and two packing the marked assemblies in boxes and addressing the boxes ready for despatch to customers. The total number of workers engaged on all three activities is therefore six. If the organisation chose, individual PBR schemes could be provided for each of these workers. Alternatively, a group PBR scheme could be used. For a group scheme to operate successfully, the operations must be balanced — i.e. with all the operators performing at a standard effort rating, there should be no build up of work-in-progress between operations and no slack time for any of the operators. To ensure that this occurs, all the operations will be studied to ensure appropriately balanced worker levels are arranged (i.e. six workers as noted above). The implication is clear. Given that the standard time for the assembly operation is 48 seconds and there are three operators, one assembly should be completed every sixteen seconds. Since there is one only one worker performing the etching operation, this operation must take sixteen seconds. Similarly, since there are two workers packing and addressing assemblies, this operation must take thirty-two seconds, or, to put it another way, must have a standard time of thirty-two seconds. Therefore, the final output of all six workers will be, provided they are working at a standard rate of effort, one marked, packed, and addressed assembly every sixteen seconds. We can show this diagrammatically, as in Figure 39.

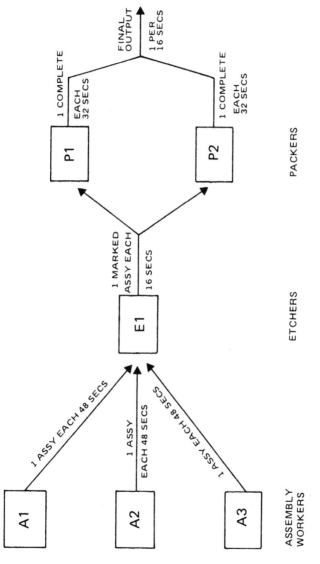

FIGURE 39 : GROUP PBR SCHEME

REWARDING EMPLOYEES

We can see that if one packed assembly is produced every sixteen seconds, the standard rate per hour will be 225. With this information the organisation could devise a payment system, either including some element of basic pay plus bonus, or entirely on a PBR system, for the group of six workers. Moreover, if the various jobs within the total task are considered to be of different levels of difficulty or skill, this could be reflected in different basic rates for the different jobs. So, for instance the assemblers may be paid at a basic rate of £1.60 per hour, the worker engaged in etching at £1.40 per hour, and the packers at £1.50 per hour, as a basic rate. However, they will all receive bonus payments, based upon the output of the whole group. Taking a very simple, single straight line basis of bonus payments, as shown below, we can calculate the earnings of each type of worker at various levels of output.

Level of Output 225 units/hour = 9000/wk.

Type of Worker	Assy Worker	Etcher	Packer
Basic Pay/hour	£1.60	£1.40	£1.50
Bonus Pay/hour	£0.40	£0.40	£0.40
Total Pay/hour	£2.00	£1.80	£1.90
Total for 40 hour week	£80.00	£72.00	£76.00

Level of Output 300 units/hour = 12000 per week

Type of Worker	Assy Worker	Etcher	Packer
Basic Pay/hour	£1.60	£1.40	£1.50
Bonus Pay/hour	£0.53	£0.53	£0.53
Total Pay/hour	£2.13	£1.93	£2.03
Total for 40 hour week	£85.20	£77.20	£81.20

The rate of output of the whole group, upon which bonus is calculated, will be constrained to the level achieved by the slowest type of worker. On this basis, the job of the worker doing the etching becomes critical, since if his rate of production drops, the bonus for all the workers in the scheme will drop. If the rate of production of one of the assemblers drops, then it is possible that this can be counteracted by the other two assemblers working faster. A similar situation exists with the packers.

With this method of payment, the workers are concerned with the final output of the group, since it is upon this that their own bonuses are based. The main concern of the management is also the final output of the group, since this constitutes the saleable product. Since the workers have a vested interest in the output of the group, they may be expected to ensure that all members of the group do their utmost to maximise the bonus, but this is not necessarily so. (See Chapter 9.) From the point of view of the management, such group PBR schemes may be attractive for at least two reasons. Firstly, the level of effort of the employees may be kept high and policed by the members of the group scheme themselves. Secondly, the cost of administration of the bonus scheme can be significantly less than the costs of administering a number of individual PBR schemes.

Measured daywork schemes of payment

Measured daywork schemes are systems of payment where the earnings of the workers vary by the quantity that they produce (the output they achieve), but where the management control the total output. The basis of these schemes is that a fixed payment is made to group members (although these payments may be different for various levels of skill) for achieving a performance level or output rate. The payment to be made for a specified level of output is mutually agreed, in advance between the management and the workers within the scheme. The payment is only withdrawn if failure to meet the specified target can be demonstrated to be the fault of the operators. These schemes of payment may be suitable for quite large assembly lines for instance where management wishes to maintain customary effort levels and specified levels of output. These schemes can provide for flexible operation by the workers, since it is in all their interests to meet the specified level of output and thus achieve the fixed bonus payment. It is attractive to operators, as it provides stable earnings, and is convenient for management, as they control output. It does, however, require very good supervision and good training of group members, since existing group members will be reluctant to accept operators into the scheme who do not pull their weight, and may therefore jeopardise the chance of earning the fixed sum bonus.

Added Value schemes of payment

The operation of Added Value schemes of payment can be quite complex and require a fair degree of understanding of, what might loosely be described as, accounting principles. For this reason we will attempt to do no more than briefly outline the general concepts. Before looking at Added Value systems of payment we must briefly define the term Added Value itself. Added Value is *the value added to materials and other purchased items, which provides, as a result of the productive activities in*

275

the organisation, the sum out of which wages, salaries and administrative overhead expenses are paid, leaving any surplus as profit.

Central to schemes based on Added Value is the establishment of the ratio between wages/salaries (known as employment costs) and Added Value. This calculation can generally be made from existing accounting information, and is done historically, say for a period of five years, so that a consistency in the ratio is assured. This ratio becomes the norm against which future performance is compared.

The difference between the ratio established as the norm, when applied to Added Value for a given period (usually one month), and the actual employment costs in that period, is available for distribution to employees. The percentage of this 'saving' paid to employees varies from scheme to scheme. Commonly the split between employees and organisations varies with the ratio of employment costs to Added Value. In other words, the employees' share of improvements in each organisation is roughly equivalent to their contribution to the Added Value generated. Some organisations allocate a certain proportion of total improvement to a reserve account, the function of which is to maintain bonuses during deficit months, since bonus is normally distributed monthly. Some organisations distribute bonus in equal shares to all members, others distribute it in proportion to basic pay. Employees are kept informed of how their efforts are affecting the organisation's productivity by regular publication of ratios reflecting organisational performance.

Added Value schemes of payment, which are an attempt to involve employees in the overall financial performance of the organisation, are clearly applicable to all employees and can be operated in addition to other PBR schemes.

Profit sharing

Like Added Value schemes, the operation of profit sharing schemes can be complicated. For this reason we will again just consider the general principles involved.

The underlying beliefs regarding profit sharing are that if an employee benefits personally when the organisation for which he works is profitable, and that his benefits are in some way proportional, then he will be motivated to make the organisation more profitable through his own efforts. Moreover, if he has some capital interest in the organisation, he will desire its long term profitability in the same way that normal shareholders would (i.e. shareholders see the benefit in two component parts, the dividend paid on shares and the appreciation of share values).

There are three main methods of profit sharing:

(i)   Payment of cash bonuses to employees in some proportion to the profitability of the organisation;

(ii)   Payment of cash as in (i), but combined with the issue of shares to employees;

(iii)   The issue of shares only in relation to the profitability of the organisation.

While profit sharing through share issue schemes is not a new innovation, it has in the past tended to be limited to employees in senior management and executive positions.

Considerations in the Choice of Payment System

Bearing in mind the important organisational objectives which are to be achieved through the payment system, it is important that appropriate systems are devised and used. We have looked at various types of payment system and, whilst there is no such thing as the perfect system, we can identify the general circumstances in which one type of system will be better than another. For payment by results systems to have a reasonable chance of operating successfully there are certain requirements. These requirements may be summarised as:

(i)   The payment system must be easily understood by those to whom it is applied;

(ii)   Earnings must relate clearly to efforts and results;

(iii)   Bonus earnings must be made promptly after the effort has been put in by the worker;

(iv)   Rates of bonus earnings should not be subject to change;

(v)   The most efficient methods should be found before installing the scheme;

(vi)   Those who set standards (work study engineers) should be competent and recognised as such;

(vii)   An efficient grievance procedure must exist;

(viii) Levels of pay must be agreed for times when there is insufficient work;

(ix)   Bonus should be applied to all jobs and should yield the same for similar levels of effort;

(x)   The system should somehow recognise differential skills.

Time-rated systems of payment are better than PBR systems when:

(i)   The amount of work is not easily measurable;

(ii)   Output is outside the control of the workers;

(iii)   Delays in the supply of work to the worker are frequent;

(iv)   There are frequent changes in the working methods;

(v)   Quality is more important than quantity.

In conclusion, when payment systems are being devised, consideration must be given to:

(i)   The type of organisation, its products, markets, and cost structures;

(ii)   The quantity, versus quality, of output required;

(iii)   The type of labour employed;

(iv)   The type of labour relations;

(v)   The capability of the supervisory staff;

(vi)   The attitudes of the workers.

Section 6

Industrial Relations

CHAPTER 18 : INDUSTRIAL RELATIONS

CHAPTER 19 : LEGISLATION ON INDUSTRIAL RELATIONS

Chapter 18 deals with the conduct of Industrial Relations at the workplace, putting it briefly in a wider context. It begins with some important definitions and outlines the frames of reference on which our understanding and expectations are based. The process of collective bargaining at the organisational level is considered, together with the range of negotiating and other activities associated with the process. Chapter 19 is concerned with the impact of the State and its agencies on the conduct of Industrial Relations, including legislation and the role of ACAS in arbitration, conciliation, and mediation.

Chapter 18

Industrial Relations

Most textbooks on the subject of Industrial Relations devote a lot of space to an analysis and description of the main parties and institutions to Industrial Relations. To obtain a sound understanding of this complex subject, it can be argued that, not only is this essential, but that it must be understood in its historical and political context. Whilst recognising this, we realise that space does not allow us to delve into the subject in the detail that it deserves. However, no textbook on people in organisations would be complete without some treatment of the subject.

Let us define Industrial Relations itself as: *the system of rules which govern employment, and the formulation and operation of those rules by the parties and institutions concerned with them.*

These rules will cover many different aspects of employment; some will be formally written, some less formally recorded (but equally important), and some will exist as a result of minimum standards set by legislation on employment.

Many definitions have been given for a trade union, often in the context of Acts of Parliament. Such definitions are very precise, but often lengthy. A simplified version of the definition used in the Trade Union and Labour Relations Act 1974 becomes: *An organisation that consists of workers of one or more type, the principal purpose of which is to regulate the relations between the workers and their employers, or the association to which their employers belong.* The number of trade unions registered with the Certification Officer at 31st December 1986 was 375, of which about 100 were affiliated directly or indirectly to the Trades Union Congress (TUC).

We define a shop steward as *a worker who is elected by his fellow trade unionists, in the place of work, to represent their interests in that place of work.* The rules concerning who is eligible to become a shop steward and the process for his election are made by the trade union and normally embodied in their formal set of rules. The functions of shop stewards are generally similar amongst trades unions and include:

(i)   the collection of union dues from members;

(ii)   the recruitment of new members;

(iii)   communication between the workers, employer, and trade union;

(iv)   negotiation of agreements on behalf of the members he represents;

280

(v)   representation of his constituents, both collectively and individually, in their dealings with the employers (usually the managers).

Most trades unions have full time officers, ranging from District Secretaries to General Secretaries and Presidents. In some these are elected positions, in others they are appointments. Most full time officials are employed chiefly as negotiators, though some have administrative duties as well.

The Trades Union Congress (TUC) is a permanent association of British Trades Unions, founded in 1868, to consider questions of importance to trades unionists and give publicity to such matters. The main function of the TUC is to exercise influence on behalf of its affiliated trades unions. The TUC operates through its Annual Congress, its General Council, and its full time officials, led by the General Secretary.

Employers' associations are organisations of employers (usually within one industry) which seek to assist, influence, or control the Industrial Relations decisions of member firms. Such associations sometimes have other functions completely divorced from the area of Industrial Relations. Probably the best known employers' association is the Engineering Employers' Federation (EEF) which negotiates, on behalf of its members, with the Confederation of Shipbuilding and Engineering Unions (a negotiating body representing the Trades Unions with members employed in the Engineering Industry). The subject of these negotiations, known as National Agreements, set minimum standards on pay and conditions to be applied to EEF affiliated members and the unions with which they deal domestically. There were 148 Employers' Associations registered with the Certification Officer on 31st December 1986, although there are many more.

The confederation of British Industry (CBI) was founded in 1965 (though similar bodies had existed before). Its objectives are to provide for British industry the means of formulating, making known, and influencing general policy on industrial, economic, fiscal, commercial, labour, social, legal, and technical questions.

A Frame of Reference for Viewing Industrial Relations

Industrial Relations is a subject about which people hold and express strong views. Discussions are often highly emotional. Our concern is to try to consider the subject objectively and analytically. Unfortunately, few of us are completely open minded, partly because our lives are affected by what happens in industrial relations, and partly because most of our knowledge and experience of it is obtained through the mass media, whose portrayal often borders upon the hysterical. Industrial

281

Relations is often shown as being exclusively concerned with conflict — conflict between workers and management; conflict between the trades unions and employers; and sometimes conflict between workers and trades unions, or between one group of workers and another. Whilst Industrial Relations is not exclusively concerned with conflict, it is certainly an important aspect and makes a good starting point for considering the subject.

Firstly, we must accept that, whether we like it or not, conflict *does* exist within industry, and we will view it in two ways. For this purpose we use the term *frame of reference,* i.e. we will consider conflict from two separate frames of reference known as the *unitary* frame of reference and the *pluralist* frame of reference. Much of what we say here is based upon the work of Allan Fox (1966) in his research paper presented to the Donovan Commission. Whilst two frames of reference have been put forward, described and used here, it would be misleading to suggest that there are no other frames of reference which could be employed equally usefully. Indeed Fox, in a later work, provides a critical appraisal of the pluralist ideology and finds it wanting. Having sounded this warning, we will continue with just the two frames of reference since, for our purpose, they are illuminating. Any reader who is particularly interested in ideology is referred to the works of Fox (already mentioned) and R. Hyman (1978).

The Unitary Frame of Reference

It is easy to understand why managements may hold a unitary frame of reference. Many of them see their organisations as being analogous to a team, with all the team members (i.e. all the workers and managers) striving towards the achievement of common goals. This position can be justified by arguing that what is good for the organisation is also good for the employees. If the organisation performs well and prospers, then so will the employees, and vice versa. Equally, if the organisation does not perform well all parties, including the workers, will suffer. In the long-term this last statement is difficult to refute.

The idea of a team sums up the unitary frame of reference, that of oneness, in which the members have common objectives which they pursue, under the direction of the team leaders (i.e. the management). We are all familiar with the phrases used by adherents to this frame of reference — such comments as 'all pulling together towards a common goal for the common good'; 'the need for high morale'; 'esprit de corps'; and 'teamwork'. Industrialists, interviewed on radio or television during industrial disputes, often bemoan the 'lack of team spirit'.

If one holds a unitary frame of reference then other features are implicit. The first of these is that the management must be totally accepted by the workers as leaders of the team. The workers must accept that the managers know best what is good for the organisation and, therefore, by implication, for them. The workers must accept managerial decisions unquestioningly. If we consider this last point and ask ourselves 'Under what circumstances would we unquestioningly follow a leader?', we are likely to come to the conclusion that we would only do so if we had a high degree of personal confidence in, and loyalty towards, that leader. Unless this was the case, we would probably want to have some say ourselves in what we should or should not do.

Managers who hold a unitary frame of reference place importance on inspiring leadership, on building up subordinates' loyalty and, most of all, on promoting the idea of a harmony of purpose.

How then do managers holding a unitary frame of reference explain the existence of conflicts? Quite simply they only have two answers available to them. Firstly (and quite commonly nowadays), they put it down to poor communications. In doing this they accept some of the responsibility for the conflict. What they say is, 'If only we had been able to communicate better with our workers, then they would have understood that what we intended to do, or have done, is for their benefit'. Or to put it another way, the whole conflict is a result of a most unfortunate misunderstanding.

The second explanation is less generous. This runs along the lines that the management has done all it possibly could to show the workers that the course of action proposed, or taken, is the right one for the organisation (and, therefore, also for the workers), but that this has been rejected because of the action of a handful of militant, extremist agitators who, by devious means, have managed to mislead the general workforce.

This leads us finally to consider how those holding a unitary frame of reference view trades unions, since it is usually through trades unions that the decisions of management are challenged. A common view of such people is that at some time in the past trades unions were necessary, but nowadays, in the age of enlightened management, they are superfluous. If pressed on the question of whether all managements have such an enlightened and benevolent attitude towards their workers, they will claim that the law provides more than adequate protection for employees.

The Pluralist Frame of Reference

Social scientists have long abandoned the unitary in favour of the pluralist frame of reference, which they see as being more realistic and, therefore, a more useful analytical tool. Here the organisation, and indeed the whole of industrial society, is seen as containing many *related* but *separate* interest groups. These groups have interests which on some occasions coincide and on others are in conflict. Once we accept this we can also accept that within a single organisation, at any given time, there will be groups with leaders whose objectives will be different. The act of management now becomes the maintenance of the equilibrium between these potentially conflicting objectives.

Some critics of pluralism have pointed out that such an equilibrium can only exist, in any meaningful way, when the power of groups representing the conflicting objectives are relatively equal and balanced. In simple terms this may mean the relative power of trades unions and employers. It may in practice be exceedingly difficult to obtain any objective measure of such power. Notwithstanding this problem there can be little doubt that the objectives of the principal parties in industrial relationships are unlikely to be congruent at all times.

Let us look now at what is involved in a full acceptance of the pluralist concept. Firstly, the way trades unions are viewed is quite different. Trades unions are automatically seen as the logical groupings of workers to promote their interests. Such interests are not confined to their rate of pay, but extend to all matters which affect them. Trades unions' attempts at regulating what might have been seen as management prerogatives in the control of the workforce, will be viewed as equally legitimate. This aspect of control will encompass the areas of management authority in deploying, organising, and disciplining the workers. In doing this, the union represents the workers who are affected by management decisions, and it is in these areas more than any others that management must accept that there are other forms of loyalty within the social system it governs (i.e. the organisation). This loyalty will be of workers towards the union, as personified normally by its shop stewards. Another difference, which is likely to be important to the workers, is that they will be giving their loyalty to a shop steward whom they elected, rather than a manager or supervisor in whose appointment they had no say. Thus, not only does the existence of a union provide a vehicle for the expressions of the workers' viewpoint, it also throws up leaders who often enjoy their loyalty. On occasions when the interests of the workers do not, from their point of view, seem to be best served by the actions of management, it is hardly surprising that loyalty will be greater to the trade union and shop stewards than to the organisation and its managers. We can conclude that, from time to time, conflict is inevitable. In fact, given the social relationships, we can say that conflict is endemic. That is not to say that unions introduce conflict into the industrial scene: unions merely provide an organised form of expression for sectional interests that would exist anyway. The representation of sectional interests is the basis of our parliamentary democracy, of which we are so proud. In terms of an analogy, trades unions fulfil the role of opposition where management play the role of government.

We must avoid falling into the trap of confusing pluralism with dualism. So far we have spoken about managements and unions as if each were in themselves entities with a single and united purpose. This is far from being the case. Within management itself conflicts exist between various levels of management; various functions of management (for example the marketing managers and the accountants may well not see eye to eye over expenditure on advertising); and between individual managers themselves. Similarly, the union and its members (the workers) sometimes come into conflict. Certainly one group of workers may be in conflict with another, where both groups are members of the same union. For example, production workers may feel that certain well-paid finishing-off operations should be performed by them, whilst workers in the quality control department may feel that the work should be theirs. Disputes between unions in an organisation are far from being unknown. These often revolve around the argument of who does what (known as *demarcation disputes*); whether a particular job should be undertaken by one group of tradespeople, who are members of one union, or whether it should be done by another group, who are members of a different union. Finally, there are disputes between officers of the union. For instance the full time officials may, for reasons of union policy, want their members to take one course of action, whilst the shop stewards recommend a completely different course to the workers.

Once we accept a pluralist frame of reference, we cannot see the organisation as one big happy family (or team), but rather as a complex system of interrelationships between the overall objectives of the organisation and those of the individuals within it. Conflict is, therefore, inevitable and needs to be managed so that organisational objectives can be reconciled with group beliefs and aims. The dynamics of this internal struggle are, by and large, beneficial to the maintenance of the vitality and efficiency of an organisation.

The Importance of the Frame of Reference

There are three main reasons why the frame of reference we hold is important:

(i)   it determines how we expect people to behave;
(ii)   it significantly affects our reactions to people's behaviour;
(iii) it is significant in determining the methods we use when we wish to change other people's behaviour.

Let us look at each of these reasons and compare the effects of holding a unitary with a pluralist frame of reference. Firstly, then what difference does our frame of reference make, in the question of how we expect people to behave? Suppose the management have just bought a new machine to increase the efficiency of one particular operation. By improving efficiency, costs can be reduced and profit increased. This is clearly in the best interests of the organisation. Someone holding a unitary frame of reference would automatically expect the workers to be as pleased about the acquisition of the new machine as are the management. Unitarists would expect the workers to provide every assistance in its introduction and operation as they will improve profitability, and make the organisation stronger, which will be good for them since, at the very least, their jobs will be more secure.

Someone holding a pluralist frame of reference would view the purchase of the machine differently, especially in the way he would expect the workers to behave. He needs to know how the new machine will affect the workers. Will it affect the numbers employed in this operation? Will it affect the speed at which the operation is carried out? Will it affect the workers' pay? Will it affect the degree of control the workers have over the operation? Should the answers to any of these questions be seen as unfavourable by the workers themselves, then he would not be surprised if their reaction to the new machine was hostile. He would not automatically expect the workers to be enthusiastic.

To consider the second reason for the importance of the frame of reference we will continue with the example of the new machine. Let us assume that in some way the workers see the new machine either as a threat to them, or as a potential threat. (This could be in terms of their earnings, or the amount of overtime they will have available, for instance). Their actions are as hostile as they are able to make them even though they may be in a position where they cannot refuse to work on the new machine. They may seem to go out of their way to create problems for the machine's effective operation. They may refuse to agree on manning levels, or pay levels, which may on the face of it seem to be quite obvious (i.e. the machine may be designed to have just one operator with a clearly defined level of skill). The reaction to such behaviour by someone with a unitary frame of reference, could well be one of exasperation at the pig-headedness of the workers. Their actions would be seen as irrationally hostile, causing problems where none really exist. The unitarist may be unable to see any reason why there should be disputes over manning levels. He may concede that if the new machine's introduction were to lead to redundancy, then the workers' reluctance to accept it would be more understandable, but since the management have given assurance that no-one will be made redundant and that everyone displaced will be re-deployed without loss of earnings, there is no justification for the workers' behaviour.

The person holding a pluralist frame of reference will react quite differently. He will not be surprised by the behaviour of the workers. He will try to understand the underlying reasons. He certainly will not see it as pig-headedness or irrationality. He will look for the workers' rationale, because he will assume that they have one. This does not mean that he will concede their claims, it merely means he will accept that the workers see them as genuine and legitimate, and he will react accordingly.

Finally then, let us consider the third reason for the importance of the frame of reference held. Continuing our example we will look at the actions unitarists and pluralists are likely to take in the situation presented by the workers' hostility.

Since the unitarists will see the workers' claims as invalid and irrational, they are likely to see no alternative but to assert their managerial prerogative and insist on manning levels and types of worker operating the new machine. From their perspective, there is no point in entering into negotiation on the subject, since the matter is cut and dried, there being only one acceptable solution, that being the one put forward by the management. In any case they will argue, once the dust has settled, the workers will see that management was right, that they had nothing to fear, and that the introduction of the new machine was in everyone's long term interest.

The pluralists will accept that they should give the workers the opportunity to express their point of view and attempt to convert the management to it. However, they will recognise that the new machine's introduction is in the best interests of the organisation, and that their role as managers is to maximise its long-term efficiency. They will not fool themselves though that what is good for the organisation is necessarily good for its workers, and certainly not necessarily going to be seen as being good by the workers themselves. The managers holding a pluralist frame of reference will expect to argue their case.

As observers of Industrial Relations, we should beware of making assumptions about disputes, for instance, which are based upon the unitary frame of reference. We should always question the bold assertion that one side or another is acting totally unreasonably and, finally, we should beware of the over-simplification of issues to which the mass media are prone.

Collective Bargaining

Let us start by taking the definition provided by Allan Flanders. He defined collective bargaining as *an institution for regulating labour management as well as labour markets'* and said that as such *'collective bargaining is essentially a rule-making process'* and that this is a feature *'which has no counterpart in individual bargaining'.*

To take this last point first, it is essential that right from the outset we appreciate the significant difference between collective bargaining and individual bargaining.

An example of individual bargaining is the process of buying and selling. Suppose you are buying a secondhand car privately and, therefore, do not expect to get a guarantee. What process will you go through?

Firstly, you buy appropriate newspapers and magazines to find out what cars, of the type you want, are for sale. Having identified what appears to be what you want, and having checked that the car is still for sale, you go and look at it and meet the vendor. You inspect the car, have a test drive in it, and come to some conclusions about its condition and how much you are prepared to pay for it. The vendor of the car knows how much he is prepared to sell it for. You decide that you think it is worth about £500, but its owner may be asking a price of £550. You offer the seller £500, which he may reject. You say you are prepared to go as high as £520, but no higher, and then you haggle over the price. At the end of this you may or may not agree on the price, so a bargain may or may not be struck between you. Let us look at both circumstances. Firstly, let us assume that you agree on a price of £525. The process from hereon is fairly straightforward. You pay the money, he gives you the car, registration documents, and so on. To all intents and purposes that is the end of the deal. Neither party is likely to apply additional conditions to the other (i.e. you are not going to tell him how he should spend the £525 and he is not going to tell you that you must not use the car on Wednesdays, for instance). Having completed the transaction, that will be an end of it. Secondly, let us assume that you cannot agree on a price. You keep your money and he keeps his car, and you go your separate ways.

This then is the first difference between what we may call individual bargaining and collective bargaining. In individual bargaining, once the bargain has been struck, the parties to the bargain have no more to do with each other (at least in respect of the transaction). There is no ongoing relationship between the parties and, if no agreement is reached, it is of no consequence.

This is the opposite situation to collective bargaining where, once the bargain has been struck, the parties to the bargain (usually the workers and management) have a continuing relationship. This means the bargain, whatever it may have been about is just one of the many that have been, and will be, made between the management and the workers. In many instances bargains that have been struck before have an influence upon those which are to be struck now. In some organisations, where collective bargaining is a strongly established method of operation, most of the features making up the relationship between management and workers will have been formed through the institution of collective bargaining. In these organisations the effect of previous bargains on current bargaining will be strong. The reason for this is that collective bargaining is essentially a rule-making process, i.e. rules governing the conduct of the parties to the bargaining.

Before we go on to explore the areas of rule-making, we should note one other significant difference between individual and collective bargaining. In individual bargaining we said that in the event of the parties concerned being unable to reach agreement they part company, and that is an end of the matter, but it is not the case in collective bargaining. If no agreement on the subject can be reached, unless both parties are prepared to drop the matter, it can only be deferred. It is unlikely that both parties will want to drop the matter entirely, since at least one of them (i.e. either management or workers) felt the need to reach some agreement in the first place.

To return to our definition of collective bargaining, we have distinguished between individual and collective bargaining, but we have not dealt with what is meant by the terms 'labour management and labour markets', nor have we really discussed their regulation or why collective bargaining is *essentially* a rule-making process.

If we think of the term 'labour market' in the way that economists would use it, it may help us to understand what is meant. When an economist uses the term market he means *the place and the process by which the demands for, and supplies of, some commodity or factor of production are reconciled at a price.* Labour is a factor of production and the term labour market describes the process of reconciling demands for labour with supplies to arrive at a price. By the term price for labour we mean the price at which labour is sold by those who have it, to those who want it. This, in the broadest sense, is the level or rate, of pay. Economists tell us that with a system of perfect competition the price of a commodity or factor (in this case labour) will be that point at which the demand curve for labour crosses the supply curve of labour. This is known as the equilibrium price. Let us take an example and assume that the supply of the factor is fixed, and imagine there are just 100 workers. Now, let us assume that the demand for labour is greater than 100, perhaps 110. This means that the total demand of all the people who want labour (i.e. the employers) is for 110 workers. If the current price of labour is £160 per week we might expect the price to rise. Because the demand for labour exceeds the supply, an employer who has fewer workers than he needs will try and attract workers away from other employers by offering to pay more. This process will continue, with the price of labour continuing to rise, until one or more employers decide that they are not prepared to pay any more and they will cease to bid for workers. This has the effect of reducing the demand for labour. Once the level of demand falls to the same as the level of supply, a new equilibrium price (level of pay) will be established. This may be £180 per week.

Conversely, in a situation where the supply of labour exceeds the demand, the price of labour should fall. Suppose the total demand for labour from all employers is for 90 workers. The number of people available and willing to work may be 100 and the going rate for labour (i.e. the price which equals the pay) is £160 per week. In a perfect market we would expect the price of labour to fall until either of the following, or a combination of both, occurs:

(i)   The price of labour, that is the level of pay, falls so much that 10 workers withdraw from the labour market, i.e. they are not prepared to sell their labour at that price. This may mean that they are unemployed and remain so.

(ii) The price of labour falls to an extent that new employers are attracted into the market. Seeing that the price of labour is low, a new employer may decide to employ workers, where previously he thought it too costly. The demand for labour may thus be increased to the 100 workers level.

Eventually a new equilibrium price will be arrived at. This could be £140 per week.

We have described the labour market in simple terms, albeit in a very theoretical way. We have now to see how collective bargaining regulates this labour market. Regulation occurs in two ways, directly and indirectly. Collective bargaining *directly* regulates the labour market through the process of workers and employers agreeing the price of labour.

Let us look at the two examples we took earlier, but add the process of collective bargaining. In the first example we had a situation where demand for labour exceeded supply which tended to force the price of labour (i.e. levels of pay) up. Under these circumstances organised labour, that is trades unionists, will be keen to bargain collectively with employers to agree a minimum rate of pay. This is a good time for them to press their claims, since there is a natural tendency for pay levels to rise due to demand exceeding supply. Employers may be prepared to agree to this, because in so doing they may keep other employers out of the market, and so avoid the demand for labour growing even more. Moreover, they will try to ensure that the minimum level agreed is the level that is in fact applied (and not exceeded) by organisations. Employers will not be over-enthusiastic about the idea of pay increasing.

When the relationship between labour demand and supply changes so that supply exceeds demand, there is a natural tendency for the price of labour to fall. However, through collective bargaining, the minimum price has been fixed at a level which, according to the natural market mechanism is artificially high.

Let us put figures to the collective bargaining process in this example. Assuming that the minimum level of pay for labour is agreed at £165 per week, £15 per week less than the actual pay received when the new equilibrium price is reached. This can be explained by a reluctance on the part of employers to concede any more than they need. When the situation changes, and demand for labour falls to 90 workers, the price remains at £165 per week, but there are 10 workers unemployed. Employers obliged through the previous collective bargaining agreement to pay more for their labour than they might have had to on the open market will attempt to get the best value for their money in other ways, probably through increases in labour productivity.

Since much of the *indirect* regulation of the labour market occurs through what we may call the *regulation of labour management,* we will now look at this and return to its indirect effects upon labour markets a little later.

The term labour management means the way in which management controls labour. It is mainly concerned with the rule-making process and not only has an effect upon the labour market aspects of collective bargaining, but is also affected by them. To understand this two-way relationship let us return to our example. Through the process of collective bargaining, a minimum rate of pay for workers was agreed at £165 per week. This was £15 per week less than we might have expected labour, through organised trades unions, to press for. At the time of negotiation the unions may have felt it prudent to agree to accept a lower minimum rate of pay in exchange for some other concessions. An example of this would be where workers and management agree that there will be no changes in working arrangements or methods introduced by the management, without the unions first agreeing to them. In this way the unions attempt to protect the actual working conditions of their members. Another example of such an agreement may centre upon the question of possible redundancies in the future. In the event of management seeing the need for redundancies, they may wish to dispose of those workers who are least useful. Management and union may (through collective bargaining) reach an agreement that, should some workers need to be made redundant, the basis will be that those volunteering should be released first, and thereafter any extra redundancies should be on the LIFO basis (i.e. the *last* people to be employed by the organisation should be the *first* to be made redundant).

Both these examples show how the process of collective bargaining has set rules for the way in which management deals with its workers. Since these rules do not necessarily reflect the way management would themselves like to act, they could be seen as an encroachment on management prerogatives. We must remember though that they are agreements freely entered into.

Neither of these agreements in the area of labour management have an effect upon what we have called labour markets. A third example of the regulation of labour management has an impact on labour markets. Suppose at the time that the demand for labour exceeds the supply, the unions and management of an organisation agree upon a minimum rate of pay £165 per week for a particular group of workers. From what we have previously said, we know that the unions could have pressed successfully for an extra £15 per week. The workers who make up the union membership may feel that it would be better to sacrifice this £15 on minimum pay in exchange for something else. They may feel that in the medium term they would be better to conclude an agreement with the management which says that only workers of a certain kind will be employed in the future. An example of this may be where skilled workers, through collective bargaining, agree that certain designated jobs will only by filled by workers who have served an apprenticeship. In doing this they are protecting themselves by ensuring that only skilled workers do certain jobs, but additionally they are limiting the number of people who could potentially fill the jobs should they become vacant. This, on the face of it, does not seem to be a very significant gain by the workers or concession by the management. However, let us consider what could happen in the future. Suppose the demand for semi-skilled workers falls but the supply remains constant, then the price of such workers would fall, and the management may be able to recruit such semi-skilled workers and train them to do the skilled job. (The training may be perfectly adequate for the purposes of the organisation). Alternatively, the semi-skilled workers may have concluded agreements such that their minimum pay has also been guaranteed, but there are still more workers available than there are employers wishing to employ them. In this case the management may wish to employ and train a semi-skilled worker. If, however, the skilled workers have concluded an agreement that only workers who have completed an apprenticeship will be employed in the type of work, it effectively limits management's action. If the demand for skilled workers exceeds the supply of 'time served' (i.e. those who have completed an apprenticeship) workers, then the skilled workers are in a position to negotiate an increase in their pay. So, whereas it may be cheaper for the management to take on semi-skilled workers and train them to do the skilled work, they may find that instead of doing this they have to increase the pay of all the skilled workers in order to attract the extra skilled workers they need. This type of situation is often referred to as a *restrictive practice* and we will look at it later when we deal with productivity bargaining.

Let us look at the interaction of labour management and labour market aspects of collective bargaining. Agreements concluded which apply rules concerning the type of worker who can be employed on a particular job are themselves concerned with labour management. That is, the rules limit the ability of management to do as they wish. They have another effect and this is to effectively limit the supplies of labour available to the organisation. This is because, once the agreement has been reached, the organisation can only employ workers who meet the specified entry requirements to the jobs concerned. The numbers of these workers may be limited and, if the demand for workers of this type exceeds the supply, the effect will be for the price of labour (i.e. the rate of pay) to rise. We can see then how an aspect of collective bargaining, which is concerned with labour management, has effects on labour markets. We must not forget, however, that the agreements were entered into by both parties at a time when the labour market was biased in favour of one party, but that they (the workers) did not exploit this direct advantage to the full. We can see that the regulation of labour market aspects of collective bargaining can be either direct or indirect.

Types of Agreement

Not surprisingly, the outcomes of collective bargaining are known as collective agreements. Before looking at the two types of agreement, known as *substantive* and *procedural* we should consider the parties to these agreements. In general terms the parties to collective bargaining are employers and organised labour. This bargaining can, and does, take place at a number of levels.

Industry level bargaining is normally carried out between employers' associations and trades unions, or groups of trades unions. Employers' associations will have full time officials to bargain on behalf of the member organisations. Trades unions will normally have full time officers, representing the members of their unions, who are employed by organisations belonging to the employers' association. Industry level bargaining can result in both substantive and procedural agreements. These agreements tend to set minimum standards within which the parties agree to operate. At this level of bargaining *substantive* agreements are likely to set minimum levels of pay, holidays, length of working week, and so on. *Procedural* agreements at this level are often nowadays limited to general guidelines on how matters should be dealt with by negotiators at other levels of bargaining, although sometimes they may be quite specific.

The next level of bargaining is known as *company level bargaining*.

This is carried out by senior managers on behalf of the owners for the employers' side. For labour, bargaining is carried out by the unions, which may mean either full time officers of the union (having a special responsibility for the workers in their trade union who work for that particular organisation), or senior shop stewards of the union working within the organisation. Alternatively it may be that the workers' representatives are a combination of both full time officers of the union and senior shop stewards. Both substantive and procedural matters will be dealt with at this level. Agreements at this level, like industry level bargaining, tend to be formal, with the resulting agreement being written up and signed by the negotiators. Substantive agreements at this level tend to be more specific on holidays, hours of work and so on. Procedural agreements will often be confined to areas common throughout the organisation, examples are agreements for the avoidance of disputes, or on redundancy.

The third level of collective bargaining is known as *workplace* or *plant bargaining*. At this level the bargaining on behalf of the employers will be conducted by the managers of the Plant. Very often the Personnel or Industrial Relations Manager will play a leading role. For the workers, bargaining will be conducted by a group of senior shop stewards from the plant. Such groupings of shop stewards may be known as Works Committees. Staff employees may be represented by a different group of shop stewards than the hourly-paid employees, and both groups may conclude the annual pay deal, in which basic levels of pay, for different grades of worker are agreed. Procedural agreements may cover redeployment of workers, selection methods, the basis on which training will be given, and so on.

The last level of bargaining is that carried out by line managers or supervisors and the shop stewards in their departments. This is known as *workshop bargaining*. At this level there may be little scope for concluding significant substantive agreements. However, if there is a payment by results system, agreements between workers and their representatives (shop stewards) and the supervisors, on the time allowed for specific jobs, will be conducted at this level. Procedural agreements will be confined to matters of interest to the particular workshop-allocation of overtime work, for instance. Such agreements will be taking place virtually all the time between shop stewards and line managers and supervisors. They will often be informal and unwritten, but just as binding on the parties concerned as if they have been written and formally signed. Agreements of this kind may be so informal that they are just taken for granted by both sides. Such 'agreements' are often known as *custom and practice*.

INDUSTRIAL RELATIONS

Substantive Agreements

As we have seen, substantive agreements are concluded at all levels of collective bargaining. The main areas covered are pay, hours of work, holidays and fringe benefits. They are mainly concerned with the regulation of the labour market aspects of collective bargaining.

Procedural Agreements

These are made to regulate the conduct of parties to an agreement (usually workers and their representatives and managements). Procedural agreements are concluded at all levels of collective bargaining. At the higher levels they will almost always be formal, written agreements specifying how the parties should behave under various circumstances and conditions. At the level of the shop floor, where the 'bargaining' is carried out by the supervisor and shop steward, it is most unlikely that they will be written, and indeed they may not even be seen by the parties as agreements. At this level they may be no more than the accepted method of dealing with some particular situation. It is only when one of the parties, either the supervisor or the workers, wishes to change the arrangements that the other side points out that there is a de facto agreement, established through custom and practice. Let us look at an example of the kind of procedural agreement that comes about through custom and practice. Suppose that within a workshop there are five different jobs, A,B,C,D,E, all of which pay the same amount of bonus and are undertaken by workers of the same grade. Over a period a kind of pecking order of jobs may develop. Thus job A may be considered the least attractive job and the one given to new employees. The jobs range in attractiveness to the workers from A to E. Suppose one of the five workers in the group leaves, and that he worked on job C; the procedure will be for the worker doing job B to take over job C and the worker doing job A to take over job B. The new worker will be taken on in job A. Remembering that all the jobs are at the same grade and all pay the same bonus, it may seem that this arrangement is, at least, illogical and, at worst, unnecessarily costly since, in this example, three people have to learn new work (the workers now performing jobs A,B and C). But, it has become the custom though there is clearly no formal agreement. If a supervisor brings the new worker straight into job C he has not contravened any formal agreement, but he has broken an informally recognised custom and practice. The workers may react with hostility and insist that there was an agreement to operate the old way. One result of this action may be for the custom to become formalised into a written agreement. In fact, many procedural agreements at the level of workshop bargaining are only formalised after their legitimacy as a custom has been challenged.

Let us now consider more formal procedural agreements at plant level, which embody both custom and practice and follow guidelines that have been agreed, perhaps at company or organisational level. The procedure for the avoidance of disputes is an example. At the level of the organisation, an agreement may be made for dealing with disputes between individual workers and management. At this level it may do little more than specify that there should be no more than four stages to the procedure and that it should not take more than eleven working days. Details will be worked out at plant level by local management and the senior shop stewards. Therefore, different plants may have slightly different details to their procedure, but will all conform to the general pattern agreed at company level. The procedure at one particular plant may be as follows:

Stage 1   If an individual worker is unhappy about something he should first approach his supervisor, who will respond within one working day.

Stage 2   If the worker and supervisor are unable to resolve the matter to their joint satisfaction, then the individual worker can enlist the support of his shop steward. Both worker and shop steward will see the supervisor and discuss the matter. The supervisor will respond within one working day of this meeting taking place.

Stage 3   If the three people (supervisor, worker and shop steward) are still unable to resolve the matter, a meeting will be convened of the supervisor, his departmental manager, the personnel officer, the individual concerned, his shop steward and the senior shop steward for the department concerned. This meeting will take place within 3 days of a failure to reach agreement at Stage 2. The parties to this meeting will attempt to resolve the problem.

Stage 4   Should the matter remain unresolved, a final meeting will be convened within 5 days. It will be chaired by the Personnel Manager and attended by the Chief shop steward for the whole plant, the senior shop steward who attended Stage 3, and the shop steward for the department concerned. From the management side, the departmental manager and his superior will also attend. If these people are unable to reach agreement, then the domestic procedure for the avoidance of disputes is exhausted and the parties can use sanctions to try to resolve the matter (i.e. they can take some form of industrial action). (We should note that prior to the procedure being completely exhausted, neither side should take any action against the other.)

It is likely that a number of such agreements will be concluded at plant level and will cover not only matters concerning individual workers, but also those concerning groups of workers; all the workers in one department or area; and throughout the plant. They will all follow clearly prescribed stages and, in some cases, may involve full time officers of the union and representatives from the employers' association.

This type of procedural agreement lays down clear rules as to how the parties should behave when dealing with matters over which they disagree. It is an agreement which limits the freedom of unilateral action of both management and workers.

Disciplinary Procedures

This type of procedural agreement warrants special attention for three reasons:

1. It is central to the notion of the employer's right to control his workers.
2. Because of (1), it is also central to the concept of collective bargaining for the regulation of labour management.
3. It is an area in which the State (i.e. Government) has seen fit to set some rules through legislation and provide some guidelines, through a Code of Practice issued by the Advisory Conciliation and Arbitration Service (ACAS).

It is clearly management's responsibility to ensure that there are adequate disciplinary rules and procedures and that discipline is maintained. If these rules and procedures are to be effective, they must be accepted as reasonable, both by those who are covered by them (the workers) and those who operate them (the supervisors and managers). It is desirable, if not essential, that all parties concerned, including trades unions, should be involved in the development and/or revision of the rules and procedures covering discipline and dismissal. This makes them an appropriate subject for collective bargaining.

Guidance has been provided by ACAS in *Code of Practice 1 : Disciplinary Practice and Procedures in Employment.* Whilst the Code of Practice does not have the status of law, it is a very important document. To quote from the Code itself:

> 'A failure on the part of any person to observe any provision of a Code of Practice shall not of itself render him liable to any proceedings; but in any proceedings before an industrial tribunal or the Central Arbitration Committee any Code of Practice issued under this section shall be admissable in evidence, and if any provision of such a Code appears to the tribunal or Committee to be relevant to any question arising in the proceedings it shall be taken into account in determining that question.'
>
> (Employment Protection Act 1975, Section 6(11.))

In this section we shall limit ourselves to quoting the essential features of disciplinary procedures as set out in the Code of Practice.

> 'Disciplinary procedures should not be viewed primarily as a means of imposing sanctions. They should also be designed to emphasise and encourage improvements in individual conduct.'

Disciplinary procedures should:

(a)   Be in writing;

(b)   Specify to whom they apply;

(c)   Provide for matters to be dealt with quickly;

(d)   Indicate the disciplinary actions which may be taken;

(e)   Specify the levels of management which have the authority to take the various forms of disciplinary action, ensuring that immediate superiors do not normally have the power to dismiss without reference to senior management;

(f)   Provide for individuals to be informed of the complaints against them and to be given an opportunity to state their case, before decisions are reached;

(g)   Give individuals the right to be accompanied by a trade union representative, or by a fellow employee of their choice;

(h)   Ensure that, except for gross misconduct, no employees are dismissed for a first breach of discipline;

(i)   Ensure that disciplinary action is not taken until the case has been carefully investigated;

(j)   Ensure that individuals are given an explanation for any penalty imposed;

(k)   Provide a right of appeal and specify the procedure to be followed.

The Code of Practice goes on to make recommendations on how the disciplinary procedure should be operated, providing an outline which management and trades unions will supplement. This key area of management control should be arranged through joint consultatio and negotiation between management and workers, and not left merely to management to exercise its unilateral prerogatives. It should be encompassed by the institution of collective bargaining.

Productivity Bargaining

Let us use Allan Flanders' (1969) definition of Productivity Bargaining — *'a type of collective bargaining in which an increase in the price of labour is associated with an increase in its productivity, regardless of how the latter is achieved'*. In previous sections we have used the term 'price of labour' to mean the same as pay — we will continue to do this. When we talk about an increase in labour's productivity we mean that each man produces more output in the same time. Increases in productivity can be achieved in a variety of ways including:

(i)   the worker puts more effort in and produces greater levels of output in the same time;

(ii)   the working arrangements are so reorganised by management that the number of workers required to perform a task is reduced, thus leading to greater output per worker;

(iii) the management can introduce new plant and equipment, which results in increased output in a given time. This new equipment may involve the same number, or fewer workers in the task. The output per worker is increased;

(iv)   some combination of the 3 ways noted above.

We see from the definition that it does not matter how the productivity is achieved, it can still be the subject of productivity bargaining. To some people this may seem wrong. Why should workers be paid more, unless they have worked harder? To these people the only acceptable form of productivity bargaining would seem to be based on (i). We suggest that individuals holding a unitary frame of reference may be prone to think this way. Consider this situation. The management currently employ one worker on a task. In this particular task the worker can produce 100 units of output per hour. The management spend a considerable amount of money buying a new piece of equipment which speeds up the operation so that 200 units per hour can be produced. Moreover, whereas the previous method of manufacture involved the worker in hard physical labour the new equipment is very easy to operate. Why, under these circumstances, should the worker expect to be paid any more money? Yet, under our definition, such a change in working arrangements might be dealt with through productivity bargaining. Before we go on to discuss this we need to introduce and define the term restrictive practices:

Arrangements imposed by employees under which labour is not used efficiently, there being no social or economic justification as far as society as a whole is concerned.

On first reading this may sound nothing short of the workers unreasonably trying to wreck the economic efficiency of the organisation, if not the economy as a whole. The key to understanding the definition of restrictive practices lies in the words 'there being no social or economic justification as far as SOCIETY AS A WHOLE is concerned'. This does not mean there is no social or economic justification as far as the workers themselves are concerned. People who hold a pluralist frame of reference can understand how something can be socially or economically unjustifiable from the point of view of society whilst being perfectly justifiable as seen from the viewpoint of the workers concerned, perhaps a better term would be, *'protective practice'*. In other words one person's protective practice may be seen by another person, if not most other people, as a restrictive practice. This does not mean that pluralists accept that restrictive practices should continue, but that they find it acceptable that changing restrictive practices may be a difficult process in which compromise is called for.

Perhaps the best known cases of restrictive practices involve *overmanning*. Here we have a situation where workers insist on maintaining worker levels, even though changes in technology, for example, no longer make them necessary. Take the case of firemen on diesel and electric trains. There can be no social or economic justification for firemen, since there are no fires for them to keep burning on diesel trains. As soon as a diesel engine replaces a steam engine there should, theoretically, be one fireman surplus to requirements. This seems to be a good idea, unless you happen to be the fireman who no longer has a job. He is not concerned with a mere increase in efficiency but whether he has a job or not. Given his point of view, he may well not react to the introduction of diesel engines in the same way as the rest of us. His prime consideration will be the protection of his job and he would argue that it is no fault of his that his job is redundant, so why should he suffer? One could hardly expect him to welcome the introduction of diesels. If he accepts that diesel engines are going to replace steam engines, he is going to do all he can to protect his position. He will band together with other railway workers and, if they need convincing, which they may not, he will use the argument, 'Firemen are made redundant by this round of technological change, next round it will be drivers'. He is unlikely to have too much difficulty in convincing his brother/sister trades unionists that they are better off to make a united stand. The likely consequence is that the railway workers generally and the footplatemen in particular, will insist that they will only work on diesels if the old manning levels, operated on steam trains, are maintained. If the employer agrees to this, he is agreeing to what he knows is overmanning. If he does not agree, he will not get his diesel trains into operation, because no-one will operate them. Hard line unitarists may argue that the employers should insist on reducing manning levels on the introduction of diesels and face the inevitable industrial strife. They would be overlooking the fact that the one side, (i.e. the employers) would be fighting for increased efficiency, whilst the other side (the workers, and more particularly the firemen) would be fighting for their very survival, and thus feel they have nothing to lose.

Once having agreed to overmanning, management cannot expect to change the rules unilaterally at some later date. They must look for ways of improving productivity. The quickest way to improve productivity is to eliminate the overmanning, but it was part of the agreement for introducing diesel engines. So what can management do? In crude terms they can buy out the overmanning at some later date when they are in a position to offer, through a productivity agreement, the right package of safeguards to satisfy the workers. This example is a gross oversimplification of what could happen and is not intended to reflect what occurred within British Rail, but merely to describe how restrictive practices occur and how they may be related to productivity bargaining.

A second example of a restrictive practice and its relationship to productivity involves *demarcation* and its opposite *worker flexibility*. Let us assume that an organisation employs both electricians and machine tool fitters for the maintenance of its plant and equipment. Traditionally these workers belong to different skilled trades and are represented by different trades unions. When a machine breaks down and needs maintenance the work may be electrical in nature, but involve some fitting work on the mechanical aspects of the fault. In other circumstances, the fault with the machine may be mainly mechanical but, since it is powered by electricity, involves a small amount of simple electrical work. The traditional way of dealing with both these maintenance tasks is for a tradesman of each skill to attend to the machine. Under this arrangement the electrician does all the electrical work whilst the machine tool fitter does the mechanical work. In jobs where the amount of electrical work to be done is small and relatively simple the organisation will be paying an electrician to do this work, while the machine tool fitter stands by and waits. More importantly, when the machine tool fitter is doing the major part of the work the electrician is standing by. The opposite situation could just as easily apply. This kind of demarcation is clearly costly in terms of highly-paid craftworkers. Management would prefer a situation where each trade undertook simple tasks which traditionally are within the work domain of the other. Neither trades union is likely to be keen on this idea, since potentially it threatens the jobs of their members. From the point of view of the electricians, if machine tool fitters carry out electrical work, the organisation may end up employing fewer electricians, and vice versa if electricians undertake machine tool fitters' work. Here then is a situation where there is scope for a limited cross trades working productivity agreement. Both groups of workers will be paid an increase, in return for their agreement that members of the other trade can carry out specified tasks which have been traditionally associated with their own trade. The long term effect of such an agreement would be that, given the same volume of work, there would, in total, be fewer machine tool fitters and electricians employed, but that those employed would be paid more.

The Process of Negotiation

Before we look at the stages of the negotiation process we will consider briefly what the purposes and general objectives of negotiation are and how these fit into the scene of Industrial Relations.

We have established that the parties to Industrial Relations may not have similar goals and objectives and that sometimes these objectives may be fundamentally incompatible. We may also conclude that there is usually a desire to maintain some sort of dialogue, if only because their relationship is likely to be a continuing one. It is against this background that Industrial Relations negotiations take place.

The purpose of negotiation is to achieve, through discussion and argument, an agreement which is acceptable to all parties concerned. This is not always going to be possible. Sometimes the best that can be hoped for is to provide an agreement which is not unacceptable to all parties. We refer to *all* sides, not *both* sides, recognising that matters under negotiation are often of interest to a number of groups, and that sometimes these groups will polarise into management and union blocks or homogeneous groups. From now on, for the sake of simplicity, we will refer to negotiation as if it only involves two parties. (We must avoid falling into the trap of confusing pluralism with dualism.)

The subject matter of negotiations is often of interest to large numbers of people, both workers and managers. It is rarely, if ever, the case that all who have an interest in the outcome of the negotiations are present whilst it is being conducted. For this reason, the negotiators themselves are merely performing the roles of representatives. Herein nearly always lies a difference between the negotiators themselves. Management negotiators are not elected by a heterogeneous group upon whose support they are dependent. Union negotiators, especially shop stewards are entirely accountable to the members who elect them. Both sides at the negotiation are trying to achieve the best possible result for those they represent, but both should recognise there is little merit in destroying the other negotiators. If management negotiators take shop steward negotiators 'to the cleaners', the result could be that the workers will refuse to accept the outcome of the negotiations, and replace their negotiators with new shop stewards who may, from the management's viewpoint, be even more difficult to deal with. If union negotiators annihilate their management opposite numbers, they too may find themselves dealing with new people. Negotiators should always remember that they may have to return to their groups and sell them something they are not very keen to accept.

There are normally three stages to the process of negotiation:

(i)	Preparation;
(ii)	Encounter;
(iii)	Follow up.

Preparation

The first stage of preparation for both sides is to define their aims. Obviously they do this separately, but both should follow the same format. Each side should specify what they would ideally like to achieve from the negotiation, then what they would reasonably expect to achieve and, finally, their fallback position (that is the minimum possible result that they would accept). Wise negotiators also try to anticipate the equivalent three positions of their adversaries.

Very often negotiations will cover a number of areas, some substantive matters and some procedural. It is advantageous if the agenda for the negotiation can be agreed in advance. We have all heard the expression in Industrial Relations matters: 'talks about talks'. These almost always mean agreeing what will be included on an agenda and what will not. Both sides will not only want to consider what they want on the agenda but also its order. Some negotiators prefer to deal with matters over which there is likely to be little disagreement first and move on to more contentious items; others prefer to keep the 'easy to agree matters' in reserve to use as make-weights in the final bargain.

The next step is to collect and analyse data on each item for discussion. For procedural matters this will mean checking through all existing agreements, both formally written and informally understood, to see what impact they may have on the subject under negotiation. Consideration will be given to any relevant legislation or any guidelines provided by the government, government agencies, employers' association or trades unions. Opinions will be canvassed of those who would be affected by the procedural changes, should they be agreed.

INDUSTRIAL RELATIONS

Many negotiations concern substantive matters and, to prepare for these, data collection and analysis can be a major exercise. The kind of information required will include:

(a) Movements in the cost of living, changes in the retail price index;

(b) Comparison with local organisations. Has the organisation's position in the pay league table deteriorated, improved or stayed the same?

(c) Comparison with the rest of the industry in which the organisation operates;

(d) The labour position locally, in conjunction with the organisation's need to recruit personnel. Does the organisation have difficulty recruiting labour?

(e) Have any nationally negotiated agreements been implemented, are pending implementation, or are likely to come into effect in the lifetime of the agreement that is about to be negotiated. (For example, minimum pay agreements nationally may have an effect upon the organisation's total pay bill;)

(f) The structure of the organisation's costs — how significant are labour costs? This is considered in conjunction with anticipated financial performance;

(g) Changes in the positions of different groups of workers in terms of their internal pay differentials.

There will be items on the agenda about which the negotiators, for one side or another, feel they have a very strong case. There will be others where they feel their arguments are less persuasive. Now is the time, before the face-to-face negotiation takes place, to prepare the strategy and, to some extent, the tactics of the negotiation. Planning an argument to be presented and information to be made available will be done at this stage. This planning will mean trying to anticipate the strategy and tactics of the opponents.

A strong negotiating team must be assembled, team members clearly understanding the role they are to perform, whether it be main spokesperson, listener, expert in one area or another, or note taker. Many negotiations are seriously hampered by having too large a group; some trades unions' negotiating groups have been known to number nearly 50. It is impossible for fifty people to negotiate at the same time. It is not possible to specify perfect numbers, but certainly both parties to a negotiation should keep the numbers down to single figures. If the numbers become too large, no negotiation takes place in formal sessions, merely sets of statements from each side.

The final part of the preparation stage is to arrange a suitable venue. Neutral ground may have some advantage but, wherever the negotiation is to take place, it must be free from interruptions (such as telephones) and also enjoy facilities for negotiators to adjourn and be able to make contact with the people whom they represent. Just as important as the place, is the time allocated. Many negotiations founder because one party or another tries to enforce unrealistic deadlines.

Encounter

The encounter stage of negotiation tends to have various phases, which are often punctuated by adjournments. At the commencement of most negotiations there is some posing by both parties — often this amounts to 'sabre-rattling'. Any agreement between the parties seems impossible. But, by the very act of going to the negotiating table, both parties tacitly understand that there is room for movement and compromise. Most negotiations start with the spokesman for each side strongly asserting his case. Both sides will refer to the groups they represent as being adamant that the views expressed by the negotiators are their last words on the question, and that circumstances make it impossible to move from this position. Management negotiators will refer to the financial position of the organisation, the marketing prospects, and the possibility of the organisation pricing itself out of the market, if any concessions are made to the workers. Workers' representatives acting as negotiators will declare that they have been mandated by the workers to obtain the amount claimed and not a penny less, that tempers are running high amongst the workers, and that they themselves are having the greatest difficulty in avoiding industrial action being taken.

Each side often appears to be taking virtually no notice of what the other side is saying. In fact, at this stage, there is virtually no dialogue but assertions, followed by counter assertions. The temperature of the negotiations may seem to be rising, but really each side is closing ranks, an essential prerequisite of bargaining. Despite the fact that little attention seems to be paid to the other side, each is trying to evaluate the strength of the other's conviction. Surprisingly, after the initial bout of sabre-rattling, both sides are likely to declare that they recognise there is no personal animosity between them as individuals, but they are performing a representative function.

The second phase of the encounter stage is often slipped into by one side asking for further clarification on a point the other side has just made. It is then common for an adjournment to be sought so that the implications of that particular point can be discussed.

The importance of an adjournment at this stage cannot be overstressed, since it may perform at least three functions:

(i)   it may signal the conclusion of the first phase of the negotiation, with each side displaying its strength to the other.

(ii) it provides both parties with the opportunity to confer within their negotiating teams and to agree amongst themselves an evaluation of the opposition's position.

(iii) it provides for each side to reconsider their priorities and tactics.

The second phase of the encounter stage is often called the 'thrust and parry stage'. This phase differs from that earlier in that individual negotiators start trying to sell their ideas to their opposite numbers. The whole tenor becomes more personal. Movements of a conciliatory nature are almost always prefaced by remarks that the negotiator is stepping outside the mandate he has been given and that, whilst this is the case, he cannot make any commitments on behalf of those he represents, but that even so it seems worth looking in more detail at the matter under discussion.

It is at this phase of the encounter that the movements by both parties start — very tentative at first — with each side expecting the other to compromise at about the same rate they feel they are. This is a very sensitive state which is heavily dependent upon the individual skills of the negotiators. The main skills are associated with being sensitive to the feelings of opposing and fellow negotiators. Attempts at speeding up this phase can have disastrous effects. The side which feels the other is trying to go too fast suspects that they themselves are giving too much and getting too little in exchange. They dig in their heels and virtually stop further progress. The degree of trust built up has been destroyed. Negotiators from either side do have one thing in common at the personal level, they will both have to return to the groups they represent and report how well they have done, and they are both going to be judged by their respective groups. The similarity of circumstances will build up some bond between them from which trust can be developed.

It should become clear at this stage whether there is room for agreement, i.e. whether there is enough common ground between the two groups for them to settle on a mutually acceptable position. It is possible that there is no common ground, in which case the negotiators will fail to agree and industrial action may follow. We will look at various forms of industrial action later in this chapter.

If there is common ground, then it is up to the management representatives to make an offer. In major negotiations it is unusual for the first offer to be accepted in exactly the form that it is made, though adjustments to the offer must be marginal or the credibility of the negotiators suffers.

The Follow-Up Stage

It is essential that what has been agreed is clearly understood by all. Therefore, a clear written statement of the agreement, which is checked and agreed by both groups of negotiators, and drawn up straight away before memories fade, is often initialled by both sides. Under the rules of the union or the arrangements prevailing at the time, both sets of negotiators may need to have the agreement ratified by the people they represent. It is only when both groups have agreed to accept the terms laid out in the statement that the negotiators will sign on behalf of their group, and only then can the agreement be said to be concluded.

Industrial Action

Sometimes in the course of negotiation, particularly in the first phase of the encounter stage, the exhibition of strength will go beyond the stage of talking. At this time, one side or the other may take some action to convince the opposition of their strength or determination. This action on the part of the workers may involve sanctions falling short of strike action, like banning overtime or working to rule. A great variety of sanctions may be threatened and some may be used. The workers may mount token stoppages of work, as part of the 'softening up' process, or the management may declare small scale redundancies. These may appear to represent a breakdown of negotiations, but this is not always the case. For the workers, sanctions inevitably cost money, and are used only when necessary. The cost of management taking sanctions against the workforce may have a less obvious financial effect.

If it becomes clear during the negotiating process that there is no common ground for agreement, sanctions may be applied in earnest in an attempt to force the other side to give ground. Sanctions of this kind tend to be either lockouts, where the employers effectively suspend the employment of the workers, or strikes, where the workers withdraw their labour.

Strikes

Let us define a strike as *the collective withdrawal of labour initiated by the workers*. A strike is an extreme form of industrial conflict classified into three main types, *official, unofficial and unconstitutional*.

307

INDUSTRIAL RELATIONS

The official strike is a *stoppage of work initiated or supported by the trade(s) union(s) concerned, when a group of employees acts together, to bring pressure to bear upon an employer to resolve a grievance or grant terms and conditions of employment which they wish to enjoy.* (Trade(s) Union members on official strike sometimes receive payments from union funds.)

An unofficial strike is *one that takes place without the permission of the body authorised under the union rules to sanction strike action.* It is not uncommon for unofficial strikes to be made official retrospectively. That is, the strike having taken place, or continuing, is sanctioned by that body in the union which, according to the union rules, has the power to declare official strikes.

An unconstitutional strike is *one that takes place before the procedure for the avoidance of disputes has been exhausted.*

Organisations can experience unofficial strikes, unconstitutional strikes, unofficial strikes which are subsequently made official, and occasionally unconstitutional strikes which are made official.

The main value of the strike lies in its use as a threat.

Strikes are clearly costly to workers and managements almost inevitably publicly deplore their use. Sometimes employers may not be averse to having the workers on strike, perhaps because of lack of work.

The right of a worker to withdraw his labour is seen as a fundamental one in our democracy, and yet is almost always described as anti-social behaviour by the media. Such terms as 'holding the country to ransom' are used. It is interesting to wonder why it is that such emotive terminology is rarely levelled at other groups who through their actions, though perhaps less openly performed, behave in a way which is detrimental to the economic well-being of the country. Whilst not suggesting that workers taking strike action is in the interest of the general public, it is proof of a degree of liberty that exists within a country.

The strike and lockout are overt forms of industrial conflict, which we have recognised as endemic in industrial society. Either taking place for a prolonged period indicates such a fundamental conflict of interests that normal processes of compromise through negotiation are unable to bridge the gap.

Third Party Intervention

By third party intervention we mean the activities of the government and government agencies and their effects upon industrial relations. The main effects of third party intervention have in recent years been in three areas:

INDUSTRIAL RELATIONS

(i)   Incomes policy;

(ii)   Legislation affecting the relationship between the main parties;

(iii)   The provision of bodies and machinery, in attempts to assist in the conduct of Industrial Relations.

Incomes Policy

Incomes policies have come in all shapes and sizes since the second world war. There have been pay freezes, statutory incomes policies, voluntary incomes policies, and cash limits in the public sector. In the main these have been greeted unenthusiastically by Trades Unions, who have advocated the use of free collective bargaining as the method of determining members' incomes.

Incomes policy has a direct effect on collective bargaining in the substantive areas, although its effects often continue after the incomes policy itself has been abandoned. The argument usually runs that incomes policies, which set artificial limits on the incomes that can be negotiated, merely build up a backlog of pay claims, and that as soon as the controls are removed there is a free-for-all. Incomes policies have their critics and supporters, but one side effect seems unquestionable and that is that in the early stages of voluntary incomes policy the number of working days lost through strikes declines.

Chapter 19

Legislation On Industrial Relations

During the last quarter of the last century, and for the first 60 years of this century, the role of Government was essentially non-interventionist in Industrial Relations. Attempts were made by various governments to regulate the conduct of the parties to the employment contract; these occurring notably during the two world wars, though generally what might be called the 'voluntary principle' was maintained.

We will concern ourselves mainly with legislation which has been enacted since 1960 and look at some of the more significant parts of the Acts of Parliament surviving today. (We will not consider Acts of Parliament which have subsequently been repealed, though their importance cannot be ignored in any detailed discussion of this subject.) Much of the legislation introduced by Conservative Governments, and some considered by Labour administrations, has been viewed by sections of the Trades Union movement as hostile to their interests. Conversely, some of the legislation introduced by Labour Governments has been viewed by some employers as against their best interests.

The Employment Protection Act 1975, as amended, provides certain basic rights for an employee in his contract with an employer. Amongst the main aspects of this Act are two concerning the contract. The first covers the right of employees to notice of termination by their employer. Employees who work more than sixteen hours each week are entitled to one week's notice after they have worked for the employer for 4 weeks. After they have completed 2 years' service with the employer, employees are entitled to 2 weeks' notice. Thereafter, for every completed year of service, the employee becomes entitled to one more week's notice, up to a maximum of 12 weeks' notice for more than 12 years' service. These are minimum standards which can be improved upon through the process of collective bargaining.

The second main aspect concerning the contract is that the employer must give a written statement within 13 weeks of the employee starting work. This statement has to give the names of the employer and employee and the date when employment began. The statement then has to specify the following particulars of the terms of employment:

(i)   The scale or rate of pay, or the method of calculating pay;

(ii)   The interval at which payments are made (i.e. whether pay is weekly or monthly);

(iii)   Any terms and conditions relating to hours of work;

(iv)   Any terms and conditions relating to:

        (a)   entitlement to holidays, including public holidays, and entitlement to holiday pay;

        (b)   incapacity for work due to sickness or injury, including any provision for sick pay;

        (c)   pensions and pensions schemes;

(v)   The steps to be followed in any grievance which an employee might have;

(vi)   The date on which a fixed term contract is to end;

(vii)   The title of the job which the employee is employed to do;

(viii)   The period of notice the employee is obliged to give and entitled to receive.

The written statement must contain an additional note to inform the employee of any disciplinary rules applicable to him, and to indicate the person to whom he should apply if he is dissatisfied with any disciplinary decision. The additional note must also state whether a contracting out certificate under the Social Security Pensions Act 1975 is in force for the employee's job.

The object of the written statement and the additional note is to give employees a clear understanding of their rights and obligations under their contracts of employment.

The second major piece of legislation on labour management was the Redundancy Payments Acts of 1965 and 1969. The general purpose of the Acts was to require employers to make lump-sum compensation payments, called 'redundancy payments', to employees dismissed because of redundancy. The size of the payment to be made is determined by the amount of pay each employee normally received, his length of service with the employer, and his age at the date at which he was made redundant. Like the Contracts of Employment Acts, these Acts set minimum standards which can be, and quite often are, improved through negotiation.

The Trade Union and Labour Relations Act 1974 had the main purposes of repealing the Industrial Relations Act 1971, and defining the terms 'Trades Union', 'Independent Trades Union', and 'Employers' Association'. The Act provided definitions for the terms 'collective agreement', 'official of a trade union', and 'union membership agreement' (closed shop agreement). The Act also provided protection from the law of tort for individuals and trades unions who are *acting in contemplation or furtherance of a trade dispute,* though this protection for trades unions was modified by the 1982 Employment Act. The first schedule of the Act, which deals with unfair dismissal, is of interest. The right of an employee not to be unfairly dismissed had first been enacted in the Industrial Relations Act 1971. It was re-enacted in this Act and has subsequently been modified in the Employment Acts of 1980 and 1982.

The law now states that employees have a right not to be unfairly dismissed and that those who think they have been may seek a remedy by complaining to an industrial tribunal, within three months of the effective date of termination. Industrial tribunals are independent judicial bodies which deal with complaints concerned with employment and covered by the legislation. Each consists of a legally qualified chairman and two lay members, one appointed by an employers' panel and one appointed through the TUC. The procedure of tribunals is designed to be orderly but simple and flexible, there being no necessity for parties appearing at tribunals to be legally represented.

For a tribunal case on unfair dismissal the employee must show that he has in fact been dismissed. Dismissal is deemed to have occurred in three circumstances:

(i)   where the employer terminates the employee's contract with or without notice;

(ii)   where a fixed term contract expires without being renewed (the Employment Act 1980 set the minimum length of fixed term contract for which the parties can waive the employee's rights to claim unfair dismissal at one year);

(iii)   the employee resigns because of the employer's conduct (i.e. where the employer showed no intention of being bound by the terms of the contract, thus making it intolerable for the employee to continue working for him). This is known as *constructive* dismissal.

In the Trade Union and Labour Relations Act, dismissal would only be considered by a tribunal as being fair if the employer could show that it was for one of the reasons listed below:

(i)   a reason related to the employee's capability or qualification for the job;

(ii)   a reason related to the employee's conduct;

(iii)   redundancy;

(iv)   a statutory duty or restriction which prevents the employment being continued;

(v)   some other substantial reason which could justify the dismissal.

Under the Employment Act 1980 the question of whether a dismissal is fair or unfair shall no longer depend on whether the employer shall satisfy the tribunal that he acted reasonably, it will depend on, whether in the circumstances, including the size and administrative resources of the employer's undertaking, the employer acted reasonably or unreasonably in treating the reason as sufficient in dismissing the employee.

Only employees with more than two years' service can complain to an industrial tribunal on the grounds of unfair dismissal. Tribunals can provide three possible remedies for unfair dismissal:

(i)   Reinstatement (employee treated as if he had never been sacked);

(ii)   Re-engagement (the employee is to be re-employed, but not necessarily on the same terms and conditions);

(iii)   Compensation (consisting of a basic award, using the same basis of calculation as the redundancy payments award, and a compensatory award, based on the employee's loss arising out of dismissal).

In 1974 the Health and Safety at Work etc. Act was introduced. Whilst this Act does not attempt to directly regulate Industrial Relations, it has had some effect upon the relationship between employers and trades unions, by safety representatives and their participation in safety committees. Safety has traditionally been an area in which shop stewards have taken an interest. The importance of the Health and Safety at Work Act, and the subsequently published Codes of Practice on Safety Committees and Safety Representatives, is that it formalises the role of the shop steward/safety representative. It places certain responsibilities and obligations on the safety representative but, just as important, places obligations on the employer to take note of and respond to the appeals and requests of the safety representative; and to deal with him through safety committees and in the day-to-day maintenance of a safe working environment. This may improve the standing of the shop steward/safety representative in the eyes of both management and workers.

The most important piece of legislation affecting individual employee rights to be enacted in recent years is the Employment Protection Act 1975. As well as defining employees' rights, the Act established a number of statutory bodies including the Advisory Conciliation and Arbitration Service (ACAS), the Certification Officer, the Central Arbitration Committee (CAC) and the Employment Appeal Tribunal (EAT).

In terms of employee rights, the Act established minimum standards in areas which might normally be covered by the process of collective bargaining. This does not mean that they cannot still be the subject of collective agreements, but that the minimum standards have been set by legislation. Employees now have statutory rights:

(i)   to be a member of an independent trade union;

(ii)   to have time off to carry out trade union duties;

(iii)   to have time off for certain other trade union activities;

(iv)   to have time off for public duties;

(v)   to have a written statement giving the reason for dismissal;

(vi)   to have an itemised pay statement;

(vii)   to guarantee payments, under certain circumstances;

(viii) to be paid for suspension on medical grounds under statutory provisions;

(ix)   to maternity pay;

(x)   to not be dismissed on grounds of pregnancy;

(xi)   to return to work after pregnancy;

(xii)   to payments of debts following insolvency of their employer.

On the 1st November 1978 the Employment Protection (Consolidation) Act came into operation. This brought together in a single Act of Parliament all the individual employment rights previously contained in the Redundancy Payments Act, the Contracts of Employment Act, the Trade Union and Labour Relations Act, and the Employment Protection Act. It in no way altered the rights conferred by those laws, it simply consolidated them into a single Act of Parliament.

In the General Election of May 1979 the Conservative party replaced the Labour party as the Government. They introduced legislation in the form of the Employment Act 1980 which, as well as introducing new features in the field of labour law, also modified existing legislation. The main purposes of the Act are:

1(1)   To encourage the wider use of secret ballots in trade union elections and votes on other important issues, such as deciding on strike action;

(2)   To enable the Secretary of State to publish Codes of Practice containing guidance for improving Industrial Relations;

(3)   To provide greater protection for individual employees where a closed shop is established;

(4)   To limit lawful picketing to a picket's own place of work;

(5)   To restrict other forms of secondary action, such as blacking or sympathetic strikes;

(6)   To provide protection against secondary action specifically designed to force workers into union membership against their will;

(7)   To amend employment protection legislation, where experience has

shown that it is not working properly, and where it has discouraged employers (particularly in small firms) from creating new jobs. (The main effects of this are felt in the areas of unfair dismissal and maternity rights);

(8)   To provide a new right for pregnant women not to be unreasonably refused paid time off from work for ante-natal care.

In 1982 the Conservative Government introduced a second Employment Act. This Act made further changes to the law regarding the closed shop. The main impact is with respect to unfair dismissal of a worker for non-membership of a trade union in a closed shop. As well as increasing significantly the amount of compensation payable, the Act also creates additional circumstances in which it would be unfair to dismiss an employee who refused to belong to a trade union where a closed shop agreement was in existence. The most significant of these additional circumstances is where a closed shop agreement has not, in the five years preceding the dismissal, been supported in a secret ballot by 80% of the employees covered by it or by 85% of those voting. If, as many believe, this part of the legislation is as much, if not more, concerned with an attack on the closed shop as a defence of individual rights, then it will be interesting to see how the case law develops.

The 1982 Act also modifies the law on the dismissal of strikers. If strikers do not return to work, then those remaining on strike may be dismissed, providing, firstly, that all those taking part in the action at the same establishment were dismissed and, secondly, none are offered re-engagement within three months.

The 1982 Employment Act also makes void any term in a commercial contract which requires a person to use only union labour in fulfilling a contract.

The main effect of the 1984 Trade Union Act is to require trades unions to secretly ballot their members before taking industrial action. If industrial action is taken without such a ballot having taken place; and yielded a majority in favour of taking the action; then the immunity that the trade union might enjoy against claims for damages against its funds by parties incurring losses as a result of the action, is lost. In other words a trade union organising a strike for which there has not previously been a secret ballot majority amongst the members concerned runs the risk of having substantial damages awarded against it, by the courts.

In addition to this a trade union which attempts to organise industrial action, without holding a ballot may find that an employer, or other party who may be affected by the industrial action obtains an injunction from the courts restraining the union from taking the action.

If the union ignores an injunction then it is acting in contempt of court for which it may suffer penalties which can take the form of severe fines.

INDUSTRIAL RELATIONS

Since 1960 there has been a considerable amount of legislation which has either attempted to directly control the actions of the parties to Industrial Relations, or has affected areas which are dealt with through the processes of collective bargaining.

Since 1980 there has been a greater preparedness on the part of employers to use the law as it applies to Industrial Relations conflicts. This contrasts generally with the behaviour of employers in the early 1970s (B. Weekes, 1975). This use of the law is occurring to the extent that some observers feel that the traditional voluntarist system of Industrial Relations may be changing to the extent that the term no longer accurately describes the situation. Such changes in employer behaviour may be related to the relative strength of trades unions which itself is affected by the unprecedently high level of unemployment in the 1980s.

Bodies set up to assist in the conduct of Industrial Relations

The best known body in Industrial Relations is the Advisory Conciliation and Arbitration Service (ACAS). To quote from their annual report, 'ACAS was established as a statutory body under the Employment Protection Act 1975 on 1st January 1976. It is charged with the general duty of promoting the improvement of Industrial Relations and in particular, of encouraging the extension of collective bargaining and the development, and where necessary, reform of collective bargaining machinery. The Service is directed by a Council whose Chairman and nine members are appointed by the Secretary of State for Employment'.

The service that is provided by ACAS is impartial, confidential, and free of charge. Before ACAS was set up, conciliation in complaints to Industrial Tribunals was carried out by officials of the Department of Employment.

As well as having a duty to try and conciliate in complaints by individuals against their employers made to Industrial Tribunals, ACAS has a role in *collective conciliation*. Collective conciliation involves ACAS in providing help to employers and trades unions to reach mutually acceptable settlements to their disputes. Conciliation comes about by voluntary action by the disputants and agreements reached through this process are their responsibility. The conciliator tries to help the parties find common ground upon which they can make a settlement. In addition to conciliation, ACAS will arrange or provide the services of arbitrators and mediators. *Arbitration* differs from mediation in that the parties to arbitration agree to accept the findings of the arbitrator in advance. In this way he acts as judge, informing the parties of his decision. Arbitration may be carried out by a single person (often an academic with industrial experience), or a board of arbitrators. ACAS apply three rules before they will appoint an arbitrator. Firstly, both parties to the dispute must agree to use the arbitration process and to be bound by it. Secondly, conciliation must have been considered as a method of resolving the problem and must have been rejected. Thirdly, any agreed procedures between the parties for the resolution of problems must have been exhausted.

The Central Arbitration Committee (CAC) is a permanent independent arbitration body set up under the Employment Protection Act. The CAC carries out arbitration on references made to it from ACAS.

Mediation, the third service offered through ACAS for collective conciliation, may be seen as a 'halfway house' between conciliation and arbitration. ACAS apply the same three pre-conditions to using mediators that they use for arbitrators but, unlike arbitration, the parties to the dispute are not bound by what the mediator recommends.

All these services provided by ACAS are free of charge and given by staff of the service, or people appointed to panels by ACAS. Most disputes are dealt with through the conciliation process with relatively few referred to arbitration or mediation.

Section 7

The Organisation In Context

The last section on Industrial Relations suggested that processes within the organisation are deeply influenced by external factors — notably Government intervention. This final Section develops this point by discussing a range of external influences and their effects on the structure and functioning of organisations. Chapter 20 provides a theoretical framework for such a discussion by examining the concepts and assumptions inherent in a systems perspective of organisations. In Chapter 21 the impact of technology on the individual, as in the case of the assembly-line worker, and on the organisation, as illustrated by Joan Woodward's work, is reviewed and the phenomenon of resistance to change is analysed. Chapter 22, on organisational change, treats change as inevitable and concentrates on possible sources, for example market forces, Government regulation, and social attitudes. This leads to a description of strategies for change, with particular reference to organisation development (OD) techniques.

Chapter 20

Systems

Your experience of education is significantly affected or influenced by your family background. Sociologists have shown that parental attitudes, social class, and aspirations can have a very important influence on the quantity and type of education a child receives. Similarly, we know from reading newspapers or hearing the news, that education is also tied up with politics. In Britain the majority of the population experiences education which is financed and controlled by central government and local education authorities. We can see, if these statements are reproduced diagrammatically, that there is an overlap or interrelationship between these three sectors of society — the family, education and government.

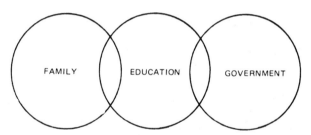

Figure 40 : Education system — basic

We can carry this investigation of interrelationships still further. Why are you doing this course? You may be doing it purely out of interest, but the majority of people believe that their career prospects will be enhanced by obtaining qualifications. On the other hand, many industrialists are on record as having commented on the content of educational courses and the utility of educational qualifications. Certainly it is common to talk about education as being an investment which a country makes for its future success. Thus we can extend our diagrammatic representation to include industry in Figure 41.

The 1944 Education Act included provision for religious education in schools, and there are many schools in this country which are closely linked to a particular religious denomination, Church of England Schools, Roman Catholic Schools, Jewish Schools and so on as shown in Figure 42.

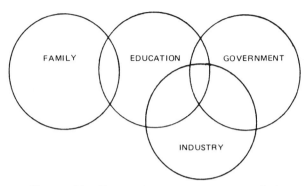

Figure 41 : Education system — extended

Taking education as our focal point, we can see that it is significantly influenced by, and influences, the ways in which industry affects the government, and so on. Indeed, we can point out many ways in which each institution in society affects, and is affected by every other institution. This set of interrelationships and interdependence of institutions, and therefore of individuals was seen by early sociologists, such as F. Tonnies (1955) and E. Durkheim (1933), as characteristic of industrial societies and brought about by the process of industrialisation. Durkheim referred to this interdependence as leading to *organic* solidari-

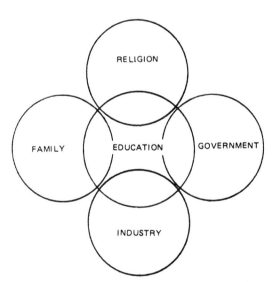

Figure 42 : Education system — complex

ty in industrial societies, as opposed to the *mechanical* solidarity which existed in pre-industrial societies.

Why did Durkheim talk about organic solidarity and what did he mean? If we think in very simple terms about an organism, such as a human body, it is made up of different parts; a heart, a liver, a brain, bones, the circulation of blood and so on. Each of these parts has a particular 'job' to do, or role to play in maintaining the organism — it is specialised — and yet each part is dependent on the others. For example, if the heart stops beating and blood containing oxygen does not reach the brain, the brain cannot work. Similarly, the liver plays an important part in determining the 'quality' of the blood circulating. Thus each part of the body has a specialised job to do, and yet all parts work together and are interrelated in their overall job of keeping the body alive and healthy. So, when Durkheim referred to organic solidarity, he was comparing society to a living organism — a system made up of interrelated but specialised parts which work together for the maintenance of the whole.

L. Von Bertalanffy (1968) went further than this and pointed out similarities between the human body and machines, for example. He laid the foundation for systems theory as it is used today.

Let us take the car as an illustration. From what we have considered so far, it is fairly clear that a car is made up of a large number of different parts which are specialised and yet which work together to make the car work, as in the human body example outlined above. Yet the similarities go further. A car needs certain 'raw materials' or *inputs* in order to function, and these are petrol, oil, air, and water. The normal human being similarly needs certain 'inputs' of food and drink and air to breathe. Indeed, when we talk about a car suffering from 'petrol starvation' or a person feeling 'run down', we are unconsciously accepting and using this very comparison. What happens next? In a car these inputs are 'processed' by internal combustion, just as the respiratory and digestive systems of the human process his inputs. As a result of this processing in

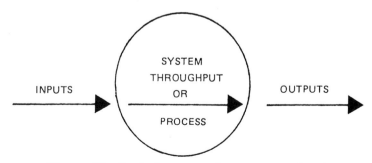

Figure 43 : Basic features of a system — simple

the car or the human, energy is produced, along with waste materials. These latter 'outputs' are disposed of through the exhaust pipe in a car, or its human equivalent!

We can use this simple model of a system to consider a business organisation. A company making jam will have inputs of raw materials, for example, fruit, and sugar; people to make and sell the jam; and equipment; as well as money to pay for the process. These inputs will come together in the organisation in the conversion or throughput stage, and then, finally, outputs will be produced — such as the finished product, jam; people who are retiring, leaving jobs, or who have been made redundant; and money, for example in the form of wages. Although this picture is highly simplified, and therefore somewhat incomplete (for example one may consider staff training to be a form of throughput), it does exemplify the application of these three features of a system in the organisational context.

The very idea of inputs and outputs suggests the next essential feature of a system, and that is its environment. The success of our jam manufacturer will be, at least in part, dependent upon the price he must pay for his raw materials; how effective he is in recruiting staff; and the price he can demand for his finished product. Thus the *environment* in which an organisation, or any other system for that matter operates may be of great significance. For any organisation, environmental aspects such as the industrial relations climate, the price of the pound vis-a-vis other currencies, the supply of labour in a particular area, are important variables which affect its success.

Figure 43 should perhaps be modified in the light of this additional information.

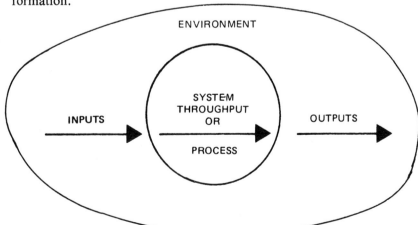

Figure 44 : Basic features of a system — extended

We can similarly see the impact of the environment on a system by using the other examples referred to previously. The outside temperature will affect the performance of a car, especially if it is highly tuned. The amount of choke a car needs to start may be affected by the outside temperature; the grip of the tyres will depend on the amount of wet or ice on a road; and the water in the radiator may boil if the outside temperature is high. The human body too, will be affected by environmental conditions — your energy may be low on a hot, humid day; you may develop a headache in thundery weather; and the altitude may similarly affect your performance, as athletes training in high altitudes have found.

Another property of systems is that they tend to operate in a cyclical nature — there are cycles of events. It is commonly accepted that the human body is subject to biorhythms, cycles of potential for high or low activity, and psychologists have done significant work on circadian rhythms, cycles of sleep and activity, which are important in the study of stress and in the effectiveness of shift work patterns. A car operates on a particular cycle of firing — pistons do not go up and down at random, but follow a particular pattern. The business organisation, too, operates according to particular timed patterns of events. You can see in Chapter 14, on Management by Objectives, that certain cycles of events occur. Budgets, too, are subject to fairly tight time-schedules, tied to the end of the financial year, for example. A serious drop in share-price may occur for an organisation which is late in publishing its half-yearly or annual accounts. Even the products which an organisation makes are subject to this phenomenon of cycles, and both economists and marketing specialists refer to 'the product life-cycle', taking cognisance of the fact that products go through phases of growth, maturity and decline, which will have implications for an organisation's need for Research and Development, advertising, and marketing resources. Another cycle, which is apparent in many organisations, is a Planning cycle. Most large organisations construct a five year plan which states where the organisation 'wants to go' and how it plans to get there. This plan is usually operated on a 'rolling' basis, in that it is updated annually on the basis of any changes internal or external to the organisation. Related to this need for an organisation to respond to changed conditions is the concept of *equifinality*. This property of the business organisation as a system means, in a very simplified form, that there are many means to achieving the goals. To use a very simple example, more money may accrue to an organisation either by cutting costs, or raising the price of its goods or services (although the success of this will be significantly affected by the elasticity of demand for the product or service), or the organisation could try to raise capital from its shareholders. Similarly a basic goal of 'improved effectiveness' could be achieved by a variety of means, such as automation, improved training, a different strategy of selection of staff, or improved motivation.

The concept of equifinality is one which must be grasped by students of Business Policy, for it implies that there is rarely 'one right answer' to any firm's problems. Rather, one has to decide where the firm should be in, say, five years time and the best strategy to adopt, in the light of the prevailing circumstances and the current information available to the planners.

One type of information which is vital to planners, and indeed to any system for that matter, is *feedback*. Again, a very simple description of feedback is information concerning the system's output which may subsequently affect its input. Perhaps the most familiar usage of the term feedback to you as a student will be in the context of written assignments. Let us imagine that you have to hand in two essays — the first one next Monday and the second in two weeks' time. Being a model student, you must work hard at your first essay and hand it in on time. Let us assume however, that your lecturer is not such a model person, and he does not hand back your essay before the next one is due. What effect would this have on your performance in the second essay? What do you think the main problems might be? On the other hand, if you do receive your first essay back before you start to write the second one, what difference would it make?

Usually a marked essay has some sort of comment on it — perhaps concerning the length of the essay, perhaps the grammar; it might ask you to quote your references in a bibliography at the end, it may ask you to use ink rather than pencil. The feedback you receive on your first essay should help you to be more successful in your second one — hopefully you will not make the same mistakes again.

By receiving adequate feedback, your performance as a student should be enhanced.

Writing essays is, of course, a very important part in determining your success as a student, but it is not such an expensive process as a company launching a new product. Feedback is vital to any organisation if it is to be successful, and feedback may be collected in a variety of ways and for a number of different purposes. Most computerised management information systems will give the manager up-to-date feedback on how long it takes customers to pay accounts, thus enhancing the information available on cash flow. Sophisticated systems of stock control will provide feedback on stock turnover and the most profitable lines, together with economic order quantities. Market research is frequently concerned with collecting feedback on potential new products from potential customers, while reports from salesmen who are out in the field can frequently furnish feedback about company image and competitors' activities.

Feedback can have a more direct impact on the organisation as a system. If we return to our simple diagram of the organisation as a system, and concentrate on one type of input and output, namely people as employees, we can see an important feedback loop: The feedback loop in Figure 45 suggests that people as 'output' are affecting the people as 'input'. How might that occur? Imagine that you are looking for a job. There is one large company near you which appears to be an attractive proposition and you apply for a job there. One evening before your interview you are sitting in a pub and two men on the next table mention

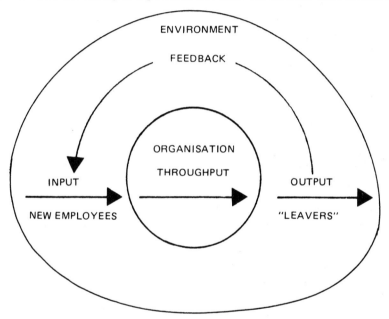

Figure 45 : Basic features of a system — complex

the name of the company. You naturally listen in to what they are saying. What would be your reaction if you learned from their conversation that they, and two hundred employees like them, had just been made redundant? At best you might be concerned about the stability of the firm and your potential job in that firm — at worst you might withdraw your application.

Another example of this direct feedback link can be seen in terms of finance, in that the more successful a company is in selling its products, the more cash it has coming into the organisation as an input.

If we return to our initial discussion of organisations as systems, we must bear in mind that we are considering interrelationships between the parts which make up the whole — in the case of organisations these inter-relationships will be between the different departments which make up the organisation, or different groups of products or individuals. Another property of systems which will affect these interrelationships and which also incorporates the concept of feedback, as outlined above, is that of *homeostasis*. Homeostasis means a tendency towards equilibrium, and it also implies that if change is introduced in one part of a system, then the other parts will, in time, tend to change, such that eventually the same relationship exists between the parts as before. One very simple example of this can be seen in pay negotiations. If we take three groups of workers:

Group A earn £x   per week
Group B earn £x + 15% per week
Group C earn £x + 20% per week

Group A then negotiates a pay rise of 9%. This means that:

Group A earn £x + 9% per week
Group B earn £x + 15% per week
Group C earn £x + 20% per week

It is more than likely that the workers in Group B and C will object to their pay differential being eroded and they will, in turn, put in for a pay rise. The situation for that particular pay round will probably settle at around the following:

Group A   £x + 9% per week
Group B   £x + 9% + 15% per week
Group C   £x + 9% + 20% per week

Obviously this is a highly simplified view of what happens in pay negotiations, as a variety of other intervening variables would need to be taken into account, but it does illustrate this concept of homeostasis or dynamic equilibrium, since we can see that the workers end in the same position relative to one another, although at a higher level of pay. Thus homeostasis refers to the concept of 'dynamic equilibrium', suggesting that, although the quantities involved may change, for example, the nature of the relationships will remain constant.

How does the management of an organisation use or apply this systems perspective? Let us take a practical example of an organisation which is experiencing a high rate of labour turnover. The management may decide that it should investigate this problem by looking into the job content, supervision, and working conditions of the groups most at risk in labour turnover terms. They would study the relationships between work groups and between departments. They would study the relationship between training given and skills demanded in particular jobs. They would investigate the relationship between supervisory style and numbers leaving, and whether improved supervisor training might remedy the problem.

This type of investigation is very common to work organisations, and the systems framework provides a number of suggestions for fruitful and worthwhile areas of investigation, particularly in the field of relationships between individuals, groups, and the processes designed by the organisation. A specific example of this kind of study was undertaken by some researchers at the Hawthorne plant in America, where the investigators started by looking at a great many of the factors mentioned above — supervisor/subordinate relationships, relationships between group members and so on.

Closed and Open Systems

This approach to investigating organisational problems is known as a *closed* systems approach — because it views the organisation as a total environment to be investigated. This can be a very useful approach, but it has many critics, who claim that often we can only understand problems within an organisation if we view them from a wider environmental perspective. If we return to the labour turnover problem, it should be apparent that, before it can be known that there is a problem of high labour turnover, some comparison must be made. Do we have a high rate of turnover compared to a time in our company's past? Do we have a high rate compared to other firms in our area? Do we have a high rate compared to other firms operating in the same kind of industry? By taking the latter two comparisons, we are acknowledging the importance of the environment in which the organisation is located, and in doing so we are moving towards an *open* systems approach to organisations. The open system model stresses the relationship between the organisation and its environment. Thus the problem of high labour turnover may be investigated through the study of internal organisational processes, and also of relationships between the organisation and its environment. Thus we would need to look at the state of the employment market generally, and specifically in relation to our locality. We would study the rate of growth or decline of our industry, to see how attractive it appears to our labour force compared to other industries. We would need to look at our wage rates and compare them with other companies' wage rates.

The major problem associated with this open systems approach is just where do you halt your investigation? How many environmental influences can you take into account before the cost of the investigation far outweighs the cost of the labour turnover? Not only that, but where are you going to draw the boundary, the outside limit, of the environment which affects your organisation. If the majority of our labour turnover is among immigrant groups, our boundary may have to extend to the cultures from which our workers originate. Similarly, a purchasing problem may have a boundary encompassing the world as far as sources of raw materials are concerned. Much as we would like to pursue the perfect investigation, the implications of adopting a fully open systems model for organisationally related problems are so enormous that such a model remains an aspiration rather than an actuality.

Having pointed out the significance of environmental influences, and therefore the dangers inherent in the closed systems approach, and yet realising the practical difficulties of the open systems model, we must consider a third possible variant, that of the *partially* open systems approach. In adopting this approach we acknowledge the importance of environmental variables, as well as our own restrictions in terms of time, cost, and other resources, so we deliberately and carefully choose which environmental variables we will study.

P.R. Lawrence and J.W. Lorsch (1967) investigated the relationship between organisational effectiveness, organisational structure, and environmental conditions. They chose three environmental variables to study — the Market, Technology, and Research and Development activity. By definition, since this partially open systems model is a compromise, it is not perfect, its obvious and major flaw being its dependence on the researcher's skill in identifying the most significant environmental variables to study and in ignoring the peripheral or unimportant ones. It is, however, the model most frequently adopted in the study of organisations and their problems.

This chapter has outlined some of the major features of systems, with specific reference to organisations as systems, and has provided a few examples of how this approach can be applied to the study of organisations. Before we leave this topic, it is important that some of the weaknesses of such an approach are discussed. Three such weaknesses will be outlined — firstly, the impersonality of the systems approach; secondly, the harmonious frame of reference it represents; and thirdly, the paucity of its explanatory value.

A systems approach to the study of organisations may be criticised because it tends to assume that organisations have an independent life of their own, and thus it does not pay much attention to the people who are employed in the organisation and particularly who shape, direct and manage the process or procedures within it. In other words, the systems approach *reifies* the organisation, thus we may talk of inputs, processes, or outputs without seriously considering management policies to direct and control these. We have a Manpower Planning cycle, or a five year plan, not because the organisation 'needs' them, nor because the organisation as a system has to work that way, but because *people,* top management, have decided that these are desirable features. So we must guard against reifying the organisation, and we must always bear in mind the crucial importance of human need and intention in organisational life.

Secondly, by its relationship with the organic analogy, comparing the structure and functioning of the body and the organisation, the systems approach tends to imply a high degree of harmony in organisations and that disharmony is pathological — a sign of 'illness'. We pointed out that, although specialised in function, the liver, heart etc. work together for the maintenance and good of the whole body. Should a situation arise when parts of the body are in conflict, this would be perceived as highly undesirable and something that should be 'cured' or prevented very quickly. However there are many instances when conflict in an organisation is neither undesirable nor in need of a rapid 'cure' — many writers such as L. Coser (1958) have pointed out the beneficial aspects of conflict, particularly as a means to organisational change. Furthermore, it is possible to question whether an organisation is in fact made up of specialised parts working harmoniously towards the good of all, or whether it is not more accurate to describe the members of the organisation as each striving in different ways to achieve their own different objectives whilst being controlled and constrained to behave in managerially approved ways so that management's objectives are achieved before all others.

The third criticism which may be levelled against the systems approach is that it *explains* very little about the way in which organisations work in practice. In fact the systems approach provides a framework, an analytical tool, by which organisations may be studied, but as an explanatory device, as a theory which provides answers to problems in organisations, it is seen by many as being inadequate.

Chapter 21

The Impact Of Technology

Developments in the methods of production since the Industrial Revolution have meant that a very large range of goods are available for everyone to buy, but they have also meant significant changes in the nature of work experienced by the work force. The introduction of machinery has made some jobs less difficult or arduous, some jobs less skilled, some jobs more boring, and it has also meant that some jobs have disappeared completely. Today this last experience is one that is of significance in the printing industry, where people are aware that equipment is available to render a large proportion of the work force redundant. Thus, the use of automated production methods to increase efficiency means that fewer people are needed to produce the same volume of goods and, although rapidly expanding economies may be able to maintain a high level of employment, this appears to be more difficult in the stable economies of most industrialised nations.

In the twentieth century we have seen a shift away from agriculture and the other primary industries into manufacturing, often perceived as being related to the availability of agricultural machinery, as well as a drift away from rural to urban areas. More recently, since the 1960s, we have seen a further shift away from the secondary, or manufacturing sector and towards the tertiary, or service, sector. This trend is continuing, as again machinery is available to replace people in the production process, but there are indications that it will be difficult to create enough new services and craft-produced goods to provide employment for all who wish it.

Because of these trends, the terms *technological change* and *automation* have won prominent places in our vocabulary in the recent past, with the majority of the comment being directed at the problems arising out of these processes — obsolescent skills, job displacement, retraining and so on.

Studies of Technological Change

One set of studies which consider the implications of technological change for human behaviour, and vice versa, are those originating from the Tavistock Institute, particularly E.L. Trist and K.W. Bamforth's study of mining in 1951, and A.K. Rice's (1958) application of this socio-technical approach, as it is known, in India.

The Trist and Bamforth study was conducted in the coal mines, which were a scene of bitter conflict. The nationalisation of the coal mining industry had been expected to result in a diminished level of conflict, but this did not turn out to be the case, whether level of conflict was measured by overt, open conflict, or implicit conflict, as demonstrated by absenteeism. Criticisms were frequently made of the new method of getting coal which was called the 'longwall' method. Trist and Bamforth set out to identify the technical features of the method of getting coal, which might affect the response of the miners. They considered that there are three features which characterise mining, irrespective of the methods used:-

1. Mining is dark, dirty and dangerous work;
2. Geological features can, and frequently do, threaten the smooth operation of the process;
3. There are three distinct operations involved:-
    a) Preparation, which involves cutting the fresh coal in the seam;
    b) Getting, which involves actually removing the coal;
    c) Advancing, which is the process of moving the machinery, pit props and so on to the next section to be mined.

In the traditional, hand-got method of mining, a self-selected group of six or so miners would work together, often being paid on a group bonus payment system. The group or team set its own pace and regulated both its members and its output. Each member could be skilled in all parts of the total mining operation and, because each team looked after all parts of the process, the flow of coal was even throughout the day, with very little possibility of bottlenecks occurring. Needless to say, the cohesiveness of the work team was normally reinforced by their social life, and it was not uncommon, in the past, for a man's 'team' to assume financial responsibility for his family in cases of accident or even death.

The longwall method was introduced as machinery became increasingly available, and conveyor-belting and coal-cutting machinery were introduced to the mines. These innovations, which made mining resemble mass-production methods, also involved changes in the organisation of work. Now the work was broken down into a standardised series of components which were designed to follow each other in succession over three shifts, with a complete cycle being completed each twenty-four hours. The logic of production engineering dictated that, instead of each team operating all three parts of the coal mining process, each miner now became specialised as each shift became specialised. The specialisation led to the emergence of a status system amongst the miners, and a lack of cooperation between them. The problems of coordination were now severe, and if one shift hit upon a problem, and was unable to progress, subsequent shifts were held up, leading to bottlenecks in production and scapegoating among the miners. Since the groups no longer existed, the self-regulation disappeared and significant resentment grew up over the supervision which now appeared to be necessary. The other symptom of the problem, attendant upon this new production method, was that output dropped.

To summarise, technological change had necessitated a major change in the organisation of work, which had, in turn, brought about adverse reactions from the miners and a deleterious effect on their behaviour. The socio-technical approach thus emphasises the interrelationship between technology and human behaviour, particularly interpersonal or social behaviour.

A further example of the impact of technology on the experience of work is provided by C.J. Walker and R.H. Guest (1952). They studied a number of assemblers working in a newly-built factory in America. Only one in ten of the sample had previously experienced machine-paced work, and Walker and Guest elicited their responses on a number of issues related to their experience of work. Virtually all the men said that they disliked the machine-pacing work — in other words, that the worker has to keep up the pace at which the conveyor belt assembly line is moving, irrespective of how fast or slowly he wishes to work. They also complained that the work was very repetitive and boring, almost totally lacking in challenge. So why had these men gone to work in this apparently distasteful environment? The answer seems to lie in the fact that they could earn substantially more by working in this assembly line factory than they would elsewhere, and 75% of the workers questioned claimed to have come to work in this particular plant solely because high wages were offered. Many of the workers obtained a 50% increase in their pay in this way.

Apart from the high level of pay, the security of the job was also appreciated although the men, probably realistically, perceived little or no opportunities for advancement. Furthermore, the men experienced little social interaction at work, as the noise and layout of the line precluded most conversation, and so it is not surprising that few respondents were conscious of belonging to an identifiable work group.

Walker and Guest suggested that union membership was an important counterbalance to the impersonality and anonymity of assembly line production. L.R. Sayles (1958) was similarly interested in grievance activity of workers, and he classified work groups into four types, according to their level of grievance activity:

1.   Apathetic — characterised by disunity, often very low status;

2. Erratic — unpredictable, inflame very easily;
3. Strategic — high level of unity and located in a vital area of the production process;
4. Conservative — often highly paid craftsmen.

Sayles believed that the nature of the work group, and hence its propensity to indulge in grievance activity, was rooted in the technology it experienced.

Just as Sayles pointed out the relationship between technology and group cohesiveness and militancy, so Joan Woodward (1965) indicated the relationship between technology and administrative structure. In the 1950s she led a research team investigating aspects of organisation such as the number of levels of authority, the span of control, and other administrative features. Having established that firms show considerable differences in these areas, Woodward and her team set out to establish why such differences might occur. They considered differences in size as a possible answer, but it did not appear to be justified, nor were differences in origin. When different production methods were considered, however, there did appear to be a strong relationship between technology and organisation structure.

The product made and the market served determine whether a 'one-off' production method is used or a mass-production method. Thus the building of prototypes of electronic equipment tends to be carried out on a 'one-off' basis, while the manufacture of cars is usually done using the assembly line form of production, as this gives greater control and a lower cost.

Woodward classified production methods into three forms:

1. Unit & small batch;
2. Large batch and mass production;
3. Process production.

Unit and small batch production is normally done by more highly-skilled workers on low volume/high cost pieces, such as the more expensive types of furniture available today; or prototypes; or on units made to customers' specifications. As more and more of the same good is required it becomes cheaper to manufacture by mass production or assembly line methods.

In this case, each individual worker assembles part of the finished product before it is passed on to the next person on the line. With some products, and with the increasing application of computer controlled devices to the production field, process production becomes a viable and desirable alternative. The petro-chemical industry has used automated processing for some time now, and it is being applied to food processing and car manufacture. The main feature of this mode of production is the virtual absence of the human as production worker, as the machinery is the prime producer. Man, instead, works at programming the machinery and maintaining it.

These differences in technology account for many variations in organisation structure. Automated plants, for example, are characterised by the high proportion of administrative and managerial personnel compared with production operatives, while assembly line production is identifiably by the large proportion of direct production operatives. Unit or small batch production methods rely heavily on the skills and integrity of the production personnel themselves, and show little evidence of the tight control apparent in assembly line production.

This aspect of control leads us to another typology of technology namely that of Robert Blauner (1974). He was interested in the concept of alienation, which he defined as a general syndrome made up of a number of different objective conditions and subjective feelings and states which emerge from certain relationships between workers and the socio-technical settings of employment. Alienation he said, exists when workers are unable to control their immediate work processes, to develop a sense of purpose and function which connects their jobs to the overall organisation of production, to belong to integrated industrial communities, and when they fail to become involved in the activity of work as a mode of personal self-expression.

Thus there are 4 dimensions of alienation which may be contrasted with non-alienative states:

Powerlessness	—	Control
Meaninglessness	—	Purpose
Isolation	—	Social Integration
Self-estrangement	—	Self-involvement

Blauner gathered evidence from 4 industries based on 4 different technologies:

Printing as an example of craft technology;
Textiles as an example of machine-minding technology;
Cars as an example of assembly line technology;
Chemicals as an example of process technology.

He suggests that technological factors are paramount in their impact on aspects of alienation.

Blauner suggested that alienation has travelled a course that could be charted on a graph by means of an inverted U-curve. Thus, in the craft technology situation, the worker's freedom is at a maximum. This freedom is then sharply diminished by the advent of machine-tending systems and is further eroded by mass assembly production systems. But the case of the continuous-process industries, particularly the chemical industry, shows that automation increases the worker's control over his work process and checks the further division of labour and growth of large factories. The result is meaningful work in a more cohesive integrated industrial climate. Blauner's optimism concerning the less alienating aspects of process production technology is not unanimously upheld, as many critics have suggested that this form of production provides the ultimate in man's subjection, since he is now reduced to serving and maintaining the machine. Others have argued that automation replaces physical fatigue with mental fatigue.

Resistance to Change

Whether or not the change in production technology towards automated production is beneficial to all or not, it is certainly the case that technological change in itself can cause a variety of problems. Technological change and its acceptance or rejection by the work force is inextricably linked to the method by which change is introduced; the system of authority which it reveals; and the way in which the new production methods fit in with other aspects of the work situation. Resistance to change is a common phenomenon, often linked to the variables mentioned above, as well as to a variety of other factors, such as the real or imaginary threat to jobs and job security.

A study, which was carried out in the United States by L. Coch and J.R. French some years ago, is still a very vivid illustration of some of these points. It was set in a textile firm, where the workers consistently resisted necessary changes in methods and job content by raising grievances over new piece rates, and by restricting their output. These manifestations of discontent were accompanied by a high rate of labour turnover and absenteeism. Coch and French thought that this resistance to change might be caused by a combination of individual frustrations and anxieties, coupled with group-induced aggression. To test this out, three groups of workers were studied as further changes were proposed. The first group, as had been the case in the past, were told that the change was to be introduced and were offered no opportunity to participate in this process. As a result, the same symptoms of discontent appeared, and 17% of the group had left the company within 40 days.

The second group were invited to elect a representative who was party to management discussions about the change, and who could put the workers' point of view. In this group, where representation was encouraged, the results following the change were somewhat different in that no one left the company, there was virtually no hostility to the change process, and output targets were achieved on schedule.

The third group experienced the highest level of participation in the implementation of change, as each individual was asked to participate in this process, thus enabling them to ask questions about aspects which may have been troubling them, and avoiding the emergence of rumours which could lead to individual anxieties or group resistance to change. The results from this fully participative group were very good, in that there was a 14% increase in productivity.

Coch and French had demonstrated by their research that resistance to change can be alleviated by the workers receiving accurate information from management, and being able to participate in the implementation of change.

Whilst the work of such writers as Woodward, Blauner, and Trist continues to be very popular, and to influence the area of job redesign very significantly, a reaction against this set of ideas has emerged: it emphasises the broad orientations to work held by individuals and the fact that such orientations may be derived from outside the work place. J.H. Goldthorpe and D. Lockwood (1968) stressed the instrumental orientation of the affluent manual worker, which enabled him to tolerate repetitive and uninteresting work, provided that the money was good. The 'instrumental worker' on the assembly line certainly did not appear to show signs of the alienation Blauner would have described for him. This emphasis on workers' own values and perception has carried on in work by H. Beynon and R.M. Blackburn (1972).

Future of Technological Change

The most recent area of interest in technology has been the silicon chip and its impact on the production process, with the emphasis from the employees' side being the likely effects on employment. It has been suggested that, unless Britain innovates into this new technology at a similar rate to her overseas competitors, very high levels of unemployment will result, and this prospect has to be weighed against the redundancy which is inevitable with the introduction of the silicon chip to industry and its substitution of capital equipment for people in jobs.

Chapter 22

Organisational Change

Change is inevitable in any organisation and, even when we talk about stable or static organisations, we tend to mean that change in them is gradual rather than non-existent. Although organisations change in a variety of ways for a variety of reasons, the sort of change we will consider here may be defined as: *a planned and deliberate attempt to modify the functioning of a total organisational system, or one of its major components, usually with a view to improving the effectiveness of the organisation.* Although such a definition suggests that a part can be changed, as distinct from the total organisation, it is only in exceptional circumstances that such isolated change will occur. Normally, as we saw in our study of systems, change in one part of the organisation will have an effect on all other parts. Change can emanate from many different sources, and it is to an examination of these that we now turn.

Innovation

The introduction of new products or new technology can have a significant impact an organisation. We have already considered Joan Woodward's work relating technology to organisational structure, and it is obvious that a change from small batch to a fully automated production system is going to have implications for job design, for the proportion of white collar/blue collar workers, possibly for the hours worked and so on. Frequently this type of change in technology is associated with a change of product. The manufacture of detergents requires a different form of technology from bars of soap, just as the manufacture of the bicycle is different from that of the modern car, which may be built by robots. This type of approach can also be taken out of the factory and into the hospital, for example, where micro-surgery and computer-assisted diagnosis has meant increasing specialisation and the introduction of new jobs into the medical services. A similar change can be observed in the armed forces, where technological change has led to the introduction of new specialisms.

Changing Consumer Demands

Changed products can be brought about by changes in consumer demand, and products may rapidly be rendered obsolete by changing fashions. Microwave ovens, citizen band radios, and turbo chargers are relatively recent consumer preferences which the alert Marketing department will be ready to take up. Consumer concern about diet has led to the emergence of low calorie drinks, ranging from the traditional 'mixers' such as tonic water, to low carbohydrate lagers and cola-type drinks. Changes in buying patterns, away from the corner shop and towards the supermarket, dictated the change away from returnable, deposit bottles and towards cans or disposable containers. The application of microprocessors to the leisure industry has meant that the consumer is able to convert his television from a passive object to be viewed into a teaching machine or an active entertainment as different programme packages can be used to teach basic Maths or play 'Space Invaders'. Such developments in consumer taste can mean a rapidly expanding market in one area, with the associated growth of companies which are able to predict trends and take advantage of them, but they can also mean the demise of markets, and with them, companies who failed to perceive the impending changes.

Competition

There are very few companies which offer a unique product or service, and governments tend to take a dim view of monopoly wherever it exists. Most companies operate in a competitive market, and will frequently have to take an interest in their competitors' activities in order to survive. Many large companies have a specialised department or individual whose task is to monitor 'competitors' activities', to establish, for example, when a new product is to be launched, an existing product relaunched, or a new advertising campaign mounted.

Keeping up with, or hopefully ahead of, the competition is thus a very important source of change in the organisation, and will provide the force behind the Research and Development department.

Government Regulation

Government intervention in the running of industry has increased dramatically in the last thirty-five years. In the field of employment legislation alone, significant changes have been made from recruitment and selection, through Health and Safety at work, to redundancy and dismissal provisions. Legislation on Equal Pay and Equal Opportunities has seen the advent of more women in industry, although it would be naive to suggest that this trend results entirely from the legislation. In the financial area, too, there are regulations and recommendations concerning the disclosure of information to trade unions, the way in which information is presented, inflation, accounting and so on.

Such intervention has led to changes in such areas as personnel departments, where legal experts are frequently now employed; stock-holding policies of companies; the accounting conventions they use; as well as many others. Any move towards the introduction of industrial democracy via the statute book would obviously have an enormous impact on the structure and decision making of an organisation.

Changes in the Work Force

It may be argued that change is frequently introduced into a company through the people it employs, and changes in the environment will obviously influence prospective employees in a number of ways. There have been changes in the education system in the past 50 years which mean that all individuals now receive a different and, in most cases, longer education than formerly. The change of emphasis, away from rote learning, and towards understanding, discovery, and analytical thought means that the intellectual capabilities of the work force have changed, which has implications for the way in which they can be managed and the sort of work they can be expected to do. It is commonly believed that to be an effective manager today the individual must win the respect of his work force by his expertise, as opposed to relying on his authority simply because he is a manager.

These, however, are relatively long term trends. It is possible for change to be experienced in the organisation due to much shorter term influences. Trade union activity will frequently diminish in a time of economic recession and high unemployment, for example, just as a strike in one company or industry can result in short-time working or lay-offs in a different but related company. This is frequently observed in the motor industry.

Changes in Social Values and Attitudes

It is possible to argue that this source of change is a direct result of the former source, in that one of the causes of changes in values and attitudes has been the development of secondary education in quantity and quality over the past forty years or so. Whatever its root cause change in social values and attitudes has occurred, bringing with it significant implications for organisations. Concern for ecology may be one of the most important of such changes, in that it has led to changes in the market, with a trend towards simulated furs and cosmetics with a vegetable rather than animal base. It has led to controls on exhaust emissions in some countries, certainly to added costs for industry through controls over the disposal of waste materials, either into the atmosphere or into rivers. Some companies are now able to make a selling point of the fact that their packaging is recycled or bio-degradable. Similarly, companies are considering alternative forms of vehicle propulsion with a view to the possibility of oil running out in the future.

In all these cases, changes in values and attitudes have led to new product development, alternative production, packaging and distribution methods, and a concern, often voiced if not always put into practice, for preservation rather than destruction. Fortunately such concern has now been spread from 'Nature' in general, to groups of people who were previously disadvantaged in employment. Without debating which comes first, legislation or a change in attitudes, it is possible to argue that the two together have led to improved employment prospects for women, members of racial or religious minorities, and disabled people. Such changes have led to employment practices and employee facilities being altered to cope with both the letter of the law, as in the case of recruitment advertising and, hopefully, in many cases, the spirit of the law through employers providing toilet facilities, ramps etc., for the disabled.

Thus changes in social values and attitudes have led to significant organisational changes.

Strategies for Change

Strategies for change, or ways in which organisational change can be effected, may be classified under the following headings:

1. Change in Personnel
2. Change in Structure
3. Change in Technology
4. Organisation Development

It is quite rare for any of these strategies to be adopted in isolation, as frequently two or more are introduced at the same time. However, we will consider them initially as conceptually distinct.

Change in personnel

This strategy is normally undertaken to halt what is perceived to be a deterioration in the performance of the organisation. It involves the replacement of one or a number of the top executives. Frequently this will result in a number of replacements at lower management levels, as positions are filled by individuals known to be loyal to the new administration. It is of vital importance that the new top management gains the trust of the rest of the employees very rapidly, as such a 'Board Room Shuffle' can cause grave anxieties, insecurities and mistrust among their junior colleagues. Many studies, notably Gouldner's *Wildcat Strike,* have suggested that the new, albeit senior, entrant would be well advised to study the climate or 'feel' of the organisation before making any sweeping changes in procedures or policies, since plans cannot — or should not — be conceived in a vacuum, but rather should be developed bearing the strengths and weaknesses of the existing organisation in mind.

Changes in organisation structure

This is normally experienced in such strategies as decentralisation, 'flattening' the organisation hierarchy, or moving from one form of departmental structure (such as product organisation) to geographical or matrix organisation. A.D. Chandler (1962) suggested that over time organisations went through four stages in structural development:

a) Stage 1 consists of the small scale, owner-run organisation;

b) Stage 2 consists of the undiversified organisation which develops into a function-based organisation staffed by professional managers. In time it may develop international divisions;

c) Stage 3 is the large multinational unit, with a general service Head Office and decentralised divisions;

d) Stage 4 is the very large organisation, such as Unilever, matrix organisation being the most appropriate structure. Such an organisation must be considered as a force in international politics by the very size of its interests in a large number of countries.

We have considered the implications of organisation structure in Chapter 2, but it is interesting to note that an American Management Consultant recently claimed that large organisations in the United States change their structure every two or three years.

Changes in technology

We have already seen that a change in technology can affect organisation structure, so that a move towards automated production can mean a significant change in the proportion of blue to white-collar workers employed. This is an obvious example of how one type of change, in technology, will lead to another, in structure.

Organisation Development (OD)

Organisation Development involves the application of the techniques and theories of the Behavioural Sciences to create a climate of increasing openness and trust among organisational members. There are a great many different strategies and techniques for organisational development, and we do not have room for them all here. We will briefly look at three different forms of organisation development which contrast quite sharply, and which will, therefore, present part of the spectrum of such strategies.

a) *Group training:* this approach has as its focus the feelings and attitudes of course members, and not the transmission of knowledge. The basic assumption of sensitivity training or T-groups as a strategy of OD is that by improving the interpersonal skills and perception of the course members, who are normally of middle management grades or above, the climate and leadership style of the organisation will be improved.

Group training differs from the more traditional approaches in two basic ways:

1) the training aims to improve the skills of group members by focusing on the training group itself. The problems which arise out of the experience of working together in the training group are examined with a view to improving both the group's effectiveness and the individual's effectiveness as a group member. People are encouraged to benefit from their actual experience, hence the term experiential learning. In contrast, a case or role-play involves a situation which is either fictional, historical, or real to someone other than the trainee. The individual has to pretend to be another person. In group training the group is its own on-going case study and people are themselves.

2) in group training considerable emphasis is placed on evaluating the performance of the individual or group. This leads to experimenting with behaviour and styles of group working.

The classical form of T-group centres in the 'here and now', and aims to increase the member's insight into his own attitudes and beliefs as well as his interpersonal skills. There is virtually no structure imposed on the group and the trainer typically does not overtly take a leadership role or lead the group discussion.

J.P. Campbell and M.D. Dunnette discuss 6 objectives of T-groups:

1) to increase insight into one's own behaviour and its meaning in a social context. This includes learning how others interpret one's behaviour and gaining insight into why one acts in certain ways in particular situations;

2) to increase sensitivity to the behaviour of others;

3) to increase awareness of the types of processes which facilitate or inhibit group functioning;

4) to improve diagnostic skills in social situations, to provide individuals with explanatory concepts for diagnosing conflict, faulty communication etc.;

5) to improve ability to intervene in interpersonal situations so as to increase satisfaction and performance;

6) to learn how to learn, by improving one's ability to analyse interpersonal behaviour in various social situations.

The T-group is a small, unstructured, face-to-face group of 10-15 people. Because the trainer overtly rejects the leadership role, a vacuum is created which frequently causes hostility and frustration initially, thus leading to the necessity for considering interpersonal and group behaviour at an early stage. The following developmental pattern is often observed:

1) Forming: group members exhibit anxiety and dependence on the trainer — they attempt to discover the rules underlying the situation in which they find themselves.

2) Rebellion: hostility is directed towards the trainer and members who try to impose a structure.

3) Norming: the development of a stable group structure with clear norms and modes of conflict resolution — group cohesion develops.

4) Cooperation: the group turns to the constructive solution of problems of interpersonal relations, its energy directed towards task achievement.

It is important for the success of a T-group that a climate of psychological safety exists, such that a group member feels that the group supports him. Two important factors which may influence the generation of such a climate are:

a)   the composition of the group;
b)   the feedback process.

The composition of the group may consist of individuals from a variety of backgrounds or companies (a *stranger* group) or it may be made up of individuals from the same organisation. A *cousin* group consists of individuals from the same organisation, but different departments and different levels in the hierarchy — a diagonal cross-section of the organisation. A *brother* group consists of people from the same organisation, same level in the hierarchy, but different departments. A *family* group is made up of members of the same organisation, same department, but different hierarchical levels. It should be apparent that a 'trade-off' may have to be made between a better chance for transfer of learning to occur and greater difficulty in arriving at a useful group climate. Since unfreezing occurs by removing familiar props and customary social mechanisms, by violation of trainee expectations, and by the creation of an ambiguous, unstructured situation, it can be seen that the presence of familiar individuals with familiar roles may inhibit individual experimentation and group cohesion under the novel circumstances.

Campbell and Dunnette are insistent that feedback of an appropriate type is necessary for effective T-groups. Many group members, they claim, when confronted with the feelings and behaviour of others in a psychologically safe atmosphere, can give articulate and constructive feedback. Feedback is an important source of learning because most people have an imperfect view of themselves and their relationships with others and, by gathering information from others, the individual may be able to correct his erroneous assumptions and perceptions.

E.H. Schein and W.G. Bennis (1965) claim that a successful T-group is one in which there is a willingness to experiment; a desire to expand interpersonal consciousness; the freedom to be oneself, rather than playing a role; and the realisation that conflict resolution must occur through problem solving, rather than coercion.

One of the comments that is sometimes made about a T-group is that it is a temporary system (sometimes compared to a holiday romance!) and as such the conditions are 'accelerated' — that there is an a-typical degree of spontaneity, interpersonal risk-taking, and open expression of feelings. Thus the transfer of learning may be open to question. It is certainly true that a manager will usually only exhibit sustained behavioural change after a T-group if the organisation encourages and places a positive value on that behaviour.

Another criticism of T-groups has been made by Argyle who claims that they may do psychological damage to a significant proportion of trainees. This type of claim is difficult to evaluate, but C. Cooper (1977) presents evidence which seems to contradict Argyle's findings. Cooper concludes: 'Although we must be aware of the inherent risks of experiental learning techniques and ensure that we have the skills to cope with them, we must also ensure that these safeguards do not inhibit the potential beneficial effects of such groups'.

One of the major pieces of work evaluating T-groups was carried out by Campbell and Dunnett. They found that favourable changes in behaviour on the part of participants were noted by their work associates, and that these were still apparent 6-9 months after training. They found no conclusive evidence of attitude changes by participants, as measured by scores on objective attitude tests. There was no hard evidence to show that organisations who favour T-groups have improved in productivity. This latter point is of importance when we consider the extensive use of T-groups in an Organisation Development programme, since OD is an approach to encouraging exploration and planned development of managerial, group, and organisational processes, aiming to create an environment which will facilitate effective contributions to the organisation.

b) *Grid OD:* W.L. French and C.H. Bell (1973) described this strategy, which was designed by Blake and Mouton, as 'Perhaps the most thorough going and systematic organisation development programme'.

It is carried out in the organisation by internal members who have been trained beforehand in grid concepts — i.e. by internal change agents. It is assumed that there is an ideal model, which applies to all organisations, and the change effort has as its overall goal the movement of the organisation in the direction of this model. Grid training differs from other forms of group training in that it:

(a) has a clear structure;
(b) focuses on managerial styles and behaviours which are directly relevant to the organisational setting, rather than on participant personality characteristics;
(c) looks at organisational rather than individual development

Basically individual training is merely the initial stage of a 6-phase programme. During the first phase participants study the Grid, engage in face-to-face feedback concerning each other's management styles, and participate in structured experiments dealing with the effects of interpersonal relations upon task accomplishments. Participation in any seminar is on the cousin, or diagonal slice, basis — this permits many organisational levels to be represented while assuring that no-one interacts directly with boss or co-worker. Subsequent phases emphasise team and intergroup integration and development; the development of long range organisation goals, implementing changes to achieve these goals; and accomplishing stabilisation.

The concept of Grid training is built on a systems approach to OD and has two major parts: the improvement of communications and interaction between individuals and groups of individuals, and the production and implementation of a corporate strategy model so that the organisation can reach objectives in an effective way. Blake and Mouton regard the organisation as the primary target and not the individual or isolated groups. This distinction highlights the difference between OD and management development, where management development involves increasing the knowledge and skills of individual managers to improve their contribution to the organisation, and OD involves the creation of an environment in which all members may contribute in an effective manner.

Another characteristic of the Management Grid is the highly structured nature of the approach. Participants work through a series of activities which are highly directive but which, when followed closely, provide the necessary learning experiences. The Grid concept (Figure 46) sees the manager as being concerned with two major factors, people and production.

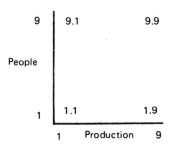

Figure 46 : Simplified managerial grid (Blake & Mouton)

The Grid OD effect, which generally takes from 3-5 years to implement, passes through the following stages:

Pre-phase 1 : Training managers are selected to be internal change agents. This takes the form of a one-week experiential laboratory with training in Grid concepts; team action skills; problem solving and critical skills; analysis of the culture of a team and of an organisation.

ORGANISATIONAL CHANGE

Phase 1 : A grid seminar is given to all managers in the organisation, the seminar being conducted by those managers trained in the previous phase, and the same topics being covered. Managers are supposed to learn in this phase how to become 9.9 managers.

Phase 2 : This is aimed at perfecting team work in the organisation, through the analysis of team culture, traditions etc., and developing skills in planning, and objective setting. Feedback is given to each manager about his individual and team behaviour. Comment on team work is done in the context of actual work behaviour.

Phase 3 : This is aimed at improving intergroup relations, moving from the usual win/lose ways of relating toward an ideal cooperative relationship. All teams with particularly important interfaces, or at least selected members of these teams, convene and go through exercises and activities together.

Phase 4 : Top management engage in strategy planning activities aimed at designing an ideal strategic corporate model. This may take up to one year, and there may be technical inputs etc. from all persons in the organisation.

Phase 5 : In this phase the organisation is restructured so that the ideal model may be implemented. Firstly, logical components of the organisation (e.g. geographical locations, product lines) are designated and each appoints a planning team. This team looks at all concepts in the ideal model and examines their implications for the component. A 'phase 5 coordinator' is appointed to each team to act as a resource person.

Phase 6 : This is instituted when phase 5 has made appreciable progress towards converting the organisation. It consists of a systematic critique of the results of the development programme and completes the first cycle.

The Grid OD is a commercial 'product' which offers management a number of easily understood 'tools' such as learning instruments and projects. It is not submitted to continuing research and revision as many OD methods are and it tends to apply its development methods in a uniform fashion in all organisations where it is applied. As can be seen from the previous discussions, the Grid method is aimed strictly at management and the emphasis for a lot of the programme is very much on upper management. Grid development is time consuming, offers no quick results, is expensive, and may call for organisational redesign. Also there is difficulty in demonstrating either that the ideal model is generally applicable, or that the method is an efficient way of achieving progress towards the model. There is no support for these claims other than from

Blake and Mouton themselves and, furthermore, the model tends to ignore questions of reward and motivation and places little emphasis on technology.

Other commentators have mentioned a major advantage of the Grid approach being its relatively low cost in that comparatively inexperienced trainers can be used. Criticisms include the apparent rigidity and inflexibility of the system, which may cause resistance, with people objecting to the 'sausage machine' principle.

c) Action Research: action research is the application of the scientific method of fact-finding to practical problems, where solutions in the form of actions are sought. It is characterised by clear objectives, step by step action taking and evaluation, and movement towards the objective in a series of planning-action-evaluation cycles. Because of this feedback element, imperfect understanding of the system operated upon is less disastrous than in previous organisation change attempts where a major change was prescribed (with varying degrees of consultation) and implemented as a single large-scale exercise. In such a strategy mismerceptions and misconceptions about the system can cause the change effort to result in a new state of the system which is considerably less adaptive, or less functional, than its original. The constant evaluation built into a series of small action steps, means that any mistakes can be detected and corrected before they become costly in themselves, or threaten the effectiveness of the project as a whole. This at least is the conceptual justification of action research. In practice there may be difficulties. Clear goal setting may be an absolute prerequisite for the success of any change effort, but the problem of measuring progress towards that goal may, in practice, prove considerable. Furthermore, it is not always possible to envisage progress towards the goal as a series of discrete forward steps. Because of the large size and complexity of many of the systems desiring change, and the limited resources for carrying it out, many action steps will be preparation for subsequent actions. It may be harder to set subgoals for these preparatory steps so that progress may be evaluated.

Such problems do not mean that the method is impractical. Rather it means that great care in goal setting and the selection of suitable measures is needed. The concept of repeated goal setting and evaluation, despite the occasional difficulties of implementations, would seem to offer the best basis yet available on which to build organisational change efforts, whatever the goals and particular change strategies selected.

Change Agent

One of the choices which has to be made in using the technique of OD is whether to use an external or an internal change agent. An internal change agent is an existing employee of the organisation who is seconded to the role of change agent for a specific period whilst the external change agent is someone from an outside group of consultants, hired at a particular rate of pay per day. One of the problems facing the manager who is trying to choose between the two is the plethora of over-optimistic claims, often made by those whose livelihood depends on selling their services to organisational clients, no matter how limited and inappropriate these services might be.

The *internal* change agent may operate from an existing Organisation Development Department, which occurs most usually within the Head Office of a conglomerate; or he may be in the Personnel Department; or he may, as suggested above, be seconded from a position elsewhere in the organisation and assigned to groups or parts of the organisation as a change agent. The role of the internal change agent may be very ambiguous, and he may have far more difficulty than an external consultant in explaining his role, since his clients may still regard him as a member of the Personnel Department, or whatever department he comes from rather than a neutral objective observer. On the other hand, the internal change agent is more likely to accept the system as it is, and to accommodate the needs (as he perceives them) of the organisation. External consultants are far less familiar with, and affected by, organisational norms. The internal change agent may also be under significant pressure to divulge information, whereas this is less likely with the external consultant. It is also possible that he will not have the same access to people at the top of the organisation, particularly if his status in the organisation was previously relatively low.

For these reasons, the internal change agent is often not in as good a position to help the organisation in its development effort as the external consultant, and in some cases, indeed, they may work together. However, provided that there is a future role for the internal change agent, that role can be extremely useful training and the use of an internal change agent in such circumstances will be far less costly than the employment of someone from outside.

External change agents can also be found in a variety of roles, from the relatively isolated trainer in a group training package, to a full-time, but temporary, contract to act as the expert in a particular problem area. External consultants may similarly vary in style ranging from the individual who perceives his role as solving the organisation's problems to the one who believes he is there to act as a catalyst, to help the organisation to learn how to solve its own problems. This continuum of consultancy styles may be represented as in Figure 47.

To conclude, a model is proposed which covers the stages involved in any organisational change programme, and is illustrated in Figure 48. In this model we are suggesting that pressure for change may derive from an

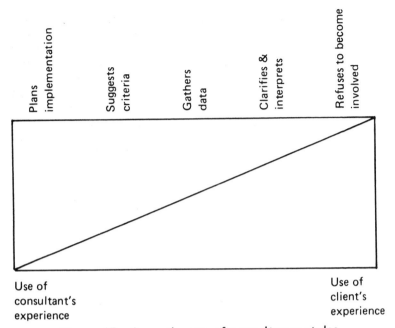

Figure 47 : A continuum of consultancy styles

internal source, such as a particular labour relations problem, or a breakthrough by the Research and Development group in the formulation of a new product; or from an external source, such as a new piece of employment or anti-pollution legislation, or a new product launched by a competitor. The pressure for change must then be recognised and translated into a specification of the area for change, which will be investigated. It has been suggested that response to change may be proactive or reactive. Reactive responses, as the name implies, suggest that the individual company 'reacts' or acts in a defensive way after environmental change has been experienced. An example of a reactive policy is a decision to introduce a competitive brand after your major rival has launched a new product, or drawing up a disciplinary procedure after the relevant Code of Practice has said you must. In other words reactive policies are drawn up *after* the event, and are thus reacting to what has occurred in the environment. Proactive policies involve significant forward planning, such that changes in the environment, in its broadest sense, are anticipated and action is taken to maximise the gain to be derived from such change, or to minimise the losses. Tobacco companies have tended to diversify as they predict a lower volume of sales over time.

ORGANISATIONAL CHANGE

Having recognised the need for change, an organisation's management will try to specify or diagnose the particular problem area, and identify the alternative change strategies (listed above) open to them, bearing in mind the limiting conditions of constraints (such as cash flow, or the present level of staffing). The change strategy which is considered most appropriate will be monitored; and success (or otherwise) will be reviewed. It is quite possible that the change which has been implemented will cause a further pressure for change and this is represented by the feedback loop in Figure 45 which reinforces the point made at the beginning of this section, that change is inevitable and normal in any organisation.

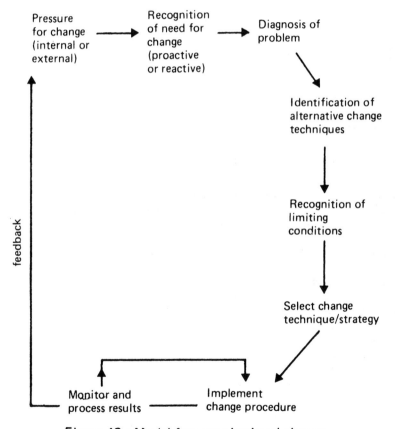

Figure 48 : Model for organisational change

References

ADAIR, John, *Action centred leadership* 1979, Gower.

ALDERFER, C.P. *Existence, relatedness & growth & human needs in organizational settings* 1972, Collier Macmillan.

ALLPORT, G.W. *Personality* 1937, Holt.

ARGYRIS, C. *Personality and organisation* 1957, NY, Harper & Row.

ASCH, J. *Social psychology* 1952, Prentice Hall.

BALES, R.F. *Interaction process analysis* 1950, Addison-Wesley

BEYNON, H. & R.M. BLACKBURN. *Perceptions of work: variations within a factory* 1972, Cambridge University Press.

BIRD C. *Social psychology* 1940, Appleton-Century-Crofts.

BLAKE, R & J. MOUTON. *The managerial grid* 1964, Gulf.

BLAU, P.M. & W.R. SCOTT. *Formal organisations: a comparative approach* 1963, Routledge & Kegan Paul.

BLAU, P.M. *The dynamics of bureaucracy* 1963, University of Chicago Press.

BLAUNER, R. *Alienation and freedom: the factory worker and his industry* 1974, University of Chicago Press.

BOGARDUS, E.S. Measuring social distances. *Journal of applied sociology* Vol 9, 1925.

BROWN, J.A.C. *Freud and the post freudians:* 1966, Penguin.

BURNS, T & G.M. STALKER. *The management of innovation* 1961, Tavistock.

CAMPBELL, J P & M.D. DUNNETTE. Effectiveness of T-group experiences in managerial training and development. IN *Psychological bulletin* (70:2) 73 - 104.

CATTELL, R.B. *Personality: a systematic, theoretical and factual study* 1950, McGraw-Hill.

CHANDLER, A.D. *Strategy and structure* 1962, MIT Press.

COCH, L. & J.R. FRENCH. Overcoming resistance to change IN *Human relations* (1) 512 - 32.

COOPER, C. IN *Personnel management January* 1977.

COREY, S.M. Professed attitudes and actual behaviour. *Journal of educational psychology* Vol 38, 1937.

COSER, L. *The functions of social conflict* 1958, Routledge.

DALTON M. *Men who manage* 1959, Wiley.

DAVIS, K. *Human behaviour at work* 1972.

DURKHEIM, E. *The division of labour in society* 1933, NY: MacMillan.

ETZIONI, A. *A comparative analysis of complex organisations* 1961, Free Press.

EYSENCK, H.J. *Dimensions of personality* 1947, Routledge & Kegan Paul.

FAYOL, H. *General and industrial management* 1949, Pitman.

FIEDLER, F. *A theory of leadership effectiveness* 1967, McGraw-Hill.

FISHBEIN, M. (ed.) *Readings in attitude theory and measurement* 1967, Wiley.

FLANDERS, A. 'Restrictive practices and productivity bargaining' IN *Collective bargaining* A. Flanders (Ed.) 1969 Penguin.

FLANDERS, A. 'The nature of collective bargaining' IN *Collective bargaining* A Flanders (Ed.) 1969 Penguin.

FOLLETT, M.P. *Dynamic administration* (edited by H.C. Metcalf & L.F. Urwick) 1941, Pitman.

FOX, A. 'Industrial relations: a social critique of pluralist ideology' IN CHILD, John (Ed.) *Man and organisation.*

FOX, A. *'Industrial sociology and industrial relations'* Research paper 3 Royal Commission on trades unions and employers associations HMSO 1966.

FRENCH, W.L. & C.H. BELL. *Organisational development* 1973, Prentice-Hall.

GILBRETH, F.B. & L.M. *The writings of the Gilbreths* Illinois: Irwin 1947.

GOLDTHORPE, J.H., D. LOCKWOOD, F. BECHHOFER, & J. PLATT. *The affluent worker: industrial attitudes and behaviour* 1968, Cambridge University Press.

GOULDNER A.W. *Wildcat strike: a study in worker-management relationships* 1954, Routledge & Kegan Paul.

GRAICUNAS, V.A. 'Relationship in organisation' IN L. Gulick & L. Urwick (eds) *Papers on the science of administration* 1937, NY: Institute of Public Administration pp 183 - 187.

HERZBERG, F. *Work and the nature of man* 1966, World Press.

HUMBLE, J.W. *Management by objectives* 1972, British Institute of Management (BIM).

HYMAN, R. 'Pluralism, procedural concensus and collective bargaining' IN *British journal of industrial relations March* 1978.

JUNG, C.G. *Analytical psychology: its theory and practice* 1968, NY Pantheon.

KATZ, D. & R.L. KAHN. *The social psychology of organisations* 1966, Wiley.

KATZ, D. 'The functional approach to the study of attitudes' *Public opinion quarterly* Vol 24, 1960.

KOHLER, W. *The mentality of apes* 1925, NY: Harcourt Brace Jovanovich.

KRETSCHMER, E. *Physique and character* 1925, London: Kegan Paul.

LaPIERE, R.T. Attitude v actions *Social forces* Vol 13, 1934.

LAWRENCE, P.R. & J.W. LORSCH *Organisation and environment* 1967, Harvard University Press.

LEWIN, K., R. LIPPITT, & R.K. WHITE. Patterns of aggressive behaviour in experimentally created 'social climates'. IN *International journal of social psychology* (10) 271 - 99.

LIKERT, R. A technique for the measurement of attitudes. *Archives of psychology* Vol 22, 1932.

LUPTON, T. *On the shop floor: two studies in workshop organisation and output* 1963, Pergamon Press.

LUPTON, T. *Payment systems,* 1972, Penguin.

MASLOW, A.H. A theory of human motivation. *Psychological review* Vol 50, 1943.

McGREGOR, D. *The human side of enterprise* 1960, McGraw-Hill.

MOONEY, J.D. & A.C. REILEY *Onward industry!* 1931, NY: Harper.

NEALEY, S.M. Pay and benefit preference IN *Industrial relations* (3:1) 17 28.

PARSONS, T. *Structure and process in modern society* 1960, NY: The Free Press.

PAVLOV, I.P. *Conditioned reflexes* 1927, NY: Oxford University Press.

PORTER, L.W. & E.E. LAWLER. *Managerial attitudes and performance* 1968, Irwin.

PUGH, D.S., D.J. HICKSON & C.R. HININGS *Writers on organisations* 2nd edn, 1971, Penguin.

REDDIN, W.J. *Managerial effectiveness* 1970, McGraw-Hill.

RICE, A.K. *Productivity and social organisation: the Ahmedabad experiment* 1958, Tavistock.

ROETHLISBERGER, F.J. & W.J. DICKSON. *Management and the worker* 1939, Harvard University Press.

ROY, D.   Efficiency and the 'fix' IN *American journal of sociology* (60) 255 - 66.

SAYLES, L.R. *Behaviour of industrial work groups* 1958, Wiley

SCHEIN, E.H. & W.G. BENNIS. *Personal-organisational change through group methods* 1965, Wiley.

SCHEIN, E.H. *Organisational pyschology* 2nd edn, 1972, Prentice Hall.

SHELDON, W.H. *Atlas of men* 1954, NY Harper & Row.

SKINNER, B.F. *The behaviour of organisms* 1938, NY: Appleton-Century-Crofts.

STOGDILL, R.M. Personal factors associated with leadership IN *Journal of psychology* (25) 1948.

TANNENBAUM, R. & W.H. SCHMIDT.   How to choose a leadership pattern IN *Harvard business review* 1958.

TANNENBAUM, R. & W.H. SCHMIDT. How to choose a leadership pattern IN *Harvard business review,* 1973.

TAYLOR, F.W. *The principles of scientific management* 1911, NY: Harper & Row.

THIBAUT, J. & H.H. KELLEY. *The social psychology of groups* 1959, NY: Wiley.

THURSTONE, L.L. & E.J. CHAVE. *The measurement of attitude* 1929, Chicago University Press.

TONNIES, F. *Community and association* 1955, Routledge & Kegan Paul.

TRIST, E.L. & K.W. BAMFORTH. Some social and psychological consequences of the longwall method of coal-cutting. IN *Human Relations* (4:1) 3 - 38.

TRIST, E.L., G.W. HIGGIN, H. MURRAY & A.B. POLLOCK. *Organisational choice* 1963, Tavistock.

URWICK, L.F. *The elements of administration* 1947, Pitman.

VON BERTALANFFY, L. *General systems theory* 1969, George Brazillier.

VROOM, V.H. *Work and motivation* 1964, Wiley.

WALKER, C.J. & R.H. GUEST *The man on the assembly line* 1952, Harvard University Press.

WEBER, M. *Theory of economic and social organisation* 1947, NY: The Free Press.

WEEKS, B. *et al Industrial relations and the limits of law* 1975 Blackwell.

WOODWARD, J. *Industrial organisation: theory and practice* 1965, Oxford University Press.

Additional Reading

BAIN, G.S. (ed.) *Industrial relations in Britain*. 1983, Blackwell.

This book which has an impressive list of contributors brings the study of industrial relations and by implication personnel management up to date from the perspective of different disciplines.

BARRETT, RHODES and BEISHAM (eds) *Industrial relations in the wider society*. 1975, Macmillan (Open University).

This book which is a collection of readings includes many classics in this field.

BRAMHAM, J. *Practical manpower planning*. 1982, Institute of Personnel Management (IPM).

This book is a very good introduction to some of the techniques used in manpower planning. It deals with the techniques in a way which should not be too daunting to non-mathematical readers.

CUFF, E.C. & G.C.F. PAYNE (eds) *Perspectives in sociology*. 1979, George Allen & Unwin.

A number of different perspectives and methodologies used by sociologists are described in this book, and their respective strengths and weaknesses are outlined. It provides a very good overview of sociological theory, although some students may find it rather complex and obscure in parts.

FARNHAM, D. & J. PIMLOTT *Understanding industrial relations*. 1979, Cassell.

This is a very useful introduction to the theory and practice of industrial relations in Britain. It locates industrial relations practices in an ideological, historical, and socio-economic context and is valuable reading for anyone interested in this aspect of the behavioural sciences.

FLANDERS, A. (ed.) *Collective bargaining: selected readings*. 1969, Penguin.

Despite its age, this collection of readings provides an excellent insight into the subject of collective bargaining, from both theoretical and practical viewpoints.

HILGARD, E., R.L. ATKINSON & R.C. ATKINSON *Introduction to psychology*. 8th edn, 1983, Harcourt, Brace, Jovanovitch.

This is a rather large, but thorough, general text on psychology. The topics we have covered in psychology are covered here in greater depth without an organisational or industrial emphasis.

PUGH, D.S., D.J. HICKSON & C.R. HININGS *Writers on organisations* 3rd edn, 1987, Penguin.

An excellent summary of the work of some of the most significant writers on organisational theory.

TORRINGTON, D. & J. HALL *Personnel management* Prentice Hall. 1987.

This book approaches the subject in a quite different and interesting way.

WORK FOR WORK

A workbook for the mature job seeker

Michael Weatherley & Michael Ryan

Designed to help managers, professionals and other mature
people to find work. Starting with self-analysis, it
takes readers through the complex process of looking for a new
job, career or business opportunity, giving sound, practical
on organising and mounting a successful search.

It is a workbook, not a textbook. Tasks are set at each stage
so that individuals can develop and test their expectations,
perceptions and skills; analyse the market; evaluate their
own campaigns; and find appropriate, satisfying work.

Work for Work is based on successful courses for the mature
unemployed. It has been helpful to those wishing to
change career or to make an effective transition into
work which is new and rewarding.

Some of the topics covered:

the database
managing your career
decision making
alternatives to employment
the interview
offers/no offers
starting work

Wire bound (for ease of use)   £6.95   isbn 0 946139 51 2

INDEX

363

365

366

370

V

Vacancies, advertising of	135-7
Valence (expectancy theory)	78-9
Validation (training)	228-9
Validity of psychological tests	161-2
Value expressive function (attitudes)	64
Values, social	245-6
Vertical communication	94
Victimisation	156
Visual communication	91-3
Von BERTALANFFY, L	321
VROOM, V	77,78-80

W

Wages (see payments)	
WALKER, C J and R H Guest	332
Wastage rate, skills	197-8
WEBER, Max	12-14
WESTERN ELECTRIC COMPANY (see Hawthorne Study)	

Wildcat strike (Gouldner)	14,341
WOODWARD, Joan	333
Work	
attitudes	124-5
groups	
autonomous	75
permanent	96
interests	123-4
measurement	41
study	203
Worker flexibility	301
Workers (see employees OR labour)	
Workforce, changes in	339
Workplace	294
bargaining	294
personality	49
Works committees	294
Workshop bargaining	294
Written communication	90-1

Y

Youth Training Scheme (YTS)	241

MRS THATCHER'S CASEBOOK

Non-partisan studies in Conservative Government policy

Terry Garrison

Well-researched case studies of ten major crises handled
by Mrs Thatcher's government.

Inner city time bomb ?
The Falklands War
GCHQ
Deregulation of the buses
London Transport - Fares Fair
The coal strike
Flexible rostering - British Rail
British Steel
The De Lorean dream
British Leyland

Includes a large section on policy analysis for managers.

Hardback binding   £19.95 (student edition/bulk £9.95)
isbn 0 946139 86 5

TUTOR'S PACK

Case notes, chronologies, commentary and other material
to supplement, support and extend the text.

Presentation looseleaf binder   £59.00 (gratis with 15 books)
isbn 0 946139 46 6

Personnel management in context: the late 1980s second edition

Terry McIlwee
isbn 0 946139 35 0   £9.90 (Students 8.90 direct)
Sewn paperback   September, 1986

A set book at many colleges for the IPM Stage 1 examination Personnel Management in Context, the first edition was 'a valuable text for personnel specialists as well as students'. It brought together:

'a large amount of relevant research in a concise, readable review.'

Jane Granatt in *Industrial Society*

'The book succeeds in its main aim and should prove a valuable addition to the reference books of those studying or teaching this subject. It should also find a place in the libraries of many personnel and training departments…The section on legislation is particularly well laid out and could prove handy in many personnel departments where a quick reminder on the salient parts of some piece of law is often required.'

John Foulds in *Personnel Management* May, 1983

Personnel management in context: the late 1980s Statistics supplement (second edition)

isbn 0 946139 40 7   £4.95   Looseleaf for ease of copying   Autumn, 1986

Tables, charts and other data to supplement and extend the book (culled from a variety of printed sources).

CASE STUDIES IN MANAGEMENT

private sector, introductory level

second edition

edited by Sheila Ritchie

A topical and interesting collection of real-life business case studies based on mainly small and medium-sized companies. There are nine mini-cases (short incident studies) and ten longer, cross-functional cases.
There is an interesting mix of products and services, from chemicals and valves to books and leisure.

Sewn paperback   £7.95   isbn 0 946139 02 4

TUTOR'S PACK

The Tutor's Pack comprises model answers, notes and other materials (including some computer programs and 6 overhead projector transparencies). All cases in the book have been tested on business management students and the notes in the Tutor's Pack build on that experience.

Bound in a presentation file with loose insert plastic pockets £49.00 (gratis with 15 copies of the book bought direct)

isbn 0 946139 07 5